Religion and Tourism

This book explores the dynamic interaction between religion and tourism in the modern world. It considers questions such as:

- Do travellers leave their religion at home when they are touring – and what happens if not?
- What are the relationships between tourism and pilgrimage?
- What happens to religious performances, places and festivals that function as tourism attractions?

Other chapters examine religious theme parks, wellness and spa tourism, the roles played by tourist guides, guidebooks and religious souvenirs and the significance of tourism as a major arena of religious encounters in the contemporary world. Surveying the growing body of work in the field, Michael Stausberg argues that tourism should be a major focus of research within religious studies.

Michael Stausberg is Professor of Religion at the University of Bergen, Norway. He is the European editor of the journal *Religion*, and his recent publications include *Zarathustra and Zoroastrianism* (2008) and (as editor) *Contemporary Theories of Religion* (Routledge, 2009).

Religion and Tourism

Crossroads, destinations and encounters

Michael Stausberg

Routledge
Taylor & Francis Group

LONDON AND NEW YORK

First published 2011
by Routledge
2 Park Square, Milton Park, Abingdon, Oxon, OX14 4RN

Simultaneously published in the USA and Canada by Routledge
270 Madison Avenue, New York, NY 10016

Routledge is an imprint of the Taylor & Francis Group, an informa business

© 2011 Michael Stausberg

Typeset in Times New Roman by Taylor & Francis Books
Printed and bound in Great Britain by TJ International Ltd, Padstow, Cornwall

British Library Cataloguing in Publication Data
A catalogue record for this book is available from the British Library

Library of Congress Cataloging in Publication Data
Stausberg, Michael.
   Religion and tourism : crossroads, destinations, and encounters /
   Michael Stausberg.
      p. cm.
   Includes bibliographical references and index.
   1. Tourism–Religious aspects. 2. Sacred space. I. Title.
   G156.5.R44S77 2011
   201'.691–dc22   2010017900

ISBN 978-0-415-54931-8 (hbk)
ISBN 978-0-415-54932-5 (pbk)
ISBN 978-0-203-85478-5 (ebk)

To my family

Contents

Acknowledgments

I remain mystified why this work should be the first book from religious studies to deal systematically with a topic which is right in front of everybody's eyes: the vibrant interface between tourism and religion. My attention to the subject was alerted not only in the field (India and Iran) or when holidaying with my family, but also on my way to work during the summer months, when I invariably passed a crowd of tourists who visited a church located next to my department in the historical center of Bergen. Musing on why these people might be showing such a keen interest in a building that I did not perceive as particularly remarkable brought a series of other questions to my mind, some of which are addressed in the present work. One of the main hurdles along the way was the need to eliminate many stereotypes about tourists and tourism that stand in the way of such a scholarly endeavor. There is a deeply ingrained suspicion of and contempt for tourists and tourism in academia even though we are all involved in tourism – consider the numerous conferences one keeps traveling to.

Where my previous monographic work mainly dealt with one religious figure (Zarathustra's "career" in early modern Europe) and one religious tradition (Zoroastrianism), in writing the present book, I found myself navigating a vast terrain covering many religious traditions and all continents of the globe. I am quite aware that my text may in some cases rest on shaky ground and that I had to rely on some sources that I had only limited means to check. Moreover, the analysis of the various examples presented in this book remains quite compressed, but my ambition was to cover a middle ground beyond yet another empirical case study or yet another ideological overgeneralization.

The present text was never planned as a book, but somewhat obstinately it has grown into one over the years. The access dates of internet sites given in the notes provide something like an implicit chronology of the work. Originally planned as an article, then as a series of articles, it was only during winter 2007/8 that I decided to reframe it as a book. Then suddenly things just seemed to fall in place but, due to other scholarly activities, the gestation of the present book took another couple of years. Partly due to the gentle reminders from the publisher, and partly because the field seemed to grow much faster than I could hope to keep pace with, I finally had to realize that this work could not possibly cover as much ground as I might have hoped for – and that I could never dig as deeply as I had wished both in terms of empirical data, analytical strategies and theoretical models. While the present book appears as a specimen of the old-fashioned genre of a monograph written in splendid isolation by the lone humanities scholar, ideally, one should think, a book like this should be co-authored by colleagues from different disciplinary backgrounds. But then it simply might not have been written at all.

Some of the ideas developed in the present book were first launched as a grant application, which was turned down by The Research Council of Norway in 2005 despite overwhelmingly positive reports. In retrospect, I am grateful to the wisdom of the Research Council for having saved me and my family the trouble of extensive fieldwork and the challenge of heading yet another research group. At some stage, I was prepared to let the topic go, but precisely at that time I happened to be invited to present my ideas at other places. I therefore wish to thank my hosts and audiences in Trondheim, Copenhagen, Lausanne and Heidelberg for making me tour and for initially providing the opportunity to stay tuned to the topic and for their intellectual input. The same holds true for my students with whom I have discussed parts of this book in my Postgraduate Research Seminar. I have also benefitted from the opportunity to present drafts of chapters to colleagues from the research group on "place" at my department and, invited by my colleague Bruce Kapferer, at a seminar arranged by the department of social anthropology. I would like to thank my friend and colleague Bjørn-Ola Tafjord (Tromsø) for having commented upon a first draft of the manuscript in early 2008. Working with Florian Jeserich (Bayreuth) on the German sister of this work has yielded additional insights. The kind assistance of some other colleagues is acknowledged in the notes. In spring 2010, Russell Adams went through the final manuscript and saved me from numerous mistakes in my English. The index was compiled by Richard Bartholomew.

I also would like to use this occasion to recall the memory of my brilliant former student Janemil Kolstø who passed away in May 2009. Janemil assisted me in conducting two studies of tourists visiting local churches in Bergen (Norway) in the summers of 2007 and 2008. He also prepared a content analysis of tourist guidebooks to Egypt, Italy and Thailand. Both projects have remained unfinished. Janemil's traumatic death was a terrible blow not only for his family but also for his friends and the academic community where he had started to make his presence felt.

During better days in my office, as a German looking out onto the beautiful town of Bergen and the Norwegian mountains while studiously neglecting my emails, I would actually find it difficult to say whether I am holidaying or working. It is a privilege to be based at an institution that still provides its employees not only the freedom but also the liberty and leisure to do research.

I sometimes acted under the suspicion that I should holiday with my family rather than spending valuable time on writing a book on tourism. I am afraid that I all too often fail to live up to the expectations of my wife and children when it comes to holidaying. At some point, it crossed my mind that this book might lead me, in a round-about way, to finally come to terms with holidaying; it is perhaps my ticket to ride for an activity that I have to date found more daunting than most. Let us see whether it has a cathartic effect. At any rate, I feel the desire of expressing my sincere gratitude to my family for nevertheless bearing with me.

Michael Stausberg
Bergen
Spring 2010

Introduction

Tourism, "the largest ever movement of people across national borders" (Urry 2002, 141), is an elementary form of modern global life. Tourism is no longer elsewhere. Despite events and crises such as the attacks on 11 September 2001 (9/11), the Kuta bombings (Bali) in 2002, the Iraq war, the 2004 Tsunami, the SARS virus, H5N1 (avian influenza) and H1N1 (swine flu), tourism remains one of the fastest-growing economic sectors and one of the world's largest sources for employment, including high income as well as less economically developed countries. Travel and tourism amount to some 12.5 percent of the gross domestic product (GDP) of nations world-wide, varying from 61.1 percent in the Maldives to 2.2 percent in Angola (Aramberri 2009, 367–76.).[1] However, the importance of tourism is not restricted to the economic sphere alone. Tourism is very much a cultural phenomenon, shaping ways in which we perceive and act in the world, extending beyond the very act of traveling.

Until now tourism and religion have often been seen as independent and mutually exclusive subjects. This book aims to correct this misconception and change the way we look at religion and tourism, to see the dynamic interaction between these closely related subjects in the contemporary world and to put this into a scholarly perspective.

While the present work is not the first to explore this area (see later for previous scholarship), it is the first religious studies monograph that does not present one particular case study but draws a larger picture by putting a variety of extant studies from different disciplines into a coherent perspective. It should be made clear at the outset, however, that this book is neither pro- nor anti-tourist, nor is it pro- or anti-religion. The book is concerned with where phenomena commonly classified as religions or religious are engaged and negotiated in tourism, and how religions engage and negotiate phenomena identified as tourism.

The present book will take the reader on a journey around the world with stopovers in many countries, and on this intellectual voyage we will encounter various religious traditions. By the end of this journey it will be clear that we can no longer ignore the fact that tourism and religion are in various ways tied together in the modern world. While it still remains conceptually possible to conceive tourism without religion and religions without tourism, in reality they are densely interwoven. The present book will address some of the main forms in which this is happening and point at some of the consequences this brings about – mainly for religion(s).

In this introductory chapter we will begin our journey with some preliminary historical and conceptual explorations. These are primarily aimed at a religious studies audience unfamiliar with tourism. Moreover, we will take a brief look at the academic point of departure for our study and will distinguish two main approaches to the field. The present work consistently builds on the second of these approaches, focusing on the connections between the cultural/material/social realities of tourism and religion rather than on their structural affinities.

Part I of the present book explores the crossroads between religion and tourism by reviewing the thesis of structural affinities between them and by examining modes of interactions between the two. A further chapter is devoted to a discussion of the relationship between tourism and pilgrimage in order to illustrate the distinction and overlap between these two spheres or systems of human communication and practice.

Part II of this book looks first at religious sites and places which have been subjected to tourist impact. We will then visit tourist spaces that quote, recreate or replicate religious universes, draw on religious tropes, or seem to create hybrid structures where holidays seemingly turn into religious experiences.

Part III shifts the focus from sites, places and spaces to peoples and religions. It first reviews religious groups that are regularly visited by tourists, and then investigates religious performances and events where at least parts of the audiences are tourists. In the perspective adopted in this book, tourism emerges as the main global arena where adherents from different religions (or from no religions at all) encounter other religions. The final part of our journey will explore some of the main mediators and media which to some extent frame such encounters before, during and after the visits.

Along our journey, before leaving each station a selection of "souvenirs" will be offered that highlight some findings of the discussions in the form of a list of bullet-points (which entails a serious reduction in complexity).

Having reached the terminus of our journey we will conclude by visiting some vantage points that will allow us to take some views on the landscape from different theoretical perspectives in which the present study can be situated. Right from the beginning of this journey, however, the readers should be aware that this voyage, as any, will be far from exhaustive, that other itineraries are possible, and that there will remain much more to explore.

Historical developments

In Europe, the history of tourism goes back to antiquity.[2] Upper-class people went on educational journeys to Egypt or other places of interest and had residences in the countryside, in the mountains or by the sea. Baiae on the Bay of Naples and Kanobos near Alexandria were luxury coastal resorts in antiquity, but there was no widespread recreational tourism in antiquity and upper-class holidaying did not continue to mediaeval times. However, mediaeval pilgrimages are popularly seen as a precursor of modern tourism. From around 1600 to the French Revolution, wealthy young British noblemen embarked on the Grand Tour, taking them to France, Italy, Switzerland, Germany and the Netherlands (later also to Egypt and Palestine) for a period of some months up to several years.[3] From an educational adventure for only a few extremely wealthy upper-class young gentlemen, trips to the continent "became commonplace among well-to-do Europeans in the first half of the nineteenth century" (Withey 1997, 104). During the 18th and early 19th centuries, the bourgeoisie followed the example of the aristocrats by developing a taste for educational journeys. Romanticism gave a new impetus to this development, with nature joining cultural heritage as a subject of attraction.

The transition to mass tourism – a distinctive feature of modern tourism – is often associated with the former English Baptist minister and advocate of temperance Thomas Cook (1808–92) and his son John Mason Cook (1834–98). Thomas Cook and Son offered package tours that made travel cheaper and more widely accessible, even for the working class, and turned traveling into a commodity open to purchase. In the 1870s and 1880s the company expanded its operations into Palestine and Egypt, the first main non-European destinations. Thomas Cook "had been driven by a belief in the ethical benefits of travel and often referred to opening Middle Eastern travel in missionary terms" (Hazbun 2007, 23) so that he continued to offer Holy Land tours even when they produced losses. His son John did not share his father's religious commitments, and was more of an imperial entrepreneur. The company started its first round-the-world trip in 1872.

Apart from individual business ventures as well as the development of new managerial and administrative skills and classes, the Industrial Revolution laid the structural foundations on which mass tourism could develop and whereby organized travel and hospitality turned into a modern industrial sector. To begin with, changing means of transportation put ever more distant places within reach and made it possible for these places to function as tourist destinations. The invention of steamships, trains, automobiles (car, bus, truck) and airplanes are important steps towards the worldwide expansion of modern mass tourism (as well as for the rise of other industries and social projects). It seems to be only a matter of time before outer space will also be widely accessible to tourists (for some it already is). In addition to transport, modern information technology has helped to connect places and people as well as to create awareness of supply and demand. Moreover, greatly improved security of travel and the prosperity of increasing numbers of people, changes in the structure of work and leisure including paid holidays have contributed to the growth of tourism as a mass activity. Last but not least, the emergence of novel means of communication and modes of visual perception such as photography have been crucial factors.[4] All these factors laid the ground for the formation of tourism as a systemic sector that integrates modes of transport and communication, economic and cultural transactions; this systemic quality distinguishes tourism from earlier forms of collective travel.

The expansion of tourism has greatly accelerated since the 1960s. Statistics indicate more than a ten-fold increase in the number of international arrivals in the period from 1960 to 2000 (Harrison 2003, 13). From 2000 to 2008 the number of international arrivals has again grown, from 682 to 924 million (*UNWTO World Tourism Barometer* 7 (1), 2009),[5] corresponding to a 35 percent increase. One notable development was the increasing number of trips abroad, with ever longer distances being covered. With the middle classes of populous countries such as China and India as well as other South Asian countries gaining in spending power that development is likely to continue.[6] In Germany, to take the example of one country with a high density of tourists, in 2004 74 percent of the adult population made an annual trip of a minimum of five days in length (in 1954 that figure was 24 percent). However, it seems that in every known society, 80–85 percent is the limit of tourist density, given that some groups cannot travel for reasons of health, money, preferences or work pressure (Steinecke 2006, 32–33).

The global history of tourism still remains to be written. Most scholarly accounts focus on Europe and North America and much of the extant literature has a Western bias. "Non-Western" countries are usually studied only to the extent of being destinations for Western tourists; the non-Western international and especially the domestic tourism in the Global South are usually neglected (Gladstone 2005, 108).[7] The focus on international travel with border crossings in official statistics probably creates a distorted image of reality, among other things resulting in a statistical overrepresentation of Europe compared to, for example, the United States (Aramberri 2009), where the number of domestic leisure trips (1.4 billion) taken in 2006 outnumbers worldwide international arrivals by some 40 percent. In a similar fashion, Gladstone has remarked that the number of domestic arrivals in countries such as China and India, respectively, exceeds the number of international tourist arrivals in the entire world (Gladstone 2005, 164). It would, however, be wrong to assume that domestic tourism always precedes international tourism. The reverse process also occurs. In Bali, for example, domestic tourism has grown considerably in the 1990s, to the point that domestic tourists even outnumbered foreign visitors (Picard 1996, 167).

For those who can afford it, mostly in Europe, North America and North East Asia, tourism has become a worldwide practice and a planetary reality. For many inhabitants of the more developed nations, East and West, touring and holidaying appear to be indispensable features of life under the conditions of modernity. One is under the impression that leisure tourism is not regarded as optional, but as compulsory, and that "getting out" is something of a social mandate. Obviously, this generally observable fact demands an explanation. As we will see below, in providing such explanations, some scholars have engaged the concept of religion.

Global agencies and disputed effects

There are several global agencies involved in the promotion and development of tourism. These include the Organization for Economic Cooperation and Development (OECD) and the United Nations – in particular the latter's agencies such as the UN World Tourism Organization (WTO). According to its statutes, first adopted in 1970, "[t]he fundamental aim of the Organization shall be the promotion and development of tourism with a view to contributing to economic development, international understanding, peace, prosperity, and universal respect for, and observance of, human rights and fundamental freedoms for all without distinction as to race, sex, language or religion".[8] In an earlier version of its website the World Tourism Organization argued: "Intercultural awareness and personal friendships fostered through tourism are a powerful force for improving international understanding and contributing to peace among all the nations of the world."[9]

This passage has been taken off the site, and many critics of tourism draw a rather different picture. Rather than understanding, critics argue that tourism strengthens intercultural stereotypes and misunderstanding; "[i]n the last two decades voices from indigenous communities began to decry tourism, cataloguing the social, environmental, cultural, and moral devastation that it often unleashed" (Harrison 2003, 13). Negative effects of tourism – also with regard to economic impacts – have of course also been discussed in the scholarly literature.[10] Even varieties of tourism with a clean image such as ecotourism have been severely criticized as oppressive (Johnston 2006). With regard to socio-cultural effects one problem is that tourism is usually embedded in larger processes of change so that it is difficult to understand and single out the tourist factor.[11]

Tourism is an easy target for theories of metropolitan neo-colonial global capitalism. The often pervasive (neo-)colonial and imperialist dimensions of much global tourism have been countered by post-colonial critique (Hall and Tucker, 2004a). Today, many tourists are actually aware of the effects of tourism, are self-critical, and show emotional reactions such as feelings of guilt or shame, and even anger as they reflect on the often negative and disruptive impacts their travel has on the region and its population.[12] Yet, tourism has at the same time brought benefits for many people and groups (Harrison 2003, 15–16). Neither uncritical tourism-propaganda nor sweeping tourism-bashing get at the whole picture. The moral and condemnatory undertones in many analyses of tourism may not be helpful to understand what is going on "out there". As always, reality is multifaceted, and reflexive scholarship needs to unmask prevailing ideologies of all sorts. Before we start to look at tourism and religion, one crucial question needs to be briefly addressed: What is tourism?

Defining tourism

The United Nations World Tourism Organization (UNWTO) has proposed the following definition of tourism: it "comprises the activities of persons traveling to and staying in places outside their usual environment for not more than one consecutive year for leisure, business and other purposes not related to the exercise of an activity remunerated from within the place visited".[13] According to this definition, which has gained something like an official status, tourism is a displacement fulfilling three criteria.

(1)   Tourism proceeds "outside the usual environment" of the traveler; this implies a destination and it excludes commuting.
(2)   The definition seems to imply that after a year of continuous stay at a location, the latter becomes part of the boundaries of the "usual environment" and does thereby no longer qualify as tourism; on the other hand, innovations in transport technologies enable people to leave the boundaries of their usual environment within a day, so that an overnight-stay is not required to qualify for tourism.[14]
(3)   Contrary to previous and alternative definitions, leisure is not regarded as the determining factor of tourism. A vast array of activities is now included, as long as their remuneration does not stem from the destination.

Religious travels such as middle- or long-distance pilgrimage are clearly covered by this definition. From a technical point of view, pilgrimage then is a form of tourism. In the present study, however, when speaking of tourism I have in mind not so much a typological category referring to any form of travel that corresponds to the three criteria given by the UNWTO but a historical category referring to a modern mass phenomenon, economic-cultural sector and aspect of contemporary lifestyles.

Not only pilgrimage, but many other activities of religious specialists and religious people in general fall into the category of tourism as defined by the UNWTO. Consider pastoral and shorter missionary travels, study and charitable trips, or participating in all sorts of religious events. In any of these forms, varieties of tourism can be found in virtually any religion. Such travels are often classified as religious tourism (see pp. 13ff).

Scholarly activities such as attending conferences, fieldwork and time spent abroad for a sabbatical also fall into the domain of the definition. Given that most people would probably object to being classified as tourists – tourism is the sort of frivolous role played by others! – most scholars would probably not be happy about being mixed up with half-naked, bronze-bellied camera-equipped creatures. Yet, aren't we scholars also equipped with our notebooks and cameras? The challenge of the comparison may lead one to reflect on one's travel behavior and work ethics, or question one's prejudices against tourism.[15] As scholars of religion we need to reflect to what extent our scholarly practice of presenting religions, for example in world religion surveys, amounts to a form of intellectual tourism.

Despite its quasi-official character, the definition quoted above can be disputed as any other; alternatively, one could point to academic conceptualizations of tourism such as those that emphasize the aspects of consumption and leisure (Hall, Williams and Lew 2004, 4–7). Even though I would not wish to make leisure a necessary precondition for travels to qualify as tourism generally, for pragmatic reasons the present study will mainly focus on leisure tourism. The voluntary and discretionary character often ascribed to tourism can serve as a criterion to exclude business-related travel. To include all forms of tourism, at least when applying such a broad definition as the one proposed by the UNWTO, would certainly go beyond the scope of a single monograph. Educational travel, the professional tours of religious specialists or various sorts of celebrations and events that involve traveling are common in most religions; an attempt to cover them systematically in the present work would amount to a world history of religions.

Two negotiated categories

From the more general perspective of critical cultural analysis, "the problematic nature of tourism as a theoretical category" (Rojek and Urry 1997, 2) has been pointed out. While the category seems to engage clear-cut demarcations from its various others (such as hobbying, strolling and culture), these demarcations, it is argued, are in fact much more complex and ambiguous. More than that, in lay discourses, the terms "tourism" and "tourist" appear to be negative and derogatory, so that many tourists (including academics) prefer to describe themselves as travelers; to some extent, anti-tourism is part of the negotiation, role-taking and rhetoric of tourists.[16] Therefore, "tourism is a term waiting to be deconstructed" (Rojek and Urry 1997, 1). As far as I can see, this warning has not had a lasting impact on Tourism Studies. This situation recalls similar and likewise effectively unsuccessful attempts to dispose of the category of religion in Religious Studies (e.g. Dubuisson 1998; Fitzgerald 2000). Just as travel seems to be the more generally acceptable term for touring, so is spirituality in lay discourse and rhetoric often used as a more positive way of addressing religious affairs.

This book is not the place to discuss these attempts, but it will indeed point to the problematic dichotomy involving one type of tourist, namely the pilgrim. As will become clear, tourism, far from being the other of religion, is a major arena, context and medium for religion in the contemporary global world. This, in fact, is the major finding of the present book. Note, however, that tourism and religion are here not understood as if they were timeless entities or naturally given; instead, they are approached as cultural and social realities (constructs/facts), i.e. as contingent, constrained and negotiated creations of human agency. Even if one denies that tourism and religion are natural entities, this is not to say that they thereby lack a systemic quality; in fact, they refer to recognizable assemblies, ordered wholes, of cultural and social interactions linked to specific social frameworks, organizations or institutions.

On a lay level, even when the validity of the category is denied by some (albeit far from all) scholars, people continue to refer to specific forms of activities as tourism and they will continue to tour – just as the category of religion is being engaged in public and private discourse, whatever misgivings the scholarly community, or some of its members, might or might not have about that. Theoretical deconstructions notwithstanding, many actors both outside and inside the academy still believe "that tourism does in fact possess a self-evident essence" (Rojek and Urry 1997, 1). This is precisely what most people, religious or otherwise, do with regard to the category "religion". As scholars, of course, we are not supposed to believe in such essences, but to develop a critical analysis. To that effect, a "deconstruction" may or may not be a healthy exercise. In the present book, it will be argued that it is a rewarding exercise to take account of "tourism" as a significant context of "religion" in the present world. The underlying conceptualization of religion puts the focus not so much on religious motivations or on categories such as "the sacred", but on religion in the shape of material and public culture, on public places and events, and on groups generally acknowledged as religious rather than on anthropological ideas such as the *homo religiosus* or the *homo viator*.

Religion in Tourism Studies and tourism in the Study of Religion(s)

Interestingly, the suggestion to deconstruct the category fell in a period of academic institutionalization of Tourism Studies, which has been a rapidly growing field.[17] There are now many departments and degree programs in this field throughout the world, and there is a vast amount of academic literature on tourism including journals, books, conference proceedings, and electronic publications (Hall, Williams and Lew 2004, 9). A fairly recent survey lists no fewer than 76 journals in the field (Hall, Williams and Lew 2004, 11–13; see Table 1.1, Chapter 1). The literature in the study of tourism has reached such a degree of complexity that there are not only bibliographies and surveys of the field and its different subfields, but recently a meta-survey surveying the surveys on the sociology and anthropology of tourism was published (Dann 2005, 3–15).

Similar to the study of religion(s), Tourism Studies as a distinct academic discipline makes up for only part of the scholarly discourse on this subject. Geography, economy, sociology, anthropology are key-disciplines that have a history of contributing to the field.[18] As with other fields, the development of Tourism Studies resulted in increasing diversification and specialization (Steinecke 2006, 28).

Travels vaguely classified as "religious" by observers amount to "one of the most significant types of tourism in the world today by volume and prevalence" (Timothy and Olsen 2006, 276). Already this simple fact calls attention to the relationship between religion and tourism. Not surprisingly the field of Tourist Studies has therefore already begun to address religion. As we shall see throughout this book, there are numerous possibly relevant case studies, undertaken from various angles and with different agendas. Some have a practical (managerial) impetus. There are so few published volumes on religion and tourism that I can briefly review them here.

The first book-length treatment of the topic was published in 1996 under the title *Tourism and Religion*. The author, Boris Vukonić, is a Professor of Economics at the University of Zagreb.[19] Although the book is concerned with the same issue as the present work, namely with the "interrelationship between tourism and religion" (Vukonić 1996, ix), the approach taken by Vukonić is quite different from the one adopted here. Vukonić, who has a fundamentally positive and optimistic view of tourism, argues that "tourism provides people with the conditions for the spiritual enrichment of the individual and his or her constant self-development as a personality" (Vukonić 1996, 18). He also claims that "[t]here is much more of the spiritual, even the sacral and religious, in the entire phenomenon of tourism than is generally thought" (Vukonić 1996, 50). In other words, he is concerned with the positive contribution made by tourism to religion and religious individuals. The idea of the *homo turisticus religiosus* is a cornerstone to his approach (see p. 13f). Moreover, his perspective is limited by a focus on Catholicism, theology and pilgrimage.[20] So far, Vukonić's book has remained the only general monograph on the topic, but in recent years it was supplemented by three edited volumes.

Some Brazilian anthropologists and sociologists have contributed to the international conversation on religion and tourism. An edited volume the title of which reads (in English translation) *Religious Tourism: anthropological essays on religion and tourism* came out in 2003 (Abumanssur ed., 2003). To give the readers an idea of that volume, here is a brief summary of some main points addressed by the six essays contained in that volume. The opening essay by Maria Ângela Vilhena praises pilgrimages as a source of renewal of life. Carlos Alberto Streil reviews the relevant terms for pilgrimage[21] and he introduces the term "religious tourism" to refer to more "external" experiences with less immersion into the sacred than is the case with pilgrimages. He notes a resistance to the term "religious tourism" among Catholics but acknowledges the attempt by politicians and administrators to transform religious events into touristic ones. Based on a review of previous studies of pilgrimages and tourism mainly in English, Streil concludes by emphasizing the unique and distinct features of pilgrimage as an experience. Edin Sued Abumanssur tries to sketch out the meaning of "religious tourism" by pointing to the historical development of mass tourism. "Religious tourism" points to the convergence between tourism and religion in events like the large-scale travels to the "national sanctuaries" of Brazil such as Senhor Bom Jesus de Iguape where religion, consumption and leisure form a "promiscuous" union. The connection and mutual interference between tourism, consumption and leisure is also discussed in theoretical terms by Emerson José Sena da Silveira with the example of visits to the Basilica of the National Shrine of Our Lady of Aparecida, for which he claims the occurrence of a "carnivalization" of the religious. Christian Dennys Monteiro de Oliveira coins two neologisms to conceptualize the development of religious tourism: *turismomonumentalidade* to point to the massive expansion of tourism and *fétur*, the combination of travel *(tur)* and faith *(fé)*, i.e. traveling faith and travel motivated by faith. The essay concludes with a table that correlates types of sanctuaries (traditional, natural, technological, festive), sites and rituals. The final essay, by Paulo Roberto Albieri Nery, does not address religious tourism but discusses walks and related pastime practices among the lower classes in Brazil. The main agenda of the volume seems to be to throw light on the perceived conceptual ambiguity of tourism and religion; the empirical material of all studies is from Brazil with an emphasis on pilgrimages or pilgrimages sites.

Tourism, Religion and Spiritual Journeys was edited by a professor of Community Resources and Development and a geographer. This book contains 18 essays, divided into two main parts (Timothy and Olsen eds., 2006).[22] Only one of the 17 contributors to that volume (T. S. Bremer) works at a Religious Studies Department. The first part explores a number of general concepts, concerns and issues in tourism with regard to religion such as spaces, religious/secular pilgrimages, retailing and management challenges. The second part contains a series of essays that analyze the official attitudes of a series of religions towards travel and tourism and pilgrimage and the status of travel within these religions.

The majority of the contributors to another edited volume, entitled *Religious Tourism and Pilgrimage Management* (2007), are part of the European Association for Tourism and Education (ATLAS) Religious Tourism and

Pilgrimage Special Interest Group, founded in 2003.[23] The authors mainly hail from tourism, hospitality and events management studies. No scholar of religion has contributed to the volume. Most chapters discuss pilgrimages. Among the 17 chapters, 8 are labeled case studies (but even most of the remaining 9 chapters can be described as case studies), from various parts of Europe and the globe. As the editors point out in their introductory essay, the volume makes a case "for a reassessment of analysis underlying religious motivations of travel and a full exploration of the pressures for sacred spaces to become venues for commercialized and festivalized arenas" (Raj and Morpeth 2007b, 13).

Studies from these two rather heterogeneous volumes will be engaged in the present work.

The latest edited volume that has come to my attention, published in 2008, is entitled *Patrimonio Cultural, turismo y religión* (*Cultural Heritage, Tourism and Religion*). As the editors of this volume, to which social anthropologists, geographers, historians and psychologists from Mexico and Spain have contributed, outline in the introduction, this work points to the enhanced importance of cultural heritage, the revitalization of rituals and reinterpretations of "religious facts". According to the editors, these related processes often depend on tourist commoditization with its tendencies towards spectacle, theming and the exotization of social facts in order to attract visitors, be it pilgrims or tourists (Díaz Brenis and Javier Hernández eds., 2008, 8). Unfortunately, very few of the contributions throw light on the actual interface between heritage, religion and tourism.

Only one Religious Studies scholar has contributed to these four edited volumes, and scholars from Religious Studies departments have so far largely shunned tourism. However, the tide seems to be turning. Two recent reference works have included entries on tourism (Schlatter 2006; Bremer 2005). Both sketch some important issues, but have a very small basis of research to build on and are therefore by necessity tentative. Thomas Bremer, the author of one of these entries, has also published a monograph in which he presents an interesting American case study (Bremer 2004).[24] In this book Bremer recounts the history of the "sacred ruins" of the Alamo and San Antonio Missions and their encounter with tourism from pre-tourist travel practices to contemporary mass tourism with more than a million tourists annually visiting the Missions. In his work Bremer points to a number of key issues many of which will also be addressed in the present book.

Shared concerns and mutual relationships

Bremer directs attention to four concerns that he argues are shared by tourists and religious adherents. First, both "demonstrate a concern for space and maintain deep attachments to special places" (Bremer 2004, 3).

Second, there is an articulation of identities. "In fact, the making of place always involves the making of identities, and, conversely, the construction of identities always involved the construction of place" (Bremer 2004, 4–5). A third feature is a pervasive concern with aesthetics: "Tourism involves a thoroughgoing aestheticization of the world. Tourists everywhere regard much of what they encounter in terms of the beautiful, the uplifting, the edifying" (Bremer 2004, 5). One of the tourists' prime worries is with authenticity as an aesthetic quality. Bremer rightly notes that "[t]he touristic concern for authenticity also frames travelers' experiences of religion" (Bremer 2004, 6). The fourth aspect is commercialization, also involving commoditization. Bremer notes "all things, all places, all experiences, become potential commodities in the tourist economy. Religion is no exception" (Bremer 2004, 6).

It is unclear what these mutually shared concerns reveal either about religion or tourism per se, or about their specific interrelations. Moreover, other points of shared concerns could be added. Consider issues such as the body, performance, time and "the other(s)". Or think of social processes such as globalization.

From his observations Bremer concludes that "distinguishing between the religious and the touristic in the modern world can sometimes seem a futile task" (Bremer 2004, 7). Indeed. Yet, just as Bremer does in the remaining part of his book, the present work takes the conceptual distinction prima facie for granted, but by doing so, we will explore various dynamic modes of the relationships between tourism and religion.

From affinities to interfaces

In the absence of any large-scale research program on religion and tourism, the only way to address the subject at present is to tap into the field of tourist studies and add some of the limited data of one's own research to it. This is what I will attempt in the present book. Contrary to Bremer's case study, and to almost all published work so far, the present book builds on a relatively large and heterogeneous sample of examples taken from around the globe as discussed in the literature available and known to me.

When reviewing the literature one can distinguish two main approaches to the study of religion and tourism. One approach theorizes structural affinities between religion and tourism, whereas the other points at the dynamic interferences between these cultural domains. Both employ different methods, have different theoretical agendas and different explanatory impacts. While the former approach explains the significance of modern tourism with regard to religious history, the latter approach points to changes in contemporary religions resulting from tourism.[25] While the former is more interested in interpretations of tourism as such, the latter approach is concerned with what happens at and as a result of the various confluences between religion and tourism. Such confluences occur around sacred sites and spaces, religious groups, performances and events as well as religious rhetoric in tourism. The conceptual distinction between tourism and pilgrimage is important for both approaches. It will therefore also feature prominently in this book.

Religious tourism and religion in tourism

In recent years, the term "religious tourism" has become increasingly widespread in popular parlance[26] and by several actors in the field: in Brazil, in particular, the term has been widely used by representatives of the church, by entrepreneurs of various sorts, by the tourism sector,[27] and by scholars, resulting in a semantic fuzziness (Silveira, 2004, 2–7). The term has gained a certain currency among Catholic intellectuals using Romance languages; for example, an Italian bishop has written a book about religious tourism (Mazza 2007)[28] and the Department of Pastoral Care of Tourism and Leisure Time of the Spanish Episcopal Conference devoted a conference to religious tourism in November 2008 in Ávila.

In the scholarly literature, the term has assumed different meanings. Often it is used without any definition. Let us briefly review some more explicit interpretations.[29] As in many typologies of tourists and tourism,[30] motivation is routinely regarded as the decisive factor for classification. The geographer Gisbert Rinschede, for instance, uses the term "religious tourism" to refer to various forms of travel undertaken exclusively or dominantly for religious motives. Pilgrimage is just one of the forms religious tourism may take. Others include attending religious conferences, festivals, conventions, etc. (Rinschede 1992; 1999, 197–221).[31]

The concept of religious tourism or "the religious tourist" is central to the book by Boris Vukonić (1996), but he adds content to motivation. For Vukonić, not every tourist who is a religious person qualifies as a *homo turisticus religiosus*, but only such a person who (a) undertakes his/her journey for religious motives and who (b) "demands that certain religious content be included in the obligatory range of touristic supply amenities" (Vukonić 1996, 75). According to Vukonić there are three main forms of religious tourism:

(1) pilgrimages
(2) religious events ("large-scale gatherings on the occasion of significant religious dates and anniversaries")
(3) "a tour of and visit to important religious places and buildings within the framework of a touristic itinerary" (Vukonić 1996, 75).

In the third case, it seems to me, "religious tourism" is embedded in other forms of tourism such as cultural heritage tourism. According to Vukonić's own premises, however, such tours and visits will only count as "religious tourism" when they are motivated by religious needs and motives.

Motivation, but not content, is the decisive criterion for "religious tourism" as the term is understood by Maria da Graça Mouga Poças Santos. She proposes using it to refer to "movements in which genuinely religious motives may co-exist, simultaneously, with others common to different types of tourism" (Santos 2003, 36). Given this state of amalgamation, the question is then how to determine "genuine" religious motives. The idea of religious travel as a separate, unmixed category still seems to lurk in the background. Nevertheless, her way of using the concept allows for such travels that include religious practices in their itinerary as well as those that are "directed especially at sacred places and buildings" (Santos 2003, 39).

In the course of this study we will encounter examples of people who travel for religious intentions, motives and reasons. Here are some common purposes of religious travels/tourism (in alphabetical order):

- education and training
- events (gospel concerts, papal visits, *melas*, etc.), fairs and expositions
- feasts and festivals
- healing and seeking other this- or other-wordly benefits
- holidaying in a religious environment (camps, etc.)
- mission and other forms of propaganda/evangelism
- pilgrimages
- purchase of religious objects
- retreats
- rituals
- seminars, conferences, meetings, conventions
- spiritual self-discovery and growth
- visits to religious authorities for counseling, confession, etc.

These and other forms of religious travels are integral parts of many religions. They are not specifically related to modern (leisure) tourism. It is therefore beyond the aims and scope of the present book to address these various forms of religious traveling in any detail, yet we will encounter some of them along our way as we explore religion in tourism contexts.

For the purposes of the present study, moreover, using prior motives and motivations as a starting point seems too static and limited a perspective. In fact, religious motives often co-exist with other motivations such as desires to get away from home, to relax, to spend time with family and loved ones, to discover and learn or to be entertained and to satisfy curiosity. Moreover, religious practices and visits to sacred places may be part of trips that were not, or at least not originally, motivated or devised as religious. Religious elements (practices, experiences, information) may even emerge on the road as persons, things, events or places are encountered on the way. The (aesthetic, auratic, charismatic) character of certain sites often does not fail to make an impression on people who just came for a brief stopover, to gaze and take pictures. Furthermore, as we shall see, religious tropes are often used to describe places and experiences. Or, as Thomas Bremer has aptly put it: "For many people, religion slips imperceptibly into touristic practice" (Bremer 2004, 144).

Accordingly, the present book will go beyond the field of religious tourism in a narrow sense. Rather, the present work will address the wider interfaces between religion and modern (leisure) tourism. Even many tourists who do not travel for religious motives and reasons are often exposed to religion on their travels. This may happen accidentally or intentionally, but such intentions are often not "religious" or "spiritual" in the first place. Consider the following two examples. Tourists just happen to be at a place where a religious festival is being celebrated (= accidental exposure to religion); tourists make it a point to visit Notre Dame on a trip to Paris (= intentional exposure to religion), but without having religious motives in mind or without the intention of performing any religious act such as praying or attending Mass in that cathedral. (They may then nonetheless light a candle or meditate during their visits – the emerging dimension mentioned above.) Exposure to religion is not necessarily the same as being affected by religious indoctrination or religious belief systems – although that can happen as well, even to the modest extent of raising questions. Exposure to religion here means encountering religion in its material side of places, events, performances, actions, and objects or their respective media representations. Tourists can focus on religion, be attentive to religion and be appreciative of religion (Timothy and Nyaupane 2009, 8).

Not only are tourists exposed to religion, but religions are for their part exposed to tourists and tourism. To return to the two previous examples. Tourists are part and parcel of many if not most contemporary religious festivals, and tourists are the main group of visitors at several religious sites in the Americas, Europe, Africa and Asia. As a reality of contemporary life, tourism affects religion as much as religions are affected by other contemporary realities such as global migratory flows and the media. This is the territory the present book sets out to explore.

SOUVENIRS FROM THE INTRODUCTION

- Modern mass tourism goes back to the mid-19th century; it is a ubiquitous part of contemporary lifestyles and cultural practice around the world; it is also one of the most important economic sectors, with ambiguous and controversial social effects.

- Religion is increasingly important for tourism – and vice versa.
- Tourism and religion are disputed categories; they are here understood as ordered/systemic social facts rather than as metaphysical entities.
- Tourism Studies and Religious Studies have both largely ignored the inter-relations between tourism and religions; exceptions confirm the rule.
- Religion and tourism share some concerns (e.g. identity).
- Standard definitions of tourism cover a wide range of travel activities undertaken by people in religious contexts.
- Religious tourism mostly refers to travel made for religious motives/purposes (e.g. pilgrimage, education, propaganda), but this book adopts a wider framework.
- Rather than taking religious motivations as our starting point, this book will address the mutual exposure of religion to tourism.
- Religion can have an emergent quality in tourism contexts.

Part 1

Crossroads

Chapter 1

Affinities

One way of approaching the interrelation between religion and tourism is the idea that both are at the same time distinct but yet overlapping realities. This will be exemplified paradigmatically with regard to general stereotypes and scholarly discussions of tourism and pilgrimage. Since religion seems to represent a prototypical feature of pre-modern or pre-industrial societies while tourism epitomizes modern lifestyles, the idea of a possible structural replacement of religion by tourism has appeared on the agenda in social theory. At the same time, it has been pointed out that tourist destinations share a history with religious elements in modern nation building, at least in the United States – but most likely also in many other countries.[1] Tourism, however, has changed alongside modernity, and just as the master narrative of modernity and modernization has been replaced by a plethora of post-modernist tales, it is no longer appropriate to speak of tourism and the tourist in the singular. As we shall see, the diversification of tourism corresponds to other metaphorical engagements of the figure and the trope of "the tourist" in post-modern social theorizing.

Tourism and pilgrimage

In the Western discursive universe, which is heavily imbued by Christian patterns that are still casting long shadows over scholarly discussions, pilgrimage and tourism occupy two diametrically opposite semantic poles. For purely heuristics purposes, these can be schematically arranged in the form of a binary structure (Badone 2004, 185; Berger 2004, 35; see Table 1.1).

A similar binary structure can be constructed for the travelers (see Table 1.2).

These schemes should not be read as my attempt at definition or as a statement about realities, but rather as an attempt to set out prevalent emic cognitive frames generally engaged in order to classify public behavior and individual intentionality. However, as an etic, conceptual division, the pair pilgrim–tourist has also been used as a point of departure and at the same time fundamentally challenged in some influential scholarly theorizing and

Table 1.1 The binary tourism–pilgrimage scheme

Tourism	Pilgrimage
secular	religious
pleasure	faith
curiosity	duty
commercial	ascetic
evil	good
material	spiritual
end in itself	progression
holiday	ritual
presence	history/myth/future salvation
modern	pre- or anti-modern
confirming	transformative
relaxing	meritorious
distraction	intensification
directed towards center	directed towards periphery

Table 1.2 The binary tourist–pilgrim scheme

Tourist	Pilgrim
profane	religious
superficial	deep
playful	committed
this-worldly	other-worldly
pleasure-seeking	salvation-seeking
hedonism	quest
consumerism	renunciation

empirical work.[2] Instead of stressing the phenomenological or ideal-typical opposition between tourism and pilgrimage, while still building on the same binary classification, some scholars have pointed towards their deeper, structural convergence.[3]

An important point of reference for a certain strand of theorizing tourism has been the work of Victor Turner and his well-known notions of *liminality* and *communitas*.[4] Originally developed for an analysis of Ndembu rituals, Victor and Edith Turner extended the application of these terms to non-tribal societies. According to the Turners the standard ritual repertoires of "historical" or "salvation" religions contain merely truncated versions of the scale and complexity of *liminality* and *communitas* (Turner and Turner 1978, 3–4). In these religions, pilgrimage shares many of the attributes that *liminality* has in passage rites of tribal societies.[5] Since the Turners regard pilgrimages as voluntary acts rather than as compulsory social mechanisms, they classify them as *liminoid* or *quasi-liminal* (Turner and Turner 1978, 34–35). At one point, they consider a kinship between tourism and pilgrimage:

[A] tourist is half a pilgrim, if the pilgrim is half a tourist. Even when people bury themselves in anonymous crowds on beaches, they are seeking an almost sacred, often symbolic mode of communitas, generally unavailable to them in the structured life of the office, the shop floor, or the mine.

(Turner and Turner 1978, 20)

In this often quoted sketch, the conceptual dichotomy between tourism and pilgrimage is importantly challenged. The crowds at the beaches – the anti-stereotype of despised tourism par excellence – are devised as a *proto-communitas* rhetorically presented with an appropriate symbolism of death. Tourism gets elevated to a *quasi-liminoid* position. It acquires the qualities of a religious quest and turns into the *anti-structure* with regard to the ordinary working-routine.

The Turnerian line of argument fell on fertile ground in the study of tourism. Several studies have illustrated how travelers from different countries formed a touristic cosmos in which "ordinary" perceptions of space and time, patterns of movement, planning of time and spending money as well as norms and goals are effectively left behind. Likewise, tourists may leave their ordinary roles of scholars, businessmen, nurses, or whatever behind and play just one "total" role: that of the tourist (Hennig 1997, 43–53). And like pilgrims the tourists return home afterwards.

Christoph Hennig has applied this approach to such types of traveling as camping and beach holidays. The beach holiday, to take that example, constitutes a social world in which "ordinary" boundaries are no longer applicable: quasi naked bodies are getting closer – much closer on the beach than what would be acceptable in ordinary social contexts, where they would also be clothed – social hierarchies are not that prominent, children and their parents play together, there is no more boundary between work and time off, or school and leisure. Even the material environment contributes to this extraordinary scenario: the sand is a diffuse and unstructured, almost by nature anti-structural type of material, and the sea evokes a set of cultural and religious imaginations including symbolisms of paradise, death and regeneration. These symbolisms are then acted out and bodily appropriated by the diving and swimming – ritual acts that are a vital part of the archetypical holiday (Hennig 1997, 27–30). Similar observations could be made with respect to holidays in mountainous regions. Hennig has even gone one step further by claiming that many travelers, consciously or unconsciously, seek salvation in the sense of transformation of identity and inner renewal (Hennig 1997, 84–85).

This interpretation suggests a rationale for collective behavior that otherwise appears rather meaningless; the ritual interpretation of tourism thereby offered an important counter-narrative to the hitherto prevailing theories that would discount tourism as a superficial kind of illusory pseudo-practice.

Precisely this makes that sort of approach attractive. At the same time, one wonders whether the intuitive plausibility of that line of cultural analysis is substantiated by empirical evidence. However, empirical studies exemplifying that approach are not entirely lacking. Anthropologist Tom Selänniemi did some empirical work on Finnish tourists in Playa del Ingles on Gran Canaria, a typical mass tourism ghost-town dominated by huge apartment-hotels.[6] Finnish tourists staying at these hotels cook their own Finnish style meals and drink their Finnish style coffee. When they eat out they prefer a place called "Casa Finlandia". Hence, there is very little exposure to local culture, apart from the beach and some shops. As data for his project Selänniemi used questionnaires, field notes, photographs and diaries that tourists had written especially for him. One of the interesting side results of his study is the emphasis on the wide spectrum of senses that are being activated by tourists. Selänniemi situates the experiences reported by the tourists within the broader category of *etalanmatka*, verbatim meaning "a trip to the South", but as a folk category referring to "a charter trip to a holiday destination where the climate is more favourable than arctic Finland" (Selänniemi 2001, 88). Selänniemi interprets this "utopian" spatial demarcation – utopian in the sense of not referring to any specific locality – as a liminoid zone. Accordingly, he provides a Turnerian reading of his materials. Despite some traces of liminoid elements in the experience of the tourists[7] Selänniemi himself provides massive evidence for the observation that the life led by the Finnish tourists can be described as "psychocentrics who travel *with and in* their culture" (Selänniemi 2001, 91).[8] The only thing that really makes a difference is the weather – the fact that it is warm and sunny even in mid-winter. Obviously it is the weather that determines the choice of location. One may doubt that the Finnish tourists – quite like most tourists for that matter – are being transformed by their experience.[9] Moreover, one has to keep in mind that Turner's notion of *liminoid* or *quasi-liminal* refers to a number of elements that are clearly not applicable to modern tourism. For Turner *liminoid* phenomena "develop most character-istically outside the central economic and political processes" and they are "subversive" (Turner and Turner 1978, 253). That does not seem to be the case with tourism.

Tourism as a modern functional substitute for traditional religion

Whereas the Turners had focused on ritual structures, but only implicitly touched upon their religious dimensions, anthropologist Nelson Graburn, probably the most influential and vociferous advocate of the "religious" approach to the study of tourism, goes a step further. Graburn is here inspired by structural analysis as devised by his teacher Edmund Leach and, on a deeper level, by Mauss' theory of sacrifice as involving a process of sacralization. Graburn presents a binary scheme according to which tourism has similar, if not the very same characteristics assigned to pilgrimage in the scheme outlined above (Graburn 1989; see also Table 1.3).[10]

Graburn refers to this pair as "two lives" that "customarily alternate for ordinary people" (2001, 44). The transition between these "two lives" is demarcated by rites. At the re-entry into the profane workday at home, "[w]e are a new person who has gone through re-creation and, if we do not feel renewed, the whole point of tourism has been missed" (Graburn 2001, 27). He argues that "the basic motivation" underlying all forms of tourism regardless of their "outward rationale ... seems to be the human need for recreation" (Graburn 1989, 36).[11] Modern tourism thereby fulfills the position held by festivals (according to the Durkheimian pattern) in traditional societies – albeit on a (collectively) individual level.[12] It is the "structurally ritualized breaks in routine that define and relieve the ordinary" (Graburn 1989, 23). In line with a Durkheimian theoretical approach to religion and inspired by Turnerian ideas of ritual (Graburn 2001, 47–48), Graburn maintains that the source of this recreation can ultimately lie only in the sacred. Tourism is the "sacred journey" and for modern Westerners "tourism is the *best* kind of life for it is sacred in the sense of being exciting, renewing, and inherently self-fulfilling" (Graburn 1989, 28). Tourism here plays the role of a modern substitute for traditional festival and religion.

A similar theoretical approach had already been outlined by the American anthropologist-cum-sociologist (later a professor of Landscape Architecture) Dean MacCannell in his by now classic study *The Tourist: a new theory of the leisure class*, first published in 1976, i.e. two years prior to the Turners' book on pilgrimage. According to MacCannell the tourist "is one of the best models available for modern man-in-general" (MacCannell 1999 [1976], 1). In retrospect MacCannell writes that his study was devised "as a new kind of ethnographic report in *modern* society, as a demonstration that ethnography could be redirected away from primitive and peasant societies, that it could come home" (MacCannell 1999, xv). According to MacCannell, tourism is a key to modern society for it restores the unity and totality of society that were lost as a consequence of modernization and the corresponding processes of societal differentiation and alienation of the individual.

For MacCannell tourism is basically sightseeing – obviously a somewhat restricted perspective – which he describes as a specifically modern

Table 1.3 Graburn's binary structure

Profane	Sacred
workday	non-ordinary
stay-at-home	touristic

ritual performed to the differentiations of society. Sightseeing is a kind
of collective striving for a transcendence of the modern totality, a way
of overcoming the discontinuity of modernity, of incorporating its
fragments into unified experience.

(MacCannell 1999, 13)[13]

Obviously, sightseeing focuses on the sights that attract the tourists.
MacCannell posits "that tourist attractions are precisely analogous to the
religious symbolism of primitive people" (MacCannell 1999, 2). It is one of
the theoretically fruitful contributions of MacCannell to have pointed out
that the sights are not just given a priori, but that places, events, or objects
first of all need to be constituted as sights. He refers to this process as "Sight
Sacralization" (MacCannell 1999, 43–48). He distinguishes five stages of
this process, beginning with the naming and marking off of the sight from
other potential sights, followed by the "elevation and framing" of it – the
putting it on display and drawing a boundary around it –, followed by its
"enshrinement", which basically extends on the previous stage. The final
stages pertain to the reproductions of the sight: first in mechanical terms
taking the form of "the creation of prints, photographs, models or effigies
of the object which are themselves valued and displayed" (MacCannell
1999, 45) and which first set "the tourist in motion on his journey to find the
true object" (MacCannell 1999, 45), followed by "social reproduction",
when geographical or social units "begin to name themselves after famous
attractions" (MacCannell 1999, 45).

Apart from giving a religious label to this process of sight *sacralization*,
MacCannell refers to the sight as a "sacred object" (MacCannell 1999, 45).
His description appears to be inspired by processes of ritual consecration
of religious objects and their *enshrinement* as pilgrimage places. In a way,
then, the tourist attractions are the "shrines of modernity" (Cohen 1992b,
49). The attractions make up for the alienation of the modern subject. In
fact, MacCannell presupposes a link between the "modern disruption of real
life and the simultaneous emergence of a fascination for the 'real life' of
others" (MacCannell 1999, 91). The alienation of the modern subjects, their
disentanglement from their own world, including their domestic contexts, sets
in motion a quest for authenticity that they cannot find within themselves:
"Modern man has been condemned to look elsewhere, everywhere, for his
authenticity, to see if he can catch a glimpse of it reflected in the simplicity,
poverty, chastity, or purity of others" (MacCannell 1999, 41). For modern
subjects authenticity is always elsewhere and has to be staged at the sights.[14]
MacCannell speaks of the "dialectic of authenticity" (MacCannell 1999, 145),
where the inauthentic self and the authentic "other" depend on each other,
and where the authenticity of the other is invariably becoming endangered.[15]

In several ways, then, in MacCannell's macro-sociological scheme the rise
of tourism and touristic performances has replaced religion as the social

process reabsorbing the modern individual into societal totality.[16] The fact that, as he points out at one place, "[t]hroughout the world churches, cathedrals, mosques, and temples are being converted from religious to touristic function" (MacCannell 1999, 43), is no mere accident but reveals deeper (socio-) logics. Moreover, he conceives of modern tourist attractions in a way similar to traditional religious shrines.

However, religion was not MacCannell's theoretical object but modern society. His aim was to explain the omnipresence of tourism as a collective and individual phenomenon in modernity.[17] As an equally omnipresent phenomenon in pre-modern societies which seemed to perish under the conditions of modernity, religion served as an explanatory factor: tourism is taking the functional place that has been left vacant by religion, and the tourist sights seem to create "an elementary impulse analogous to the one that animates the Australian's awe for his Churinga boards" (MacCannell 1999, 42) made famous by Durkheim's theory of religion. Theories such as MacCannell's are thereby implicitly imbued by the ideological assumption of the disappearance of religion in modern societies. In this regard, the theories are mistaken. If one were to derive predictions from this model, one should assume that in countries where secularization scores high tourism rates high and vice versa; this, however, is not the case: in the United States, for instance, where religion does not seem to be much on the decline, tourism is a vibrating domain, likewise in other "religious" societies.

Tourist attractions as sacred places of national religion

For the United States, John F. Sears, then the Executive Director of the Franklin and Eleanor Roosevelt Institute (New York), has published a study on religious aspects of tourist attractions in the context of the construction of an American national identity in the 19th century (Sears 1998 [1989]). He suggests that tourist attractions were especially apt for American identity formation because they appealed to people belonging to different religious fractions; they could thereby bridge America's religious diversity and create sentiments of national unity.

Sears regards tourist attractions as functional equivalents to "sacred space in archaic societies" (Sears 1998, 6). In his interpretation of sacred space he is informed by, and he also refers to, Mircea Eliade.[18] He suggests that the "Niagara Falls, the Willey House, Mount Auburn Cemetery, and other cultural attractions suggested transcendent meanings and functioned as the sacred places of nineteenth-century American society" (Sears 1998, 6–7). This interpretation is based on the following types of evidence (with regard to the Niagara Falls):

- Visitors referred to themselves as "pilgrims".
- The approach to the site was ritualized.

- The emotional reaction to the site resembled familiar patterns of religious conversion.
- The Falls were ideally regarded as the most sublime of God's creation (resulting in an appropriate reaction of religious awe).
- The sense of danger and excitement surrounding the place.
- The temporary presence of a hermit at the Falls.

(Sears 1998, 12–30)

In the case of the Mammoth Cave (Kentucky) Sears points to the experience of entering a different space and time, associations with the mythic time of creation, and images of Hades and heaven.

> Among the attractions which the nineteenth-century tourist visited, Mammoth Caves seemed particularly suited to meeting the persistent need for sacred spaces that churches, cities, and other centers of earlier times had provided.
>
> (Sears 1998, 48)[19]

Sears seems here to imply that the tourist attractions have taken the place left vacant by religion.[20] While I see no way to test this hypothesis (which strikes me as unlikely), Sears' study unmistakably points to religious tropes and patterns in the description of sites and experiences at the attractions in his sources.

Sears argues that the tourist attractions as a result of mass tourism and commercialization of travel since around 1885[21] lost their "conscious and explicit religious resonance" (Sears 1998, 10). Nevertheless, he finds that

> [T]he nation's principal tourist attractions continue to function, like temples or sacred cities or cosmic mountains, as places where, in Mircea Eliade's words, there is "an irruption of the sacred into the world". At such places tourists hope to enter a world separated from the world of their familiar, daily routine and to contact a transcendent reality.
>
> (Sears 1998, 210)

The changing faces of tourism

When reconsidering early theories of tourism (MacCannell and Graburn), one has to recall that these were formulated in the 1970s, a period which saw a rapid expansion in modern mass tourism. Tourism, however, has continued to increase and to diversify. Apart from other developments the last decades have witnessed "a rapid segmentation of the tourism market" (Harrison 2003, 27). Tourism no longer seems to provide the sort of coherent structure it had for MacCannell – if it ever did, given the multidimensional character of tourist/tourism experiences (Ryan 2002b).

The fact that increasingly more people travel ever more often – some are hardly at home anymore – has two major consequences. First, most people have quite a travel-career, they are practiced experience-hunters, increasingly sophisticated in their demands and expectations, but at the same time often reflexively ironic and playful about their own experiences,[22] an attitude that enables them to enjoy evidently inauthentic ("staged") entertainments and performances. "Genuine fakes", i.e. objects or performances which are bought or consumed knowing that they are not what they pretend to be, are nowadays not felt to be embarrassing but enjoyed as such (Brown 1996).[23]

Second, and related to that, "tourism is no longer the exceptional part of people's life" (Prentice 2004, 268). There are no hard and fixed lines distinguishing leisure, work and tourism in post-modern societies. The boundaries between work and non-work have become more fuzzy and flexible, and so have the boundaries between holidays and non-holidays. Tourism is omnipresent in contemporary society (Urry 2002, 32, 74). These two observations present an important empirical challenge to the type of structural theories outlined above: for many people the tourist experience is the ordinary non-ordinary,[24] and hence may no longer qualify for the great sacred anti-structure. Both spheres ("worlds") are connected by the mobile phone and other media.

Third, both as an economic sector and as a domain of modern lifestyles, tourism is a highly diversified reality. There are various types of tourists and tourism. Basing a theory of tourism on one of its forms only – the beach tourist and the summer holidays – therefore seems like a futile exercise. Recall some of the many varieties under which tourism in terms of main activities, attractions and motivation with related market structures now manifests itself (in alphabetical order):[25]

- academic tourism
- adventure tourism
- agritourism
- backpacker tourism
- business tourism
- collector tourism
- countryside tourism
- creative tourism
- culture tourism[26] (including arts, folklore, foods, museums, music, wine, etc.)
- "dark" or "disaster" tourism[27]
- diaspora tourism
- ecotourism

- educational tourism
- entertainment tourism
- event tourism
- gambling and gaming tourism
- heritage tourism
- hunting tourism
- medical tourism
- nature tourism
- political tourism
- sex tourism
- shopping tourism
- spa and wellness tourism[28]
- sports tourism
- technology tourism
- urban tourism
- visiting friends and relatives tourism
- volunteer tourism[29]
- youth tourism (and tourism for other age groups).

Most of these segments, many of which are combined in actual tours, again cover a wider range of diversified options. Religious/spiritual tourism (see the Introduction; pp. 13ff) could be included in this list. As will be exemplified throughout this book, religion in various forms is present on the itineraries of other forms of tourism including but not limited to cultural tourism, diaspora tourism, ecotourism, heritage, urban and wellness tourism.

This segmentation of the market and the diversification of the tourists points to "the pitfalls inherent in trying to characterize any generic tourist experience" (Harrison, 2003, 28).[30] This statement should also serve as an important caveat for any generalizations about the various ways religious elements, dimensions and experiences become part of contemporary tourism. We will also encounter new niches of tourism where religion and spirituality play a more prominent, or at least a different, role than in other forms of tourism.

From modernity to post-modernity

While several influential theoreticians of tourism regarded tourism as a modern functional equivalent or substitute for religion,[31] Polish-British sociologist Zygmunt Bauman has given a new twist to the pilgrimage tourism scheme by taking it to stand for the prevailing conditions of modernity and post-modernity respectively. As Bauman sees it, pilgrimage is a suitable metaphor of modern life, the great project of meaning-making, identity-building and saving for the future (Baumann 1996, 19–23). In contemporary (post-modern) society, however, "life-as-pilgrimage [is] hardly feasible as a strategy and unlikely to be chosen as one" (Baumann 1996, 24). The modalities of post-modern life and society demand other guiding metaphors, and for Bauman "the stroller, the vagabond, the tourist and the player offer jointly the metaphor for the postmodern strategy moved by the horror of being bound and fixed" (Baumann 1996, 26). Like the vagabond, the tourist is constantly on the move and does not belong to the places where he goes, but unlike the vagabond he goes there on purpose. This purpose "is new experience; the tourist is a conscious and systematic seeker of experience, of a new and different experience, of the experience of difference and novelty – as the joys of the familiar wear off and cease to allure" (Baumann 1996, 29). This quest for experiential novelty, on the other hand, is mitigated and domesticated "by the profusion of safety cushions and well marked escape routes" (Baumann 1996, 29). The strange/other does not frighten anymore. Unlike the vagabond the tourist has a home to turn to, but on the other hand the tourist's never-satiated appetite for ever more new experiences corresponds to "the fear of *home-boundedness*, of being tied to a place and barred from exit" (Baumann 1996, 31).

This account echoes some familiar themes from the study of unchurched religion, new religiosities, or reflexive spiritualities. If it were not already used as a niche in the tourism branch, one could consider "spiritual tourism" as an alternative to well-known metaphors such as the "spiritual marketplace", "patchwork religion", or "vagabonding religion". One may think here of the changing destinations for the spiritual tourist-seeker, the constant search for new spiritual experiences, and a basic curiosity seeking constant experiential enrichment rather than the one, once-in-a-lifetime, transformative experience. The pilgrimage to the great goal of life is replaced by the touring selves which are bound to remain the same after returning (Bruner 1991). "Everyone's on the move ... : dwelling-in-travel", to borrow a quote from a post-modern theorist (Clifford 1997, 2).

Note that the terms "pilgrimage" and "tourism" are here used merely as metaphors for social processes.[32] The present book is not interested in "the tourist" as a theoretical model or metaphor, but in some of the myriad things that happen at the confluence of religion and tourism "out there" in the global (post-)modern world.

SOUVENIRS FROM CHAPTER I

- Tourism and pilgrimage, the tourist and the pilgrim, are often conceptualized as a binary structure with opposite and corresponding attributes.
- Some scholars have challenged this scheme by pointing to the structural convergence between tourists and pilgrims; tourist behavior is interpreted in terms of liminality and *communitas*, but the utopian zones often do not lead to transformative experiences.
- An influential theoretical approach, informed by Durkheimian theory and secularization narratives, interprets tourism as a functional substitute for religion, but does not have religion as its theoretical object nor as its subject matter.
- Religious tropes and patterns are engaged in the perception of tourist attractions, but this does not imply a replacement of religion by tourism.
- Tourists have become experienced travelers and tourism has witnessed a diversification to such a degree that macro-theories of tourism, the tourist and the tourist experience seem questionable; this also challenges religionist readings of tourism.
- Religion comes into play in different branches of tourism.
- As a metaphor for post-modern life and identity construction, the tourist can also be engaged as a metaphor for post-modern spirituality, but the present book is interested in tourism as a social fact and not as a theoretical metaphor.

Chapter 2

Interfaces

The present book is concerned with the interfaces between tourism and religion(s) – i.e. the ways and places where these two "systems" meet and interact. Such interfaces may take the form of impacts or interferences. The notion of impact refers to the effect of one domain on the other. Religion can have effects on tourists, and tourists as much as tourism can have an impact on religions, religious places, performances and people. Tourism may also benefit from religion, and religion may build on tourism. In many cases, therefore, the interface is rather an interference, understood here (like in physics) as "[t]he mutual action of two waves or systems of waves, in reinforcing or neutralizing each other, when their paths meet or cross".[1] In actual fact, however, it may be difficult to neatly distinguish impacts from interferences.

In the present chapter we will address some interrelated questions serving as starting points of our journey through this neglected territory. To begin with, we will need to be reminded that even though tourism is generally perceived as a profane activity, tourists are not a priori a-religious people. As we shall see, the religious needs of the travelers (and those working in travel-related workspaces) can be catered to by special churches and parishes, but may call forth further institutional provisions. When traveling, many religious people will continue to practice their religion, but while traveling special needs sometimes arise that require religious coping, be it because of things happening on the way or back home. Religious objects, symbols, sites and personnel may be present at some transitional spaces within tourism including airports and hotels. Obviously, their religious preferences and values to some extent influence decisions taken by tourists. Yet the question imposes itself whether tourism, itself regarded as secular activity, leads to a "secularization" of the people engaged in it – a question which so far for the most part has been studied with regard to host communities. Last but not least, while tourists are by definition "persons traveling to and staying in places outside their usual environment" (see p. 6), these travels may actually bring people home – in a narrow or much wider sense linked to the performative construction of identities. At that point, the rhetoric of pilgrimage once again enters the travel scenario.

Religious people on travel

Some religions make travel mandatory for several reasons – most prominently in cases of compulsory pilgrimages. On the other hand, religion may
restrain the travel choices and behaviors of its adherents, for instance by
imposing purity rules. In extreme cases religious concerns may prevent
believers from traveling altogether. Also in terms of religious worldviews and
ideologies religions have different attitudes to traveling and tourism.[2]

Once people travel, however, they rarely leave their religion at home. Even
in such an apparently profane setting as tourism, people do not automatically stop practising their religion. Believers will continue to practice
their faith and tourists seek "possibilities of satisfying their religious needs",
as Vukonić puts it (1996, 59). Anecdotal evidence has it that at least some
people resume an interest in the church while holidaying.[3] For others, the
very situation of traveling creates situations of emotional confusion, stress
and unpredictability that may call for religious responses; health issues
during the trip and the death of friends or relatives back home are issues that
may require religious coping.[4]

Some groups of travelers relax their attitude to religious observances, once
they are no longer under the control and surveillance of religious communities and authorities.[5] In order to be able to travel, people who wish to
remain committed to mandatory rules of their religion, on the other hand,
have certain requirements. Often, these pertain to dietary regulations. Many
Muslim tourists, for example, wish to eat only *halal* food and they also like
to get information on the prayer times at the respective destinations. For
many Jewish travelers, access to *kosher* food is important.

In Michigan (USA), resorts catering particularly to Jewish tourists were
started in the 1920s. Many of these resorts adopted *kosher* food regulations
and observed the Sabbath. The fact that Yiddish was spoken was considered
another advantage (Ioannides and Ioannides 2002, 20). Already in the 1880s,
Jewish resorts had been established in the Catskills and Adirondacks near
New York and, since the 1920s, when Jews started to purchase "Christian"
resorts, the so-called "borscht belt" in the Catskills developed into a Jewish
holiday area dominated by "Yiddishkeit" of an Eastern European flavor
(Bajohr 2003, 161).

Besides accommodating ritual and social needs the main reason for the
creation of separate holiday resorts, however, was the fact that Jews were
denied access to American tourism facilities. Up to World War II, or even
longer, American holiday resorts enforced strict anti-Semitic entrance
policies; "signs in vacation areas specifically prohibiting Jews from renting
holiday homes" or "No Hebrew Accommodation" were not uncommon
(Ioannides and Cohen Ioannides 2004, 104). This phenomenon is known as
"resort anti-Semitism".[6] As late as 1956/57, according to reports from the
Anti-Defamation League some 30 percent of hotels in the United States did

not take in Jewish patrons; in the states of Maine, Vermont and New Hampshire 56 percent of hotels would refuse to accommodate Jewish guests (Bajohr 2003, 162).[7]

In recent decades, as a result of diminishing racial boundaries in the United States, these resorts have lost their function and largely declined;[8] most Jews nowadays spend their holidays at the same domestic destinations that also attract non-Jews, in particular Florida. Moreover, luxury hotels and resorts take the special needs of their Jewish guests actively into account. Luxury hotels, resorts and spas routinely have special Passover offers, and Passover travel has increased strongly in recent times (Ioannides and Cohen Ioannides 2002, 22). When it comes to group-specific destinations, "old neighborhoods" within the US, where they or their parents had lived previously, have emerged as new destinations as well as the countries, mostly in Central and Eastern Europe, which their parents, grandparents or ancestors left as they migrated to the States (Ioannides and Cohen Ioannides 2004, 105).

Tourism Studies sometimes addresses the needs of religiously committed tourists. Take an empirical study of the religious needs of Christian tourists in Israel as an example. The agenda here is to provide strategic tools for the accommodation sector to attract new customer segments and improve competitiveness (Weidenfeld 2006).

In line with the segmentation of the tourist market, specialized agencies have emerged that cater to the requirements and demands from specific religious groups (Cohen 2003b, 156). In the case of the Jewish market, there are a variety of agencies offering heritage tours, solidarity missions, Jewish cruises (i.e. cruises with Jewish quality entertainment, religious services and *kosher* food), Jewish single tours, exotic or adventure tours (such as an African Kosher Safari Tour), and educational tours (Collins-Kreiner and Olsen 2004, 280–86).

"Faith-based tourism", also referred to as "faith tourism", "religious tourism" or "Christian travel", is currently developing into a major new market force in the United States. Since Christian books, music and films have turned into a significant segment of American consumer culture, it is to be expected that the same will happen with Christian travel. Protagonists of this line of business talk about a market worth US$18 billion, with some 300 million potential travelers. Christian travel appears to be dominated by small-scale organizations and entrepreneurs. Meanwhile, a "World Religious Travel Association" was started to assist its members including tour operators, travel wholesalers, cruise lines, destination marketing organizations, suppliers, travel agents, religious organizations, group planners and travelers with networking, education, increased visibility, etc.; the World Religious Travel Association also hosts an annual World Religious Travel Expo and Educational Conference. Recently, some major mainstream travel agencies apparently began catering to that clientele. There are also some travel magazines such as *Going on Faith* and *Travel with Spirit* that seek to inspire their readers to plan faith-based holidays.[9]

Apart from offering trips to "religious" destinations and events such as Israel and Oberammergau, faith-based travel seems to operate along thematic lines where standard forms of tourism are either supplemented or modified in line with a religious agenda. An example of the former is where Christian elements are integrated into ordinary travel schedules such as when water-rafting is supplemented by the singing of devotionals after meals. An example of the latter, i.e. the adaptation of established forms of tourism to perceived religious values, are "Christian cruises", where cruise ship bars don't serve alcoholic beverages, casinos are darkened and fashion shows display "modest" fashion. Another format for "faith-based travel" is to incorporate religious forms of travel such as pilgrimages and mission into leisure frameworks.

Tourist churches and parishes

Churches were engaged in tourism at an early date. In the north of England, besides pubs and clubs, churches helped to organize tours for their members by hiring an excursion or holiday train and by providing facilities (Urry 2002, 24). For the United States, the World Religious Travel Organization reports that 50,000 churches and religious organizations currently offer some forms of travel programs.[10]

Starting from the early history of modern tourism, the religious requirements of tourists have led to the establishment of special churches catering exclusively to the needs of tourists. Already by the 1840s, Florence had an English church (besides a newspaper and a reading room holding London newspapers) that served the massive influx of British tourists who obviously would not rely on local Catholic churches (Withey 1997, 88). (They visited the Catholic churches nevertheless, albeit for other purposes.) Similar institutions can be found in other popular destinations, for instance in Switzerland.

Sometimes churches are built without there being a special parish for tourists. An example is a church for summer tourists built on the East Frisian island of Norderney (Germany) in 1931 by the well-known German architect Dominikus Böhm (Hoff 1962, plates 284–89).[11]

Places like the Canary Islands witness a continuous presence of large numbers of tourists, some of whom stay for extended periods of time, especially during winter, as second homes, places of recovery or after retirement.[12] As a result, there are some tourist churches that are part of migration-infrastructures such as newspapers, clubs, associations, shops and other services in the main tourist centers. While the majority population on the Canary Islands is Catholic, the tourist churches belong to different branches of Protestantism and national groups, mainly British, German and Scandinavian.

The first Anglican churches were started in the late 19th century – All Saints in Puerto de la Cruz/Tenerife (1890), Holy Trinity Church in Las Palmas/ Gran Canaria and St. George in Santa Cruz/Tenerife (1903) (Gonzáles 2008, 72). The German and Swedish churches were established around a century later. The first pastor was sent to the Canary Islands from Germany in the 1970s, and he was later assigned the task of starting a parish that was formally established in 1988. In 2005 separate parishes were established for the Northern and the Southern Islands. This "German language church" aims to provide community, conversation, services and ministry for people staying on the islands who are interested in using the German language (i.e. not just German nationals).[13]

There are also religious communities of other Christian churches and denominations in the Canaries. The tourist parishes have only marginal contacts with the Spanish churches (Gonzáles 2008). Although numbers are difficult to obtain, among some tourists one apparently finds a renewed interest in religion and church life, possibly as an escape from the monotony of tourist lifestyles (Diez de Valesco 2008a, 21), but also as a means to establish social networks. These tourist congregations are an interesting phenomenon because they are rather stable in their demographic composition, although their "membership" is continuously shifting.[14]

Non-Spanish churches or other foreign religious organizations also cater to the needs of non-nationals working in the tourism sector. Moreover, apart from churches there are other providers of religious or spiritual services in operation on the Canary Islands, which thereby become an extension of the religious landscapes of Northern Europe. At the same time, the sun and beach tourism is being extended to the niche market of religious/spiritual tourism, perceived to be a growing market segment for the Canary Islands (Diez de Valesco 2008b, 307).

Sometimes religious groups use tourism facilities as a draw for their own (passive) adherents but also as a means to reach broader audiences; this interpretation has been suggested by Francisco Diez de Velasco for the Hotel Kadampa in a rural setting near Malaga (Andalusia). Apart from its name, which does not sound "religious" for those not familiar with contemporary Buddhism, this hotel advertises itself as a standard hotel situated close to whatever this tourism region has to offer in terms of cultural and natural attractions;[15] at the same time, it is the main center of Kadampa Buddhism in Spain, housing the publishing division of the group, offering courses and selling religious paraphernalia. Moreover, right behind the swimming pool there is a *gompa*.[16] None of this is mentioned in the advertisements of the hotel, which thereby serves simultaneously as a standard hotel and a religious outreach center.

The case of the German Lutheran church that sent a minister to the Canaries has already been mentioned. There are some more organized strategies. Consider the Norwegian Seafarers' Church (Sjømannskirken), which represents the Norwegian Lutheran state church abroad. It was founded in 1864 under the name of the Norwegian Seafarers' Mission. Originally its mandate was to provide pastoral care for the seafarers abroad. The organization greatly expanded its orbit after World War II. In 1980, on the request of the bishops of the Norwegian state church, it changed its mandate to provide services to all Norwegians staying, or living, abroad.[17] Tourists are now a main target group. Tourists visit its churches not only for religious reasons, but also when they need help, company, a familiar environment or merely seek a place to stay. The church now advertises itself as "your home abroad" – and that includes tourists as much as non-tourists. Since late 2008, the Sjømannskirken has a new consecrated church in Arguineguín on the southern coast of Gran Canaria, and the new church has apparently become quite popular among seasonally resident tourists who flock to the church to read Norwegian papers, get together with fellow Norwegians and have some Norwegian food. The church has also been a popular site for Norwegian couples to get married, and it offers six weekly dates for holding weddings.

Apart from tourist organizations made of and for tourists, many religious communities and organizations such as parishes themselves are developing various travel activities benefitting from tourism infrastructures. Parishes travel to pilgrimage or other religious sites, often in the same region, and they undertake educational trips. Christian parishes have a tradition of mutual visitation, in order to exchange experiences and opinions, to network, and to worship together (Neumann and Rösener 2006, 154). The Bergen Cathedral parish, for example, regularly exchanges visits with its sister parish in London, and the two parishes together arrange trips, for example to Canterbury.[18] Moreover, the staff sometimes holds meetings out of town. Visiting other parishes, we were told in an interview, is generally perceived as rewarding and inspiring. Given its beautiful location and church buildings, in recent years the Bergen parish was also contacted and visited by congregations from Sweden and Denmark. While this is merely a local example, it seems reasonable to assume that tourism is by now a standard activity of religious communities and organizations at least in Europe, but possibly the world over.

In Germany, according to figures provided by one of the largest travel agents specializing in Biblical and other religious trips, German parishes on average conduct 1.5 trips of several days and around four day trips. This amounts to some 500,000 parishioners traveling annually (Neumann and Rösener 2006, 154). According to a 1998 national survey, traveling is also part of the usual activities of US American congregations: 45.5 percent of congregations and 62.5 percent of attendees reported an overnight trip during the past year (Chaves 2004, 230), but the data does not specify what kind of trips these were. The question was not replicated in the 2006–7 survey, but two new questions were added. Asked whether a group from the congregation had in the last year travelled in the US to assist people in need 30 percent of the congregations, containing 50 percent of attendees, reported that they did; service trips abroad were somewhat less frequent (25 percent of congregations, containing 42 percent of attendees). The data does not specify how many people went on these trips; typically only a small group from a congregation may go on such trips.[19] These figures testify to a great deal of traveling overall, and congregations may well make trips for other purposes than assisting people in need.

Simultaneously with the immense growth of international tourism after World War II, specific ministries have developed at airports.[20] These ministries cater both to the needs of travelers and to those working at the airports (the latter apparently being more difficult in the case of large airports). There have been chaplains at Heathrow airport (London) since 1946, and in 1952 a Catholic airport chapel was dedicated by the Catholic archbishop at Boston Logan International Airport. Similar initiatives soon followed. In 1961, the first meeting of airport chaplains took place when the Catholic priests of Brussels and Paris Orly airports met. This was followed in 1967, when ten airport chaplains gathered in Brussels, which was the starting point for the formation of the International Association of Civil Aviation Chaplains (IACAC). This is a networking organization that now has members at some 130 airports around the world, including two in Turkey (the only Middle Eastern country) as well as Bangkok, Hong Kong and Singapore, representing Asian countries. While the original kernel consisted of Catholic priests, the organization soon assumed an ecumenical character and it now considers itself a multifaith organization. To become a member, one does not have to be a Christian, but one needs to be active in airport ministry and one has to be approved by some official authority of one's denomination or religion. While all members of the executive board are Christians, the IACAC also has some Jewish and Islamic members.[21] Moreover, the airport chaplains typically find themselves serving adherents of different religions, whenever required, so that multifaith ministry seems to be quite common in practice. While there is no standard set of services, for travelers airport chaplains deal with several issues including prayer, counseling, travel assistance, provision of communication and a wide range of emergency responses (from individual cases to disasters). Apart from this international multifaith association, the Catholic Church has also established a National Conference of Catholic Airport Chaplains in the United States and a Secretariat of the European Catholic Chaplaincies in Civil Aviation.

The International Association of Civil Aviation Chaplains has devised a logo – a figure of a kneeling person, apparently in prayer – used at many airports as a signpost directing people to the respective religious facilities, which many airports are equipped with. Among the world's ten busiest airports by passenger traffic (figures for 2008 provided by the Airport Council International)[22] nine are provided with religious facilities – Los Angeles

International Airport (LAX) being the exception. Among the ten airports, Tokyo International Airport (HND, not to be confused with Narita!) and Beijing Capital International Airport (PEK) are the only non-Euro-American airports. While I did not find any reference to religious facilities on their respective websites, internet websites such as Flickr and YouTube reveal pictures of an impressive temple at PEK (search under Beijing Airport Temple) and a "Shinto Shrine" at HND (search under Shinto Shrine Haneda), which in the Japanese original is referred to as "airport shrine"; besides Japanese and English, the sign is also written in Chinese and Korean, which is surprising since a Shinto shrine would normally only be frequented by Japanese.[23]

In the West, in most cases, the ritual space is referred to as a chapel, alternatively as a prayer room.[24] At London Heathrow (LHR), in the land-side area, one finds both a chapel – St George's Chapel, opened in 1968 – and several other facilities, including a multifaith prayer room (opened 30 years later), which is above the chapel, at street level. According to Marion Bowman, services held at the chapel "are often very flexible – for example a memorial service with readings from the Sikh scripture"[25] – but the official airport website (www.heathrowairport.com> Airport information> terminal information> worship) only lists regular Catholic services, and Anglican and Free Church services "by arrangement", without specifically mentioning any other religious traditions. LHR also has some airside facilities in the terminals. While the airport provides the space, the chaplains are financially supported by the religious groups. At other airports, chapels can also be qualified as multifaith. Take the Interfaith Airport Chapel, incorporated in 1980, at Hartsfield-Jackson Atlanta International Airport (ATL). On the airport's website (http://www.atlanta-airport.com > Passenger Information > Customer Service > Religious Services[26]), the chapel is described as "a sanctuary in the world's busiest airport". While the "Interfaith Airport Chapel is available to all faiths for reading, meditation and prayer", Christian services are held twice a week, and it seems that the chapel does not display any devotional items from Judaism, Buddhism, Hinduism and Sikhism. At O'Hare International Airport Chicago (ORD), there is an Interfaith Chapel, which is described as "a peaceful oasis" and "as a place for silent prayer, as well as a place for worship and liturgies; and a place to bow your head in prayer while lifting up your heart and spirit".[27] The multifaith chapel, which was first started as a Catholic place, is currently served by a Catholic, a Protestant and a Muslim chaplaincy. At Paris Charles de Gaulle (CDG) and Frankfurt International (FRA) airports there are not only different chaplaincies but also different religious spaces – namely Catholic, Protestant, Jewish and Muslim at CDG and Catholic/Protestant (ecumenical), Greek Orthodox, Jewish and Muslim at FRA. While religion appears as a multifaith sphere at some airports (in Britain and the United States), it appears in the disguise of bounded communities at others (in France and Germany).[28]

While there is a "Prayer Room Plane" (a separate level with prayer rooms for different religions) at Taipei airport,[29] there are mosques at airports in many Islamic countries.

Also some airlines based in countries with a predominantly Islamic population address the religious needs of travelers. Premium lounges of Etihad Airways (based in Abu Dhabi) at Frankfurt and Heathrow and the Gulf Air lounge at Bahrain International Airport are provided with (Muslim) prayer rooms, and Saudi Arabian Airlines even has a prayer space within their aircraft. Some airlines based in Southeast Asian countries such as Indonesian Airlines and Malaysia Airlines carry prayer cards.

Responses by religious and other public institutions/ organizations

The case of airport ministries is evidence for the active involvement of churches in matters of tourism. In this section, we will briefly outline some other reactions such as:

- efforts to meet the religious demands by tourists
- strategies by religious organizations to put tourism on their agendas
- tactics to downplay the salience of religion, and to emphasize religious freedom and diversity in the context of tourism promotion
- endeavors to align tourism with religious value systems
- attempts to make use of religion for the promotion of tourism.

To begin with, religious groups and institutions make a contribution to tourism by making their sites available to tourists. Recently, several church organizations have taken initiatives to increase the availability of church buildings to travelers. Churches in Finland, Sweden, Norway, Denmark and Estonia share an initiative to keep roadside churches open during the summer months. In 2005, 265 churches in Finland were committed to be open for five hours on five days a week for five weeks during summer. This initiative is coordinated by a network, to which participating churches pay a membership fee (Neumann and Rösener 2006, 140). In Germany, the regional Protestant church of Lower Saxony (Hannoversche Landeskirche) has introduced a sign that marks churches pledging to be available to the public at least five days a week for a couple of hours during summer. Other regional churches have adopted that sign and, in 2006, 480 churches held the sign (Neumann and Rösener 2006, 96, 113).

The Norwegian Seafarers Church (see p. 35f.) is an example of a large-scale religious organization that has put tourism on the agenda. In this respect, the Catholic Church is not lagging behind. Apart from encouraging tourists to partake of the rituals (sacraments) offered by the local church wherever they are (Vukonić 2006, 239), the Catholic Church has developed an overall policy with the "intent to reach tourists, who do not travel for an express religious purpose, with a religious message on their tour, especially during visits at sites of worship, and transform them, as it were, from mere observers into participants" (Cohen 2004b, 157; see also Petrillo 2003). As pointed out by Vukonić, "there has been no pope after World War II who has not spoken, either in passing or directly, about tourism" (Vukonić 1996, 163). The Catholic Church has not only published opinions and instruction about tourism and the relation between tourism and the church, but has also convened various meetings on tourism and it has established special institutions, including a Pontifical Commission on Migration and Tourism in 1970 (Vukonić 1996, 162; Mazza 2007, 157–64). According to the Pastoral Constitution promulgated in 1988, tourists, together with refugees, migrants, nomads, circus workers, seafarers and people working for airlines and in airports fall within the pastoral concern of the Pontifical Council for the Pastoral Care of Migrants and Itinerant People.[30]

In addition, various national committees have been established. In France, the main destination country for international tourism, the Catholic Church had by 1962 established a unit for Tourism and Leisure Pastoral Care (Pastorale du Tourisme et des Loisirs). According to its website,[31] this ministry not only wishes to respond to the religious needs of those visiting religious sites, but also those admiring nature, seeking silence and calm, families who are gathering for special occasions, sportsmen and, last but not least, those working in the tourism sector. The different dioceses have adopted a variety of strategies and measures to locate pastoral care in the context of tourism.

Not only Christian organizations develop strategic responses to tourism. While "most Islamic nations, particularly in the Middle East, have been reluctant recipients of tourism growth" (Timothy and Iverson 2006, 188), there is now an increasing receptivity to tourism in the so-called Muslim world, which so far has had a very minor share of global tourism revenues. Even countries with Muslim majority populations have an economic interest in the development of tourism; accordingly governments of countries such as Egypt, Malaysia, Morocco, Turkey and the United Arab Emirates, which are the top destinations among countries with Islamic majority populations, have tried to accommodate tourism. At the same time, tourists and tourism have been an issue in domestic policy and discussions on the Islamic identity of some of these nations.

A content analysis of official tourism promotion materials issued by leading destination countries with Islamic majority populations has shown that while Islam is acknowledged as a factor in all materials (with the exception of the official website of the Indonesia Ministry of Culture and Tourism), they consistently emphasize topics such as religious freedom, freedom of worship, tolerance, diversity, co-existence, hospitality (including religious laissez-faire), international lifestyle, or, as in the case of Tunisia, they point to the limited direct impact of Islam on holidaymakers. Moreover, in all materials the "space allocated to Islam is limited in comparison to the amount of text and pictures depicting physical environments, nonreligious dimensions of cultural heritage, and more modern amenities. The tendency is for Islam to be relegated to the periphery" (Henderson 2008, 143).

Turkey is an interesting case in this context because of an organized attempt to make use of the religious capital (or heritage) of the country in order to reach out to a different group of customers. In 1995, the Turkish government launched the project of "faith tourism". On its official website, the Turkish government declares:

> There is a myriad of important Islamic, Christian and Jewish sites scattered around Turkey, making the country an attractive destination for faith tourism.[32]

The Ministry of Tourism had some years previously launched a "Faith Tourism Project" as part of an "Ecopromotion" project developed by this Ministry "with the aim of diversifying Turkish tourism products" (Aktaş and Ekın 2003, 159). Given that so far only 52,000 visitors, i.e. 0.75 percent, of the total number of tourists visiting Turkey (in 1993) came to Turkey for religious purposes, the tourist agencies obviously saw a niche market with a strong growth prospect.[33] In order to enhance the attractiveness of Anatolian religious sites as destinations on tourist routes, tourism experts from the Akdeniz University in Antalya, one of Turkey's key tourist regions, have prompted a number of adaptations. Among others, their scheme includes the following suggestions.

- Activities such as St. Nicholas Festival in Demre should be supported, ... new activities about the important religious personalities such as Virgin Mary and St. Jean should be arranged. Moreover, these activities should possess international dimension.
- In the activities of advertisement and promotion, especially the religious associations should be focused.
- Famous personalities not only of Muslim communities, but also in the entire world (Yunus Emre, Pir Sultan Abdal, Hacı Bektas, Mevlana) should be introduced to the faith tourism market and the annual ceremonies of them should take on an international dimension.
- The House of the Virgin Mary, Seven Churches and St. Peter Church, having great importance in Christianity, should be developed as a pilgrim center with the support of the Pope in the Vatican.

(Aktaş and Ekın 2003, 160)

These suggestions are remarkable in several respects, including their emphasis on Christian festivals, sites, personalities and the proposed tourist ecumenical alliance with the Vatican. As expected, Armenian Christianity remains conspicuously absent.[34] The scheme clearly illustrates the desire to exploit religious resources for touristic purposes, to provide an international promotion of local or regional events and sites in a tourist framework, and even to invent new "activities" around religious resources by creating destinations. While this is a scheme devised by academicians, it is a clear example of a global mentality of the tourist industry.

On an international level, the first international meeting on tourism in Islamic countries, arranged by the Organization of the Islamic Conference (OIC) was held in 2000 in Isfahan (Iran). The official designation was "The First Session of the Islamic Conference for Ministers of Tourism". It was attended by representatives of 31 countries and some international organizations including the World Tourism Organization (WTO). In its first declaration it recognized "the need for support and coordination in archaeological and antiquities' issues" (Al-Hamarneh and Steiner 2004, 178).

In March 2007, the Cultural Heritage News Agency (CHN), an organization administered by the Iran Cultural Heritage, Handicrafts and Tourism Organization, controlled and funded by the Government of Iran, arranged an "International Conference on Tourism in Islamic Countries". In its "Final Declaration", it suggested that "by the year 2010 which has been called the Year of Tourism of Islamic Countries, all the 57 member states of the Organization of Islamic Conference (OIC) present some fundamental plans for attracting tourists".[35] Moreover, it expressed the hope to establish "a permanent think tank for tourism of Islamic countries" and to create "an organization under the name of 'Organization of Tourism of Islamic Countries' as one of the affiliated organizations of Islamic Conference Organization to pave the ground for promoting tourism among the member states".[36] The Declaration also voiced a special concern with the use of media facilities and "image-making" in order to effectively attract tourists to Islamic countries.

In this context, there also emerged the concept of "Islamic tourism". Among others, it is propagated by the London-based Arabic/English *Islamic Tourism* magazine, which was launched some hours before the attacks on September 11, 2001 (Al-Hamarneh and Steiner 2004, 179–80). In part, the concept of "Islamic tourism" aims at redirecting tourism from Western-style consumption and Western-style destinations to Islamic sites and behaviors and values. Some elements of Islamic tourism such as alcohol-free accommodations, gender-segregated transportation, leisure and wellness facilities, and on-site prayer rooms are already established in Saudi Arabia and Iran (Al-Hamarneh and Steiner 2004, 180).

In Europe, state agencies are also involved in building bridges between religion and tourism. Take the example of some German federal states. In the north-eastern federal state of Mecklenburg-Vorpommern, from 2002 to 2005 a project administered by the Ministry for Agriculture and sponsored by the European Union aimed at developing local churches as tourist attractions by making them part of travel routes; these routes were provided with road signs and pocket guides were published. In this manner, 166 village churches became part of 24 routes. This project hoped to make hinterland regions more attractive as destinations (Neumann and Rösener 2006, 163). In 2003, the Ministry of Economic Affairs and Employment of Saxony-Anhalt sponsored an initiative to explore the development of "spiritual tourism" in and to this federal state. In this connection, it is worth noting that only 20 percent of Saxony-Anhalt's population belongs to a Christian church. (Saxony-Anhalt formerly was part of the GDR.) This may explain the choice of terminology ("spiritual" rather than "religious" or "Christian" tourism). As part of this initiative, a theologian conducted a study on the feasibility of developing the rich heritage of monasteries in Saxony-Anhalt into a resource for (spiritual) tourism (Schwilius, Kasper and Volgenandt 2009).

Apart from religious, state and interstate organizations, even the United Nations can become agents for the promotion of religion(s) in tourism contexts. In November 2001, the United Nations Economic and Social Commission for Asia and the Pacific (ESCAP) held a Seminar on the Promotion of Buddhist Tourism Circuits at Kisarazu in Japan. In order to harness the full potential of tourism and its alleged development benefits, the ESCAP recalled the need for strategic planning and the challenge as "to how Asian people's cultural and religious heritage could be linked to tourism development".[37] Here is where Buddhism comes into play, and the ESCAP member countries "have recognized that it might be possible to join hands in promoting Buddhist circuits as a way to ... give tourists and local people a better understanding of the Buddhist heritage".[38] This initiative also acknowledges the fact that many tourists traveling in Asia are Buddhists. This implies the existence of a specific set of religious interests and needs and a market force to reckon with. However, even India, where Buddhism is strong in some few regions only, began pitching Buddhist destinations (Johnston 2006, 114).

Preferences and values

In settings with sizeable Muslim populations, the contrast between forms of behaviors commonly associated with Western-style leisure tourism concerning dress-codes, food-regulations, gender-roles and gambling on the one hand and Islamic norms on the other has received a fair amount of attention. This, however, is less of a particular problem with regard to Islam than is commonly observed, for similar contrasts can be observed with regard to conservative varieties of several religious traditions, including Christianity.

Given the increased globalization of tourism, scholars from applied Tourism Studies have attempted to take stock of various factors that determine cross-cultural host–guest interactions with a view to improving the "product" and "customer satisfaction" and to develop new marketing strategies (Reisinger and Turner 2003, 30). Cultural differences have been analyzed with regard to a large number of aspects including the following:

- patterns of recreation
- leisure behavior
- benefits derived from travel
- recreation choice criteria
- perceptions/stereotypes/images
- values
- interaction rules
- contents of tour packages
- importance of food
- expected service quality.

(Reisinger and Turner 2003, 30)

In their book on cross-cultural behavior in tourism, Yvette Reisinger and Lindsay Turner list various determinants of tourist–host contacts and types of intercultural tourist–host contacts. They point to different cultural values and attitudes as well as rules of social interaction and modes of perception including stereotyping and ethnocentrism (Reisinger and Turner 2003, 34–174). However, although mentioned a couple of times, religion does not feature prominently in that book, which thereby bears witness to the general neglect of religion in Tourism Studies. Let us look at some exceptions proving the rule.

It seems evident that, apart from explicit religious needs, religious preferences and values have an impact on tourism. In his study of Branson, Missouri, Aaron Ketchell (2007) observes that many American tourists make it a point to travel to destinations which are perceived as supportive or at least unthreatening to their religious preferences. The affirmation of Christian values also underlies the booming of faith-based travel (see p. 33f).

Unwelcoming attitudes by host cultures may lead people to change their traveler patterns. Muslims, especially from Arabic countries, have changed their holiday destinations in the aftermath of 9/11 (11 September 2001) as a result of them increasingly facing negative reactions and attitudes in European, North American and Australian airports and hotels. Dubai and other Emirates as well as Oman, Qatar, Lebanon and Syria have benefitted from the resulting reorientation of travel patterns (Al-Hamarneh and Steiner 2004). Moreover, Malaysia has attempted to promote itself as a Muslim-friendly destination (Timothy and Iverson 2006, 201).

In destinations with Muslim populations, violation of dress-codes by women such as wearing of bikinis outside of hotels and resorts, behaviors in

public spaces like the display of bodily intimacies such as kissing, the violation of gender segregation and the widespread use of alcohol have led to
recurrent frustrations on the part of the host communities. For Tunisia,
Dubai and Kenya it is reported that some of this is considered to be
an offence towards Allah. However, negative attitudes towards visitors are
caused not only by the actual behavior of tourists, but also by a variety of
factors such as political developments, global media coverage and
networks of radicals and radical education and propaganda (Dłużewska
2008, 52–67).

It is a standard research agenda of the social-scientific study of religion(s)
to study the extent to which religion – usually measured in terms of self-
reported religious affiliation, behavior, or preference – influences attitudes,
behaviors and decisions in non-religious domains. This type of research has
also been done with regard to religious effects on tourist choices. One such
study has evidenced the (not altogether surprising) hypothesis that different
degrees of "strength" of belief have some impact on the visitation patterns of
heritage sites and that members of two different religions react differently
to a heritage site which enjoys a different status in these religions (Poria,
Butler and Airey 2003).[39] Another study has shown that religion and
religious beliefs (alongside gender) have a significant effect on US American
college students' attitudes towards drinking, drugs and casual sex during
spring break holidays (known for being prone to extreme behaviors and a
perpetual party atmosphere at the most popular destinations): "[S]tudents
identifying themselves with certain religions exhibit widely liberal (or conservative) attitudes compared to others. Hence, their destination choices
might be influenced accordingly" (Mattila et al. 2001, 198). The latter
hypothesis can then be applied to develop marketing strategies for destinations
(and this is maybe why the study has been done in the first place).

Starting from the theoretically plausible premise that "religious worldviews" such as Confucianism, Daoism and Chinese popular religion have
implications for people's travel behaviors,[40] a study of tourism and religion
in East Asia has likewise identified challenges for tourism management,
marketing, resort and hotel design, staff relations as well as environmental
ethics (Guo 2006). According to the author, who is trained in public
administration, the idea, common to Eastern religions or religious philosophies, that "life's journey is one of highly group-oriented structures" possibly
manifests itself "in the preference for group tours among Chinese, Japanese
and Korean people instead of exclusive individual travel, which is more
common among Western cultural groups" (Guo 2006, 135). As attractive as
this suggestion may sound, it seems that it has not been empirically tested.
One also wonders to what extent it reflects common East/West stereotypes.

Nonetheless, different travel behaviors in different cultures need to be
explained, and religion may well be a factor here. An interesting, though
largely hypothetical, example is the different decisions among Western and

Asian tourists with regard to traveling to areas affected by the 2004 tsunami. The fact that Asian tourists were much slower to resume traveling to the reconstructed areas than their Western counterparts has been tentatively explained by the pervasiveness of popular (folk) religion in Asia, namely the belief in dangerous ghosts, especially of persons who died from drowning, and taboos imposed on behavior; this increased the perceived risk of a travel decision for Asian tourists, where this was not the case for Westerners (Huang, Chuang and Lin 2008).

Secularizing effects on host communities?

Since mass tourism is a specifically modern phenomenon and modernity is often held to lead to secularization, it might be assumed that tourism directly or indirectly has secularizing effects. Indeed, the Israeli sociologist Erik Cohen, one of the most prominent voices in the nascent field of Tourism/Religion-Studies, stipulates that tourism in general has a "secular-izing" impact in the sense of "a weakening of the local adherence to religion and of the belief in the sacredness and efficacy of holy places, rituals, and customs" (Cohen 2004a, 156; quoted approvingly by Olsen and Timothy 2006, 13).

This idea seems intuitively plausible, insofar as the encounter with religious diversity is traditionally held to lead to the decline of religious plausibility structures. However, apart from this theoretical premise and prediction probably being wrong, I am aware of very few studies that actually support this hypothesis.[41] The studies quoted in this regard, moreover, point to the host communities rather than to the travelers.[42]

One case study cited by Olsen and Timothy as evidence for the secularizing thesis (Olsen and Timothy 2006, 13) is an essay by Susan Beckerleg on the village of Watamu at the heart of the Kenyan tourist region. At Watamu, as in many tourist destinations throughout the world, the local population, especially the youth, is affected by a dramatic rise of HIV as well as alcohol and drug (heroin) consumption and addiction. These behaviors are generally regarded as effects of the presence of tourists and tourism. In several ways, then, tourism has (indirectly) threatened the traditional value system of this Islamic community in Kenya. Beckerleg describes this as "[l]oss of parental control" over their children, many of whom work on the margins of the tourism industry (Beckerleg 1995, 26); in other words, tourism endangers traditional patterns of socialization and cultural transmission as well as control over territories and resources. Since Islam is a key dimension of the cultural value system, tourism implicitly/indirectly also threatens religion (= Islam).[43]

However, the interesting aspect of Beckerleg's paper, at least as I read it, is not so much the negative impact of tourism on parents' control over their children and the underlying value system, but the fact that an Islamic revival movement, the Tabligh, actually provided the youth with new options and role-models:

> Until recently young people entered the world of tourism, easy money and drugs almost as a matter of course. Now a fashionable alternative is being presented: the life of a pious, sober, socially active Muslim, with the promise of paradise after earth.
>
> (Beckerleg 1995, 38)

In other words: Religion (= Islam) may be indirectly threatened by the impact of tourism, but at the same time it presents a direct cultural resource to deal with the problems in its own terms.

Because of the observed negative impacts of tourism some religious groups may choose not to get involved in the tourist business at all. Apparently, this was the case with the Waswahali in Kenya, a group that, while in several ways predisposed to enter the tourist market, partly for religious reasons seems to have adopted a "hands-off policy on tourism in general and working in tourism enterprises in particular" (Sindiga 1996, 425), in order to avoid the perceived and real negative effects of the trade, including sexual behaviors and drug/alcohol consumption.

In other places, a strategy to avoid conflicts has been to segregate tourists. In the Maldives, tourists are insulated by spending their holidays on previously uninhabited separate resort islands. "Visits by locals are discouraged", and the tourists "can only visit a selected number of locally inhabited islands, including the capital island Male', on a guided tour of the islands" (Domrös 2001, 374–75). In that manner, "contact between the hedonistic tourists and the Muslim population" is minimized (Timothy and Iverson 2006, 190).

Recovering homelands (diaspora tourism)

Tourism is a movement away from home, but at the same time many travelers return to their former homes – be it students on low-budget holidays or families visiting relatives (sisters, brothers, grand-parents, etc.). Homeland-trips are a feature for many migrants, with people looking for their ethnic "roots" or wishing to uphold their diasporic links to the homeland (if they can), or to trace the genealogies of their families (such as Irish Americans traveling to Belfast and Dublin for genealogical research). Diaspora tourism has by now become a branch of tourism (Coles and Timothy eds., 2004).[44] Diaspora tours to India and China have become increasingly visible, and "it is estimated that over half a million Jews travel to Israel each year, comprising approximately 20 percent of all visitors to Israel" (Collins-Kreiner and Olsen 2004, 281).

When traveling to their home countries, people often visit ritual sites such as temples and churches in the places they have grown up, or where their families originate from.[45] People perform ancestral ceremonies in their home villages, or they have religious ceremonies such as initiations and weddings performed "back home". Some scholars have noted – among others for Ireland, Poland and Portugal – that homeland trips can be made in conjunction with pilgrimages to pilgrimages centers in the home countries (Rinschede 1992, 53).[46] These pilgrimages thereby often get an ethnic or nationalist flavor. Zlatko Skribiš has shown how for some Australian Croatians during their homeland trips the pilgrimage town of Medjugorje can come to embody the notion of the surrogate ideal home that is nowhere to be found any longer: the journey home thereby extends into a pilgrimage and the visit to the pilgrimage center becomes a strategy and site for negotiating diasporic identities, where the purchase of souvenirs also plays an important tangible role in that the material objects bought at Medjugorje come to represent the homeland inside their Australian homes (Skrbiš 2007).

While this is a process that may occur among migrants, homeland-trips may also be an outright strategy devised by organizations to strengthen the ethnic identity of children and adults. It has been pointed out that youth visits to Israel support awareness of Jewish identity in adulthood. In Israel, there is a variety of short-term programs available for young people and adults; these programs combine cultural, educational, recreational, religious and tourist elements; correspondingly, Jewish organizations in the New World, mostly in the United States, are engaged in arranging such trips (Mittelberg 1999).[47] Over the past six decades, over half a million Jewish youth have come to Israel from around the world. During their tours, sponsored by several organizations that represent the entire ethnic, ideological and religious spectrum, participants engage in recreational, educational and religious activities. A study of two volunteer programs in Israel has shown that "[t]he participants' ethnic identity as American Jews became stronger during and after their Israel volunteer tourism experience" (Ari, Mansfeld and Mittelberg 2003, 23). The authors comment on this finding with regard to the potential of that experience to generate return visits.[48] Similar homeland trips will in the long run probably be explored, adjusted and developed by other migrant religious communities.[49]

In addition to this sort of trip, overseas study programs in Israel – a kind of long-term educational tourism – are quite common. Visiting student programs usually involve a variety of activities such as tours, visits and planned encounters in addition to the strictly academic work. Some 90 percent of visiting students to Israel are Jewish, and the decision to study in Israel in most cases grows out of the students' past experiences and education (Cohen 2003a, 37, 43). According to a study of the reasons why American Jewish students come to Israel, "the academic factor emerged as the least important motivation for undergraduate visiting students" (Cohen 2003a, 39). Religion was given the second lowest rating of the reasons rated as "very important". In contrast, touring received the highest number of "very important" answers (66 percent, versus 49 and 38 percent for the religious and academic factors respectively). According to the analysis provided by Cohen, students with religious motivations are mainly concerned with Jewish issues and Judaism, while those with tourist and other motivations are more interested in Israel and Israelis (Cohen 2003a, 43). Behind those citing touring but not religious factors (31 percent) and those citing religious but not touring factors (29 percent), those referring to religious and tourist factors simultaneously were the third largest group (25 percent) (Cohen 2003a, 40).

Let us consider two other examples of homeland trips: Zoroastrians touring Iran and African-American US citizens traveling to Western Africa. The emergence of homeland-tours can be observed among the Indian Zoroastrians. As legend has it, in the aftermath of the Islamic conquest of their home country (Iran), the Zoroastrians fled on a boat to India where they were accepted by a generous Hindu ruler. In India, they became a clearly distinguished ethnic-cum-religious community, known as the Parsis. For many centuries, there was very little contact between the Iranian and Indian Zoroastrian communities. Later on, priests started to exchange letters in which the Iranians provided instruction to the Indians. Since the late 18th century, thousands of Iranian Zoroastrians moved to India, where they became a sub-group of the Parsi community (known as the Iranis). In the course of the 20th century, stimulated by the politics of the Pahlavi-emperors, some individual Parsis settled in Iran. However, it was only after the establishment of the Islamic Republic (in 1979), which led to a new wave of emigration from Iran, that Parsi groups regularly started to tour Iran. Since the early 1990s going to Iran is a realistic and desirable option for many Parsis, and a good number have already undertaken the trip, several repeatedly, while others contemplate going soon. Currently, there are a handful of tour-operators. Several tours to Iran are now offered every year, especially in the Indian holiday season during May (which coincides with a pleasant travel season in Iran). The operators put different emphasis on these tours. On the one hand, there are those known for luxury, sumptuous food and culture; on the other hand, there are those emphasizing competent guidance, taking groups to special sites, and even offering religious expertise. One operator makes it a point to take along some knowledgeable priests who provide religious input and ritual services during the tour. In Iran, all Parsi groups invariably visit Mount Damavand, the main fire-temples and also the shrines and pilgrimage places for which there is no counterpart in the Indian (Parsi) version of Zoroastrianism. These sacred sites of Iranian Zoroastrianism have by now become part of the religious geography of the Parsis. According to my observations in Iran (1999, 2002, 2003), there is surprisingly little contact between Parsis and Iranian Zoroastrians during these trips and since many Parsis keep on complaining about the "flat" Iranian food, some operators now even arrange for Indian food to be served. The tours are clearly all Parsi affairs with Iranian and Iranian Zoroastrian scenery, but they stir a theoretical interest in Iran among the Parsis. Some tour operators support local projects to strengthen the sacred sites visited by their groups. At many Iranian Zoroastrian places one now finds traces of Parsi impact such as Parsi devotional objects (items not used by Iranians) put up at the shrines.

While the Parsis return to the homeland from where their ancestors were said to have fled, African-Americans return to the homelands from where their ancestors were deported. Here is one important example. Elmina Castle in Ghana, erected by the Portuguese in 1482 (now a World Heritage monument), served as a prison for slaves; exiting through the castle's infamous "Door of No Return" they would be transported abroad. Apart from its function in the slave trade, the Castle also served as trading post, military fortification, colonial administrative center, prison, school and office (Bruner 1996, 292). The Castle is now an important tourist site in Ghana. Many modern Ghanaians appreciate the Castle for its long history and wish to have it properly restored to make it attractive to tourists. Restoration projects started in the 1990s. However, this enraged African-Americans who, among other issues, objected to the collaboration with agencies perceived by them as neo-colonial and imperialist.[50] African-American travelers who visit the Castle rather "want the castles to be as they see them – a cemetery for the slaves who died in the dungeons' inhuman conditions while waiting for the ships to transport them to the Americas" (Bruner 1996, 293). For them, the "homecoming is not just to an ancestral land but also to sites of traumatic memory ... For many African Americans, no matter what their ideological divisions might be, these places resemble shrines and are attributed a strong potency for cathartic healing" (Schramm 2004, 138). Most African-American visitors to Elmina Castle have profound emotional experiences at the site, often amounting to considerable sadness and pain. For many, religion serves as a powerful resource in this process: "Many of the diaspora visitors found comfort in their faith in God. Many turned to their faith while at the fort as a way of dealing with their pain" (Timothy and Teye 2004, 119). Given the intensity of their emotional experiences, African-Americans objected to what they regarded as a Disneyfication and desecration of the "shrine" when the Castle was renovated.[51]

The situation, as anthropologist Edward Bruner remarks, is quite complex and full of ironies.

> When diaspora blacks return to Africa, the Ghanaians call them *obruni*, which means "whiteman", but the term is extended to Europeans, Americans and Asians regardless of skin color, so it also has the

meaning of "foreigner". This second meaning is also ironic, since the diaspora blacks see themselves as returning "home".

(Bruner 1996, 295)

The capture of the slaves and their homecoming is also staged in specific events, which cannot be analyzed here.[52]

Interested parties in Ghana are effectively trying to develop the niche market of African-American travelers. Consider the following quote from a columnist on www.ghananet.com:

> We should be able to establish Ghana as a Mecca for our African-American brothers and sisters who were unfortunately uprooted from Africa and transplanted on a strange land several centuries ago. This will invariably be a win-win situation for both Ghanaians and African-Americans as it will bring in much needed foreign exchange for Ghana's development while helping to heal the souls of our estranged brothers and sisters. An annual pilgrimage to Ghana should be seen as a spiritual exercise … [53]

However, Ghana is facing increasing competition. Homeland travels from the tourism-pilgrimage spectrum are now taking African-Americans to Guyana and other places in the Caribbean as well as to South Africa, the Gambia and Senegal (with Gorée Island as another former slave trade center-cum-castle and current UNESCO Heritage Site). In 1995, the World Tourism Organization (UNWTO) formalized the decision "to rehabilitate, restore and promote the tangible and intangible heritage handed down by the slave trade for the purpose of cultural tourism" (Teye 2009, 180), and the Slave Route Project was started.

While there was concern about a perceived possible Disneyification of Elmina Castle, another irony is that the world's largest fast food chain McDonald's, apparently in an attempt to reach out to the African-American consumers as a new target group, in 1994 sponsored an African-American homeland tour, which took a group to Senegal and the Gambia. Arriving in Senegal, the group was welcomed by the words: "You are on a pilgrimage, not a safari" (Ebron 1999, 916). Paulla Ebron, who participated in this identity journey, has provided a stimulating analysis of the pilgrimage process this group went through. Important steps included the visited to Gorée Island, where a prominent participant said prayers and poured libations, and a naming ceremony where all participants were offered a new African name (Ebron 1999).

The homeland-trips sketched in this chapter can be described as instances of cultural, diaspora, migrant or heritage tourism, or as pilgrimages. Let us now once more take a look at the interfaces between pilgrimage and tourism.

SOUVENIRS FROM CHAPTER 2

- The interface between the systems of tourism and religion takes the forms of impact and interference.
- Religions can make travel mandatory.
- Religious rules and requirements can restrain travel behavior of believers and may create the need for specific tourism facilities and resorts.
- Religious discrimination can affect tourism, sometimes leading to the formation of separate holiday resorts.
- Some people resume an interest in religion while traveling; for some others the situation of travel creates specific religious needs.
- Specialist tour agencies cater to tourists with a special interest in matters of religious identity and also mainstream service providers may take care to meet religious needs of guests.
- Religion-based tourism has turned into a growing segment of the tourism market.
- Religious communities, congregations and groups unfold various travel activities.
- Since the early days of tourism churches were built and congregations were started at tourism destinations; churches have set up special ministries for tourists.
- Tourism hubs such as airports are often provided with ritual/religious facilities and sites of religious services and ministries, often of a hybrid or multifaith kind.
- There are (seasonal) tourism diaspora communities.
- Public, international, governmental and intergovernmental organizations have taken steps to encourage tourism to Islamic and Buddhist countries.
- Religious attitudes, preferences and values have an impact on tourists' behavior and decisions.
- Religious prejudices and stereotypes both in the host community and among travelers will affect travel behavior.
- The hypothesis that tourism has a secularizing effect on host communities has not been substantiated empirically; religious values can be threatened by tourism, but religions may also be a resource to deal with tourism; another conflict-avoidance strategy is segregation.
- Religious practices are often part of homeland and diaspora tourism.
- Trips to homelands can affect the religious identities of the travelers and can have an impact on the host communities.

Chapter 3

Pilgrimages and tourism

Ideal types and conflations

In a technical sense pilgrimage qualifies as a form of tourism (see the Introduction, p. 6). In an earlier chapter we have charted the position of the tourist versus the pilgrim and of tourism versus pilgrimage on the mental map of scholarship (see Chapter 1; p. 19f.). These binary schemes also permeate non-academic language games. Travelers from a variety of religious backgrounds (Catholics, Muslims, Hindus as well as New Ages, pagans and others) employ the pilgrim/tourist scheme to negotiate their experiences.

Classification and the negotiation of experiences

The category pilgrimage refers to a wide range of travel practices. The following are merely some of its main varieties. Pilgrimages can be:

- short term or long term
- local, regional, national or international
- compulsory or voluntary
- with open or limited access
- bound to specific dates or undertaken anytime
- undertaken alone or with smaller or larger groups
- organized individually or as part of package tours
- made with a variety of means of transportation
- made for a variety of motives such as accompanying others, leisure, seeking healing, vows, etc.

As a notion, "pilgrimage" generally provides a frame for specific motivations, expectations and experiences. By merely referring to themselves as "pilgrims" some people denote their "journeys as being special and set apart from the profane world" (Digance 2006, 45). This setting-apart, or framing, can be achieved by forms of behavior such as the wearing of special clothes or the chanting or recitation of religious text that mark this type of travel as an extraordinary or a religious venture. This marking of bodies and behaviors is in most cases immediately apparent to observers. Pilgrims and pilgrimages are also recognized by authorities in charge of pilgrimage routes and sites by issuing certificates or passes. In Japan, pilgrims have special books in which they collect stamps and inscriptions from the temple/shrine visited during pilgrimage. Pilgrimage passports are also issued on the pilgrimage to Santiago de Compostela.

Pilgrimage is often undertaken out of a sense of duty, or with the hope of obtaining special rewards. Others go on a pilgrimage because it provides them with a socially respectable framework to pursue interests such as making brief escapes from home, having a holiday, experiencing scenery and engaging in hobbies such as photography.[1] In some cases, however, the expectations and framework associated with pilgrimages seem to deter people from referring to themselves as pilgrims, even though they may appear to be exactly that to outsiders (Gladstone 2005, 173). In other cases, travelers claim to be pilgrims because they have specific motivations or expectations, although the trips are not advertised as pilgrimages.[2]

The distinction between pilgrims and tourists is an important one for most receiving institutions. Pilgrimage sites may well acknowledge the fact that they are visited by tourists and they may take active steps to be attractive to tourists as well. Alternatively, pilgrimage sites can be managed in such a way as to put tourists in their place in order to maintain their primary character as pilgrimage sites. This is done, for example, by imposing certain restrictions on behavioral and body display typical for religious sites in general (see Chapter 4). Take Mount Athos for example, where admittance is administered by the authorities in such a way as "to encourage genuine pilgrims while deterring mere tourists" (Andriotis 2009, 68).

In everyday language and publicity pilgrimage tropes can be employed rhetorically in order to mark an experience, a place, or an attachment as potentially extraordinary. There are "pilgrimages" to sports and arts events and places. Accordingly, the word Mecca, a prototypical pilgrimage site, is colloquially used to designate a range of special sites such as "the Mecca of fishing", "the Mecca of diving", "the Mecca of speed", "the Mecca of gaming" or "the Mecca of jazz". The examples are innumerable. And the rhetoric is ambivalent, since some may use the word metaphorically, as if to emphasize the importance of their trip, while others will use it performatively, in order to frame the trip as a special event. In fact, a series of new pilgrimages have arisen in the contexts of sports, politics, music, and in relation to sites of disasters, tragedies, death and mourning.[3]

Pointing to the ideological, discursive and rhetoric dimensions of the tourism–pilgrimage dichotomy does not necessarily preclude its fruitful application in scholarship when critically reframed as an ideal–typical distinction. Like other ideal–typical concepts and distinctions, the terms can be used in a comparative manner in order to interpret reality and to describe historical changes. A study by Doron Bar and Kobi Cohen-Hattab of changes in travel-patterns to Palestine by late 19th and early 20th century travelers to Palestine can be read in that manner. By comparing Catholic and Orthodox "pilgrims" from Russia, Greece, Armenia, Egypt and Catholic European countries to "modern tourist pilgrims" (i.e. overwhelmingly Protestants hailing mainly from the United States and Northern Europe), the study has brought to light a number of characteristic differences between the two groups:

- motives ("more varied and complex" motives for the modern tourist pilgrims) (Bar and Cohen-Hattab 2003, 33)
- the selection of travelers (religious background versus social status)
- the itinerary (Palestine "as part of a general tour of the Mediterranean" (Bar and Cohen-Hattab 2003, 135) for the modern tourist pilgrims)
- the choice of sights (modern tourist pilgrims wishing "to see and experience all that Palestine could offer") (Bar and Cohen-Hattab 2003, 133)
- the timing of the visits (in suitable weather for the modern tourist pilgrims)
- the religious aims of the visit (authenticating and reconfirming beliefs rather than expiating sins), if any
- participation in ongoing rituals and festivals (distance versus immersion)
- the choice and nature of accommodations
- the choice and activities of the guides
- the kind of information sought in and provided by guide books.

Other studies would add further factors to this list including the importance attributed to material comfort such as the quality of food, accommodations and visitor facilities (rated higher by tourists than by pilgrims) or the importance assigned to access to ritual space at the destination (rated higher by pilgrims) (Shi 2009, 207, 209). Bar and Cohen-Hattab describe the modern Protestant visitors as a hybrid between the pure types of the pilgrim and the tourist, "a unique blend of the sacred and the secular" (Bar and Cohen-Hattab 2003, 143). As we shall see, this blend is probably less "unique" than the historical geographers had imagined.

The popularity of pilgrimages

Sociological typologies or metaphors and single developments notwithstanding, there is no empirical evidence for the assumption of a general structural replacement of pilgrimage by tourism.[4] As a matter of fact, pilgrimage is "as popular as ever, experiencing a market resurgence around the globe over the last few decades" (Digance 2003, 143).[5] This development has been observed across cultures and religious traditions (Reader 2007, 211). Not only do more pilgrims arrive at pilgrimage sites than ever before, but Ian Reader has also drawn attention to "an increasing media interest in the phenomenon of pilgrimage" (Reader 2007, 213–14). In a feedback loop this not only reflects the increasing number of pilgrims but gives it further impetus. Moreover, the widespread use of pilgrimage talk in the media has resulted in travelers being prone to classifying some of their trips as "pilgrimages", which contributes to blurring the boundaries between "religious" and "secular" or "traditional" versus "alternative" pilgrimages (Margry 2008, 19).

Although pilgrimage, from a European-Christian perspective, seems to be a prototypically medieval phenomenon, many of the largest pilgrimage centers in Europe are in fact genuinely modern developments. Far from being relics of pre-modern religious history they are important, yet all too often overlooked, elements of modern religion. Modern means of transportation[6] and the other factors relevant for the development of modern tourism (see the Introduction; p. 3f.) have facilitated the modern upsurge in pilgrimages (Reader 2007, 216). On the one hand, pilgrimages have been propagated by religious organizations such as the Catholic Church to promote their confessional programs (Margry 2008, 15), while they, on the other hand, can also be regarded as effects of globalization and as a typical expression of the modern necessity for individuals to find meaning for their lives and the modern emphasis on autonomy (Reader 2007). In any case, rather than being antithetical to pilgrimages, modernity in its different varieties around the globe ("multiple modernities") seems to reinforce pilgrimages:

> Some pilgrimages might indeed be driven into extinction by modernity, but the institutions and landscapes of many traditional pilgrimages are being reshaped, and new ones are generated by global political and economic forces, industrialism, reliance upon expert systems of technology and transportation, and secular formations of knowledge.
>
> (Campo 1998, 42)

However, Reader argues that modern pilgrimage does not point to a resurgence of organized, established, institutional religion, but rather he suggests that "pilgrimage may have flourished ... because of its capacity to provide a way of dealing with individual needs without commitment to organised traditions and even with the rejection of religion as an organised entity" (Reader 2007, 226). A similar point is made by Sandra de Sá Carneiro with regard to the new popularity of the pilgrimage to Santiago de Compostela among Brazilians; according to her interpretation, more than a revitalization of Catholic pilgrimage, the open format of the pilgrimage allows its accommodation of diverse demands and interests (Sá Carneiro 2003).

That said, the dynamics of this process should not be framed in antithetical terms. Historically speaking, one can observe an agglomeration of individual religiosities or spiritual practices onto established religion. In many cases one finds a dialectic between institutional and non-institutional experiences such as when established religion only reluctantly, or after initial resistance, embraced pilgrimage sites and used them for its own propaganda, or when the protagonists of institutional religion at the same time appear to share features of what are generally held to be forms of alternative religion (Bochinger, Engelbrecht and Gebhardt 2009; Knoblauch 2009).

In the context of the present book it is worth recalling that pilgrimage technically is a branch of the tourism sector.[7] By 1900, Lourdes, one of the most popular modern pilgrimage towns, is said to have become "an economically developed tourist city replete with an abundant variety of religious goods and services" (Kaufman 2005, 2). Many of the established pilgrimage centers draw enormous numbers of travelers, not all of whom consider themselves as pilgrims or even as traveling for religious motives. Fátima in Portugal, for example, reportedly attracts some four million visitors annually, Santiago in Spain slightly more, Lourdes in France five, and the Marian sanctuary of Aparecida in Brazil now reports more than eight million annual visitors. These numbers rank them among the most powerful travel destinations of their respective countries. Note that Lourdes has the largest number of hotels and guesthouses in any urban center in France outside Paris, ranking before Nice and Marseille (Rinschede 1986, 30). And these well-known places are only the tip of the iceberg among the thousands of pilgrimage centers in Europe,[8] many of which have a purely regional outreach. Consider also the various spin-off pilgrimage sites based on Fátima and Lourdes in various other countries such as the United States.

Moreover, it is not only pilgrimage centers that attract tourists, but also pilgrimage events. One example is the pilgrimage performed by some 10 to 15 thousand Romanies (otherwise known as gypsies) in the fishing village Les Saintes-Maries-de-la Mer in Southern France. It seems that "[m]any villagers regard the Romani pilgrimage as an unwelcome invasion and occupation of their community" (Wiley 2005, 137). The Romani pilgrimage in turn attracts thousands of tourists (and many journalists), whose expenses generate considerable revenue for the village. The local tourist office actively promotes the pilgrimage event, apparently in a manner that evokes it as a heritage event and by casting it in a semi-exotic and semi-Romantic light (Wiley 2005, 150–53).[9] At the same time there are also posters that foreground the villagers and assign the Romanies to the background in the visual frame (Wiley 2005, 147, fig. 15). It seems that the different parties are linked in a chain of mutual interests: the pilgrims need the sacred buildings and spaces of the village as its stage, the village benefits from the pilgrimage as a tourist attraction in terms of revenues, and the tourists in turn come to enjoy both the pilgrimage and the village.

On a global scale, the impressive visitor numbers quoted for European pilgrimage centers like Fátima, Santiago and Lourdes are even low when compared to places like Kyoto and the main Indian pilgrimage centers. Indian and Japanese varieties of modernity have definitely stimulated pilgrimages. In almost all parts of the world pilgrimage has increased massively during the second half of the 20th century with numbers often pointing to a 20-fold increase in a 50-year period.

Obviously, pilgrimage builds up infrastructures that can be used for tourist purposes – or vice versa. However, pilgrims do not always avail themselves of tourism facilities. Two marketing scholars have analyzed the economic impact of the Rocío Pilgrimage (also known as Pilgrimage of the Dew) in Andalusia (Spain). They found that the impact of the pilgrimage is rather insignificant, given that most pilgrims opt for private accommodations and because only around 1.3 percent of the pilgrims made use of hospitality services for the supply of food and beverages (Gil and Curiel 2008, 428).

The lack of tourism related infrastructure also sometimes restricts access for pilgrims. For example, the restricted number of accommodations in Czestochowa (Poland) during the Communist period curtailed the number of pilgrims who could stay there for more than a day (Jackowski and Smith 1992, 105). The restriction of pilgrimages, of course, was in line with the policy of the government.

Pilgrimage is the main type of domestic tourism in India, with probably far more than 100 million Indians embarking on such travels annually:

> In India, an entire industry has grown up around this form of travel, complete with specialized travel agencies, particular types of accommodation (*dharamshalas*, *chattis*, *sarais*, *gurudwaras*), specific kinds of eating places, and a array of gift and souvenir shops specializing in religious paraphernalia.
>
> (Gladstone 2005, 8)

In the Global South, pilgrimage is often linked to the domestic informal sector in the travel business (Gladstone 2005, 170–94). Again in India, pilgrims share the travel infrastructure (such as means of transportation) with tourists, and many travel agents specialize in pilgrimage as much as they do in special forms of leisure travel such as sightseeing (Gladstone 2005, 177–78). However, the international tourist industry also derives many benefits from pilgrimage – and vice versa.

The neat interplay between tourism and pilgrimage is illustrated by the following example from the early history of modern tourism. Since 1869 the Cooks organized tours to Palestine and in 1882 they were contracted by French Assumptionist Fathers who were unable to find any Catholic organization that could match the facilities provided by the Cooks to arrange the round trip of over a thousand French Catholic pilgrims to the Holy Land; as a result it remained for the Cooks to organize "the largest pilgrimage to Palestine since the Crusades" (Shepherd 1987, 184). Once basic tourism infrastructures were established, they could be utilized to arrange pilgrimages of hitherto impossible dimensions. Note that Cook also opened a branch in India organizing tours for Muslims to Mecca (Gladstone 2005, 17).

The impact of the massive increase in the number of pilgrims has ramifi-cations for the performance of pilgrimage rituals. In some Indian pilgrimage centers pilgrims have to queue for many hours for a *darshana* or are now allotted slots by IT-based systems. The increasing number of visitors also has an impact on the natural and cultural ecology of pilgrimage sites, especially since the increased number of visitors often goes along with a considerable population growth in pilgrimage towns. Settlement patterns and urban spaces have likewise changed along with the economic structure (Rinschede 1999, 216–20). At many places dramatic changes in the form of settlement have occurred with villages experiencing rapid urbanization. In the Global South in particular, the extremely high visitor flow and urbanization have exerted a strong pressure on already strained ecological resources, for instance with regard to basic services (water supply, sewerage and waste), pollution and congestion, but often also natural resources such as forests or lakes.[10]

Modern (re)invention of pilgrimages

Not only are traditional pilgrimage sites attracting more visitors than ever before, but new pilgrimages and pilgrimage centers keep on emerging. The tourism industry clearly benefits from these developments and appears as an interested party here.

In several religions the emergence of new pilgrimage centers is part of the usual process of religious innovation. Tombs of saints or similar figures endowed with divine agency are easily transformed into pilgrimage sites.[11] The places of residence of successful gurus and similar divine figure invariably attract huge crowds. Apart from innovations in traditional religions, modern religions such as the Baha'i Faith,[12] Latter Day Saints-Christianity (Mormonism) (Olsen 2006b, 266), and Tenrikyō (Ellwood 1982) as well as currents such as Spiritism (Rocha 2006), New Age (Ivakhiv 2003), and the Goddess Movements (Rountree 2006) have likewise established pilgrimage practices.[13]

The inventions of pilgrimages have been an important Catholic response to modernity and modernization. More recently, with the World Youth Days the Catholic Church has created a new type of global pilgrimage event. By drawing on the occasion of the United Nations International Youth Year (1985) Pope John Paul II launched these five-day-long celebrations which not only Catholics are invited to attend. So far, ten World Youth Days have been held in different countries around the globe; the number of attendees has varied between 400,000 (Santiago de Compostela, 1989) and 4,000,000 (Manila, 1995).[14] A similar kind of event, albeit with fewer participants, is the Catholic World Meeting of Families held every third year in various cities around the globe. According to press reports some 7,500 "pilgrims" from 98 countries attended the opening ceremony of the sixth meeting in Mexico

City in 2009.[15] Without the modern tourism industry that provides the means of transport, accommodation and logistics, such events could not be held.[16]

Traditional pilgrimages have also been renewed. The Camino, the pilgrimage to Santiago de Compostela, has a long tradition that has been reanimated since the late 19th century (Frey 1998, 237–54). In the late 1930s, Francisco Franco propagated the figure of St. James and Santiago de Compostela as part of his new nationalist political project. In 1987, the year after Spain had joined the European Community, in order to achieve greater social cohesion, stimulate European identity and sponsor tourism, the Council of Europe started to develop themed routes that cross two or more European countries. The first such itinerary to be developed was the Santiago route (Smith 2006, 67–68). Another main factor was the Holy Year of 1993, the 1,000th Anniversary of the discovery of St. James' tomb. In the same year, the Route of Santiago de Compostela was inscribed in the World Heritage List.[17] The millennial celebrations fell in a period when Spain had launched a "Framework Plan for the Competitiveness of Spanish Tourism" (1992–95), part of which involved the regeneration of routes such as the east–west route of the Camino, amounting to a revitalization of the route of Santiago (Morpeth 2007, 158–59). The route was marked with signposts in the form of the scallop shell, the former badge of the pilgrims, and the regional government constructed a 3-meter-wide main route which avoided roads, built-up areas, agricultural land and rubbish tips. In this way, the reconstructed Camino "constitutes a very much more definite itinerary than was ever the case in the Middle Ages and is also far more clearly demarcated than at any time in the past" (Murray and Graham 1997, 516).

Several theories have been proposed to explain this revival, but it is clear that political motives (on regional, national and European levels) have played as prominent a role as any attempt to promote regional tourism; in fact, after the revitalization of the Camino, tourism has become one of Galicia's main economic sectors (Santos 2002, 44).[18]

Additionally, the pilgrimage to Santiago has been re-popularized by some best-selling literary works. To begin with, the global best-selling esoteric-spiritual novel *O Diário de um Mago* (1987; *The Pilgrimage* in English) by Paolo Coelho has raised awareness of the Camino among new audiences worldwide and must have contributed significantly to its popularity (Sá Carneiro 2003).[19] The book, which is reportedly based on the author's pilgrimage to Santiago, provides a semi-fictional account of the protagonist's esoteric initiation into the order Regnus Agnus Mundi undertaken under the guidance of a master and culminating in the obtaining of a mystical sword. In 2000, the American actress, activist and author Shirley MacLaine published a report of her pilgrimage to Santiago (*The Camino: a journey of the spirit*; European edition, 2001, under the title *The Camino: a pilgrimage of courage*). MacLaine, who is an important protagonist of the so-called New

Age Movement, did not regard her trip as a religious pilgrimage, but rather as a spiritual journey which she describes as "a mythological and imaginative experience" (MacLaine 2001, 10) and "a walking meditation" that was to "be the end of a big part of my life and the beginning of a new one" (MacLaine 2001, 255). In Germany, a 2006 book by the actor and comedian Hape Kerkeling about his pilgrimage to Santiago in 2000, which sold more than three million copies, turned out to be one of the biggest bestsellers of this type of book ever. In his book, which in 2009 was also published in English (*I'm Off Then: losing and finding myself on the Camino de Santiago*), Kerkeling reports that many travelers he met on the road were making their trips as a result of having read the books by Coelho and MacLaine. Since 2006 his book has had the same effect for many German travelers and the number of German travelers has increased. Kerkeling tells about the bodily and emotional challenge of walking the Camino, which evokes powerful memories and he describes the pilgrimage as an experience beyond his control. While he makes fun of traditional Catholic pilgrims walking the Camino, he also reports having had repeated personal encounters with God, so that the book turns out as a semi-religious book written by a person who, although raised as a Catholic, rejects institutional Christianity (Stausberg 2010, 58–59). In that respect, the book may well reflect a typical trait of contemporary European religiosity or spirituality, which may in part explain its success (Knoblauch and Graff, 2009).

The success of the revitalization of the Camino has now "spawned a range of other cultural routes based on religious themes or containing significant links to religious themes" (Richards and Fernandes 2007, 232). Think of the Baroque Route in France, the Via Francigena from Northern France to Rome, and the Monastic Influence Road across Europe, all of which are supported by the Council of Europe. Moreover, there are several direct offshoots of the Camino, for example in Germany.

In Brazil, in the early years of the present century, several new pilgrimage routes were created – modeled on the Camino. An analysis of the internet presentation of five such routes has pointed to the extent to which these pilgrimage routes are devised to appeal to tourist sensitivities by accommodating ecological, cultural and historical dimensions that can be of interest to potential travelers; moreover, the religious appeal of the pilgrimages is articulated in terms of a discovery of the self, with reference to giving space to reflection, introspection and experiences – a rhetoric usually associated with the New Age type of spirituality (Sá Carneiro 2004).

In other countries, pilgrimage is reinvented as social practice and former pilgrimage centers that were stripped of this status are being revived as pilgrimage destinations. In Norway, for instance, where the Reformation had curtailed pilgrimage in the 16th century, the Norwegian Lutheran State Church at present promotes former pilgrimage sites,[20] most notably to the Nidaros Cathedral in Trondheim, in the pre-Reformation period one of

Northern Europe's most important Christian pilgrimage sites (Kollandsrud 1998). In the late 1950s, pilgrims started to arrive from Sweden, but from the 1990s onwards pilgrimages became a project on the part of the Church of Norway, in conjunction with municipalities, local history associations and the tourism sector. As a result, several pilgrimage routes have been recreated since the 1990s. The Ministry of the Environment appointed the Directorates for Natural and Cultural History to retrace and reconstruct the pilgrimage route from Oslo to the Nidaros Cathedral. An association called Confraternity of St. James (Pilegrimsfellesskapet St. Jakob[21]) is actively advertising pilgrimage.[22] Pilgrimages were also promoted when a Norwegian princess made pilgrimage to the Nidaros Cathedral prior to her marriage in the cathedral in 2002, a media event during and after the pilgrimage, when the princess published a book on her experiences. In popular discourse, the new routes are addressed in the framework of searching for the religious roots of personal and national identities, as an exploration not only of outer, but also of "inner landscapes", where being on the move is not restricted to the pilgrimages but has become a biographical project.[23]

This development strikes one as quite remarkable in the light of the Norwegian Protestant traditions, but similar reinventions of pilgrimages can be witnessed in other Protestant countries as well. The island of Iona in the Inner Hebrides (Scotland) with its Abbey, for example, has emerged as a prominent destination for Protestant travelers.

Among Protestant travelers, Israel clearly enjoys a privileged position as a religious destination. Thomas Cook had helped to turn Palestine into a tourism destination. Cook offered different tours, among them Biblical Educational and General Tours that were "designed specially for Ministers, Sunday school teachers and others engaged in promoting scriptural education" (Shepherd 1987, 180). Cook's tours "combined visits to Holy Places, the missions and their schools, and 'biblical excavations'"; "the parties carried not only maps and guide books but bibles and hymn books, and sang as they went" (Shepherd 1987, 180). These were clearly religious trips. Protestants still make up around half of the Christian pilgrims to the Holy Land (Shepherd 1987, 180). There are various branches of Protestant pilgrims traveling to Israel, including Evangelicals, Fundamentalists and Christian Zionists.[24] Tourism and pilgrimage are now Israel's leading service industry (Collins-Kreiner et al. 2006, 23).

In Christianity, pilgrimage is increasingly emerging as a Protestant as much as a Catholic religious practice, albeit with some characteristic differences (Fleischer 2000).[25] There are travel agencies catering to pilgrims from both backgrounds.[26] While some Protestant groups, such as the American Methodists, have their specific religious geography that includes specific pilgrimage sites (Tweed 2000), many pilgrimage destinations Protestants travel to either have a Catholic background or are shared with Catholics. In Israel, however, many Protestant pilgrims avoid sites revered by Orthodox

and Catholic pilgrims and resent many of the structures built there
(Collins-Kreiner *et al.* 2006, 92).

In Europe, seven of the most popular pilgrimage towns located in seven
different countries (France, Germany, Greece, Italy, Poland, Portugal, Spain)
have formed a network called "Coesima: European pilgrimage sites". As
part of the working program of this network, besides the study of pilgrims
(frequency of visits, motivation, expectations, etc.), its website mentions "the
mutual promotion of all these places as diversified touristic destinations"[27]
as one of the aims of the network.

Not only are pilgrimages gaining a more prominent place in the European
religious landscapes, but it seems that we are witnessing the blossoming of
an international, cross-denominational awareness of sacred destinations.
Consider the existence of materials such as a French tourist guide book
to places of religious and spiritual interest throughout Europe (including
Eastern Europe and the Caucasus region) (Fournier 2004).[28] On a global
scale, several publications make religious sites around the globe accessible
to readers and potential travelers. Colorful examples include the book
Sacred Earth: places of peace and power by the photographer Martin
Gray (2007), who according to the www.amazon.com product description
"spent the last 20 years on an amazing pilgrimage: he visited 1,000 sacred
sites in 80 countries around the world" (accessed 10 January 2010).
Gray also has a website (www.sacredsites.com) that according to the www.
amazon.com author profile "has received more than 6 million visitors"
(accessed 10 January 2010). Gray also works for the *National Geographic*, a
magazine which probably stimulates many people to travel. The *National
Geographic* has also published a volume with a strikingly similar title,
namely *Sacred Places of a Lifetime: 500 of the world's most peaceful and
powerful destinations* (2008). In the preface, Keith Bellows, the editor-in-chief
of the *National Geographic Traveler Magazine*, invites the readers to use
the book as a starting point to embark on decisive, religious/spiritual/magic
travels:

> It's a book not about spirituality or religion, but about those places that
> channel the wisdom of the ages, of far-flung cultures, and unique
> perspectives. This book explores the new magic – magnetic destinations
> that have the power to change and move you ... Travel is more than a
> journey of paces and spaces. It should also move your spirit.
>
> (Bellows 2008, preface)

On the internet, one finds various resources including "an online catalogue
and travel guide to more than 1,200 sacred sites, holy places, pilgrimage
destinations, historical religious sites, places of worship, sacred art and religious architecture in 48 countries around the world".[29] Religious places have
become accessible as tourism destinations on a planetary scale.

Pilgrimages are also becoming cross-denominational in a new sense. Consider the American "Insight Travel Buddhist Pilgrimage" tour operator that offers Buddhist pilgrimages to destinations in the Himalaya (Ladakh, Bhutan, Mount Kailash, Nepal), India, China and Japan. The pilgrimage leaders are for the most parts Western intellectuals, who practice Buddhism or/and have relevant educational background (e.g. from Buddhist Studies, Comparative Religion, Chinese Studies). On the frequently asked question section of the operator's homepage it is stated that most customers traveling with this operator "have shared an interest in experiencing travel as pilgrimage".[30] Moreover, although the operator refers to itself as "Buddhist" and has adopted the 7th-century Buddhist monk, traveler and scholar Xuanzang as its logo and role-model, the answer to the question whether one has to be a Buddhist to participate, or whether only Buddhists go on these pilgrimages, is a clear "no":

> Our travelers have come from a wide variety of spiritual expressions; Buddhist, Hindu, Taoist, Christian, Jewish. Others prefer no definitions at all. Most have an interest in meditation if they aren't actual practitioners. They are quite an eclectic and fun-loving group of people who often stay in contact with one another after the pilgrimage ends.[31]

Blurred boundaries and the touristification of pilgrimages

Not only this last example illustrates that the distinction between pilgrimage and tourism is often blurred in travel practice. Here are some instances of overlappings:

- pilgrims and tourists share the same travel infrastructure
- travelers combine pilgrimages with family vacations or other forms of holidaying or vacations[32]
- pilgrims visit tourist attractions while on pilgrimage (e.g. pilgrims to Lourdes visiting Andorra and Biarritz)
- tourists visit pilgrimage centers when on holidays (such as visitors to the Atlantic coast of Portugal visiting Fátima)
- tourists and pilgrims mix in restaurants, souvenir shops and other consumer activities
- travelers split their itineraries in sections travelled in the role of pilgrims while other sections are travelled in the disguise of tourists, or walking as pilgrims during the day-time and enjoying gourmet food and fine wines at night
- pilgrimage centers are provided with non-religious entertainment facilities (such as the cable railway and the funicular in Lourdes)

- pilgrimage sites entertain strategic alliances with cultural institutions and organizations
- organized pilgrimages provide days off used for visiting nearby tourism facilities such as museums.

Tourists may sometimes slip into the role of pilgrims,[33] while pilgrims may temporarily step out of their role of pilgrims and adopt that of tourists; this role-switching may give them "a brief respite from the pressures of being on display" (Reader 2005, 239) and it can also help them to cope with tensions arising from being together with other pilgrims. Tourists, however, may subsequently discover an inner change to have occurred when traveling to pilgrimage destinations. Where pilgrims may occasionally be put off by tourist overcrowding and "trivialization" – pilgrims themselves more often than not contribute to the creation of such problems in the first place – for tourists the presence of "real" pilgrims, i.e. travelers provided with the relevant insignia (clothes, etc.) and behavior is itself an attraction, or increases the attractiveness (qua authenticity) of the place.[34] In many cases, the display of devotion and religious fervor does not fail to make an impression on visitors.[35]

The present conflation between pilgrimage and tourism is a recurrent topic in recent scholarly literature.[36] As stated by Campo: "In the late twentieth century, the two are seldom easily distinguishable. Pilgrimage often invites tourism, while tourism entertains the possibility of pilgrimage experiences" (Campo 1998, 53). The conflated reality of tourism and pilgrimage is not a characteristic only of the West. It has repeatedly been noted for Japan where temples and shrines "operate simultaneously as tourist, religious and cultural institutions" (Reader 1991, 160) and where pilgrimages are part of "having a nice day out with the family" in the countryside (Reader 1991, 159). Ian Reader gives the example of the Seven Gods of Good Fortune pilgrimage route on the island of Awaji, established in 1973. Reportedly 200,000 travelers per year make day tours by bus, where the visit to the temple, undertaken mostly in the hope of achieving this-wordly benefits, is embedded in "a tour of the island and its scenic spots in a package arrangement that combined tourism and religious pilgrimage" (Reader and Tanabe 1998, 199). Consider also a case study of the Japanese mountain village Hongū Chō, located in a well-known pilgrimage area; the village itself has a famous shrine. This village has now become popular with urban tourists because of its hot springs. John Knight notes how different local constituencies attribute quite different meanings to the visits to the village, depending on how one regards the visit to the shrine – as part of an ordinary leisure trip or as key to a spiritual journey (Knight 1996, 170). In India, to take another example, many people who look and behave like pilgrims claim to be tourists, possibly because pilgrimage has been a dominant model for traveling. Middle-class families combine pilgrimage with leisure and consumer activities and while on holidays they make it a point to visit pilgrimage centers

(Gladstone 2005, 173). Also in Europe, some main pilgrimages take place during the festival holiday season.

The fusion of pilgrimage with leisure and consumption activities promises to stimulate commercial activities. It is therefore actively encouraged. Saudi Arabia, for example, "is developing a new strategy for tourism that is based on an updated interpretation of pilgrimage that includes leisure activities in addition to the traditional pilgrimage visits to the Holy Sites" (Al-Hamarneh and Steiner 2004, 180). Similar attempts are made in other Muslim countries. Apparently one hopes that this will stimulate pilgrimage tourism.

The fuzziness of the borderline between pilgrimage and tourism should not be dismissed as an exclusively modern phenomenon. Both with respect to motivation and conduct, medieval pilgrimages were not at all the purely pious religious affairs they are often believed to have been. They were not all "immune from forms of commodification and criticism commonly ascribed to much later periods and more secularized forms of travel" (Kaelber 2006, 49–50).

As we have already seen in the case of Palestine (Bar and Cohen-Hattab 2003), there is (and maybe always has been) a common hybrid of tourism pilgrimage, where pilgrimage includes elements of ordinary travel and vice versa. With regard to historical developments, however, it has been pointed out that pilgrimages are nowadays, especially in industrial countries, more intimately linked to other forms of tourism than was previously the case. They are now often multifunctional travels, often with close ties to ordinary or cultural tourism, as trips undertaken for the sake of company with family and friends, or also for national or political interests (such as the assembly of Portuguese migrant workers during holidays at Fátima) (Rinschede 1999, 220–21). In other words: even when and where tourist elements were part of pilgrimages, the travels were still framed as pilgrimages, while the format is nowadays more open. This development is not to be misunderstood as a "secularization" of pilgrimages, but more properly framed as a response towards tourism infrastructures unavailable in earlier times.

In the case of the Brazilian new pilgrimage routes, pilgrimages are devised in such a way as to accommodate tourist sensitivities (see p. 61). In other cases, one may speak of a touristification of established pilgrimages. This includes such characteristics as specific ways of marketing the destination as well as

> limited engagement of visitors with rituals, commercial organization typical to package tours, particular way[s] of marketing the destinations, and the consumerist behavior of visitors. There is a substantial shift from the notion of journeying to quick and easy trips.
>
> (Shinde 2006)[37]

Kiram Shinde has analyzed the consequences of such transformations in a study of Vrindavan, the pilgrimage center of the complex of Braj, a region (some 150 kilometres south of Delhi) having hundreds of sites connected to the mythology of Krishna and literally thousands of temples. Reportedly, Braj attracts some 3.5 million visitors annually. For many, the journey through Braj is nowadays undertaken by car. Obviously this has led to environmental problems (Shinde 2003) and a transformation of the ecology of the entire event. Shinde refers to it as "sacred sightseeing". Moreover, the touristification of the pilgrimage (site) has led to the timing of the travel decreasing in importance with visitors traveling there throughout the year, even outside the traditional dates for pilgrimages.

Similar observations apply to the recent history of many other pilgrimages. Tone Bleie, for example, has pointed to some changes in the pilgrimage to the Manakama Temple in Gorkha (Nepal) as a result of greatly improved access to the site due to the introduction of a cable car. Changes include the greater prominence of joint meals and drinks in hotels and restaurants, the increasing "getting out" character of the trip, and the relaxation of caste related purity rules with regard to food preparation, drinking of water and social exchanges. Furthermore, the changed modes of transportation have led to a loss of engagement with the surrounding landscape and modifications in the experience of temporality (Bleie 2003, 183).

It seems that the ecological impact of pilgrimages, e.g. with regard to pollution, congestion as well as water quality and supply, is more powerful in the Global South than in the North. Kinde has recently analyzed such changes with regard to the South Indian pilgrimage center of Tirumala-Tirupati. One factor emphasized by Shinde is the change in the temporal dimension of the travels: while traditional pilgrimages are often seasonal events, the touristification of pilgrimage sites has resulted in a relatively steady stream of visitors throughout the year (with the pilgrimage seasons being mere peaks in a constant influx). This change, Shinde argues, is of great ecological significance since the ecological resources are constantly under pressure and the ecosystem has no chance to renew its resources as would have been the case under seasonal strain only. There are social factors as well. The increased demand for tourism-like consumption among visitors has led to the increased supply of consumer goods, which in turn has facilitated the access to these goods among the local population, whose demand has, in a spiral-like development, likewise increased as a result of their improved incomes generated from the greater number of visitors (Shinde 2007, 557–58).

The process here referred to as touristification of pilgrimages has also been observed for the pilgrimage route to Santiago, the Camino. Apart from use of the itinerary by travelers who are primarily motivated by non-religious leisure activities such as walking or biking, tourists do not necessarily follow the route from single starting shrines heading to the destination. In the process of touristification of the route different travelers now use various points of entry and exit, and they may only travel portions of the route, without necessarily ever reaching Santiago. Moreover, several villages in the area try to stimulate travelers to spend more time there by offering additional attractions (Murray and Graham 1997, 521–23).

Tourism in pilgrimage arenas: two case studies of dispute, accommodation and resistance

This touristification of pilgrimages is not always uncontested, especially when the changes go along with the emergence of new groups of travelers who can be more easily identified as tourists (rather than the more inconspicuous transitions in the behavior of the traditional audiences). The debates and different interests at play in such matters can be illustrated by an example from another ancient Indian pilgrimage site, namely Pushkar, a small town of some 12,000 inhabitants in Rajasthan. This case was studied by Christina A. Joseph and Anandam A. Kavori (2001).[38] Pushkar has a lake that is mythologically linked to Brahma; the god is said to have dropped a lotus in meditation into it or to have bathed in it. There is also a famous Brahma temple. The site around the lake at Pushkar is described as the *vedi* (sacrificial area) of Brahma's *yagya* (sacrifice) – marking it as a ritual space *par excellence*. At the lake, one finds step-like embankments (*ghats*), where the pilgrimage priests, the *pandas*, perform *puja* for their clients, the pilgrims.[39] Moreover, Pushkar is famous for the *Pushkar ka mela*, a large-scale event held round November: a cattle and, in particular, camel fair held at full moon. At the same time many believers attending the fair take a bath ("a holy dip") in the lake, hoping for their past sins to be washed away.[40]

Like many Indian religious centers, Pushkar emerged as an international tourist destination when hippies arrived there in the early 1970s. Initially, there was some local resistance to accept non-Indian tourists. This resistance has since somewhat eased, and the sacred geography of the town has increasingly been interspersed by tourist infrastructure. Ever since the Rajasthan government tried to "capitalize on the state's colorful religious and cultural festivals" (Joseph and Kavoori 2001, 1001), Pushkar has become a well-known tourist destination with reportedly ten thousand international tourists being among the large crowds attending the fair in 2004.[41] International tourists, however, are clearly outnumbered by domestic travelers. For 1998, the total number of both groups of tourists together was estimated as one million (of whom only 5 percent were international visitors) (Gladstone 2005, 183–84).[42]

The presence of international backpackers has created a trade-off for the domestic visitors, for many of whom the backpackers are an "attraction" in their own right (Gladstone 2005, 186). At the same time, as elsewhere, by their sheer physical presence international tourists pose a challenge at the sacred places. Exchanging gazes and even taking part in rituals may threaten the purity of the site and endanger the religious economy. At the same time, the tourists are a powerful new market force, even for the *pandas*, many of whom now readily perform *pujas* for tourists. After all, the donations given by tourists amount to around four times the money they earn from their traditional clientele. The *pujas* have adapted to their new clients. The tourist *puja* has been abridged "and is conducted in Pidgin English with a few Sanskrit religious *slokas* ... thrown in for effect" (Joseph and Kavoori 2001, 1001). While photography at the *ghats* is officially prohibited, for those tourists who have a *puja* performed, the restriction is not enforced (Joseph and Kavoori 2001, 1001–2) – and the desire to take pictures will thereby encourage tourists to hire a *panda* and have a *puja* done. While some temples maintain the traditional restriction to bar tourists from entering, most others have opened their doors to tourists, and "[t]he sight of tourists lounging and smoking inside temples is a visual testimony to this cultural commoditization" (Joseph and Kavoori 2001, 1002). Foreign tourists have now become part of the religious scenery and economy, partly also drawing religious service providers (*pandas*) away from their traditional services to "commercial ventures catering exclusively to the tourism trade" (Joseph and Kavoori 2001, 1002) such as transforming parts of their homes into small hotels or guesthouses and restaurants, for which the foreign tourists represent the largest market (Gladstone 2005, 189–90).

These adaptations are by no means uncontested, though, and many deem the implications from the "tourist interactions ... distasteful and demeaning" (Joseph and Kavoori 2001, 1003), not least from a religious point of view – the "perversion" of the *tirtha* (pilgrimage site) into mere tourism. Religion, however, not only seems under threat, but at the same time it also offers powerful means of cushioning the accommodations by blaming them on cosmic transformations. Hence, many actors ascribe the changes to the disastrous effects of *kalyuga*, leaving them no other option for survival. At the same time it provides an explanation for the presumed lack of devotion among the pilgrims (Joseph and Kavoori 2001, 1003). On the other hand, when addressing local concern, the very same priests who make a living from the tourists are often the most critical towards them. There are signposts requesting the tourists to adapt their behavior to the requirements of a religious site – e.g. by leaving their shoes at a distance from the *ghats*, to wear "proper" dress and to refrain from bodily intimacies such as kissing and the use of drugs (Gladstone 2005, 190–91, fig. 6.9). Such public statements on the one hand attempt to maintain a minimum standard of behavior. On the other hand they function to discharge the specialists catering to the tourists from the unpleasant duty of enlightening their customers on these very issues. A religious rhetoric thereby serves different and partly contradictory purposes (Joseph and Kavoori 2001, 1004).

While all this allows for a certain *modus vivendi*, Hindu nationalists can happily exploit that sort of a predicament for their political agenda.

When "Save Pushkar" committees conjure up the danger that the tourists' presumed inappropriate behavior not only desacralizes the *tirtha* but may also spoil the local youth, the government is called into action – and the touristification of a religious site at the same time sustains and strengthens a national political project and religious nationalism (Joseph and Kavoori 2001, 1005–6).

Another example of public debates and conflicts concerning the touristification of pilgrimages is reported by Nelson Graburn for Kyoto (Graburn 2004). In this case the government tried to capitalize on the travelers in order to raise money for a larger program of historic preservation. A scheme was devised according to which the 40 most popular tourist attractions (37 of which were temples and 2 were shrines) were designated as "tax collectors" that were supposed to collect a small amount per visitor. When the tax was implemented in 1985, "[t]he Kyoto Buddhist Association, which represented 1,100 of the temples, rebelled by asserting that these were *religious institutions*, not *tourist businesses*, and that their visitors came to *worship*, not to *gaze*" (Graburn 2004, 133). The distinction between tourism/business and religion/worship is here employed in emic discourse[43] and the government is implicitly criticized for touristifying the religious institutions – although the temples were comfortably generating large incomes from the entrance fees/donations paid by the travelers.

Since the government persisted in its efforts, the situation escalated and while 25 of the temples eventually decided to pay the tax, 12 other temples (which happened to be by far the most popular ones) refused and closed their doors for 115 days leading to an economic crisis in the city because many travelers cancelled their trips. Afterwards, the temples opened for three months, but they "would only admit visitors who 'donated' their entrance fees in special envelopes printed with the declaration that the donation had been specially invited by the Association to Remove the New Tax" (Graburn 2004, 134). When the temples closed their doors again, tourism once more fell off. Apart from the resulting economic crisis, shouting matches and fights erupted creating atypical public disharmony, thereby worsening the standing of Kyoto as a destination.

Eventually, the city government had to give in and the temples were reopened. However, "[i]n the aftermath, many temples put up signs saying that visitors were to enter for religious purposes … Some temples raised their 'entrance fees' to unprecedented heights … and made the visitors perform *shakyo* (tracing sacred Buddhist texts in ancient characters) or other religious acts before allowing them to tour the gardens or see the sights" (Graburn 2004, 135). Thereby, in Kyoto resistance against the touristification of pilgrimage seemingly resulted in a pilgrimization of tourism: When the temple officials adopted the emic distinction between tourism/business on the one hand and pilgrimage/religion on the other, this legitimizing rhetoric led to putting emphasis on the latter so that the tourist gaze was framed by ritual acts and by requiring religious practice. This case once again illustrates that it may be difficult to "objectively" and categorically distinguish between religion and tourism, while the distinction makes much sense for the actors to use; this rhetorical mise-en-scène may then in turn lead to practical changes.

SOUVENIRS FROM CHAPTER 3

- The pilgrimage/tourism distinction serves individuals and institutions to classify and negotiate forms of behavior, expectations, experiences and motivations.
- This distinction can play different, sometimes contrasting and conflicting, discursive, ideological and rhetorical roles; it can also be used as an ideal–typical analytical device in scholarship.
- There was a massive increase of pilgrimages in terms of numbers of pilgrims and pilgrimage centers across the globe and across religious traditions in the modern age.
- There has been a diversification of forms of pilgrimage and types of pilgrimage events.
- New pilgrimages are started and previously abandoned pilgrimages are being revived.
- There has been increased media attention towards pilgrimage and a greater awareness of sacred destinations.
- The distinction between pilgrimage and tourism is often blurred in travel practice and there are various ways of overlapping between the two; sometimes this is a side effect of travel patterns, sometimes it is desired by authorities to stimulate either tourism or pilgrimage.
- An extreme form of overlapping results is a touristification of pilgrimage where pilgrimage assumes traits of travel and travel behavior typical of mass tourism.
- While tourism and tourists are often despised by pilgrims and pilgrimage authorities, tourism and pilgrimage seem to mutually reinforce each other.
- The interface between tourism and pilgrimage results in processes such as accommodation, dispute, negotiation and resistance.

Part II

Destinations

Chapter 4

Religious sites and places

While the so-called spatial turn in the humanities has as yet to fully gain ground in the study of religion(s),[1] space has emerged as an important topic in recent scholarship. One of the axial changes in the contemporary understanding of place in the study of religion(s) is the shift from sacred space to taking place.[2] Rather than theorizing religious space as inherently sacred (as places of epiphanies or hierophanies), one now explores issues such as the dynamic mechanisms that turn space into "sacred" space, the status of space in religious practice, the social and political functions of "sacred" spaces, and the constructions, negotiations and contestations of "sacred" spaces in religious, political and other public discourses. Tourism, whatever else it may be, is a spatial practice, requiring temporary movement in space. It is a mobile, ambulatory, trans-locative or locomotive and, to some extent, iterative practice.[3]

In the previous chapter we discussed the types of situations that arise when pilgrimage sites become tourism destinations and when pilgrimages become touristic. With this chapter, the discussion will move out of the pilgrimage orbit altogether. While there are forms of travel and tourism that deliberately remain in the ambulatory mode ("on the road"), where the trip, as it were, is the destination or where traveling has become the preferred way of life (such as the housetruckers or "new travelers"), in its standard form tourism is a route, or a transit, to a single or multiple destination(s), chains of destinations, or to and within destination areas.[4] The present chapter discusses other religious sites that function as tourism sights or attractions,[5] especially where sights/attractions are more or less important ingredients of destinations[6] (as Notre Dame is an attraction in Paris, which is a destination).

As noted in a previous chapter, in one of the founding texts of Tourism Studies, Dean MacCannell (1999 [1976]) has referred to the transformation of any given place, event or object into a tourism sight as "Sight Sacralization" (paralleling the process whereby places or objects gain a status of respectively religious/sacred places and objects). Contrary to MacCannell who points to the quasi-religious status of tourism sights in modern society, the present chapter, in line with our focus on interfaces rather than affinities and substitutions, looks at established religious sites and places that simultaneously function as tourism sights or attractions. Chapter 5 will in turn focus on resorts or attractions that are created as tourism enterprises and look at some mythico-religious spatial imageries that are cast on landscapes, regions and countries in the context of tourism.[7]

The present focus on single sites does not intend to downplay the importance of landscapes and nature in tourism contexts, be this as attractions and destinations-cum-religious-sites or as important features of the setting of other attractions. Single sites are in many places part of landscape settings and natural environments, the scenic or aesthetical qualities of which increase their attractiveness as sights, attractions or destinations – also in pilgrimage contexts.[8] In the West, Romantic notions of "nature" and "the sublime", which were important for the formation of the "tourist gaze" (Urry 2002), often have imbued the experience of natural sceneries with supernatural attributions. The trope of sublime nature, for example, is a recurrent topic in late 19th and early 20th century elite tourism sources from the United States, and the trope is usually indexed with notions of the presence of God, transcendence or spiritual renewal (Shaffer 2001, 277–78, 291, 302–3). Ideas such as these are probably no longer part of specific classes or religious orientations, but are widely shared by various groups of travelers.

Religious sites as tourist attractions

In 1988, churches, cathedrals and other religious sites were ranked third among the six most popular leisure pursuits for overseas visitors to Britain, just behind shops and markets and restaurants and cafes (Urry 2002, 47–48). There is no reason to believe that religious sites have become less attractive during the past 20 years or so, and this is by no means typical for Britain alone.

In a survey conducted at tourism destinations in the coastal region of Ostfriesland (Germany) in 1994, around half of the respondents claimed that they would visit a church during their stay. Almost two-thirds of the respondents expressed their agreement with the statement that they enjoyed going to churches of another faith. For around a third, their visit was not planned. Around a fourth said that it was their interest in architecture and the arts that led them to visit the church; at the same time, a fourth also declared that they visited the church in order to pray. Forty percent said that they were seeking a peaceful place that had led them to visit the church, while the statement that most respondents agreed with was that they simply wanted to know what the church looked like inside (Lukatis and Hieber 1996, 38–41). Curiosity, then, appears as the main motive for visiting churches – and the very fact of visiting other churches was perceived as appealing by a vast majority of the visitors. This also reflects the complexity of churches – and the same could be said about many varieties of religious places – as places of cultural heritage, history, identity and memory, as locations of specific soundscapes (such as silence) and aesthetical density (from the olfactory to experiences connected with architectural impressions such as the sublime), as representations of virtues and localities of lifecycle transition, to name only some prominent aspects.

For Japan, Ian Reader has observed that international as well as domestic travelers there are routinely encouraged to visit shrines and temples by guidebooks, tourist offices, friends and family (Reader 1991, 134). Similar observations probably apply to many countries, but I know of very little "hard" data in support of the extent that religious sites are part of tourist travel patterns. An exception to this is data collected in France in 2002, indicating "that almost 40 percent of individual cultural tourists had visited a religious monument in the previous two years. This rose to almost 50 - percent for those traveling in tour groups" (Richards and Fernandes 2007, 217).

Local residents often take their friends and visitors to such sites and act as local guides – and from time to time locals also visit religious sites for motives that are not primarily religious: religious sites serve not only as tourist but also as visitor attractions (Rotherham 2007, 77).

It has repeatedly been pointed out that pilgrimage sites not only attract pilgrims, but also "ordinary" travelers who happen to visit these places for various reasons, without a primarily specific religious motivation. This is the case with many other religious sites as well. Such non-religious motives include:

- to pass the time during rainy days
- relaxation (church benches are often welcome when walking around cities)
- the closeness of religious sites to intersecting points in transportation networks (such as the Cathedral in Cologne next to the train station)
- hunting for souvenirs
- interest in culture (architecture, arts, music) and (national) history
- landscape setting and vantage points.

In tourist settings, accordingly, many religious places are generally not primarily visited for their specific religious qualities, i.e. as places to perform rituals or to create religious experiences, but more often because of their apparent or assumed history and historical significance and their aesthetical dimensions – including their architecture, arts, their sheer size (Vukonić 1996)[9] and other spatial features including their landscape setting and location, i.e. their landmark qualities and the scenery (Hanna 1984).[10] As cultural sights, religious sites are among the favorite motifs for tourist snapshots.

Many churches are provided with notices identifying their main features of interest; in that way the attractiveness to visitors becomes part of the organization of sacred space.

Some sites fulfil several, if not all of these criteria at the same time. Consider the basilica of the Sacré Coeur in the tourist district of Montmartre, Paris (France). Started as a pilgrimage site (Jonas 2001), it began to attract tourists at the time of its construction, which began in 1875; the "exotic Romano-Byzantine edifice" (Jonas 2001, 115) was completed in 1914 and consecrated in 1919 (Pearce 1999b, 58). In the early 1990s, Sacré Coeur received about six million visitors a year; that is more than the Louvre and the Eiffel Tower respectively (Pearce 1999a, 83). The site has historical importance as a national shrine, begun in the aftermath of the defeat of Prussian Germany, as a project of penance and national moral and spiritual renewal, and was consecrated after the victory of World War I. It is also a monument of Catholic self-affirmation in what was perceived to be an immoral and areligious public space, since it is paradoxically situated in a district known for its bohemian lifestyle and frivolous entertainment. Hence the site is "the locus of an ongoing dialogue between the publicly sacred and the outrageously profane" (Jonas 2001, 104). Besides its religious significance as a place of ongoing worship (since 1995 taken care of by a Benedictine community), its massive size, imposing architecture and artistic features (such as the monumental mosaic – reported to be the largest in the world – and its famous organ), the basilica also attracts visitors because of its parvis that allows for one of the best-known panoramic views over the skyline of the megapolis.

Many religious sites have served as tourist attractions since the early days of the tourism industry. Some other places (for instance in Nepal) only came to be exposed to tourism as late as the 1990s.

Turning religious buildings into tourist attractions sometimes leads to modifications in their access and use among the local population. Here is one example. In the context of the exhibition Magna Hispalensis, which was held at the Universal Exposition in Seville in 1992, the ecclesiastical authorities decided to restrict access to the Patio de los Naranjos, a courtyard within the complex of the cathedral, to the visitors to the exhibition which had transformed the cathedral into a large museum complex. This restriction, however, was maintained even after the exhibition was over. The Patio is now in practice only accessible to tourists, while the local population no longer has free access; the Patio has thereby lost many of the functions it used to have, and the local population, in turn, has lost an important multifunctional space. Protests staged by local initiatives have so far been unsuccessful (Hernández Ramírez 2008).

The development of tourism sites sometimes required the de-development of their environment.[11] In some extreme cases, local populations are even displaced in order to make way for tourists and tourism. "Villages near the

Borubudor and Prambanan temples complexes in Indonesia were forcefully removed to make way for the development of these sites for tourism" (Timothy and Nyaupane 2009, 61). Those who resisted were intimidated by the military. The fact that the displaced groups did not use these temples for religious purposes does not make their displacement more acceptable.

Some religious sites in general (and not only places of pilgrimage) are among the most popular tourist attractions around the world.[12] Recall the figures given for the basilica of Sacré Coeur earlier. Here are some further examples from Europe. With 13.5 million annual visitors (figure for 2006),[13] Notre Dame cathedral in Paris is reported to be "the most popular tourist attraction in Europe" (Shackley 2001, 1)[14] – ahead of Disneyland Resort Paris (annually roughly 12.4 million visitors). Boris Vukonić refers to Notre Dame as "a tourist temple" (2006, 249). Several other churches in Europe such as cathedrals in England, France, Germany and Italy – including the major churches in Rome (first of all St. Peter's Basilica) – fall into the same category. According to figures from 2000, cathedrals amounted to 19 of the 50 most visited buildings in the United Kingdom, and 5 of the 10 most frequently visited historic properties in the UK were cathedrals (Rotherham 2007, 67).[15] While most of the tourist churches are scheduled monuments, the Temple Expiatori de la Sagrada Família originally designed by the Catalan architect Antoni Gaudí (1852–1926) is still uncompleted; completion is expected by 2026. According to a 2004 newspaper report, the unfinished church had 2.26 million annual visitors,[16] reportedly making it Spain's most visited monument.[17]

All these churches are high profile places. At the same time, there are innumerable low key examples (Rotherham 2007, 69) that are not sought out as attractions in their own right but that help to turn regions into attractive destinations. Consider rural churches in Britain, France or Germany that are visited on the road or sought out for day trips. Taken together, these minor churches welcome impressive numbers of visitors. At least 10 million visits were made to English parish churches in 1983 (Hanna 1984, 5). Given the decline in rural economies such as farming and forestry in many places and the parallel increase in the importance of the leisure industry,[18] churches may well be an important resource for regions to market themselves as destinations.

Using Tourism Studies terminology, the high profile churches can be referred to as "primary nuclei" – that is attributes of places, which are influential in making the decision to visit the respective place. Apart from these, there are "secondary nuclei" – i.e. attributes known before visiting the place, but which were not decisive for the choice of itinerary. An example for this category are various churches in Rome; few people travel to Rome in order to visit Santa Maria Maggiore, but the church is still well-known. Last but not least there are "tertiary nuclei" – that is, such attributes unknown before the visit, only to be discovered on the road, often by means of signposts, or after arrival at the destination[19] or visited in connection with a neighboring attraction.[20] In Rome, this may apply to the Chiesa di S. Prassede located in close proximity to Santa Maria Maggiore. As an example for this category, the contiguous attractions as it were, one can point to a church in Bergen (Norway) up on a hill close to my department. This church (Johanneskirken) is a relatively high and imposing neo-Gothic building which is clearly visible from the main square of the town, and hundreds of tourists walk up the steps to the church every day during the summer months. The tertiary nuclei can often become relevant experiences because they involve the pleasure of discovering something new – and because the encounters with such places are less pre-determined by well-defined horizons of expectation and available pre-visit information. Visits to such places are often impulse visits.

Here are some categories of religious sites serving as tourist attractions besides churches:

- shrines
- synagogues
- pagodas
- monasteries
- temples
- caves
- mountains
- groves
- sites associated with (persecuted) religious minorities or religious deviance[23]
- mosques
- stupas
- ancestral halls
- pyramids
- ashrams[21]
- lakes
- islands
- cemeteries and other burial places[22]
- towns and sites of violent conflicts, including battlefields.[24]

Most of these places are not only visited by culture and heritage tourists, but make up part of the schedule of almost every category of tourists. Although this has not been empirically tested, it may well be surmised that many people, at least in Western Europe, visit religious sites more often on their travels (i.e. as tourists) than at home (i.e. as Sunday worshipers). However, this fact is never mentioned in official statistics of religious behavior and accordingly is never reflected upon in discussions of secularization or rivaling theories.

It was one of the groundbreaking insights of MacCannell's *The Tourist* (1999 [1976]) that attractions (sights) are not given as such, but require tourists traveling to them as well as markers flagging them as sights. This has been followed up in subsequent research. There are markers that are located at various points on the itinerary, from pre-visit to post-visit, which play different roles and have different functions in the touristic process (Leiper 1990). The use of markers varies according to the geographical origins of the tourists, their socio-demographic characteristics and their chosen form of travel. It seems that markers to some extent "pull" travelers toward the attractions (Richards 2002, 1061–62). They also involve various media and media representations.

Markers are used by and appear in advertisements. Often, images of religious sites meet the eye of the potential traveler already before departing: Notre Dame, St. Peter's and the Sagrada Familia visually represent the destinations Paris, Rome and Barcelona respectively. In one way or the other, religious places and people are part of a wide range of promotional materials including travel magazines, travel programs, advertisements and brochures for many destinations.[25]

Religious sites are marketed and promoted by various branches of the tourism industry. To begin with, they are "used prominently in tourism promotional literature" (Olsen and Timothy 2006, 1). Here is one example (from 1983) to illustrate the blending of expectations and domains of eroticism, religion and relaxation: "Bangkok with its dreamy tropical scenery, glittering temples and easy-going beautiful people."[26] www.bangkok.com (accessed 10 July 2007) juxtaposes "the skyline alongside dazzling historical temples, and luxury hotels". The link leads to a page that declares: "Bangkok's dazzling temples are a unique part of the capital's heart and soul. A visit to Bangkok would not be complete without seeing at least two of them." The status of temples and statues in tourism contexts also finds its expression in their being transferred to the design of other tourism spaces such as hotel lobbies and rooms, sometimes to the extent of kitsch such as when they form parts of lampshades (Selwyn 1993, 121). (Similar observations can be made in other parts of the globe.) This reflects the attractiveness of religion as a parameter for creating a theme for destinations, where religious sites and motives can work as notable aspects of the scenery and the setting. For tourists visiting Thailand, tourism management/hospitality research has identified Buddhism as a "minor motivation", ranking in importance behind motivations such as special interests, novelty seeking, good value food/shopping/things to do and deals on tour promotion/ currency exchange (Rittichainuwat, Qu and Leong 2003).

Some religious sites have become famous tourist attractions because of their remarkable traits. In India, for example, the temple complex of Khajuraho, located some 620 kilometers south-east of Delhi in the state of Madhya Pradesh, has been one of India's main tourism attractions for several decades. This development greatly increased after the government opened an airport close to the site in 1978 (Ichaporia 1983, 83). The 20 or so remaining Hindu and Jain sandstone temples of Khajuraho, which were inscribed on the UNESCO World Heritage List in 1986, are famous for their blending of architecture and sculpture, and apart from the beauty and excellent craftsmanship of the sculptures, some of the temples are famous for the explicit erotic motifs of some of the sculptures. Most of the temples of the Khajuraho complex had not been used for most of their recent history, and they have now become tourism temples, to which one has to pay an entrance fee. Apart from domestic and international tourists, many Buddhist, Hindu and Jain pilgrims pay visits to the complex while on pilgrimage (Ichaporia 1983, 84). The tourist development of the site finds its ultimate expression in a 50 minute sound and light show on the history of the temples, narrated by a Bollywood star (Amitabh Bachchan). The show is held every night, first in English, then in Hindi, at the Western group of temples. The event is organized by the tourism department and there is an entrance fee where foreigners are charged four to five times the amount paid by Indians.

In many, if not most, places "ordinary" tourists clearly outnumber pilgrims or "religious tourists" (Olsen and Timothy 2006, 12). Heritage church buildings in many European city centers are nowadays predominantly used by tourists and locally known as tourism churches. The church administrators are aware of and often quite explicit about that. Douglas Pearce refers to a statement by the head of the French Catholic Unit for Tourism and Leisure Pastoral Care saying that "our churches have become tourist products" (Pearce 1999a, 84).[27] Moreover, this source claims that for the French people the churches have become "places of memory" (Pearce 1999a, 84) – possibly implying a distinction between actual religious practice on the one hand, and memory on the other, reflecting processes of religious transformation or "secularization" (from religious practice to cultural memory). In other parts of the globe, previously dormant or deserted religious sites such as the Tengboche monastery in Nepalese Sherpa country have been filled with new, albeit different, life (Shackley 1999).[28]

For their part, public administrations often invest funds in the renovation of religious buildings in order to make their countries, towns or regions more attractive to travelers. For some countries these investments can be a heavy burden.[29]

One of the most spectacular instances of this development has been the reconstruction of the Frauenkirche in Dresden, one of the city's main landmarks, which at the time of writing is listed as one of the top places to visit on Germany's official tourism website (www.cometogermany.com), where Cologne Cathedral is ranked as the number one site. The project of reconstructing the Frauenkirche served many purposes, not the least political ones, but it was clear from the outset that tourists would make up the main group of users – and this is exactly what has happened. The church policy seems to reflect this in its strategy of the "open church", inviting everybody to enjoy the church space.[30] The reconsecration of the church was an international media event.

For the United States, Paula Kane has recently commented:

> Cathedrals remain an important part of American cityscapes, but only insofar as they participate in the sanitized theatrical effect that cities

hope to use to attract tourists. Cities that can advertise themselves
as having heterogeneous religious traditions and diversity of architecture
hope to use this marketing contest to succeed economically. The quality of
Moneo's design easily enables Los Angeles to sell it as a must-see piece
of architecture for visitors,[31] but the Archdiocese will have to work to defend
the sacrality of the building against the city's desire for theatrical display.

(Kane 2006, 149)

Similar processes can also be observed in other parts of the globe, even in
countries whose governments do not have a reputation for being sympathetic
to religion. In the former German Democratic Republic, the reconstruction
(1975) and subsequent restoration of Berlin Cathedral (destroyed by air raids
during World War II) was a first significant project towards the maintenance
of church buildings, and Berlin Cathedral soon became an important tourist
attraction (Neumann and Rösener 2006, 83). Turning to the present, consider the case of China, where Buddhist, Confucian and Daoist sites have
regained a new status as public spaces in tourism contexts. The Temple and
Cemetery of Confucius and the Kong Family Mansion in Qufu (in the
Eastern Shangdon Province) are a case in point. The Red Guards had been
allowed to damage the site during the Cultural Revolution, but the Open
Door Reforms from 1978 led to a new emphasis on tourism, encouraging the
rehabilitation of numerous cultural and religious sites; as a result of this new
policy, by the early 1980s Qufu saw a large inflow of investments into tourism accommodations. In 2004, the town had 4.5 million domestic and
170,000 international visitors (Yan and Bramwell 2008, 978), the vast
majority of whom came for the Temple and Cemetery of Confucius.

In 1980, the Kongzi Research Center was founded in Qufu and, in 1984,
three thousand selected Chinese and foreign guests attended the birthday
ceremonies of Confucius, with the populace filling the temple ground, and
the statue of Confucius that had been demolished by the Red Guards was
restored (Jensen 1997, 12). This is part of a process where ceremonies
previously performed at the temple slowly re-emerged, albeit at first in the
form of carefully filtered performances such as a cult dance show performed
annually as part of the program to celebrate the birthday of Confucius.
Possible religious dimensions and interpretations were carefully avoided and
excluded:

... the event was allowed to be held after it was agreed that during the
ceremony the temple door would be shut so that nobody could pay
homage to the statue of Confucius, homage would not be paid on bent
knees, and the lead ceremonial role would not be taken by a descendent
of Confucius.

(Yan and Bramwell 2008, 981)

The program was later extended, and subsequently new ritual forms were developed that became increasingly modeled on historical records (Yan and Bramwell 2008, 981–84).

There are many further examples of the re-emergence of temples as public tourism spaces in China. In Beijing, for instance, famous religious sites such as the White Dagoba Temple (Baita Si), the Temple of Heaven and the Temple of Confucius are now accessible to tourists for an admission fee, apparently as part of an attempt to attract tourists and their money. Throughout China, "a close link between the recovery of Daoist temples and the nation-wide expansion of the tourist industries" has been observed (Chi-Tim 2003, 418). Note that the vast majority of these tourists are domestic travelers or overseas Chinese visiting home.

The revenues gained from tourism via religious sites are sometimes being reinvested not only in preservation, renovation and extensions, but occasionally also in massive displays. In 1996, for example, the Yuanfu Wanninggon temple at Maoshan, in Nanjing, "decided to build the largest bronze statue of Laozi in the world" (Chi-Tim 2003, 418); the giant bronze statue, 33 meters high, was opened to the public in 1998.

Moreover, the vague hope of attracting tourists can, in conjunction with other (political, social, economical, etc.) interests, contribute to the establishment of new temples. The Daoist Huang Daxian temples in Jinhua, in the Eastern coastal province of Zhejiang, are an interesting case in point. Five such temples were built in the 1990s, as a result of the establishment of mutual contacts with authorities and worshipers of Hong Kong's Wong Tai Sin Temple, one of the largest and most famous temples of the city. The saint worshiped in this temple originated from Jinhua, but, much to the surprise to the visitors from Hong Kong, Wong Tai Sin (Huang Daxian) was not a popular figure in his home area and few locals knew about him. Jinhua party cadres perceived that as a golden opportunity to connect to the Hong Kong people; the cadres "became active in reviving religion and in transforming spaces relating to Wong Tai Sin into sites and attractions" (Chan 2005, 68), and intellectuals and business people also became involved. In the course of events, five temples dedicated to the saint were built. Among them was Chisong Daoyuan, built by a female Taiwanese factory owner, investor and Wong Tai Sin worshiper high up on a mountain slope. Based on her connections with the Taoist Association of Taiwan, Taoist priests regularly visited the new temple and tour groups came from Taiwan. Chisong Daoyan was designed as a resort area including a hotel, several restaurants and facilities for various activities. That made the temple popular with Taiwanese "religious" tourists who

> came in religious tour groups searching for their own roots and those of the gods worshiped in Taiwan's temples as well as simply to enjoy beautiful scenery … These Taiwanese visitors were also customers at the

bamboo-constructed souvenir shops, incense stalls, and restaurants and teahouses, and felt nostalgic about these recreated heritages.

(Chan 2005, 71)

At the same time this example illustrates the interplay between religious tourism and other tourists. According to Selina Ching Chan, "[d]uring peak periods, such as the birthday of the saint, Labour Day and National Day, 30,000 to 40,000 tourists come to the temple" (Chan 2005, 74). The majority of these, of course, are local visitors, who are attracted by "free admission, beautiful scenery, recreational facilities, accessible location, and many shops, restaurants, and teahouses" (Chan 2005, 74). Some, but not all, worship in the temple and interviewees "emphasized the fact that Wong Tai Sin was popular in Hong Kong but had now returned home to Chisong" (Chan 2005, 74). It is his fame in Hong Kong and the attractiveness of the location that bring the visitors to the site.

Not all attempts to attract tourists by building temples are successful (Chan and Lang 2007). At Huang Peng village in Jinhua, a private researcher who later set up a research group established that Huang Daxian originally came from Huang Peng. Subsequently, the memory of the saint came to be reinvoked in the village by establishing places and objects linked to the saint in terms of religious and cultural heritage. Local food specialties were ascribed healing powers and acquired new names that established links to Huang Daxian. These attempts culminated in the project, started in 1992, of building a temple dedicated to Huang Daxian and the temple was opened in 1995. The project, it seems, was motivated by the hope to develop the faltering economy by attracting overseas investors and travelers – tourists and pilgrims – who might find their way to Huang Peng via the famous temple in Hong Kong. In addition, heritage attractions such as a museum-like house, where materials associated with the saint were displayed were set up, and a festival related to the saint was started. However, for various reasons (discussed by Chan and Lang 2007) the expected popularity of the temple and the village as a tourism destination did not materialize. In that sense, the project failed.

Also, Buddhist temples in China are beneficiaries of the joint forces of religious revitalization and tourism boom. Consider the Chan Buddhist Shaolin monastery on Mount Song (one of the Taoist Five Sacred Mountains) in the Dengfang district of Henan Province. Famous for its association with martial arts, the monastery had been abandoned for years after the Cultural Revolution when the monks were jailed and the buildings purged of Buddhist materials. It is now a major tourism attraction visited by 81 percent of the some 3.2 million annual visitors to Dengfeng city along with the early Taoist Zhongyue Temple in its vicinity (Mu *et al.* 2007, 108). The case of the Wutai Mountain in Shanxi, which has been strongly promoted as a tourism attraction, illustrates the increasing commercialization of religious sites as a result of their exposure to tourism. Many hotels, restaurants, shops, stalls and street vendors operate on the mountain with its surviving 43 monasteries. Interviews conducted by Fangfang Shi point to ambivalent reactions to this atmosphere of commerce and sense of commercialization. Some respondents approved of the commercialization since it, among other reasons, created a livelier atmosphere and because they felt that it might even help to create an interest in Buddhism among visitors. Other respondents, however, were disapproved by the commercialization, partly because it was seen as a threat to the religious character of the site, and partly because of the unpleasant degree of haggling that had started to occur (Shi 2009, 209–10).

Chinese state policy has it that religions must be economically self-supporting, and temples may develop commercial activities that benefit from the increasing numbers of tourists and worshipers. A case study of the revitalized Nanputuo Buddhist temple in the south-eastern coastal city of Xiamen mentions tourism-generated revenues such as gate receipts, a vegetarian restaurant, photo booths and souvenir shops (Ashiwa and Wank 2006, 343) – invariably leading to discussions with the state apparatus on how to reinvest these revenues. The temple is a centerpiece in the campaign launched by the Religious Affairs Bureau to contribute to the development of the market economy of the Xiamen Special Economic Zone. It seems that the state authorities assumed "that the revival of religion encourages economic investment by overseas Chinese" (Ashiwa and Wank 2006, 348). Overseas Chinese may come to China as tourists or in order to worship their ancestors; once there, the reasoning goes, these visitors discover business opportunities and get involved. Accordingly, city officials single out the Nanputuo temple "as a famous scenic site in tourism campaigns" (Ashiwa and Wank 2006, 348).

Not only are extant sites increasingly supported by the Chinese authorities, but

> some localities have created their own Buddhist holy places, apparently as business ventures, by such means as the construction of massive bronze or copper images, approached through a funnel of tourist facilities to which a small temple has been appended.
>
> (Birnbaum 2003, 444)

Business here is not created around extant religious sites, but apparently religious sites are created in order to attract tourists.

In Hong Kong, where tourism amounts to the second largest source of foreign currency (Cheung 1999, 576), temples, rural shrines and ancestral halls have been renovated. Preservation of religious sites is funded and supported by the Hong Kong government. They are marked and developed for the tourism industry (Cheung 1999, 572). According to Tik-sang Liu, the function of these buildings changes after renovation. In other words, the buildings are preserved, but not their functions: "the religious center is turned into a museum and is open to the public ... and formerly religious buildings have become a cultural resource for the Hong Kong tourist industry" (Liu 2003, 392). Instead of arenas for local religious practice, some buildings are part of a so-called Heritage Trail created in 1993 for tourist consumption. Interestingly, while originally promoted by the Hong Kong Tourist Association "for international tourists who are looking for the real 'old China,' with traditional folk religion, ancestor worship and lineage family organization" (Cheung 1999, 577), the Heritage Trail soon became popular among domestic tourists, to some extent as part of a discourse on "Hongkongese" that became especially virulent in the context of governmental transition.

The Taiwan Tourism Bureau provided data pointing to the popularity of temples and temple fairs as visitor and tourist attractions. According to these findings, the Taiwanese rank temples/temple fairs second to exhibitions as cultural activity, before festivals and sports. "Among foreign tourists visiting Taiwan, 37.66% visit a temple or temple fair" (Chang and Liu 2009, 1). Because of competition between the 11,275 officially registered Taiwanese temples, temple administrators add dancing, plays and acrobatics to the temple performances to attract visitors to their respective temple. Moreover, markets "selling snacks, calligraphy, antiques, religious products, and traditional arts and crafts have been established around numerous temples" (Chang and Liu 2009, 1).

In the Lao People's Democratic Republic, where the government has promoted tourism development since 1990 and where tourism now is one of the top foreign exchange earners, the government has taken steps to designate selected temples as tourist attractions. Active steps were taken to ground this agenda among the religious specialists. Experts from the National Tourism Authority of Lao PDR even "offer lectures to monks at the Buddhism College on tourism issues" where "[p]articular attention is given to the temples as prime examples of the people's cultural and religious heritage".[32]

For Burma (Myanmar), Janette Philp and David Mercer have shown how the military junta has invested in preserving and renovating Buddhist sites in a political project meant to attract foreign tourists. To domestic audiences, however, the same project served to propagate the idea of a unified nation (Philp and Mercer 1999).

While all the examples considered so far referred to actual religious structures, Joy Hendry reports an example of a different sort for Japan. In 1973, a hotelier on the island of Shōdoshima "decided to promote both tourism and philanthropy by building a replica of a Greek temple at the highest point of the island and planting a park of olive trees around it" (Hendry 2000, 46). The island of Shōdoshima, a popular destination for domestic tourism, has grown olives since the early 20th century, and according to Wikipedia "olive-related merchandise is quite popular with tourists".[33] In this case, however, apparently the olive trees were chosen for the symbolism of peace of the olive branch, and the structure was intended as a contribution to planting a culture of peace after the devastation of the war. Interestingly, the Greek temple actually contains a Shinto shrine, which is here dressed up by way of a Greek theme. A desire for peace and for welcoming more tourists jointly led to the creating of a hybrid religious site rather than dressing up actual places.

Emerging religious involvement

When tourists enter the scene, they invariably perform the standard set of tourist rites such as sightseeing, photographing and souvenir-hunting (Bremer 2006, 32). However, these same practices are also part of pilgrimages.

Many tourists visit sacred places with no prior intention or specific motivation to worship (although that may be the case for many others). Nevertheless, at least in somewhat familiar religious environments many perform basic religious acts such as kneeling, saying a short prayer, meditating in front of pictures, lighting candles or (especially in East Asia) using instruments of divination.

The special character of certain sites does not fail to make an impression on people who just came for a brief stopover, to gaze and take pictures.[34] Furthermore, religious tropes may be used to describe places and experiences (as illustrated by Sears' study of 19th-century America). Or, as Thomas Bremer (2004, 144) has put it: "For many people, religion slips imperceptibly into touristic practice."

A study of visitors to four cathedrals in England supports that point of view when it notices a "contrast between the generally minor importance of religion in attracting visitors to cathedrals and its relative high importance in describing their overall feeling or perception of their visit" (Jackson and Hudman 1995, 43). Well aware that many travelers visit churches while ever fewer people attend services, the Church of England attempts to capitalize on this and hopes that "visitors to churches present opportunities to draw new people to the faith, or to claw back those that have slipped away" (Rotherham, 2007, 68).[35]

A number of churches – 10 percent of the English parish churches in a 1983 sample – are able to provide some kind of "pastoral ministry to visitors, which involves someone being present in the church both to welcome visitors and to help with their problems" (Hanna 1984, 7). A 1977 study of English cathedrals also quoted representatives of the cathedrals as saying that visitors should get an opportunity to be immersed in the religious dimensions of the buildings, for example by inviting visitors to join worship; while one spokesperson at Winchester Cathedral hoped that "the spiritual values will 'rub off' on the visitors", at Rochester Cathedral the opinion was voiced "that the Cathedral is a major place of evangelism" (Hanna, Marris and Lefley 1979, 94–95).

At the main tourist churches in Paris, texts placed at the entrances point to attempts to evangelize the visitors.[36] At Sacré Coeur, for example, "more than two million small multilingual texts are distributed each year stressing the origins and purpose of the basilica and offering three short prayers for non-Christians, non-Catholic Christians, and Catholics" (even lapsed ones) (Pearce 1999a, 86). The former chaplain of the church emphasized that Sacré Coeur saw itself as a "meeting place" between visitors and worshipers, believers and non-believers (Pearce 1999a, 86).

A recent sociological study cites evidence that many "rank-and-file Americans ... have been prompted to think about spirituality by participating in the arts or by being exposed to the arts as consumers" (Wuthnow 2003, 18). Since tourists often encounter religious art, for example when visiting a cathedral, it can be surmised that their visit will prompt spiritual or religious emotions, stimulate reflections or trigger reflexes such as memories based on sensual reactions (recalling smells, etc.). Such sensations are often sparked off by the specific atmospheres created by religious sites – and experiencing the "atmosphere" of places is often mentioned as an important motivation for visiting sites (see, for example, Richards 2002, 1055). Atmospheres, which are experienced by bodily immersion, have the power to stir emotions (Böhme 2006). Many churches and other religious sites have specific atmospheres, often in marked distinction from surrounding spaces. These are created by varieties of architecture that form different textures of sound and light exposing visitors to different spatial dimensions; in combination with perceptual features such as smells and by evoking memories of past experiences with sacred spaces this often appeals to visitors and creates moments perceived as significant.

There is overwhelming anecdotal proof of the ability of art and liturgies in generating "spiritual", "reflective" or "religious" moods that deeply touch or move tourists who did not come for that experience in the first place. As far as I am aware, such perspectives on the emergent effects of tourism on religion and spirituality have not yet been explored systematically.[37] In fieldwork conducted at a church in Bergen in 2007, Janemil Kolstø observed that the mood among visitors to the church changed consistently whenever the organist rehearsed on his instrument; visitors would remain longer, sit longer on the benches rather than walking around, and would apparently became more meditative.

Threats to sacred places and management challenges

The author of a study of travelers to Israel was surprised by the "high proportion (66%) of non-pilgrims who visit holy places" (Fleischer 2000, 321).

The overlap and distinction between places used for religious, tourist and possibly also other purposes creates a "simultaneity" (Bremer 2006, 32)[38] that poses a number of practical challenges such as screening worshipers from tourists but also fundamental concerns, for instance with regard to questions and politics of identity and authenticity.[39]

Another issue is that of commoditization. Geographer Daniel Olsen claims that the transformation of religious into tourist sites "changes the meaning of sacred sites from that of worship and contemplation to that of leisure" (Olsen 2003, 99). However, apart from the questionable distinction between leisure and sacred time or the sacred and the profane – as if one could not contemplate in leisure contexts – meanings are not ontologically given to places but ascribed to them and embodied in practice by different groups of users. Hence, the sites as such do not necessarily change their meanings (as if these meanings were inherent in these spaces), but some people use sites for worship and contemplation while others use them for other purposes. Rather than simply shifting their meanings from religious to touristic, they are developing into "multi-use sites" (Olsen 2003, 100) – if they have not already been that for a long time, as is the case with the large cathedrals (Pearce 1999a, 84). Meanings can also change for individuals during visits or after visits, when a tourist gets into a spiritual mood or a religious visitor is drawn into tourist behaviors. Last but not least, the borderlines between the aesthetic and the sacred are often blurred; even if a place is visited because of its expected beauty, the artwork is religious in nature and can under certain conditions also be perceived as such.[40]

The growth in the number of tourist visitors leads to extra work for the staff at these sites. Large and important religious structures in terms of visitor attraction that can afford it have some kind of administrative structure in place for the management of visitors. In English cathedrals, already in the 1970s new jobs were created to meet the demands posed by tourism. These jobs included shop and refectory managers and assistants, public relations officers, information officers, visitation officers, guided tours secretaries, etc. (Hanna, Marris and Lefley 1979, 90). Also smaller sites have some administrative facilities (Woodward 2004, 181). Besides the staff, many sites engage the work of volunteers. In 1983, a third of English parish churches had volunteers for helping visitors (Hanna 1984, 7). Major cathedrals could call on more than 100 volunteers from their parish (Hanna, Marris and Lefley 1979, 90), many of whom acted as guides.

Administrators of religious sites often provide services that highlight the specific features of the respective site. For churches and cathedrals in the UK such services include guided tours, guidebooks, brochures, leaflets (sometimes in foreign languages), notice boards, displays or exhibitions, welcomers/stewards, education programs and children's programs (Woodward 2004, 181). Visitors are sometimes directed along recommended routes through the buildings and in many churches particular works of art are often highlighted and illuminated.

The process that turns religious places into tourist destinations puts various forms of pressure on the respective sites and the religious communities worshiping there, especially since "[v]ery few sacred sites were constructed to cope with the visitor numbers they now experience" (Shackley 2001, 54).

The local clientele of the site, if any, may be proud of its success or else be put off by all the foreigners who may easily become the majority of users of these sites and who are often regarded as behaving inappropriately[41] and even sometimes as ritually impure. All this may (or may not) lead to decreased participation on the part of the local users.

Access to many sacred sites is restricted when ritual activities are being performed. This is the case in many churches in Italy. Another prominent example is the Taj Mahal, one of the icons of planetary tourism, which is at the same time a UNESCO heritage site and a religious building. On Fridays, this site is open only for Muslim worshipers and closed to ordinary tourists.

Noise, traffic and congestion, overcrowding (think of the over 30,000 daily visitors streaming through Notre Dame!), inappropriate dress and behavior (from the point of view of the religious communities) are some of the main disturbances encountered at most places once they get exposed to tourism.[42] They may diminish the experience of worshipers, threaten the religious character of sites (and thereby, ultimately, their attractiveness as destinations) and may lead to tensions between residents and tourists. Large numbers of visitors impose practical requirements such as restroom facilities.[43] The crowd, however, is not only seen as a disturbance for the locals – in some cases they are hardly involved at all – but also, if not primarily, for the tourists themselves: the presence and behavior of other tourists is often commented upon negatively by fellow tourists.

Annoyances and nuisances apart, tourists may actually damage the places they descend upon. Almost inevitable ecological consequences include general wear and tear, microclimatic change, garbage, pollution, erosion and accidental damage, often caused by the desire to physically connect to the site (by touching, etc.).[44] This desire is especially strong at many religious sites, where the touch of some object is often held to confer blessings. Moreover, at many religious sites one finds what has been termed "ritual litter" caused by ritual acts such as the burning of candles, the offering of flowers or even animal sacrifice (Timothy and Nyaupane 2009, 59). Equipment such as flash cameras, heavy walking boots and modern means of transport (from cars and coaches to helicopters) also do their share of damage.

Moreover, theft and destruction (often motivated by the desire to take away an original/authentic piece of the site as a souvenir), removal of offerings, graffiti and vandalism such as "breaking pieces of buildings or statues, spray-painting over sculptured reliefs, carving names or slogans, or burning" (Timothy and Nyaupane 2009, 59) are common occurrences at many heritage sites including religious structures.[45] In English parish churches in the period from 1979 to 1982 "more than half of the churches in the survey had suffered from theft and nearly half from vandalism" (Hanna 1984, 9). Since many religious sites have long opening hours but little security, they are heavily exposed to these dangers (Shackley 2001, 39). The same problems of visitor impact are encountered at tourist as well as at pilgrimage sites where visitors often are especially keen to establish physical contact.[46]

Some of these problems may be dealt with by specific counter-measures. In extreme cases, the site is temporarily shut down.[47] In order to counter theft and vandalism, security systems are installed, while smaller churches lock away or fence off valuable moveable objects, or arrange for volunteers to guard the building in turn (Hanna 1984, 96).

In order to counteract inappropriate dress by visitors, religious-cum-tourist sites often seek to impose dress-codes: The "prohibition of shorts is a worldwide phenomenon and few sacred sites allow unlimited amounts of flesh to be displayed" (Shackley 2001, 34). There is also a "very widespread view that unrestricted photography is inappropriate in a sacred place" (Shackley 2001, 35). This is motivated by the desire to affirm the religious (sacred) character of the space. This kind of message is also reinforced by other media or markers such as billboards or leaflets, often admonishing people to keep silent.[48]

Cultural Resource Management scholar Myra Shackley has pointed out that

> [m]any religious sites ... have rigidly hierarchical clerically-dominated management structures which may have functioned in the same way for thousands of years. Such structures are largely unaffected by modern management trends ... Some sacred sites seem not to be managed at all, and merely exist in a management vacuum where things happen by custom and nobody is too bothered with achieving specific targets.
>
> (Shackley 2001, 90)

In her book, written from the point of view of Tourism Management Studies[49] Shackley analyzes several strategies for controlling visitor flows employed at sacred sites. Apart from types of available means of transport and vehicle management to the sites,[50] visitor flows at the sites and within the buildings are influenced or controlled by means of zoning, entrance fees and pay perimeters. Other techniques include queue controls, temporary closure or diverting visitors to other sites, forcing all visitors into guided tours, restricting or increasing visiting times, establishing visitor centers, shortcutting walking distances, and specially designed visitor flow routes (Shackley 2001, 55–75). As soon as sites exceed their so-called "optimal visitation level", Shakley argues, the experiential quality of the visitation is diminished, visitors get dissatisfied and upset, and even "the physical fabric of the site may be adversely affected" (Shackley 2001, 66).

At the same time, it seems that contrary to most other tourist destinations the absence of basic facilities and efficient management does not deter visitors. "In management terms they break all the rules for success", as Shakley (2001, 94) candidly remarks.

She argues that visitors to religious sites "are motivated by quite a different set of factors from those of visitors to any other site of the heritage attraction market" (Shackley 2001, 94). I don't know whether there is empirical evidence to support that idea, and I am skeptical about the underlying theoretical assumption, which seems to be based on a questionable theoretical legacy (why should religious sites trigger specific motivations?). Instead, one may argue that it is exactly the absence of apparent management skill that at least in part can create the impression of an increased authenticity of a religious site (since religion and skilful strategic management are often regarded as antithetical). Paradoxically, the less commercialized religious places appear, the greater their commercial success.[51]

Maintaining and running religious-cum-tourist sites can cost tremendous amounts of money which often needs to be collected from visitors. Admission (if levied), collections, donations and retail including the sale of souvenirs are some of the more common ways of merchandising to generate revenue. Sometimes the space is let for private ceremonies such as weddings.[52] Although British cathedrals, to take an example of extremely popular religious-cum-tourist sites numbering more than 30 million visitors per year, make substantial revenues from tourism, their overall balance suffers heavy losses largely due to the maintenance and upkeep of the fabric of these structures, requiring them to devise new strategies of generating income (Shackley 2002).

Given a widely shared dichotomy between religion and commerce and the generally accepted idea – at least in Europe – that religion should be free for all, the question whether or not to levy admission fees appears as a recurrent matter of dispute. (See also the case from Kyoto discussed earlier; p. 70f.) In Bergen (Norway) some years ago the church administration decided to levy an admission fee for one church (Mariakirken) that is famous for its artworks and a popular visitor attraction. In an interview with us, the Dean explained that the revenue from this is used to keep the other churches open for several hours per day and to offer basic facilities during the tourism season.[53] During fieldwork at Mariakirken in summer 2008 we encountered several cases where visitors would rather avoid visiting this church than pay entrance fees, while others paid grudgingly. Many, however, did not seem to mind. In Venice, the discussion on the levying of entrance fees led to a new development. Some 13 congregations started a non-profit management project called

Chorus, which managed their churches from 10am to 5pm Mondays to Saturdays and from 1pm to 5pm on Sundays as if they were a museum (with admission, tickets, guards and typical techniques of presentation). At the same time, special spiritual zones and some side-chapels are accessible to people who want to pray. Outside of these time-slots the sites function as churches. Chorus has some hundred members and friends, 24 employees and a series of volunteers. It attends to some 500,000 visitors a year and from the income generated by Chorus in the period from 1998 to 2004 800,000 euros were invested in the restoration and preservation of the churches (Neumann and Rösener 2006, 167).

In some places visitors are charged admission to see some parts of the structure. This had been the case for a long time at Westminster Abbey, where visitors had to pay to see the Royal Chapel. When visitor numbers were reaching 2.5 million in 1995, the Dean and Chapter at Westminster decided to implement a new visitor scheme that included raising the admission charge by 20 percent and extending it to the whole of the Abbey. As a result overall visitor numbers declined by 60 percent (to 1 million), but gross income actually increased. Moreover, an official press release from the Abbey stated that "[w]orshippers are returning to the Abbey in increasing numbers and the tourists have shown that they much prefer the new arrangements".[54]

Especially in economically less developed countries, religious sites are sometimes made accessible to tourists in the hope of gaining substantial revenues, but these expectations are not always met. In some cases, the revenues obtained from making the site accessible go entirely into security measures to protect the site. The need to generate funding often reinforces the process of commoditization of sites "by interpretation and packaging onto everything from mugs to tea towels. There seems to be no limit to what can be commodified" (Shackley 2001, 86).

Apart from the damage or other forms of impact and changes resulting from the exposure of religious sites, tourism development may also lead to the demolition of religious structures.[55] Sometimes, this is also met with resistance. In Sanur (Bali), in 1971, the extension of the Bali Beach Hotel required the demolition of a temple, but then the priest and the congregation staged a successful campaign, which also involved ritual trance; the paralysis of a priest hired by the head of district and the subsequent death of the wife of this priest were regarded as signs of the resistance of the gods and helped to draw attention to the affair (Picard 1996, 76–77). Again in Bali, in 1993, there was a project to build a luxury holiday resort, the Bali Nirvana Resort, on the site of the Tanah Lot temple. Given its situation on a cliff this temple is a favorite tourism site as a scenic spot to witness sunsets. This project was met with an unprecedented wave of protest, the opponents unanimously insisting "that Tanah Lot is a symbol of Bali throughout the world and that the Balinese see it as a symbol of their identity" (Picard 1996, 193).

Eventually, a compromise was reached and the Indonesian Hindu Council (Parisada Hindu Dharma Indonesia) decreed in 1994 "that no building could be built within a two kilometer radius of the Tanah Lot temple" (Picard 1996, 194). Michel Picard notes that "several villagers from the surrounding area have for some time refused to sell their land" but that it was "not land but religion that has rapidly emerged as the issue at the heart of the controversy" (Picard 1996, 193). Apparently, religion was able to mobilize people for a common cause. However, one wonders whether it was religion that helped to turn this issue into a larger cause, or rather the fact that the temple was a symbol for Balinese and a successful cultural resource for tourists and domestic visitors. Currently, the area surrounding the temple can only be entered by buying a ticket. There are several restaurants and souvenir shops in the area, but the temple as such is shielded from tourist consumption; as stated on the website:

> Do not entry to the temple, except you want to pray with balinese uniform. [sic!][56]

Minority attractions and religious self-representation

Many sacred places serving as tourist attractions belong to a mainstream religion or one of the various religious groups operating in social contexts characterized by religious plurality or pluralism. As we have seen, other sites belong to religions that may have once been dominant, but can no longer claim this position in society. Still others are only testimonies of the past religious history of a place or a people. In these cases, the tourism attractions serve as landmarks on the map of memory. In yet other cases, tourism attractions belong to religious minorities.

Granting access to their sacred places for minorities comes at the risk of losing intimacy and therefore requires techniques or management efforts to control the impact, but their appearance on tourism maps also provides enhanced visibility (and also some income) to religious minorities. Let us visit some groups and places.

In Iran, during my travels in the late 1990s and the early 2000s I was under the impression that international tourists, who visit places belonging to Zoroastrianism, were appreciated by the Zoroastrian community partly because the tourists possibly alerted international attention to that vulnerable religious minority.[57] National (mostly Muslim) tourists were likewise welcome to visit the major temples. Zoroastrians seemed to be content that visitors did not perceive their religion as paganism or superstition but appreciated it as an important part of the cultural and religious heritage of the country. For Zoroastrians, visits by tourists provide one occasion to actively display their history and religious beliefs to visitors in order to disseminate their own views of their religion (as against popular ignorance or misinformation) and to elicit sympathy. The main fire-temple in the town of Yazd, one of the traditional strongholds of the religion, is now neatly distinguished into a frontstage for visitors and a backstage area accessible to Zoroastrians only. From both angles one can see the main temple-fire, but there is a glass window between the fire and the frontstage tourism hall, probably in order to prevent attempts at desecrating the fire.

In the city of Haifa in Northern Israel the main tourist attraction and quasi-symbol of the city, the Baha'i gardens, belongs to a religious minority which otherwise pursues a low-profile policy in Israel – the Baha'is have no formal community in Israel. The terraced Baha'i gardens were opened in 2001. They center on the gold-domed Shrine of the Báb, an imposing landmark that serves both as a pilgrimage place for Baha'is and as a tourist attraction for non-Baha'is. The Baha'i authorities have taken great care to shield the pilgrims by providing them with exclusive access to some parts and by restricting visiting hours for tourists. Spatial and temporal arrangements are made in such a manner as to avoid interaction between pilgrims and tourists (Gatrell and Collins-Kreiner 2006, 771). The national government regularly brings VIP guests to the gardens. In this way, the Baha'is are implicitly showcased in the context of political propaganda – a fact presumably perceived by the Baha'is as safeguarding their position in Israel. It seems that the site is a place of pride for the local residents, very few of whom are Baha'is. The gardens are invariably part of any tour schedule in Haifa. Some buses only stop briefly, mainly for the scenic beauty and the view, but there are also guided tours. The guides, however, are not themselves Baha'is, and their presentation primarily focuses on the aesthetic dimension of the site rather than on its religious aspects (Gatrell and Collins-Kreiner 2006, 771; Collins-Kreiner and Gatrell 2006, 43). The Baha'i authorities are not using tourist visits for proselytizing, but they carefully stage the visits, provide basic information about the faith and create an aesthetically appealing image of the religion. Probably for many people who happen to travel to Israel and care to visit Haifa, the gardens will be a first encounter with the Baha'i Faith and provide a lasting impression.

Following the routes of Baha'i history, we move from Iran, via Israel, to the United States. In October 2008, I visited the oldest extant of the currently seven Baha'i temples in the world, "The Baha'i House of Worship" in Wilmette, Illinois, completed in 1953. This impressive dome, surrounded by gardens, on the shore of Lake Michigan, is reportedly visited by around 250,000 visitors annually.[58] Although prayer services are held daily at the temple, the structure does not fulfil any specific ritual need for the local Baha'i community, but its aesthetical qualities clearly serve as a means to impress the "beauty" of the Baha'i religion on visitors. The architecture is decorated by religious symbols of and quotes from the message of the Baha'i Faith. Near the entrance information brochures on the Baha'i Faith in around a hundred languages are placed for visitors to take with them. Printed gratis postcards requesting further information from the Baha'i National Center are also available, and different sorts of books and other materials can be purchased or taken home for free. The temple clearly is a site of information about and propagation of the Baha'i religion for tourists visiting the Chicago area.

Let us conclude this section by referring to a case where a religious group that faces persecution in its homeland – just as the Baha'is do in Iran – tries to benefit from tourism to change public opinion. In Taiwan, members of Falun Gong have recently started to flock to tourist sites and to set up exhibits around these sites in order to alert the growing numbers of tourists from mainland China to the destiny that their religious group is facing in China. Tourism and tourist attractions are here engaged as strategic sites to campaign against religious discrimination, but it is unlikely, or at least unclear, whether this kind of outreach will have any effect on the situation in China.[59]

The UNESCO World Heritage List: a global canon of tourist sites

Religious sites serving as tourist attractions are a global phenomenon. Moreover, there is a sort of global canon of the world's most prestigious heritage sites: the UNESCO World Heritage List, which as of April 2008 lists 851 properties in 141 states.[60] The vast majority (660) of the sites are categorized as cultural properties. Most of these sites which are to be conserved/preserved are also main tourist attractions and the designation of a place as a World Heritage Site creates symbolic capital that can be exploited in tourism contexts (in addition to stimulating local/regional/national pride and self-consciousness); the label "is a highly valued promotional tool for developing tourism" (Timothy and Nyaupane 2009, 11).

A large number of World Heritage Sites can be classified as religious places. Apart from the World Heritage List, there are also lists of heritage buildings on a national scale. In China, to take one lesser known example, 180 nationally preserved cultural heritage sites were designated, out of which 80 (= 45 percent) "are religious tourist destinations. In the first and second classes of 84 national level tourist sites, 63 of them are related to religion" (Mu *et al.* 2007, 105).

The creation of the UNESCO World Heritage List originally resulted from UNESCO's attempt to preserve some endangered sites. The creation of the World Heritage List was sparked by a campaign aiming at the preservation of the Egyptian Abu Simbel temples that were threatened to be flooded when the Aswan High Dam was being built in the 1960s. As a result of the worldwide campaign launched by UNESCO, in an extremely costly operation the Abu Simbel and Philae temples were taken apart, moved to a higher location, and put back together piece by piece. In that shape, they can now be visited by tourists, and New Age travelers and other may perform some rituals at these sites.[61]

As of April 2009, 186 States Parties have ratified the World Heritage Convention. Among other things, by signing the convention the states pledge to conserve the World Heritage Sites situated on its territory and to protect its national heritage. As the UNESCO website points out "[w]hat makes the concept of World Heritage exceptional is its universal application. World Heritage Sites belong to all the peoples of the world, irrespective of the territory on which they are located."[62] This globalization of cultural capital, the legitimate owner of which is humankind, finds itself in a constructive symbiosis with tourism as a way to explore this universal heritage.

Power places

Apart from the well-established or recovered pilgrimage centers a new global set of places has emerged since the 1960s, the so-called "power places".[63] The category of "power places" includes sites such as (moving from the Americas towards Australia) Cusco,[64] Machu Picchu, Yucatan, Sedona, the Devil's Tower, Stonehenge, Crete, the Egyptian pyramids, Mount Everest, the Taj Mahal, "mystical Tibet", Mount Kailas, Mount Fuji, the sacred mountains of Bali (Agung, Batur, Batukao and Abang), and Ayers Rock (Uluru) – to name but some of the best-known ones.

The open list of the "power places" reflects the process in which cultural resources of the world are perceived to be part of the universal human heritage; the power places are something like a religious heritage list. In fact, many of the sites mentioned earlier are listed on the UNESCO World Heritage List. These "power places" are often at the same time national tourism icons and sites of archaeological activities and concern, but also pertinent landmarks on the mental and spiritual global map of the New Age, various paganisms or other forms of contemporary religions (Druids, Goddess Movements, etc.). There are various guidebooks to these "power places" and numerous small-scale tour operators offering to arrange tours to these sites (Attix 2002, 54). Just as other tourists perform their tourist rites at the World Heritage Sites, New Age and pagan travelers perform their spiritual practices at many of these places; in several cases New Agers operate travel agencies or other businesses catering to tourists at the sites.[65] Nowadays, "New Age and other nature and self-religionists comprise a major world market for tourism" (Timothy and Conover 2006, 143), which has acquired a certain level of specialization (Pernecky and Johnston 2006). There is clearly an overlap and probably also a mutual reinforcement of tourism and the New Age Movement. Besides traveling to special places, elements of New Age tourism include purposes such as attending fairs, festivals and gatherings, visiting special service providers and purchasing spiritual goods, attending courses and traveling to retreats or other centers.

However, the appeal of these "power places" is not restricted to one religious group only. New Agers, pagans and adherents of other religious groups are not always in harmony with each other. In fact, there is a fair amount of rivalry among different groups usually subsumed under these umbrella terms. Importantly, various pagan groups have different concerns with the power places, some supporting the preservation ethos propagated by most traditional management agencies and archaeologists, some objecting to it; some engaging in private rites, others in public rituals; some trying to avoid a visible impact on the sites, others not; etc. (Blain and Wallis 2007).

Christians and adherents of other "traditional" religions likewise visit these places, albeit often, but not necessarily, with different expectations. Moreover, concepts, narratives, and practices that one would have associated primarily with the New Age have now gained a much wider currency even in contexts that prima facie do not belong to these New Age milieus.[66]

New Agers, pagans and other newcomers also compete with established religions for the ritual appropriation of space. Consider Glastonbury, one of the most prominent New Age destinations. Apart from the variety of "alternative" religious and spiritual options available at Glastonbury, the town also has a prominent Christian legacy and likewise is a Christian place.[67] In addition, the town is a major tourism destination.

Adrian Ivakhiv finds that New Age visitors have developed a specific form of "encounter" with these "power places" that puts a high value on "tuning to" and "openness" to signs and signals as "a different form of 'place practice' than the Cartesian relationship embodied in photography, sightseeing, and other forms of commodification" (Ivakhiv 2003, 106–7). A recent study of Machu Picchu has analyzed some features of the practices performed by spiritual pilgrims who carefully distinguish themselves from adventurers and "regular" tourists. To begin with, in order to grasp the "essence" of the place and its "energy", New Age visitors like to enter Machu Picchu at night, entering when the guards are asleep. Moreover, the visit to the site is often preceded by a physically challenging four-day trek, or even by running the "Inca trail" in the course of just one day in order to reach the kind of psychosomatic state required for obtaining the right sort of spiritual experience. To quote Alexandra Arellano: "The visit requires sacrifice, challenge, physical endurance and a wide range of multidimensional embodied performances that convert 'touring' into 'performing' and give way to a self-transforming experience" (Arellano 2007, 94). Self-challenge and going to the limit are also common in other forms of contemporary tourism.[68]

Contests and negotiations

The appearance and promotion or partial rejection of tourism at religious sites invariably raises the questions of ownership, control and power in complex situations with several interested parties such as religious leaders and participants, participating or non-participating local inhabitants and communities, local business people and retailers, government, management authorities, archaeologists, tourism agencies, investors, tourists and others who all make different claims on sites and spaces by engaging them in different sets of discourses and practices. The interested parties are not just locals, but often operate on a national or even transnational level. Religious sites transformed into tourism destinations are therefore naturally contested sites. In many cases, this contestation can be resolved or kept stable by negotiations and adaptations. In other cases, however, the contestation leads to clashes and legal as well as political battles. Legal decisions will then need to be enforced by site managers or the police.

Several examples of such conflicts have in recent decades involved indigenous people (i.e. minority first nation peoples subjected to colonial history) whose self-assertion of ownership and ritual use of places sometimes coincided with their increasing popularity among other visitors. Let us take a look at two cases – one from the US and one from Australia.

The so-called Devils Tower, a monolith dramatically rising above the surrounding terrain in Wyoming (USA), is regarded as a sacred site by numerous Native American tribes, some of whom perform Sun Dances at the mountain around the month of June and individual Vision Quests throughout the year. At the same time, the spectacular mountain is highly popular among climbers who, however, have occasionally "taken pictures of Native American ceremonies, removed prayer bundles, and intruded on solitude."[69] In 1906, Devils Tower and the area around it were established as the first national monument of the United States. It is the property of the United States. Since the early 1990s management plans were drafted to resolve conflicts resulting from the simultaneous appropriation of the site by climbers and Native Americans. The Final Climbing Management Plan for Devils Tower National Monument (1995) stipulated that "[i]n respect for the reverence many American Indians hold for Devils Tower as a sacred site, rock climbers will be asked to voluntarily refrain from climbing on Devils Tower during the culturally significant month of June".[70] It also stated that the management might consider other options, including mandatory closure during June, if voluntary closure did not work out. Some climbers who did not refrain from climbing in June challenged approval of the Final Climbing Management Plan for violation of the Establishment Clause. The United States Court of Appeals ruled (26 April 1999) that as the climbers "have alleged no injury as a result of their claim the FCMP [Final Climbing Management Plan for Devils Tower National Monument] improperly establishes religion, we hold the Climbers have no standing to sue in this case".[71] In practice, though, the park management will need to balance the needs of the (500,000) tourists and 6,000 climbers on the one hand and the some 20 Native American Plains tribes on the other.[72]

A similar conflict has arisen in Australia. Uluru, also known as Ayers Rock, is an impressive landmark in Central Australia (located 1431 kilometers south of Darwin by road and 440 kilometers south-west of Alice Springs). This sandstone rock is a World Heritage Site and Australia's most prominent natural icon. As such it is prominently featured on covers of some guide-books and infinitely photographed, preferably with the view of the rock silhouetted against the sky – a view which for many symbolizes the "real" Australia. At the same time, the Uluru is an important place for the Anangu, the traditional owners of the area to whom Uluru was handed back in 1985. Since then the Uluru-Kata Tjuta National Park has been managed jointly by the Anangu and Parks Australia staff. Tourism is grow-ing in the area since the 1950s. Currently, it receives more than 400,000 visitors a year (Hueneke and Baker 2009, 477). Most visitors spend one night in the resort and virtually all watch the sunset. Apart from observing, photographing and walking, motorbike and helicopter tours around the mountain are also available. There is also a range of new activities such as Sounds of Silence tours or gourmet dinners prepared by chefs out in the desert.[73]

A phenomenological study (Ingram, 2005) has shown that even for many tourists who apparently did not belong to the "religious" category the experi-ence of the rock was special. Respondents referred to the sight as "impressive", "overcome by the sheer immensity", "you really felt small in its presence", and "awe-inspiring". These words are bordering on what is often qualified as constituting "religious" experiences and, indeed, one respondent said: "I felt that there was something sacred … just something special."[74] These state-ments once more point to the potential emergence of religious experience or rhetorical tropes in touristic settings.[75] Since "nature" has emerged as an important codeword in religious/spiritual discourses and practices, religious experiences are not only to be had when visiting religious sites or attending religious performances, but also when encountering spectacular landscapes (see also Shackley 2004, 72).

For many (if not most) tourists, climbing the rock is a desired part of the trip. It seems to resonate with themes of test, challenge, quest, center, exploration and conquest. These may equally touch on the dimensions of sports or spirituality. The Anangu, on the other hand, are opposed to the tourists climbing the rock, mainly as this is against the ancestral order of things, the *tjukurpa* (encompassing tradition, law, morality, cosmology, religion) and is held to desecrate the mountain.

Although climbing is not formally prohibited, in various ways the Anangu ask visitors to refrain from climbing. This message is increasingly spread to more and more tourist agencies – not all of which were sympa-thetic to the Aboriginal point of view and sometimes even explicitly chal-lenged it, encouraging tourists to climb the rock and "take it easy" (Robinson 2001, 41–42). It seems that still over a third of the visitors opt for climbing the rock (Hueneke and Baker 2009, 482). By way of the entirely Aboriginal owned Anangu Tours Pty Ltd operation (started in 1995), one of the largest employers of Aboriginal people, the Anangu are promoting alternatives to the climb (du Cros and Johnston 2002). For the alternative walks advertised by this company it is suggested that the Anangu guides will share traditional bush survival skills, but also creation stories and explanations of symbolism of rock art (all provided in the aboriginal language with English interpretation). Interestingly then, the Anangu are prepared to share some of their myths and symbolic explanations as long as the rock remains untouched. They trade skills, myths and explanation of art for sacred space. Many visitors, who feel deprived of a sense of achievement, will not regard this as a valid replacement (Shackley 2004, 71).

A special problem, however, is caused by spiritual or New Age travelers who consider Uluru as part of their own spiritual cosmology. They therefore feel entitled to override the restrictions imposed by the park management, for instance with regard to the performance of their own rituals or remaining at the site overnight.[76]

At Mount Shasta in Northern California, which is considered a sacred site among the Wintu and some other Northern Californian Native American people, but is nowadays predominantly used by "spiritual pilgrims", i.e. people who consider it a major center for spiritual power and who perform various kinds of ritual activities there (such as prayer, worship or creating an altar), the indigenous and New Age groups as well as environmentalists and others formed a coalition to successfully stop the development of a ski area on the mountain (Huntsinger and Fernández-Giménez 2000). In order to succeed the legal case had to be made on the basis of Native American use, but it was supported by other groups; this coalition overshadowed other disagreements the groups might have, such as when Native Americans object to some forms of ritual appropriation of the mountain by the "spiritual pilgrims" and others. However, there seems to be a "culture clash" between the pilgrims on the one hand and the Forest Service on the other (Huntsinger and Fernández-Giménez 2000, 554).

Another problematic domain with regard to indigenous people is the notion of space. For among many indigenous people the spatial reference does not go to specific sites, but to the more encompassing notion of land (Johnston 2006, 122). Burial sites have also been issues of contention. An interesting incident occurred in Hawaii. When digging to build the new Ritz Carlton hotel in Kapalua on Maui Island in 1987, an ancient burial site that had apparently been in use until the late 18th century came to light. When as a result of an archaeological investigation the importance of this place was realized, protests were held against the erection of the hotel which appeared to threaten the peace of the ancestors buried there. Eventually, the investors obtained new building land close by, where the hotel opened in 1990. The rediscovered burial site became registered as a State Historic Place, which is

"reserved exclusively for native Hawaiian ceremonies and religious practices", as the dedication stone notes.[77] Employees of the adjacent Ritz
Carlton now offer weekly sense of place tours to the site, despite the fact that
it cannot be entered. The building of the hotel has thereby led to the rediscovery of a ritual site which after a dispute and negotiations has obtained a
new status as a protected religious space – tapped as symbolic capital by
the hotel.

While Uluru, Devils Tower, Mount Shasta and the Honokahua Burial
Site have traditional owners and users, the Egyptian pyramids are an example of religious buildings erected by religious communities that have long
since ceased to exist. Sites of this type are prone to conflict over access and
claims of ownership. Kathryn Rountree has illustrated the various contesting
practical and interpretative appropriations of Malta's Neolithic temples by
different local and international interest groups such as Maltese intellectuals
and nationalists, hunters, archaeologists, artists, tourists and the tourism
industry as well as participants in the global Goddess Movement. Foreign
tour operators somehow affiliated with the Goddess Movement are here
sometimes perceived to be in economic competition with local tourism
operators (Rountree 2002).

One of the best-known examples of the prehistoric monuments is Stonehenge (a World Heritage Site since 1986), where Druids started to worship in
the early 20th century. While this was tacitly tolerated, the appearance of the
so-called New Age travelers and their Free Festival (with over 50,000
people attending in 1984) has stirred up local opposition, resulting in violent
clashes in 1985 and 1988 and the eventual exclusion of the group from the
site (Shackley 2001, 145–47; Hetherington 2000). In 1998, however, English
Heritage (managing the site) again granted permission to a small number of
Druids and other pagans to celebrate the solstice at the site. Summer solstice 2000 was the first of a series of "managed open access" events. The
number of participants has significantly increased and now stands at
some 20,000 for weekday solstices (Blain and Wallis 2007, 86). Nevertheless,
the general conflict between different interpretations, discursive constructions
and practical engagements of the site – for instance between the
remote visual exhibition of the site aiming at its "preservation" and its
tactile engagement for current experiences – is far from resolved (Blain and
Wallis 2007).

Apart from being a site where new travelers and various modern religious
groups from the pagan and New Age spectrum perform their respective rites
and festivals, often in implicit (and sometimes explicit) competition with
each other in so far as the practices of the respective others are held to dis-
turb the celebrations of one's own, Stonehenge is one of England's most
important tourism attractions. In tourist imageries, Stonehenge epitomizes
England as much as the Taj Mahal represents India and the Great Wall
typifies China (Blain and Wallis 2007, 108). Many tourists are primed by

expectations of the site's "mysticism". Moreover, the disputed solstice celebrations are themselves a tourism attraction. The variety of ritual constructions of the event becomes part of its experience (Blain and Wallis 2007, 115). We will return to religious performances in tourism contexts in a later chapter (see Chapter 7), but we now turn to tourist forms of space-making.

SOUVENIRS FROM CHAPTER 4

- Religious sites are among the most popular tourism attractions (or parts of attraction systems) around the world.
- In some societies, people tend to visit religious sites more often when traveling than when at home.
- At some religious sites tourists outnumber other types of visitors, resulting in their changed *modus operandi*.
- Pictures of religious sites are prominently featured in tourism promotional materials.
- Religious sites are often promoted as tourism attractions, and in some parts of the world tourism has led to a revival and to the occasional establishment of sacred sites.
- The promotion of sacred sites belonging to religious minorities can provide a medium of self-presentation for these groups.
- In tourism contexts religious sites are visited for a variety of motives.
- Even if not visited for religious motives, religious tropes, reflections and experiences may emerge during such visits.
- Some religious organizations try to capitalize on the popularity of their sacred sites to promote their religious message and to attract visitors to their community.
- Sacred sites are generally considered a form of cultural heritage, owned by humanity.
- Apart from sacred sites belonging to religious groups and traditions, sacred sites of extinct religions and cultures are prominent attractions on a worldwide scale.
- Tourism at sacred sites results in various sorts of managerial issues such as matters of preservation, access and entrance fees.
- Exposure to tourism raises concerns of authenticity, commercialization and identity.
- Various interested parties advance different claims on sites resulting in the contested and negotiated character of sacred tourism sites.

Chapter 5

Tourist spaces

The sites and places discussed so far have already been in existence prior to their acknowledgment and exploitation as tourist attractions. The fact that religions throughout the world provide material culture that can be framed, packed, commercialized and commoditized into tourist products makes religions an invaluable resource for tourism and related industries.

Contemporary tourism not only transforms extant sites into attractions, but creates new attractions. Theme parks are among the most prominent strategies for constructing attractions. We will inspect some in the following pages, while we will examine some of their distant relatives, namely folk villages, in Chapter 6.

Reflecting the ubiquity of the "tourist gaze" in contemporary societies, theming, i.e. the recurrent and strategic use of an overarching theme in order to create a coherent impression of a spatial unit (from consumer venue to region), has become an omnipresent strategy of space making, even beyond tourism contexts such as theme parks. Heritage sites, landscapes, museums, musical-centers and shopping malls, some of which are now being designed as destinations in their own right (sometimes even having hotels on their property), seem to adopt features of theme parks. Most multifunctional themed environments are characterized by professional management or stimulation of emotions, for example by music and the creation of sounds and smells, animation, accent lighting and scenic architecture (Steinecke 2006, 266).

As a strategy of space making, theming can also be applied to extant sites. Parts of cities are themed; in tourism contexts such themes are often created in the form of walks (e.g. "Jewish Frankfurt"). In this way, single sites are themed by becoming part of thematic routes, like single monasteries being linked to a given route.

Sometimes, tourism agencies try to attach a special dimension to what are otherwise rather inconspicuous sites in order to make them more unique. Take the attempt by the Finnish Tourism Board to market Finnish Lapland as "Santa Claus Land", where planners developed a Santa Claus Village claiming (as did rivals in a number of other countries), that it was the "original" home of Santa Claus (Pretes 1995).[1]

Regions or landscapes are often themed by a pervasive usage of orna-
mental elements that utilize "traditional" architecture or elements of interior
design. As we already have seen with regard to Bangkok, on a minor
scale, tourist institutions such as hotels, especially hotel lobbies and restaurants often display typical features of the cultural context such as the
uniforms worn by servants and other employees in the service industries.
Sometimes these elements refer to religious themes. As an extreme example
one may point to the King Kamehemeha Kona Beach Hotel on the Big
Island of Hawaii that has a reconstructed religious/ritual site (*heiau*) incorporated into the hotel grounds which is accessible to the public as well as
guests during in the daytime.[2] Indigenous culture, and to some extent also
religion, serves as "a marketing vehicle whereby the hotel portrays itself as a
guardian of tradition" (Linnekin 1997, 226).

In the present chapter we will encounter some further instances where
regions and landscapes are charged with religious rhetoric in order to create
"induced images" that make them more appealing as destinations. Note that
such destination images, which were at first deliberately created in order to
make locations more attractive for outsiders, may eventually be appropriated
by local inhabitants themselves. Ubud (Bali) is "a prime example of a place
initially distinguished by Western fantasies and whose promotional image,
confirmed by its touristic success, has ended up imposing itself on the local
population as a reality" (Picard 1996, 89).

Moreover, there are tourist landscapes that have long enjoyed a mythological status on the mental map, often grounded in well-established exotic,
colonial and Orientalist images and discourses. Contrary to induced images,
in Tourism Studies jargon these can be called "organic images" (Gunn 1997,
37–38). Moreover, as we shall see, some tourist places are deliberately
designed and rhetorically signposted in such a way as to become something
like tourist-pilgrimage sites. But let us start our itinerary by visiting another
typical tourism space, namely museums.

Museums

In the days before the advent of mass tourism, museums provided forms of
surrogate travel (Smith 2006, 87). Although museums were not initially
established to serve tourism, they function as tourist attractions or "nodes of
attractions that form the recreational geography of a region" (Kirshenblatt-
Gimblett 1998, 132).

Visiting a museum is part of many tourist itineraries, and tourists are
among the main visitor clientele for museums. Concurrently with the rise of
mass tourism after World War II, there occurred a spectacular growth in the
number of museums around the world. Recent changes in the set-up of
museums such as a change from auratic display to audience participation
and from collection to communication, the increased usage of interactive

and multimedia technologies, experience design, theming strategies, special events, and commercial activities including catering and retail, etc., make it "difficult to distinguish between museums and other kinds of visitor or tourist attractions" (Smith 2006, 88; see Urry 2002, 119–20). While museums have started to become more like theme parks, other institutions, including shops, have started to present themselves as museums (Urry 2002, 119).

In many museums, visitors (including tourists) encounter a variety of religious objects, albeit mostly under the label "arts" or "crafts", "archaeology", etc. In fact, many of the pre-modern items on display in museums originate from religious contexts or/and presents religious motives. It is only in recent decades that the sacred character of many objects has been acknowledged and recognized as necessitating special care. In the Code of Professional Ethics issued by the International Council of Museums in 1986 religious objects are subsumed under the larger category of "culturally sensitive material". In its current form (approved in 2004) the passage reads as follows:

> Collections of human remains and material of sacred significance should be acquired only if they can be housed securely and cared for respectfully. This must be accomplished in a manner consistent with professional standards and the interests and beliefs of members of the community, ethnic or religious groups from which the objects originated, where these are known.
>
> (§§ 2.5; 3.7; 4.3)[3]

Museums have adopted several strategies to respond to the fact that an object stored or displayed in a museum, despite the generally accepted non-religious character of this location, may still be considered sacred by a given religious community (Paine 2005, 6244); museums may:

- insist on its secular value as an exhibit
- retain the object and treat it in a special way such as giving visitors an opportunity to engage in a ritual way with it
- return it to groups that claim ownership and want to use it for ritual purposes[4]
- periodically move the object to a religious site and context.[5]

This is similar to how many religious sites are being perceived in tourism contexts. Yet many religious communities consider religious objects as "inalienable sacred" (Gaskell 2003, 150), i.e. as resistant to deconsecrating by museification. Sometimes museums, for different reasons, invite ritual specialists or religious authorities to consecrate objects to be displayed.[6] In some cases, ritual or religious objects are specifically produced to be displayed in museums, and sometimes rituals are held in museums. Both are the case with Japan's National Museum of Ethnology ("Minpaku") in Osaka, which was constructed in the wake of and on the site of Expo70. Anthropologists were employed to set up the museum. Prayer posts from aboriginal Australia were made for the museum, and so were some ritual objects from the Ainu (Hendry 2000, 159–61). In addition, "every autumn *kamuinomi*, libation worship to the gods, is solemnly celebrated in the Ainu display house" by a ritual specialist (Ohtsuka 1997, 112). The former resident anthropologist in charge of the exhibition made it clear that "[t]his is no pantomime ... and is necessary because these *are* Ainu objects" (Ohtsuka 1997, 112; original emphasis). If the rituals were not performed, he seemed to suggest, the objects would lose their Ainu status and hence their value as exhibits.

There are many religious buildings – in particular, churches – that have either parts serving as museums (often former treasuries) or museums attached to them. In the cities of Siena, Florence and Pisa in Tuscany, already in the late 19th century, cathedral museums were started in buildings adjacent to the cathedrals, which now serve as important tourist attractions. Among other displays, the museums contain objects originally placed, or meant to be placed, within the cathedrals. In a way, then, these museums are extensions of each respective cathedral, and according to Grace Davie "it is impossible to say" where, exactly, the cathedral ends and the museum begins (Davie 2000, 164).

Some churches, for example in Rome, function simultaneously as a museum and a church. Some Jain temples, both in India and elsewhere, have a sort of museum connected to them that illustrates Jain history and faith (Paine 2005, 6245). Another notorious example is the much-disputed Yasukuni Shrine in Tokyo with its attached museum of the (military) history of Japan, the Yūshūkan. The museum-cum-shrine is visited by many domestic and international tourists for a variety of reasons – including curiosity, to make a political statement, to perform a patriotic act, etc.

Several museums, including but not limited to museums of liturgical items, are housed in buildings that were formerly used as ritual sites such as churches.[7] In some cases, the former churches are no longer required by the respective religious communities, and transforming them into museums is one way of preserving the buildings by giving them a new, yet from the churches' perspective non-offensive, function. The museums, in turn, reside in premises considered as majestic or worthy.

Some transformations of liturgical into museum space, however, occurred under specific political circumstances, powerfully backed up by anti-religious or secular ideological programs. The Kazan Cathedral on the Nevsky Prospekt in St. Petersburg (built in the early 19th century, modeled after St. Peter's Basilica in Rome) was transformed into a Museum of Atheism in 1932, some years after the church had been closed for services.[8] In 1992, following the collapse of the Soviet Union, once again services were held in the Cathedral, and the museum has changed name and location (see p. 112). Similarly, Hagia Sophia, one of Istanbul's tourism highlights, was originally built as a church but transformed into a mosque in 1453, and in 1935 Mustafa Kemal Ataturk converted the building into a museum.

In both popular and academic discourse, art museums are sometimes compared to churches or described as "secular cathedrals" or "cathedrals of culture", visited with "religious awe" in order to enact "civic rituals" (Kirshenblatt-Gimblett 1998, 137–38). The United States Holocaust Memorial Museum in Washington (reportedly visited by more than 30 million visitors since its opening in 1993) is said to "take on the character of a shrine" (Paine 2005, 6245), and among certain visitors it may well evoke religious responses.

While the Holocaust Museum foregrounds the tragedy of a religious community, it is not a Jewish museum. Jewish ritual objects were first publicly displayed at the Exposition Universelle in Paris in 1878 (Rauschenberger 2004, 145). International Expositions or World's Fairs have been some of the earliest tourist destinations ever since Thomas Cook arranged the travel of 165,000 travelers to the 1851 "Great Exhibition of the Works of Industry of All Nations", and are another kind of tourism events where religion is present and represented in various forms. Restrictions of space prevent us from pursuing that line further in the present work.[9]

The first Jewish Museum was established in 1897 in Vienna. These days, there are some 150 Jewish museums around the world.[10] In Brooklyn, New York, a Jewish Children's Museum was opened in 2004. These museums are important points on the itineraries of Jewish travelers; one survey of 3,000 Jewish households in Greater London from 2002 "found that 24 percent of the respondents reported having visited a Jewish museum outside the UK in the previous 12 months" (Collins-Kreiner and Olsen, 2004, 281).

There are museums dedicated to the lives of important religious personalities such as Luther and Melanchthon Houses in Wittenberg or John Knox's House in Edinburgh. These museums are important attractions for the respective cities. Some 70 percent of all tourists in Wittenberg visit the Luther House, which together with two prominent churches makes up the core program of visitors (Seidel 2006, 34). Martin Luther is used to theme and brand tourism in the federal state of Saxony-Anhalt, which has developed a Luther Route. In a recently published advertisement the Minister of Economic Affairs and Employment refers to Martin Luther as a mainstay brand for the federal state.

Apart from religious personalities, religious scriptures, especially the Bible, are also themes for museums. An early example is The Amsterdam Biblical Museum (Bijbelsmuseum), originally founded in 1851. Since 1975 it has been housed more prominently in two historical buildings in central Amsterdam. These days, there are several Bible museums in a variety of countries including Australia, Hungary, Israel and the United States. Similarly, there are museums of Islamic arts all over the world, many of which are advertised prominently in tourism contexts.

Some religious communities maintain museums and some religious groups use the medium of museums to get their message across. Think of the much disputed Creation Museum set up by (Young Earth) creationist evangelists in Petersburg, Kentucky, in the vicinity of Greater Cincinnati Airport (within one hour's flight of the majority of the American population). The museum promises to bring "the pages of the Bible to life"[11] and does so by state-of-the-art technical means. The museum is reported to have received half a million visitors within the first nine months of opening its doors to the public in May 2007.[12] Tourism, museums (packed with high tech media displays) and religious apologetics-cum-evangelism are here forming a powerful alliance.[13]

On the other side of the ideological spectrum, there are museums with a cross- or multireligious outlook based on liberal religious attitudes. Take the Swedenborgian New Church inspired Glencairn Museum in Bryn Athyn, Pennsylvania[14] (USA) which sees its primary role as a "teaching museum" (Gyllenhaal 2006, 135). The museum moved to its present premises in 1980 but the first part of the collection had been set up as a private museum in Philadelphia as early as 1879. Another, perhaps better-known and more recent example is the Buddhism-inspired Museum of World Religions in Taipei (Taiwan), opened in 2001 (Wilke and Guggenmos eds, 2008).

Tourism sometimes leads to the creation of new museums that in turn represent the religious culture of the region. Take the Museu Afro in Salvador da Bahia (Brazil), which exhibits artefacts and provides glimpses into Afro-Brazilian religious culture for people who read Portuguese. The museum is part of the regeneration of the old part of the city and a main tourist attraction.[15]

Folk villages (discussed pp. 146ff.) function as a kind of open-air museum. Open-air museums often include sites of worship. Here are some examples. In 1916, the influential Skansen museum in Stockholm (opened in 1891) bought Seglora kyrka, an 18th-century wooden church from the western Swedish province of Västergotland, which was to be demolished and replaced with a stone church. Similarly, The Norwegian Museum of Cultural History (Norsk Folkemuseum) in Oslo (established in 1894) manages the 13th-century Gol stave church which was demolished in its original location when the local congregation had desired a larger and more modern church; later on, four replicas of the church were erected – two in Norway and two in the United States (one in the Epcot theme park in Walt Disney World in Orlando/Florida and one in the Scandinavian Heritage Park in Minot/North Dakota). Services are held in Seglora kyrka in Skansen open-air museum on some holidays and on selected Sundays. Moreover, sometimes music and devotions are performed in the church, which suggests, to some extent, that it remains a functional church. The church can also be booked for christenings and weddings and for "humanist" or "civic" name-giving ceremonies. In addition to this church, Skansen also has a low-church missionary home from Östergötland (originally erected in 1898), which fulfils the same functions as the church within the framework of Skansen.

Open-air museums can be found in many parts of the world. Sometimes, it is difficult to distinguish them from folk villages and theme parks. The Meiji Mura ("Meiji village") in Inuyama, Japan, is generally classified as an open-air museum, but it also has elements of a theme park (Hendry 2000, 143–45). Opened in 1965 in an impressive landscape setting, Meiji Mura houses some 60 buildings mainly from the Meiji era (1868–1912), but also some from later periods (such as the main lobby of Tokyo's Imperial Hotel designed by Frank Lloyd-Wright). Interestingly, among those edifices restored or saved from destruction by being transferred to the museum, are three Christian churches, among them a neo-Gothic cathedral from Kyoto (built in 1890), where according to some internet sources weddings take place.[16]

Meiji Mura belongs to the local railway system, which also runs another museum and a wildlife park. Another heritage museum (or theme park) called Ancient City (Muang Boran), around 1 hour from Bangkok (and 40 minutes from Suwanabhumi Airport) was opened in 1963 by a wealthy Thai gentleman with a mission. By recreating and resurrecting Thai cultural heritage in the Ancient City the founder hoped to "remedy the existing moral deterioration of human society".[17] Crossing the boundaries between theme parks and museums, the Ancient City "provides a judicious combination of 'real' buildings and monuments, scaled-down replicas, and full-size reproductions" (Hendry 2000, 120). The museum/park, which is so large that one has to navigate it by car, contains some "116 constructions for educational purpose"[18] from all over Thailand, many of them of a religious nature such as reproductions of temples, pagodas, stupas, statues, a reproduction of the Buddha's footprint, but also new religious creations such as an imaginary reconstruction of the Sumeru world mountain. The museum/park is clearly inspired by Buddhist ideas, and at this site religion and heritage politics join forces. In its attempt to lay out the essence of Thai culture, the park can also market itself as a shortcut for busy travelers: "Just a visit to the Ancient City is comparable to a Thailand-round journey within a day [sic]."[19] The "Facilities & Activities" listed on the Ancient City's homepage also list weddings and the site displays several pictures, indicating that several religious structures in the open-air museum are being used to hold weddings, which connects the Ancient City with similar themed worlds.

Where open-air museums usually contain reassembled structures from earlier ages and elsewhere,[20] ecomuseums comprise in situ structures and objects, "and very often these include places of worship" (Paine 2005, 6245).

The Te Papa Tongarewa, the national museum of New Zealand in Wellington, which opened in 1998, aims to be a bi-cultural museum bringing Maori and white settler cultures together. The museum includes a Maori *marae* (culture house, performance and meeting space), and as explained by the website of the museum, the *marae* is presented to figure as a kind of national forum: "All people have a right to stand on this Marae through a shared whakapapa (genealogy) and the mana (power) of the taonga (treasures) held in Te Papa Tongarewas's collections."[21]

The first public museum focusing on religions in general established within an academic Religious Studies framework was the Religionskundliche Sammlung started by Rudolf Otto (1869–1937) at the University of Marburg in 1927. The collection of this museum, based to some extent on objects Otto had collected himself during his travels, was devised in explicit contrast to museums of anthropology, arts and history. The collection was intended to throw light on the specific character of religion and to present religion as a living reality.[22] Despite its title and religionist point of reference, the already mentioned St. Petersburg Museum of Atheism operated not so much as an institute of propaganda but as an institution of academic research. The museum has continued and expanded its activities in the post-Soviet era and is now called The Museum of the History of Religion. It regards itself as "a secular organization that should not become the apologist of any religious system" while at the same time it is devoted to a "social mission – the promotion of respect towards the different religious traditions" (Koutchinsky 2005, 157).

In the 1990s, two further museums of religion(s) were established. In 1991, the Musée des Religions du Monde moved from a temporary site (opened in 1986) to its present location in Nicolet (Quebec/Canada) and in 2001 it was assigned the official status of museum. The museum, according to its website, is committed to the idea of religious pluralism (which is of special significance in the Canadian context) and focuses on the similarities and differences among the "five world religions".[23]

In 1993, the St. Mungo Museum of Religious Life and Art was opened in Glasgow, Scotland, in close proximity to the Gothic cathedral. In fact, the idea for a museum of religion grew out of the original plan to open a visitor center for the cathedral (Michel 1999, 17). When the project was started, religious communities in the city of Glasgow were invited to become involved and to present objects representative of their faith to the museum (Michel 1999, 12). From the beginning, the museum stirred opposition from various quarters (Michel 1999, 17–21, 167–71).

The museum has some 450 objects. Apart from exploring "the world's six major religions" (in Glasgow, but not in Nicolet, Sikhism counts as a "world religion"!), presenting the story of religion in Scotland as well as displaying Britain's first permanent Zen garden, the museum "promotes the understanding and respect between people of different faiths and none"[24] and it hosts "free anti-sectarian workshops". The French sociologist Patrick Michel has studied visitor reactions on the basis of comments left by visitors on the "comments board". The museum won the best museum of the UK award in 1994. It counted around 750,000 visits in the period from 1993 to 1997, ranging from 130,000 to 160,000 visits per year (Michel 1999, 21). It even attracted visitors from Canada and Israel who traveled all the way to Glasgow in order to visit the St. Mungo Museum (Michel 1999, 35).

This is not the place to discuss these museums in any detail, nor the question of the representation of religion in a museum context, religious reactions to the exhibits and exhibitions, nor the politics of representing religion in museums in the context of religious pluralism. The years around the turn of the millennium have seen several high-profile special exhibitions such as "Face of the Gods" (Berlin 1998), "INRI" (Berlin 1999), "Heaven" (Düsseldorf 1999; Liverpool 2000) and "Seeing Salvation" (London 2000). The latter exhibition, at the National Gallery, which was accompanied by a television series, was visited by over 350,000 people. Letters sent to the gallery witness that many visitors were profoundly moved by the exhibition and that the mood of the space was experienced as being similar to that of a church; it seems that professed Christians, who otherwise feel themselves to be a minority in contemporary Britain, were heartened by the openly Christian theme of this exhibition (Davie 2003). The exhibition "Altäre – Kunst zum Niederknien" (Altars: art to kneel; Düsseldorf 2001), on the other hand, invited practitioners of different religions to consecrate the altars then displayed as art.[25] Museums, thereby, make religious topics present in the public space, and large exhibitions clearly target tourists beyond the local clientele.

Theme parks

Theme parks are a major product of the modern tourism industry. While Disneyland, which opened in 1955, is its main prototype, the format has undergone considerable changes and global variations.[26] Main precursors and relatives of theme parks include amusement parks,[27] folk villages, world exhibitions, fairs or expos.[28]

The theme park industry has consolidated and developed in recent decades. Disneyland has become "the largest single visitor attraction in the United States" (King 1981, 116). Its success has only been surpassed by its larger counterpart, Disney World, which opened in 1971. The concept was copied by other companies, and several smaller and specific parks came into being since the 1980s. The names of some of these parks play with magical motifs: think of "Enchanted Island", "Magic Kingdom", "Magic Springs" and "Enchanted Forest".

While Disneyland is used as a metaphor for the contemporary staging of religion in a well-known publication by Canadian sociologist David Lyon

(Lyon 2000), it seems that religion itself is not explicitly featured in the Disney Parks.[29] Disney may have good reasons to avoid explicit religion since religious adherents may well be sensitive to any salient "Disneyization" of their respective faith.[30] Other investors, however, are not as reluctant, and some religious theme parks have come into existence. Although none of them has reached a scale comparable to Disneyland and Disney World, they are worth a visit in the context of the present book.

A famous example is the now-defunct Christian theme park Heritage USA in Fort Mill, South Carolina, opened in 1978. With reported six million annual visitors in the mid-1980s it developed into the third most popular theme park behind Disney World and Disneyland (O'Guinn and Belk 1989, 227). The success story came to a sudden halt when founder James ("Jim") Bakker's (one of America's best-known televangelists) sex and financial scandals were exposed in 1987. Attendance dropped dramatically, eventually resulting in bankruptcy and eventual closure in 1989.[31]

The park housed a hotel, campgrounds, auctions, a flea market, television studios, a water park and a variety of entertainment facilities. It also had a church, a Passion Play and replicas of Old Jerusalem (O'Guinn and Belk 1989, 227). Apparently, these formally religious features were not what framed the visitor experience as religious. Rather, it seems that the park as a whole was perceived as something like a refuge for certain types of Christians, a space where people could be found sitting on benches and praying for each other, laying hands on friends in prayer, or purchasing religious literature or records without being ridiculed as in the outside world.

The place where the greatest number of people gathered was not the church but the shopping mall.[32] This is how consumer researchers O'Guinn and Belk describe its effects:

> The Main Street Heritage Shopping Mall has an "other world" quality to it. There is no natural light, only artificial blue light, and until recently, simulated clouds of carbon dioxide wafted near the top of the vaulted, three-story ceiling. The soft light gives an effect of perpetual twilight ... Dramatists use such lighting when they are attempting to convey detachment from reality, dream and fantasy states, and heaven ... The employees smile, and everyone seems unusually happy.
>
> (O'Guinn and Belk 1989, 230)

The park, with the mall at its core, is described "as a sacred consumption venue" (O'Guinn and Belk 1989, 227). The emphasis on unrestricted and self-indulgent consumption makes for a feast which is not centered on a joint meal, but on individual consumption, creating a community of purchase. Theologically grounded in prosperity evangelism, one affords oneself this-worldly "rewards".

Evangelicals have not only started theme parks but also taken over an extant one and given it a more explicit religious dimension, even if its outward impression does not immediately reveal any religious message or content. I am here referring to Silver Dollar City in the Christian tourism stronghold Branson/Missouri (see www.bransonsilverdollarcity.com) (Ketchell 2007, 56–84). In 1960, Silver Dollar City was built atop Marvel Cave, one of the large caves whose visitors often claimed to have experienced God's presence within that subterranean wonderworld. The park now reportedly attracts more than two million visitors per year. As the start-page of its homepage reveals, it offers its guests trips "back in time to the simplicity of 1880s America" – a clear example of the rhetoric of nostalgia prominent in many tourism settings. Besides the usual shows, entertainment facilities, shops, craft centers, and restaurants, the park also offers several "festivals", including "America's Biggest Southern Gospel Picnic" and "An Old Time Christmas" spectacle, reportedly of national repute. Christianity here is part of a national nostalgia, of the good old days.[33]

Religion and Christianity are neither explicitly nor dominantly promoted in the presentation of the park and that may actually help not to put off "unchurched" visitors, who can then be targeted indirectly. According to Ketchell, "[m]any of the gospel entertainers often claim that they appreciate the unique prospect of evangelizing to unchurched park visitors" (Ketchell, 2007, 76).

However, the park also adopts more direct strategies of religious transmission. It arranges some events targeting Christian youngsters, such as the Young Christians' Weekend, "an event that draws up to sixteen thousand teens for a combination of entertainment and dating, self-image, and sexuality seminars" (Ketchell 2007, 78), with Christian artist-ministers performing. It is reported that many attendees "accept Jesus" as a result of their participating in the Weekend (Ketchell 2007, 78).

An apparently marginal attraction of the park is the Wilderness Church. It is described as follows:

> This authentic country church is a vintage log chapel originally built in 1849 on Bear Creek near Branson. The structure was dismantled log by log, lovingly rebuilt in its current location, and dedicated on July 10, 1960. The giant sycamore tree that once stood on the site was hand carved into the church's pulpit by Lester Vining, and is still used today. Experience the peaceful charm of Silver Dollar City's Wilderness Church.[34]

The inconspicuous church not only serves as a visitor attraction, but as another piece of the mosaic of reconstructing the America of the good old days. This interdenominational church has one minister who holds services directed both at the guests and at employees. The services and the daily hymn-singing "regularly inspire sizeable crowds who had not come to the site for devotion, with upwards of one hundred people gathering at the church for song" (Ketchell 2007, 68).

Even if most attractions in Silver Dollar City have no explicit Christian content, the owners insist that even non-religious or unchurched employees act in accordance with "Christian values". Staff are "expected to provide a 'Christian witness' to the park's guest without 'wearing faith on our sleeves'" (Ketchell 2007, 74). In this respect, evangelization proceeds by the service ethos rather than by the content of the theme park.

While religious dimensions are not absent in Silver Dollar City, other parks are explicitly religious projects. Not far from Disneyworld in Orlando (Florida), a Christian-Biblical theme park by the name of The Holy Land Experience opened its doors in February 2001.[35] If we believe Timothy Beal, "[f]or many, it has become a popular alternative to the theme parks operated by Disney, which the Southern Baptists, Assemblies of God, and other conservative Christian groups have boycotted on account of its support of 'Gay Day' and its progressive partner benefits for gay employees" (Beal 2005, 51).[36] Based on a visit to the park in 2003, Beal reports that "[o]n a peak-season weekend day, the Holy Land Experience hosts well over a thousand visitors, nearly all of them conservative Christians" (Beal 2005, 51). When I visited the park in March 2010, higher figures were quoted to me: some 500 visitors during the Friday when I visited and around 3,000 visitors during peak days. The park remains closed on Sundays; this is, I was told, because the park would have very few visitors on Sundays. Apparently, then, the park is not visited by unchurched weekenders, but the park's main clientele are church-going Christians who would not spend their Sundays in a theme park.

According to its own mission statement, "[t]he Holy Land Experience seeks to bring the Bible to life and to educate believers and present the gospel of Jesus Christ to the world".[37] The "bringing-the-Bible-to-life" is attempted in the form of a museum of scripture (the "Scriptorium"), presentations and live-shows. The latter category includes a show entitled "The Ministry of Jesus". It is described in the following terms:

> Jesus always drew a crowd, and the miracles He performed revealed His deity and bore witness to God's power and glory. In this drama, you become part of the crowd as Jesus calls to a tax collector, heals a blind man, confronts the Pharisees and gently reminds everyone of our Heavenly Father's desire for our lives.[38]

The park contains replicas of the temple at Jerusalem and visitors are invited to stroll down Via Dolorosa all the way to Calvary's Garden Tomb, where they can rest, pray or meditate. The park does not attempt to be a geographical replica on a reduced scale,[39] but a staging of places. The visitors must be well aware of the resulting anachronisms and are invited to enjoy them. At Simeon's Corner, "at the crossroads across from the Qumran Caves", the visitors are invited to "stop by for a steaming foot-long hot dog, or a giant flavored pretzel, and grab something cold to drink".[40]

Because of "the timing and schedule of shows, visitors end up moving through the park in an order – a narrative that connects the various events, shows, and exhibits as a unified whole" (Lukas 2007, 275). Scott Lukas finds that this predominant narrative structure "carried through the park" (Lukas 2007, 275) makes it somewhat unusual, in line with its ideological/ religious project. Lukas describes the park as "an interactive site of worship" (Lukas 2007, 275). When leaving the museum ("Scriptorium") "[a] voice, perhaps of God, asks participants to reflect on their own religiosity and thus the performance of the Scriptorium ... is attached to the lifeworld of the visitor" (Lukas 2008, 150). In fact, during the shows I saw in March 2010, the audience was addressed directly and several shows were interspersed with prayers and the singing of hymns. In line with the ideological narrative of the park, the final show of the day, at 5 pm, was a 30 minutes Passion Drama ("We Shall Behold Him"). "Re-dedication report" cards were available throughout the park.

The main audience of the park, it seems, are Christians of certain persuasions.[41] It is unclear to me to what extent other visitors can appreciate engagement with the theme of worship in the purely subjunctive mood, the as-if approach to reality, as an engagement with the theme without some sort of religious commitment; it is unclear, whether unchurched people or non-believers visit the park, and how they would react to it. Moreover, I have no data on the success of this theme park in terms of achieving its religious mission. Unlike Disneyland, however, The Holy Land Experience does not need to produce shareholder value, for despite charging admissions it is a non-profit-organization. According to a newspaper write-up from 6 April 2006, a Senate Bill was passed that would grant parks "used to exhibit, illustrate and interpret biblical manuscripts" exemption from local property taxes. It was made clear that it would be difficult for other theme parks to match the rigid criteria of the bill that was tailor-made to suit The Holy Land Experience which thereby, with respect to tax, functions like a church.

Just as theme parks are no longer predominantly an American enterprise – "[b]y 2006 13 of the top 25 highest attendance theme parks in the world existed outside the United States" (Lukas 2008, 14) – religious theme parks are likewise no longer an exclusively American phenomenon. In Buenos Aires (Argentina) a Biblical theme park called Tierra Santa (Holy Land) opened in 1999. In this theme park visitors can celebrate Christmas every half hour and gaze at the marvels of creation and resurrection, which are visualized with the help of light and sound technologies.[42] My colleague Bjørn-Ola Tafjord who visited the park in March 2009 commented that the light effect displayed in the dark theater created strong effects on visitors.[43]

One of the material highlights of the park is a 4-meter high and 40-meter wide simulacrum of the Jerusalem Western Wall. In a German press report I found a note that the small votive papers deposited by visitors in the cracks of the wall are picked up once a year by employees of the Embassy of Israel who take care that they are brought to Jerusalem.[44] When it comes to "real" wishes the simulacrum apparently is perceived as insufficient. The ethnic theming of the park is underlined by restaurants serving Arabic and Armenian dishes.

In other respects, though, Tafjord commented upon the fluid boundaries between representation and participation. Priests, monks and nuns are admitted for free, as long as they wear their religious garments. The presence of monks and nuns might contribute to giving the place a religious aura; but at the same time, their free admission, as if entrance to the park was their prerogative, evokes the idea of the park being a religious space. Moreover, visitors were free to perform some basic religious acts. In front of statues of saints, signs invited visitors to light candles, if they so desired ("si desean pueden encendar velas"). Moreover, even in the theme park some religious prescripts had to be followed: when entering the mosque visitors are required to take off their shoes! Ambivalent to the point of being ironic is the warning sign placed underneath the three huge crosses at "Mount Calvary": "peligroso subirse" ("dangerous to climb").

Tafjord further noted that the number of visitors was higher than he expected. It also seems that the city of Buenos Aires has officially acknowledged the educational function of the park (according to a signpost at the entrance), and from Tafjord's observations it seems that the park is in fact used by parents to educate their children in Biblical history.

While the (Baptist/Christian Zionist) Holy Land Experience theme park in Florida and Tierra Santa in Buenos Aires operate with "authentic simulacra", some American evangelicals actually started to "theme" the original places. Sherry Herschend, the wife of one of the founders of the Herschend Family Entertainment Corporation (the owners of Silver Dollar City and other theme parks and tourism attractions), donated US$1 million to help build Nazareth Village in Israel, which opened in 2000 (Ketchell 2007, 74). The website of this enterprise states: "Based on solid New Testament scholarship and the most up-to-date archaeology, Nazareth Village brings to life a farm and Galilean village, recreating Nazareth as it was 2,000 years ago."[45] The project aims at a veritable ethno-archaeological reconstruction of what a village like Nazareth must have been at that time, and archaeology is prominently featured in Nazareth Village's web presentation. The theme park invites its visitors on "parable walks", that is, to "walk where Jesus walked and see the Holy Land in a whole new way".[46] The walks, taking approximately 1.25 hours, are guided tours in English, German, French, Italian, Arabic, Russian, Hebrew, Spanish and Finnish. The guide, it is reported, describes Galilean life in the first century as visitors meet villagers dressed in first-century costumes engaging in daily life activities in homes, in the olive press and on the farm. One walks past cultivated terraces, an ancient winepress, a watchtower, stone quarries, grape vines, old olive trees and then enters a first-century synagogue. The parables and teachings of Jesus spring to life as one hears the stories in an authentically recreated setting with donkeys and sheep meandering by or stopping to pose for petting and photos.[47]

Note the apparent paradoxical nature of the "authentic recreation" and the photographic freezing of moments, a scenario which at the same time is expected to make the teachings of Jesus "spring to life". The webpage proudly reports that October 2007 for the first time surpassed the 6,000 visitor mark for a single month.[48] The same source also refers to a project aiming at the production of a video series focusing on the Biblical prophets targeting Middle Eastern markets. The reconstructed village will here serve as the "authentic" site of the filming.

It seems that there are now plans to build a Holy Land theme park on the shore of the Sea of Galilee, at the very place where Jesus is reported to have walked on the water and fed the masses. According to a write-up in *The Guardian* from 4 January 2006, "[a] consortium of Christian groups, led by the television evangelist Pat Robertson, is in negotiation with the Israeli ministry of tourism"[49] about acquiring a slice of land on the shore of the Sea of Galilee not far from the Mount of Beatitudes where Jesus is reported to have delivered the Sermon on the Mount. Of course, there is no unanimous enthusiasm for this project among Israelis (who are aware of the plans), and some fear that the park's target group may actually be Jews, challenging them to adopt Christianity. Apparently economic interests are the principal concern in approving this project among officials. Thus, a spokesman for the Israeli ministry of tourism is quoted by *The Guardian* as having said that "the Christian market was very important for Israel's tourism industry. 'We would like to give them more of a reason to come here. We would be willing to lease the land to them free of charge and they would finance the construction.' "[50]

In these developments, India is not lagging behind. While Disney has not yet opened a theme park in India, local entrepreneurs have entered the market and amusement parks, theme parks, and family leisure centers now serve to entertain the affluent middle class. On 28 April 2005, the BBC reported that the Sagar Group of Companies, an Indian media production company, was planning to set up the "world's biggest ever mythological theme park"[51] close to the north Indian pilgrimage town of Haridwar, one of the four places where the Kumbh Mela pilgrimage, which amounts to the largest gathering of human beings across the world, is held every twelfth year. It is no wonder that it is the Sagar Group that has undertaken to establish that sort of project, given the group already owns a luxurious resort in Haridwar – the Sagar Ganga Resort – but most of all since this company has a long experience with commercializing mythology. In 1985 the company ventured into TV production and in 1987 it launched the famous Ramayana TV series. The producer and director of that series, Ramanand Sagar, is the grandfather of the chief executive of the mythological theme park supposed to "recreate great moments in Hindu mythology through hi-tech rides, an animated mythological museum, a 'temple city', food courts and a sound and light show".[52] The theme park would thereby complement the TV series. This crossbreeding of several lines of products is a business strategy successfully worked out by Disney, and here would allow a visitor to enter the realm of myth.

The project going under the name "Ganga Dham"[53] (Ganges Abode) was scheduled to be opened in 2007.[54] As its name indicates, it was supposed to be placed right on the banks of the Ganges. According to a BBC interview with Shiv Sagar, the park was supposed to attract people after they had performed their ritual bath: "People come to take a bath on the bank of the Ganga river because it is a Hindu belief that this cleanses a person … But after they take a bath there is nowhere for the pilgrims to go to learn about Hindu stories."[55] In that way, the tourist destination would supply the myth to the ritual. In addition, it was also planned that ritual services would be offered. As the BBC reported: "A center is also being planned that will enable Indians living abroad to set up remote *pujas* and other rituals over the internet."[56] Apparently, the project hoped to cater to the needs of the numerous wealthy non-resident Indians who might have wished to visit the park on their trips home. In the first place, however, the park sought to serve the immense domestic tourist market combining religion and entertainment in a novel manner and "at affordable prices", as the Sagar Company promised.[57]

While these projects have so far remained at the planning stage, in 2005 the Swaminarayan branch of Hinduism, a devotional-reformist tradition dating back to the early 19th century, opened a complex that combines a temple with elements of a theme park on the banks of the river Jammu in Delhi.[58] The complex is called Akshardham, which is a key notion in the religious vocabulary of Swaminarayan Hinduism, where the term refers to the highest form of being and dwelling of the divine. In fact, the center of the complex, which is surrounded by a high, long and impressively ornamented wall, is a large temple (mandir) with 234 carved pillars and nine domes, 136 scale-sized elephants and thousands of images and statues. Not only does the mandir represent the multitude of Hinduism, but also the construction blends several architectural styles of India so that it appears as the epitome of Indian religious culture. Under the central dome of the mandir, however, there is a huge statue of Swaminarayan, surrounded by similar statues of the so far nine gurus of this Hindu tradition. In this way, the Akshardham mandir casts Swaminarayan as the key religious figure in the Hindu religious universe. Apart from the mandir, which because of its architectural features was clearly devised as an attraction, the Akshardham complex offers several other attractions including a musical fountain, a lake reported to contain waters from 151 rivers, a magnificent garden, a 12-minute boat ride during which one learns about 10,000 years of Indian history and a movie theater with a large format screen (so far the only one of its kind in Delhi) showing a specially commissioned film about Swaminarayan's seven year pilgrimage shot at 108 locations in India and involving 45,000 people. In addition, there is a vegetarian restaurant and a souvenir shop.

According to Wikipedia, Akshardham "attracts approximately 70 percent of all tourists who visit Delhi".[59] On the homepage of the complex (www.akshardham.com) one can download brochures in eight languages – Hindi, Punjabi, English, Dutch, French, German, Italian and Spanish. The choice of languages indicates that the Akshardham park hopes to attract international travelers. While entry into the Swaminarayan Akshardham complex is free, some attractions/exhibitions require the purchase of tickets. No electronic items (including mobile phones, cameras, etc.), or bags and luggage, pets, foodstuffs from outside, tobacco, alcohol and other substances are allowed in the complex, which also imposes certain rules of dress and behavior, in line with what is usual at many religious sites. In fact, the English brochure addresses a visitor to Akshardham in semi-religious language: "Your visit to Swaminarayan Akshardham is a pilgrimage to a sacred center of India's cultural traditions and values." Note the religious trope of travel (*pilgrimage* to a *sacred* center). Interestingly, the destination is not identified as belonging to a specific branch of Hinduism – the Swaminarayan line – but as incorporating *cultural* rather than religious values and traditions, with India serving as the main point of reference rather than a specific religious creed or tradition. Swaminarayan Akshardam thereby presents an amalgamation of tourism, religious nationalism and religious dissemination.

Let us move on to the East. In the predominantly Christian Indonesian province of North Sulawesi, one finds a monument called Bukit Kasih (Hill of Love). Opened in 2002, Bukit Kasih can be described as a multifaith religious complex or a provincial religious theme park. Located some 55 kilometers south of the provincial capital Manado, the monument is in a hilly area famous for its hot springs. On the central square of the monument, there is a pentagonal column with symbols from different religions on each of its five sides and a dove of peace carrying a globe on top. In addition, the complex has five religious sites – a Catholic and a Protestant church, a mosque, a Buddhist and a Hindu temple. Moreover, two impressive images of ancestors of the Minhasa tribe are carved on the hillside of one of the peaks, while a tall white cross towers above the other peak – a feature which, the official multifaith and tolerance approach notwithstanding, seems to assign priority to Christianity as the "top religion" (Schlehe 2009, 171–72).

According to Judith Schlehe (who first drew my attention to this park), Bukit Kasih is mostly visited by day-trippers who after paying an entrance fee seek entertainment by taking a walk, enjoying the landscape, the springs, the views, having a picnic (where one can boil food in the hot springs) and purchasing souvenirs.[60] Visitors appear to be interested in the religious sites only to a relatively minor degree, and if they engage in any of them at all, they almost exclusively do so with those belonging to their own religion. The complex has created jobs for people in the neighboring village of Kanonong, which also is the home of the governor who undertook to create the complex (Schlehe 2009, 172).

Besides theme parks that put religion in the limelight, religions or elements of religions also occur in a range of other theme parks,[61] specifically in those that spotlight culture. One can distinguish between parks that represent other cultures[62] and those that represent one's own cultural heritage.[63] The Taman Mini Indonesia Indah ("Beautiful Indonesia Miniature Park"), opened in 1975 and located in East Jakarta (in close proximity to the former main airport of the city), is an example of a national theme park with a clear ideological agenda. One story has it that the park was inspired by a visit to Disneyland undertaken by the wife of the then-president Suharto. In his opening speech the president framed the park as a project aimed at stimulating nationalist feeling and developing "spiritual welfare" and "beautiful and deep meaning" beyond mere material sufficiency (Hendry 2000, 99). The park was set up to express the (then) dominant Indonesian ideology of multiculturalism with its slogan "Unity and Diversity". In the middle of the park, there is a lake with a miniature of the archipelago; moreover, there are a theater, several museums, an aquarium, an aviary and a cable car, which takes visitors for a ride across the huge park. Each of the Indonesian provinces is represented by separate pavilions with specimens of local architecture, furniture, dress, food, craft and performative traditions such as dances. A recent development is the inclusion of a section dedicated to the Chinese, who are a migrant group rather than a province.

As Judith Schlehe has pointed out, many visitors do not care much about state doctrine; rather, they come in order to attend the music and dance performances, for recreation, because of the cheap entrance fees or simply as part of groups (Schlehe 2009, 168). Tourists may also, as suggested by several people on travel-oriented websites, appreciate the park for the option of getting a glimpse of the rich and diverse cultural heritage of the archipelago at one site within one day.

As part of the public culture of the country, where every citizen has to belong to one of the six officially recognized religions – Islam, Catholicism, Protestantism, Hinduism, Buddhism and (since 2005) Confucianism – religious buildings also have a given place within the Taman Mini Indonesia

Indah; accordingly, religious sites belonging to all these religions (with the Confucian temple still under construction) and a building belonging to the Javanese Kejawen school are placed in proximity to each other. Visitors who come to the park in order to visit the religious buildings are not required to pay entrance fees, a regulation which implicitly acknowledges them as functional ritual spaces; in fact, they are actively used as religious buildings, mainly, it seems, serving people who live in close proximity to the park, in addition to some of the visitors (Schlehe 2009, 169). Weddings are held in the sites and ceremonial activities are conducted in the different pavilions. Ritual traditions that operate alongside the official religions, such as the *ruwatan* purification ceremonies for young girls, are being performed in the park (in slightly abridged versions) (Schlehe 2009, 169–70), which thereby operates as an actual religious space. This distinguishes Miniature Indonesia from the category of parks to be considered next.

Several examples of theme parks that represent other cultures can be found in Japan. Among other examples, there are parks that showcase themes from Germany ("Glücks Königreich"), Spain ("Parque España") and Russia ("Roshia-mur"). All of these are "authentic" in the sense that the parks are true to detail, often import their displays directly from these countries, employ citizens of these countries to perform, offer food, drink, consumer goods and crafts imported from these countries or have specialists preparing them on the spot; moreover, the parks house museums and employ various means to suggest that the visitors have actually entered the respective foreign country, for example by issuing replica passports (Hendry 2000, 20). In fact, visiting these parks can either stimulate trips to the "real" places, help one to select destinations or substitute for such time-consuming and expensive trips altogether. Apart from the single-country parks there are other theme parks that assemble various pieces and themes from a variety of foreign countries such as "Reoma World", which operated from 1991 to 2000.[64] With the exception of Parque España, where they screened "a film about an Andalusian pilgrimage to Rocio, which gave a very lively and life-like representation of personal involvement in the occasion, as well as superb views of the scenery" (Hendry 2000, 27), all these parks also feature religious structures. The "Oriental Trip" in Reoma World had a Greek church, a Middle-Eastern mosque, a Thai temple, and a "tolerable but very sanitized" (Hendry 2000, 34) version of the Swayambhunath stupa, originally situated west of Kathmandu city; various gods could be evoked for fortune telling. The Brothers Grimm-themed German park ("Glücks Königreich"), which operated from 1988 to 2001 (and is now abandoned), included the replica of a church reportedly visited by the Grimm Brothers in their childhood. Although generally not functional as a church, it seems that couples held weddings in the church and stayed in the honeymoon suite of the luxury hotel belonging to Glücks Königreich (Hendry 2000, 23). Apart from this instance of lifecycle rituals, where the church operated as a scenery,

Joy Hendry notes that although some parks have "apparently religious buildings such as churches, temples or shrines ... I saw no one pray at them"; she continues by giving an example of another Japanese park called Little World, which has a chapel with a gold-plated altar within a house from Peru, that "many of the visitors just walked through without a glance at the ornate altar and the depiction of the dying Christ" (Hendry 2000, 88).

Turning from Japan to Germany, the idea of a park themed around different countries has taken shape in "Europa-Park", which is located at the edge of the Black Forest and in close proximity to the French border.[65] Opened in 1975, with reported four million annual visitors Europa-Park claims to be the number two German tourist attraction behind Cologne Cathedral. An Italian section, started in 1981, was followed by other parts themed on different European countries and regions (such as Scandinavia); in addition to these 13 sections, there are others such as Adventure Land, Chocoland, Children's World and GAZPROM theme world (reflecting a global trend towards brand theming). As Europa-Park proudly emphasizes on its homepage, with its European country-themed sections "the vision of a united continent has taken shape a long time ago".[66] While the names of several attractions allude to the sphere of fairy-tales and magic, there is in fact one religious building serving as an attraction in its own right. In the Scandinavian section, there is the reproduction of a Norwegian stave church, which is described as an oasis of silence between wild-water rafting and a roller coaster.[67] The stave church can also be booked for weddings, anniversaries or other occasions. Within the church, short devotions and relaxing musical performances are held. Since 2005, the Catholic and Protestant churches have joined forces to establish an ecumenical ministry headed by two ministers. Apparently, there was a demand for that kind of pastoral service within the park, and the theme park was regarded by the churches as an opportunity for reaching out to people. The replicated religious building not only serves as an attraction and as a site for relaxation, but also as a site for religious activities of different sorts.

Destination myth

Many theme parks are artificial landscapes that allow visitors to step into different times and spaces. Yet, there are some "real" landscapes that have long had a mythical spell cast over them (such as the "power places" referred to in Chapter 4; pp. 98 ff.). As a matter of fact, tourism is to a large extent about imagined geographies, i.e. the public representations being built around certain places, which "pull" people to specific destinations.[68] British leisure sociologist Chris Rojek has pointed out that "myth and fantasy play an unusually large role in the construction of *all* travel and tourist sights" (Rojek 1997, 53). British tourism anthropologist Tom Selwyn has found it "appropriate to think of a tourist as one who 'chases myth'" (Selwyn 1996, 1).

While the tourists may chase myths, tourism marketing specialists try to use myths in the "branding" of destinations. As we shall see, the mythic status of a destination can be consciously promoted, employed and exploited by political and public entities.

An interesting case for the dynamics of mythologizing and the branding of tourist destinations comes from Tibet. As is well known, there is a long tradition of orientalizing discourse about Tibet. While Tibetan Lamaism was regarded as the epitome of a degenerate priest-religion, in Romantic discourse Tibet became part of the projection of a timeless spiritual-mystical east. This position of Tibet on the imaginary spiritual map of mankind has been strengthened by Madame Blavatsky and the Theosophist tale of the Mahatmas, keepers of the wisdom of Atlantis, who were supposed to congregate in a secret region of Tibet. A new impetus to that history of mythologizing came in the form of fiction and film. In his 1933 novel *Lost Horizon*, British writer James Hilton describes a mystical, harmonious valley by the name of Shangri-La, a paradise on earth, and a lamasery presided over by Christian and Buddhist monks and guided by a more than 200-year-old Catholic priest. The novel is still in print. In 1937 it was adapted for film and directed by Frank Capra. The film became a huge success, and the novel was published in paperback as *Pocket Book 1* in 1939. The mythical status of Shangri-La soon came to be used in wartime political rhetoric: according to information available at Wikipedia, in American war propaganda the United States claimed that their bombers targeting Japan were starting from Shangri-La (instead of mainland China) and one of the aircraft carriers used in the Pacific Ocean was named USS Shangri-La. The presidential retreat in Catoctin Mountain Park outside Washington DC, since 1953 known under the name Camp David, was named Shangri-La by President Roosevelt when it was first established in 1942.[69]

The Shangri-La myth continued to blossom ever since and the name became a household word all over the world. In a 1997 television documentary (ABC/Kane Production) with the title *The Last Shangri-La*, Bhutan is represented to be the "last" Shangri-La on the planet, and as such it is "mythologised as inhabiting a different temporality, one that escaped commodification", a "refuge from urban living" (Brunet *et al.* 2001, 245). Mythologizing representations such as these help to create a special aura around Bhutan,[70] where the government has granted access to tourists under certain restrictions meant to preserve the cultural identity of the country. In Bhutan, the government seems to pursue an active policy (termed the "middle way") of branding whereby the "product" should not be contaminated by the side effects of extensive consumption. The challenge is to "retain something of the environmental and cultural aura of 'Shangri-La', in order to prevent the term 'Shangri-La' depicting nothing more than a tourist destination's 'marketing brand', reflective of increasing commoditisation" (Brunet *et al.* 2001, 261–62).

Whereas the mediated mythic image needs to be carefully retained at one place, it is being created elsewhere. The Shangri-La myth was also known in north-western China where it seems to have acquired the status of oral history. In 1996, in Zhongdian, a previously little known Tibetan enclave of north-west Yunnan, a province of China not far from its border to the Tibet Autonomous Region, the "county began to collect evidence to make a case for Zhongdian being the 'true' Shangri-la or legendary Himalayan paradise" (Hillman 2003, 177). Some "experts" were invited to write a report on the issue, and they invented etymological proof of the case – although they must have been aware of Hilton's 1933 invention of that name.

The attempt to dress up the country in borrowed mythological clothes was clearly motivated by economic reasons. Since the late 1960s, timber had been the main economy of the province. Because of the ecological disasters caused by deforestation, in 1998 Beijing declared a complete and unconditional ban on all logging in the area. Thereby, the largest industry and employer came to an end overnight. Searching for alternatives, the government immediately started to invest into tourism which had already been booming in other parts of the Yunnan province since the 1990s. As part of these efforts, the Diqing Prefecture Tourism Bureau invested heavily in tourist infrastructure and the development of possible sites, first of all the large Song Lan Lin (Songtseling) Monastery (numbering around 800 monks) which was provided with a new car park and a new gilded rooftop (Hillman 2003, 176) – obviously in order to make it accessible for larger crowds and to make it look more attractive. Highlighting the monastery was part of a scheme that would stress the "Tibetan" character of the area: a representative street was to be designed in "Tibetan" architecture and all signs were to be in the Tibetan script in addition to Chinese (Hillman 2003, 176).

As rumours spread in 2001 that Daocheng County in Sichuan "had also requested expert advice to 'prove' that it was the true Shangri-la, Zhongdian officials sped into action" (Hillman 2003, 179). Not long afterwards, the State Council approved the name. This act was formally announced and celebrated in the Arts Festival in May 2002, the opening ceremony of which was held in front of a massive Buddhist painting (*thangka*), reportedly the biggest ever made. However, the event obtained a performative dimension in addition to visual representation. Here is a quote from Ben Hillman's description of the event:

> The first to perform was a group of Tibetan Gelupga (yellow hat sect) monks in ceremonial garb and bearing horn instruments. They completed the circuit of the racecourse before sitting in front of the *thangka* directly opposite the main grandstand at officials. Resplendent in formal robes, the monks carried musical instruments that are normally used only in religious ceremonies.

(Hillman 2003, 180)

Hillman interprets this promotion of Tibetan Buddhism by the Chinese government as a political strategy aimed at weakening the representative claim of the Tibetan government-in-exile. On the other hand, it seems that the monks were more than willing to contribute, by employing the religious-ritual idiom (note the choice of musical instruments), to the success of the event and the project it was meant to advance. In Shangri-La, religion has become part of the ethnic and nature tourism promoted by the government. The main clients are domestic Chinese tourists from urban areas, who may be seeking a holiday refuge in an "unpolluted" environment and exposure to a lost, "traditional" world (Kolås 2004, 273) branded as Shangri-La.

Obviously, all this raises many issues such as nostalgia, authenticity and also of power and hegemonic representation.[71] Our aim here is to illustrate the promotion of religious sites and performances – if not religion – in the framework of a mythologizing branding of a tourist destination. An entire area is branded and commoditized as "Tibetan" in order to capitalize on the brand for attracting domestic Chinese and overseas tourists for whom the regions, because of its infrastructure with roads and an airport, also serves as a convenient entry into Tibet. At least the monastery mentioned earlier benefits from this development in economic terms through the sale of entrance tickets, the revenue of which it shares with the government. Not quite unexpectedly, however, the rush of tourists has also led to tourist demands interfering with the ritual-religious working of the monastery. Here is what Åshild Kolås reports:

> Economic concerns have also led to a situation where tour groups and their guides are admitted to the monastery from morning to evening, regardless of what rituals are being performed. The presence of tour groups and their guides may sometimes be disturbing. The monastery has issued complaints to the local government about this, but the problem is currently far from being solved.
>
> (Kolås 2004, 275)

Island paradises

Being out of the ordinary, mythic "paradises" are located in remote or marginal areas such as high in the mountains or on an island in the sea. There are several such "island paradises" available on the global map of tourist destinations. Early examples include Bali (one immediately thinks of Hickman Powell's *Bali: the Last Paradise* (1930)), Tahiti and Hawaii. While this imagery was first inspired by Tahiti, it then came to be mass produced in the context of emergent tourism to Hawaii from as early as the 1850s. In 1888, King Kalākaua commissioned the publication of a magazine to promote the image of the island to the outside world. The title of that magazine was *Paradise of the Pacific*; in 1966, this title was replaced by the present one, *Honolulu Magazine*.[72] The conjunction of Hawaii and paradise imagery has been so pervasive that it seems almost impossible to conceive of the archipelago without engaging this cliché.[73]

While the mountain paradise of Shangri-La is linked to the imagery of a remote kind of spiritual exaltation with an air of detachment and asceticism, the island paradises are stereotypically ascribed a sensual form of spirituality with a focus on bodies and bodily movements and pleasures. This sort of spiritual "primitivism" can also acquire a powerful spiritual appeal by representing as it were the unspoiled and in many ways "naked" truth.[74] This "primitive truth" is perceived as pre-logical and non-logocentric, but expressive in a performative manner. This is in line with the sort of "soft primitivism" (Bernard Smith) "connoting such attributes as: child-like, libidinous, free, and natural" (Desmond 1999, 11). Rather than the ascetic wisdom of the immovable Tibetan masters and monasteries, here one finds a prevalence of the performative arts, most of all music and dance (see Chapter 7). Combined with other stereotypes such as that of the South Sea maiden, the descent on paradise can also have gender and sexual implications.

Contrary to the one eschatological paradise in the other world, in tourism one may experience multiple paradise destinations, and every trip may go to a different paradise. In that sense, they are marginal not only in terms of location, but also with regard to the travelers' biographies. Reaching paradise is not the final destination of the life journey, but visits to touristic paradises amount to mere breaks or stopovers, short of any prospects of ultimate salvation (Cohen 1982, 191).

The Caribbean is often perceived and actively promoted as one such "unspoiled" area that is consistently advertised as a "paradise". Promotional literature consistently employs a religious vocabulary. Think of "terms like 'spirit', 'soul', 'eternal', 'magic', 'miraculous', 'paradise', 'heaven', 'blessed' " (Mulligan 2006, 123). The Lonely Planet "Worldguide" provides the following intro to the Caribbean island of St. Lucia under its map of destinations: "A tropical Eden at the end of the rainbow – and bananas all day long."[75] Apart from such pleasures, visits to these islands (and sometimes also exposure to "native performances"), for example Hawaii, are cast as "Edenic sites for white regeneration" (Desmond 1999, 39).

In the Bahamas, a small island formerly known as Hog Island got its name changed to Paradise Island in 1962 after an American supermarket heir (Huntington Hartford) purchased it (from Axel Wenner Gren). Since the 1980s, the island has seen several new owners. Not satisfied with "paradise", however, now a new "Atlantis" is being erected on Paradise Island. Atlantis is a high-class holiday resort. In the initial flash of www.atlantis.com (which does not repeat once the cookie is registered),[76] to a meditative sound, the site takes the visitor back *in illo tempore*, saying: "When the gods ruled the earth, Poseidon created … " This post-modern creation of Poseidon, where one mythical allusion is superposed on the next, however, does not seem to tailor any spiritual product; the myth, here, rather seems to be unrestricted high-life.

Not only in the Bahamas was an Atlantis erected in paradise; in Bali, another "paradisiacal" island, a "Nirvana Resort" was built, located close to a famous temple and just 30 minutes from the airport. The inconsistency in employing the name of a Buddhist salvation goal for a holiday destination on an island proudly displaying its Bali-Hindu culture is just one of the ironies of this construction. These are the associations that the marketing people wish to create:

> Imagine a brief moment of heaven and a culture which has inspired priests, artists and poets for centuries, an island which has earned the title – "the morning of the world". Imagine valleys of emerald green rice paddy fields set in the flanks of magnificent volcanoes, golden beaches embraced by indigo-white oceanic surf or clear, still waters. Imagine a spiritual devotion which infuses every aspect of daily life, inspiring festivals and dances as charming as the island's abundant smiles. Imagine the Island of the Gods.[77]

The religious tropes are engaged to such a degree that they only make sense in a subjunctive manner ("Imagine").

The imagery and tropes of paradise amount to a cliché, yet seem to be able to continue generating desires and affections. On the other hand, the tourism paradises always risk decaying into scenes of horror and disaster for their non-tourist population. Critics of tourism have in their turn expressed concern that the unspoiled paradise may be destroyed through the impact of tourism.[78]

Sociologist Graham Dann has analyzed the construction of "paradises" in tourist brochures: "Brochure pictures wishing to portray an uninhabited paradise typically showed deserted beaches on tropical islands" (Dann 1986, 68; see also Cohen 1982, 205). When natives appear in the pictures at all, they usually appear as scenery or cultural markers suggesting authentic experience. They are also displayed as entertainers, vendors, or servants and attendants, thereby creating visual associations with slavery and colonialism. Postcolonial critique unmasks the imagery of paradise as a (neo-) colonial mode of representation and tourist "othering".

The imagery of beauty, perfection and blissful happiness links paradises to weddings and honeymoons. Paradise islands are honeymoon destinations, but have in recent years also emerged as "offshore" wedding sites. Mary G. McDonald has analyzed the booming bridal tourism to Hawaii: in 2000, more than 46,000 tourist couples, mainly from North America and Japan, "staged their wedding ceremony while vacationing in Hawai'i"

(McDonald 2005, 174). Interestingly, both groups are seeking out very different, and indeed mutually exclusive, wedding scenarios in their respective paradisiacal others: while North American couples celebrate in a relaxed manner, wearing casual dress in "natural" non-urban environments such as beaches, gardens and waterfalls or resorts recreating such environments, the exoticism of the Japanese style wedding, by now amounting to the majority of customers, lies in very formal, staged Christian style "chapel weddings". Note that these weddings have no legal import whatsoever. This type of remade wedding first became popular in Japan in the 1990s, and was then soon transferred to Hawaii, where it costs no more than at home. Japanese tour operators arrange these weddings as package trips, taking care of all the details such as limousine, makeup, clothes, photos (faithfully reproducing and disseminating the images of the exotic other), etc.:

> The bride wears a rented "Shinderea" (Cinderella) white gown with a fitted waist, long full skirt, modest bodice, cap sleeves, tiara, veil, pearls, and gloves. The bride and groom expect a sanctuary with Christian symbols, a Bible, organ music, a hymn, a minister, vows, rings, and a chance to sign the wedding registry book. ... The Japanese tourist wedding in Hawai'i is precisely the one that North American couples are trying to escape.
>
> (McDonald 2005, 179–80)

However, space in paradise is restricted, and making place for 100 Japanese tourist weddings per day is a challenge. Some churches made a business of permitting their buildings to house Japanese weddings – a business some came to regret once revenues were taxed (McDonald 2005, 183–84). However, the space made available by extant churches even at the speed of one wedding per hour was not sufficient to accommodate demand. Tourist weddings in residential areas have met with community resistance. As a result, wedding chapels were built in commercial zones such as defunct restaurants and in new properties. In that way, wedding tourism on a "paradise island" has resulted in the creation of fake or quasi-religious sites and the partial expulsion of the everyday inhabitants.[79]

Wellness, retreats and spas

Illness and health have been occasions for traveling since time immemorial. Travel to seaside resorts and spa towns during the 18th century was an early stage in the development of modern tourism. Structured and ritualized dips in the sea were considered a medical practice, and the beach was a place of healing rather than of pleasure (Urry 2002, 17). Improving the health of working people was apparently one of the motives for Thomas Cook to develop facilities for mass travel. Health resorts are timeless tourism destinations. Health resorts, spas, sanatoriums and rehabilitation clinics are an intermediary sector between medicine and tourism (medical tourism). People on rehabilitation are in a sort of "liminal" state: their separation from family, friends, neighborhood, work and hobbies is as much a challenge as getting used to new lifestyle and dietary demands (Hoefert 1993).

The concept of wellness, a neologism that combines the terms well-being and fitness, has become popular since the 1970s, and wellness tourism has proliferated enormously and internationally since the 1980s. For many wellness tourists wellness-enhancing practices such as yoga, meditation or the consumption of organic or ayurvedic food are already part of everyday life at home, while others get familiar with such practices at wellness destinations and possibly continue them to a varying degree at home.

The precise content of the concept wellness is diffuse and disputed, but there seems to be a general consensus that wellness comprises more than physical health alone. There is a bewildering multitude of ways of approaching the extra-bodily dimension of wellness,[80] and at least some of these approaches can be described as either religious or spiritual strategies of quest and self-transcendence. Tropes from a religious/spiritual vocabulary are often engaged in wellness discourses. This is also the case with wellness tourism. Consider the following examples (Graf 2008):

- wellness destinations and facilities are referred to as "temples", "oases" or are themed to evoke mythical associations
- wellness destinations are designed as extra-ordinary spaces detached from everyday life
- wellness destinations sometimes make use of religious iconography (such as Buddha figures)
- wellness destinations can turn into arenas for the experience of meaning, transcendence or connectedness to/immersion into a higher reality
- wellness practices are structured in ritual form and conceived as spiritual purifications
- the service providers sometimes function as spiritual guides
- wellness practices build on ancient and/or Eastern philosophies, practices, therapies, and recipes including Chinese medicine, Buddhist meditation and Indian Ayurveda.

In North America, indigenous American traditions and practices are being referred to and used in many spas and retreat centers (Smith and Puczkó, 2009, 125) and occasionally shamanic workshops are on offer.[81] In India, Kerala (marketed as "God's Own Country") has specialized in ayurveda-based health/spiritual tourism, resulting in an "oversell" characterized by a mushrooming of unlicensed and ill-equipped "healing centers" (Hannam 2009). Now Nepal also plans to increase investment in ayurvedic tourism hoping to rival the "success" of Kerala (Smith and Puczkó, 2009, 121).

One niche within spa- or wellness tourism, which also crosses over into New Age ambiences, is yoga tourism, which now is a worldwide business (Smith and Puczkó, 2009, 94–97). Consider the Ananda World Brotherhood Colonies for an example of a worldwide yoga network. The Ananda network was founded in 1968 by Swami Kriyananda, a disciple of Paramhansa Yogananda. There are seven Ananda residential communities (five in the US, one in India and one in Italy) that offer various sorts of courses and retreats. Apart from Ananda Yoga, the Italian colony, located in Assisi, offers courses on how to live with more energy, the Bhagavad Gita, reincarnation, meditation, vegetarian cooking, spiritual counseling, and astrology. It also arranges pilgrimages and takes its visitors on tours through Assisi, providing an alternative narrative to this Christian city.[82] India is home to numerous yoga centers and ashrams with Rishikesh as a major center. Apart from many ashrams and centers, the town also hosts an annual International Yoga Festival with attendees from more than 30 countries (Smith and Puczkó, 2009, 96).[83]

A recent study from the United States has shown that "to renew oneself" was the top motivation for yoga tourists, whose profile has been summarized as follows:

> [T]he typical yoga tourists are predominantly females in their forties, working as professionals, and with higher than average household incomes. Their jobs seem to require interacting with people, special skills as well as mental efforts. While they appear to have busy schedules with long working hours, they seem to be generally happy people satisfied with work and family and social life. They also tend to be well travelled.
>
> (Lehto et al. 2006, 32)

The participants, who preferred practicing yoga with people who shared similar interests and were often accompanied by friends, felt that yoga was giving them "spirituality, physical and mental health as well as emotional balance" (Lehto et al. 2006, 33).

Besides being a tourism niche in its own right, yoga is also offered as a sideline in many other forms of tourism. The amount of time spent on the practice of yoga varies accordingly. Yoga is on offer in spas, retreats, hotels and other establishments the world over, in the Americas as much as in Europe and Asia.

Tourism offers that address the body/mind/spirit-balance can be classified as "holistic tourism". A study from 2006 listed over 450 operators in this sector, mostly located in the United Kingdom, Spain, Greece and Turkey, but also in many other parts of the world (Smith and Puczkó, 2009, 92–94).

Wellness tourism has an affinity with New Age practices, attitudes and milieus. Consider themes such as self-development, holism and alternative medicine. Wellness is an arena for what is sometimes described as "spiritual tourists", i.e. unchurched seekers or explorers with an interest in personal development, an unaffiliated faith in some forms of non- or super-human energies and powers, who engage a range of rites, practices and objects and who commit to visiting special places and landscapes, often held to have healing or transformative qualities (see, for example, Smith and Puczkó, 2009, 149–50).

Yet, it would be mistaken to identify wellness and wellness or spa tourism as exclusively a phenomenon of "alternative" spiritualities; wellness or spa tourism (the terms are almost used interchangeably in different countries and by different organizations) (Smith and Puczkó, 2009, 3) is a niche within the ordinary spectrum of tourism products. Moreover, it seems that from a counter-culture movement New Age has to some extent become part of the cultural mainstream. Although often criticized by spokespersons of eccle-siastical organizations as egocentric and superficial body-cult, wellness as a mass phenomenon is also shared by adherents of "traditional" religions such as Christianity.[84] In Germany, Kloster Arenberg, a monastery of Dominican nuns near Koblenz has successfully entered the wellness market, as one segment of its rich hospitality program.[85]

While not directly part of the wellness and spa boom, the spectacular rise of the international spiritual retreat business since the late 1980s points in a similar direction.[86] Monasteries have emerged as active players in this market, and tourism seems to gain increasing prominence in the life of monasteries. Numerous newspaper write-ups and the existence of specialized guidebooks[87] suggest that monastery tourism is becoming better known to a wider public.

Based on her own experience in the business, Jackie Mulligan has pointed out that "spa style vacations that bring ancient beliefs and wisdoms from Asia and China to the Caribbean and other foreign shores are a relatively new, yet fast growing phenomenon" (Mulligan 2006, 121). A case in point is the COMO Shambhala Retreats – note the name! – located at such diverse spots of the planet as Parrot Cay in the Turks and Caicos, Uma Paro in Bhutan, Uma Ubud in Bali and Cocoa Island in the Maldives. In addition, there are COMO Shambhala Urban Escapes (The Metropolitan London and The Metropolitan Bangkok). The COMO Shambala at Bali is advertised in the following terms:

> It is a place where spring water is sacred, revered by Balinese for its healing properties. It is a place where guests can find space to make informed life changes that will matter for the rest of their years.[88]

Since it is reported to have a sacred spring, the mythicized destination ("Shambala") is here presented as a sacred spot. The sacredness of the spring is taken to be proved by the "fact" that the indigenous (= authentic) people (i.e. the Balinese) pay religious devotion to it and because they ascribe "healing properties" to it. (Note that miracles are a standard "proof" for sacredness of places and virtually qualifying a place to become a pilgrimage center.[89]) The alleged sacred character of the place and its potential pilgrimage qualities are furthermore stressed by claiming the possibility for a uniquely transformative character of a visit that is to take place under the shielded conditions of the resort, allowing for "informed" rather than arbitrary and uncontrollable changes to take place. Tourist spa is here advertised as a transformative journey and a tourist site is framed in terms of a pilgrimage center.

In order to be empowered by the "spiritually based healing traditions of Asia" one does not need to travel to the East, but the wealthy tourist can also find them in the Caribbean, namely in the "sanctuary" of "[t]he world's most exclusive resort" (the current slogan), the COMO Shambala at Parrot Bay in the Turks & Caicos (an hour's flight from Miami). Here the Asian derived traditions are combined "with natural therapies from the sea and earth, offering an holistic approach to the wellbeing of the mind and body", resulting in "spiritual and physical renewal", as the website formerly stated (Mulligan 2006, 121). While Asian practices move to tourism resorts across the world, as the next chapter will show, (some) tourists travel across the globe in order to encounter other religions.

SOUVENIRS FROM CHAPTER 5

- Many museums, which are major tourist attractions, store and display religious objects for visitors to gaze at and engage with; some exhibits are prepared, used and displayed in a ritual manner.
- Religion or religious artifacts are the dominant theme of several museums; some of these museums are set up for religious, political, civic, academic or other ideological objectives.
- Some museums are connected to (former) religious sites and open-air museums often contain religious structures, which are used to a different degree (often allowing for the performance or staging of wedding rituals).
- Some theme parks not explicitly themed on religion have a religious subtext or a religious agenda; they can appeal to visitors from certain religious backgrounds and/or provide a stage for religious activities and religious outreach.
- Parks explicitly themed on religion are hybrids of religious and tourism spaces and activities.
- Explicit religious theme parks simulate, stage and rearrange historical religious sites; alternatively, they can be located at historical religious sites

or present typical examples of religious buildings, which may function as they would elsewhere.

- They can also serve as sites for the transmission of religious messages or of the idea of a multifaith society.
- Parks themed on culture often contain "typical" examples of religious architecture; in most cases, these buildings are not used for ritual purposes, except the performance of weddings.
- Some landscapes are embedded in mythical discourses, which may attract tourists.
- The mythical status of some destinations may require brand management efforts, while other landscapes may be branded by mythic themes in order to become attractive destinations; religion can play a role in that kind of theming.
- The paradise-trope is engaged in many instances of international tourism.
- Several places around the world, especially islands, are characterized by a persistent engagement of the trope of paradise, sometimes corresponding to a spiritual "primitivism".
- The paradise trope is evoked in the context of honeymoons, and an offshore wedding branch has developed in some places.
- Wellness and wellness tourism, which have become a global business, sometimes engage religious tropes and themes and appropriate various sorts of practices and techniques that may have a religious background, often taken from geographically very diverse provenience.
- Some wellness establishments present themselves as religious/spiritual centers, akin to sites of pilgrimages.
- Wellness discourses have become part of the religious mainstream; traditional religious institutions such as some monasteries offer wellness programs.

Part III

Encounters

Chapter 6

Exposures

Although generally neglected in this regard, in all likelihood tourism is the most important contact zone[1] where people, in the guise of tourists (and hosts), encounter other religions (such as Japanese visiting Christian churches), different branches of one's own religion (think of Protestants traveling to Catholic countries) or unfamiliar aspects of one's own religious tradition (take Catholics from Britain or Germany traveling to Italy). To a far greater extent than the much highlighted meetings and conferences convened by various interreligious or interfaith organizations in the so-called "dialogue of religions", travel and tourism create more or less bounded spaces that allow for a range of interreligious encounters, be it within or beyond one's own culture.[2] Tourism potentially contributes to travelers developing their religious repertoires. Although in many cases tourists interact mostly with locals who primarily act as service providers,[3] tourism can stimulate formal and informal interreligious learning and it can contribute to learning about religions.[4] Tourists and locals have their views, expectations and role-specific behaviors that frame encounters. Contrary to many other forms of interreligious encounters, tourist experiences are very much bodily approaches and immersions, often steered by the desire for enjoyment and fun. There are various degrees of preparation for encounters. The actual encounters – to the extent that they occur at all – will in some measure depend on these preparations as much as on the duration of the visits. The social context of the tour likewise sets the frame for experiences.

Visiting religious sites belonging to other religions means entering their spatial reality.[5] This and other varieties of encountering (aspects of) other religious traditions such as dances, festivals, visits to sacred sites and information on religion in travel literature are discussed in different chapters of this book. The encounter with other, different, or unfamiliar religious traditions is in most cases accidental, being a byproduct of the choice of the destinations. However, as we shall see in this chapter, cross- or inter-religious encounters can also be intended, be it as the main reason for undertaking a trip or as a main feature of destinations. The spectrum stretches from gazing at a distance ("voyeurism") to complete immersion ("going native")

(Johnston 2006, 99). Last but not least, encounters can be direct (such as receiving a blessing at a religious site) or filtered by other cultural activities such as musical performances, which may contribute to making the encounter easier to process since the religious beliefs of the travelers do not appear to be an issue.[6]

While critics, probably correctly, argue that tourism rarely leads to intercultural or interreligious understanding and rather reinforces stereotypes, the fact remains that tourism is a contact zone and provides meeting points between people from different religious groups (Hennig 1997, 133). Yet, it is not always the current religious situation at the destinations which is of primary interest to the tourist; in many cases, contemporary religion is of little or no interest, or even perceived as a disturbance, while tourists enthusiastically flock to material remnants of past or alternative religious traditions. In Egypt, for example, many tourists are insulated in such a manner as to reduce contact to a minimum with local culture and contemporary Islam, while tourists are carefully navigated to the World Heritage sites of ancient Egyptian culture.[7] Rather than pointing to specific religious traditions, some countries such as Malaysia are presented by their tourism agencies as appealing destinations precisely because of the proclaimed peaceful multitude and harmonious co-existence of different religions (Hashim, Murphy and Hashim 2007). Also materials published by the Indian government, (domestic) Indian tourism trade magazines and tourism magazines consistently praise the country's "blend of religions and cultures", for example by highlighting "how people from different religions enjoy the festivals together" (Bandyopadhyaya, Moraisb and Chick 2008, 797). Nevertheless, despite this proclamation, a content analysis of the materials has shown that they "promote the idea of a Hindu-centric national identity and vilify other religions" (Bandyopadhyaya, Moraisb and Chick 2008, 804).

In Britain, there is at least one tourism agency that caters to the niche market of intended religious encounters and exposures. Founded in 1954, Inter-Church Travel – previously a subsidiary of Thomas Cook,[8] now a subsidiary of Saga Group Limited, a company offering tourism, financial and media products mainly to older people in the UK – currently specializes in tours centering on the theme of Christian (ecumenical) unity. This is how the company's website describes its services and religious aims:

> We give Christians of all ages and denominations the opportunity to travel to some of the world's most special places and share their experiences with fellow believers. This has led to greater understanding and support of each other's beliefs, opening the door to increased ecumenical fellowship and a more intimate relationship with Christ.[9]

Note that Christians are identified as the main target group. The greater understanding and mutual support one hopes to achieve by traveling will

will increase cooperation between Christian groups and at the same time intensify the religiosity of the individual tourists.

The tours arranged by Inter-Church Travel are led by a tour guide, often a member of the clergy:

> Leaders welcome Christians of any denomination and help promote an atmosphere of fellowship and inclusion, making your holiday extra special. They will also lead spiritual worship and arrange for you to attend church services, if you wish.[10]

One of the highlights from the current Inter-Church Travel catalogue are tours to the 2010 Oberammergau Passion Plays (to which the company has been arranging tours since 1960). These tours promise "a unique opportunity to share life-changing experiences and gain a greater understanding of ecumenical fellowship".[11]

While Inter-Church Travel facilitates the encounter of their customers with their "fellow believers" other agencies even try to arrange for encounters with adherents of other faiths. In Germany, Biblische Reisen has developed from a provider of archaeological tours to Biblical places (started in 1962) to arranging tours to the "great religions of the world", where they aim at direct encounters with adherents of other religions.

While the present chapter focuses on tourist encounters with contemporary religions, tourism also exposes travelers to past religions, the monuments and relics of which, as we have seen, make for major tourism attractions. Consider the Egyptian pyramids, Greek and Roman temples, and other archaeological sites, many of which are now reappropriated in ritual, religious or spiritual terms by contemporary movements, groups or individuals. The tourist attention to such sites often correlates with the importance of these sites to (religious) nationalisms. Apart from their political and nationalist significance, as we have seen, many governments sponsor the preservation of their national heritage, which often includes monuments of past religious history, as a means of attracting international tourists to their respective countries.[12]

Tourism provides a context for people, be they religious/spiritual seekers or just curious travelers, to check out various religious and spiritual options; some groups and organizations have actively embraced this possibility to present what they have to offer. In Korea, where Buddhism has (following the rise of Christianity) in recent history been relegated to the place of religious minority, several Buddhist monasteries are now offering a joint Temple Stay program, especially catering to visitors from abroad. This program, which apparently was launched in connection with the 2002 FIFA World Cup, invites participants to 24-hour, half-day or 3–4 day exposure programs, where visitors change into monks' robes, visit the sites, participate in monastic activities (meals, meditation, ceremonies, martial arts, production of artifacts), and are briefed about Buddhism and monastic life.[13] To visitors from abroad, the program offers a glimpse of monastic life[14] – and possibly a window to enlightenment – by at the same time positioning Buddhism more clearly on the religious map of Korea. In the contemporary religious landscape, however, immersion or participation programs need not necessarily be offered by "ethnic" insiders within a "traditional" geographical context. Here is one example that illustrates how such boundaries are crossed: a Professor Emerita of Religion and East Asian Studies at a reputed US university, who is a renowned academic expert on Daoism, offers "Daoist Immersion" workshops, which take place at a "spectacular" mountain setting in New Mexico.[15]

The fact that ethnic/religious "otherness" is a main attractor ("pull-factor") also for "ordinary" tourists is occasionally mentioned in studies from all around the world.[16] While the examples presented in the following sections are taken from international tourism, religious otherness also features within domestic tourism.[17] In Chinese domestic tourism, for example, among the dominant ethnic majority of the Chinese, the Han Chinese, the desire to travel "often combines with a desire to tour the 'Others' found within China's borders" (Walsh and Swain 2004, 59), many of which are to be found in Yunnan province. As a matter of fact, alongside the scenic beauty, the great variety of ethnic people in Yunnan has attracted large numbers of domestic and international tourists. While ethnic diversity may be an attractor to the region, religion also appears in theming strategies such as the decoration of restaurants or other commercial ventures with religious symbols such as paintings of deities (Chow 2005, 297–98, with figure 6).

From a case study from Poland it appears that those sacred places belonging to a different religion from that of the visitors are commonly regarded as tourist attractions:

> The most popular tourist places, because of custom and architecture, are the most different from Polish culture, e.g. Kruszyniany (near Bialystok), the center of Islam in Poland, where there are eighteenth-century mosques and cemeteries … [as well as] Grabarka and Wojnowo … in the Warmia region (a village settled by the old Orthodox Slav church …)
>
> (Marciniak 1994, 148–49)[18]

While this study seems to suggest a causal relation between religious difference and popularity of a destination, a study from New Zealand provides evidence against considering this as a potentially universal rule. For whereas Maori places, artifacts and performances have long been popular attractions for international tourists and non-Maori New Zealanders born in Northern Europe, domestic tourists in New Zealand assign a comparatively low priority to tourism products based on Maori culture. It is unclear whether this is to be explained by the lack of spatial distance necessary for creating the exotic imagery or rather by the complex and ambiguous relationship between *pakeha* (non-Maori, New Zealand culture of European ancestry) and the Maoris in contemporary New Zealand (Ryan 2002a).

Indigenous people

Not only religious sites can act as tourist attractions, but entire cultures and indigenous ethnic communities are showcased for tourist marketing of destinations.[19] Governments, in collaboration with tourism related industries and investors, often actively seek to capitalize on their marginal populations by turning them into tourism icons or exhibits (Azarya 2004, 963; Johnston 2006, 12).[20] For instance, images of indigenous people such as the Maori are used to promote New Zealand as a destination (and Maoris have been actively involved in tourism for 140 years) (Ryan 2002a; Smith 2006, 124), Sami images to promote regions in Norway, Sweden and Finland, Aboriginal images to promote Australia, and Inuit and Dene images to promote Northern Canada (Hinch 2004, 252). All of these are on display in tourist itineraries, occasionally in zoo-like settings,[21] or in folk villages/cultural parks (see next section). The display of displaced groups of people – "people watching" – was a feature in early world exhibitions. While this is no longer the case, countries such as Australia and Canada "fund Aboriginal tourism commissions nationally in order to capitalize on strong European interest in Aboriginal tourism" (Johnston 2006, 13). Around half of ecotourism brochures "portray encounters with Indigenous People or their ancestral land" (Johnston 2006, 67). In many cases, this happens without these people being aware that they are being marketed. Contemporary (eco)tourism raises many problems with regard to land rights, self-determination and intellectual property issues (Johnston 2006).

As early as the 19th century, Native Americans and their ritual traditions have been part of tourism itineraries and marketing campaigns. Native Americans were framed in amateur ethnography and in narratives of exploration and progress of civilization, where Native Americans such as the Hopis represented the "un-American", "most-primitive stage", "with ceremonies several centuries old", as one tourism brochure of the Grand Canyon area had it (Shaffer 2001, 59). Promotional materials promised the tourists experience of real, first-hand, authentic Indians, whose material culture and ceremonies recalled "an era and a lifestyle unscathed by the ravages of civilization" (Shaffer 2001, 69), while their display at the same time functioned as a powerful display of racial superiority (Shaffer 2001, 71). This tourist performance of superiority and progress had its counterpart in a trope of loss and disappearance, what Leah Dilworth has termed the "constant Indian disappearing act", making people hurry to the destination "to see authentic Indian culture before it disappears" (Dilworth 1996, 122). Similar "acts" of nostalgia are being performed the world over. In several cases, "tribal welcome ceremonies" are part of these visits.[22]

The display of indigenous ethnic cultures in the contemporary world is often part of neo-colonial, global-hegemonic power-structures and part of the persistent and "deep-seated imperialistic assumption ... that large parts of the world exist solely for the benefit of tourists" (Robinson, 2001, 43). However, again reality is quite complex, for other analyses point in a different direction, namely that tourism provides a new arena for native cultures to assert themselves; instead of destruction of culture this type of analysis discusses tourism as a stimulus for cultural revival (however one may wish to evaluate that) and the emergence of ethnic identities (see, for example, Grünewald 2002). An example are the Indonesian Toraja who "have used ethnographic tourism as a self-managed economic base for negotiating a more legitimate space for themselves within the nation state; in effect, tourism has transformed Torajans from an oppressed minority into a national asset" (Ross 1994, 86). However, it has also been pointed out that it is the Christian Torajas rather than the Hindus or adherents of Aluk To Dolo, who mainly "profit from the marketing of their culture" (Ramstedt 2004, 213).

The commitment of indigenous people to tourism also exposes them to global economic processes and can change their position in local, regional or national power structures. Consider the case of the Mentawaians living on the island of Siberut (west of Sumatra, Indonesia). Some twenty years ago, as a consequence of the establishment of regular boat connections, the island appeared on tourist itineraries, with nature, primates and "primitives" as its main attractions. According to one brochure, the island is a place where the "stone age still survives" and if one is lucky one can "witness colourful magicians performing their curing ceremonies" (Persoon 2004, 144). An exotic statement such as this is probably inspired by popular, but outdated theories according to which magic is the most primitive stage of the evolution of religion; accordingly, where there are "primitives", there is powerful magic. In fact, the religious practice of the "magicians" or medicine men (kerei) had previously been under severe attack from proselytizing religions which have promoted their own theories of religious development. The kerei had been "forced to hand in all their religious paraphernalia, and drums as well as skulls of animals kept for ritual reasons were publically destroyed" (Persoon 2004, 144). The tourists, on the other hand, came to the island precisely to marvel at the traditional religion. From superstition and magic it turned into precious cultural capital. As a consequence, the Protestant Church no longer is in a position to exert pressure on the traditional religion (Persoon 2004, 153). Similarly, a group that had been converted to Islam, but is now one of the groups most exposed to tourism, is not the least concerned with observing Islamic law and most adult men have even become kerei (Persoon 2004, 155). In this case, then, exposure to tourism has contributed to an emancipation of traditional religious practice from the pressure exerted by proselytizing religions, and governmental agencies have become more relaxed in their attitudes towards Mentawaian culture.

In tourist contexts, KwaZulu-Natal, a province of South Africa, is anachronistically (ironically/cynically) referred to as the "Zulu Kingdom". The Zulus have become part of cultural tourism promotion in post-apartheid South Africa (Marschall 2004). Tourist promotion explicitly addresses the double edge of cultural exposure to tourism: "The Zulu traditions and culture are as much a way of life as they are a tourist attraction."[23] The website promoting the Drakensberg Mountains region highlights Zulu souvenirs and handicraft, especially beadwork (and its symbolism), fighting performances, dancing and singing, and the entire package of traditions, including some religious features, which the tourists can immerse themselves in:

> Also captivating for visitors is the opportunity to witness the disciplined and dignified social structure of a Zulu homestead (umuzi). Customs pertaining to food and the brewing of beer, ancestral worship and places of burial, the dress code for men, women and children, the role of the traditional healer (inyanga), the importance of a man's cattle, the system of compensating a father for the loss of his daughter in marriage (lobola), courtship, witchcraft and superstitions are still observed.[24]

In cases where ethnic groups have a distinct religious profile, the latter may also be used to market the respective group and their religion as a destination or to enhance the distinctiveness of the attraction by this religious diversity. In the Chinese province of Yunnan, for example, the Dai, which comprise roughly a third of this ethnically diverse region, are "the only ethnic group practicing Theravada Buddhism in China" and this "cultural distinctiveness of the Dai is used by the tourism industry for advertising in Kumming, the transit stop for most Banna-bound traveling by air (45 minutes) or bus (12 hours)" (Walsh and Swain 2004, 59).

The New Age Movement and New Age inspired tourism claim a spiritual affinity with indigenous peoples, who are often regarded as embodied carriers of authentic spiritualities. In a recent analysis, Michael Hill has argued that the essentialization of the spiritual nature of one such people, the Quechuas in the Peruvian Andes, has the paradoxical effect of disembodying the wisdom allegedly incorporated in them through tourism appropriation. Some New Age travelers "de-ethnicize and de-territorialize Quechua religious culture while still relying on racial essentialisms to market an authentic 'reconstructed ethnicity' available for tourist consumption" (Hill 2008, 259). Their religion is de-ethnicized because it is regarded as part of a universal heritage and open to appropriation; it is de-territorialized because, while purportedly grounded in a specific territory, it is made accessible to tourist consumption and "spiritual" exportation.

Folk villages/cultural parks

The world over, indigenous cultures and people are displayed in so-called folk villages or cultural parks. As a term used in the tourist sector "folk village" can denote a variety of phenomena, stretching from museum-like settings (something like open-air museums[25]) or theme-park-like displays with no actual inhabitants to villages where people are actually living in a zoo-like manner.[26] Folk villages often, but not always, make it a point to display practices and performances and works of art that we would classify as religious.

Current folk villages were preceded by ethnic village displays at world fairs.[27] Typologically, they are closely related and present a naturalistic variety of theme parks, with the theme here being identical to the living people who are presented or present themselves in such villages. While, on the one hand, folk villages/cultural parks develop a coherent framework, on the other the visitors are, to a great extent, free to shape their involvement according to their interests and preferences, be it with regards to performances, displays, food, objects, etc. and thereby they provide both a "considerable variety and choice of experience" (Moscardo and Pearce 1999, 431). In fact, not all tourists seek the same kind of experience and visitors to folk villages or cultural parks may even "see direct ethnic contact as difficult or uncomfortable" (Moscardo and Pearce 1999, 431) and would rather avoid it.

Here is an example of folk village performances from China. In Hainan (off the Chinese coast) businesspeople in a Li folk village have designed dance programs, compressed into units of 30 minutes (apt for tourist consumption during brief visits), which consist of the following five components: "(1) a harvest celebration; (2) love songs by Li youth; (3) a religious ceremony for curing disease; (4) a bamboo-beating dance; and (5) visitor participation" (Xie 2003, 11).

Sometimes, in more museum-like settings, performances are intended to showcase what things have been like in earlier ages. In the Tamaki Heritage Village in Christchurch/New Zealand visitors are supposed to "[e]xperience New Zealand Maori culture and see history come to life", as the webpage claims.[28] This is achieved by a reportedly spectacular 3.5 hours performance entitled "Lost in Our Own Land" about the Maori and European heritage in New Zealand. The show displays "the changes through time, covering religion, education, family, tribal and social structures and offers insight into the differing beliefs around the relationship between people and land".[29] Tamaki Maori Village (established in 1989) is located outside of Rotorua, "one of New Zealand's primary tourist hubs" and "a 'must see destination' because of its geothermal activity and active Maori population" (Tahana and Oppermann 1998, 24). A visit to Tamaki Maori Village is advertised as a "Journey back in time to a Pre-European lifestyle experience of customs and traditions".[30] Apart from the village architecture and the bodily appearance of the "villagers", this experience is framed by the performance of welcoming rites when entering the village. The feeling is further enhanced by food and performances:

> Enjoy the night's festivities with us as you are treated to a banquet of succulent foods cooked the traditional Maori way, rediscover the Maori village as it comes alive to the sound and activities of tribal songs, dances, myths and legends and browse throughout the largest after hours tribal market place in Rotorua.

An early example of a folk village was the family-run Lalani Hawaiian Village in Waikiki (Honolulu). Opened in 1932, this reconstructed Hawaiian village "encouraged the learning of native arts, *hula*, and [the] Hawaiian language" (Imada 2004, 120). The village, which was real in the sense that its grass huts were inhabited by residents from rural districts, aimed at cultural reconstruction, transmission and education. Among other things, visitors could observe traditional cooking practices (Diamond 2008, 27). Apparently, performances for tourists, especially dances, provided the financial basis for the village so that cultural preservation met business and commerce. The director, a part-Hawaiian married to a Native Hawaiian, selected young performers who would at the same time work with tourists and learn from the resident experts. Among these indigenous experts living in the village, there was a noted *hula* (dance) teacher whose repertoire included dances that had been rarely performed publicly in the preceding decades (Imada 2004, 121–22) (see also Chapter 7; p. 174). During World War II the Lalani Hawaiian Village was taken over by the military; after the war it was reopened and stayed open until 1955 (Imada 2004, 142).

In 1963, the Polynesian Cultural Center (PCC), which is a hybrid of a folk village and a theme park, opened on the north shore of Oahu (Hawaii), near the Sunset Beach coast, the dream destination of global surfing culture, and some forty miles from Waikiki, "the grand signifier of mass recreational tourism in the world today" (Ross 1994, 43). The PCC has reportedly attracted over 33 million visitors during the past 45 years. According to Andrew Ross, the PCC "has served as a model for many similar commercial ventures in the business of ethnographic tourism ... and as an inspiration for indigenous tourism developments" (Ross 1994, 43–44). The Polynesian Center offers reconstructions of six "typical" villages held to exemplify ideal versions of the main Polynesian cultures presented in a timeless, pre-contact mode. The PCC also has some other attractions and shows and it invites its visitors to be ethnographic investigators and "to learn something about the customs that differentiate one island from another" (Ross 1994, 49). The first aim of the Center is to "[p]reserve and portray the cultures, arts and crafts of

Polynesia", as the Mission Statement puts it,[31] and to allow visitors to experience these cultures.

From the information I was able to gather from a distance, apart from a Fijan "spirit house", the religious dimensions of the Polynesian cultures are not highlighted. Note, however, that the Center is operated by a religious group, namely the Church of Jesus Christ of Latter Day Saints (LDS), whose missionary activities in Polynesia go back to the mid-19th century. The church started a temple in Laie in 1915 (dedicated in 1919), which nowadays is one of the attractions in the PCC.[32] According to the official history of the PCC, the idea to set up a Cultural Center emerged from a highly successful fundraising feast with "Polynesian entertainment" performed by church members since the 1940s. The Center was built by over 100 "labor missionaries" and is now part of a larger educational infrastructure sustained by the church.

As the website states, the second aim of the Center is to help provide "educational opportunities for students at the adjoining Brigham Young University Hawaii. Since the Center opened on October 12, 1963, nearly 17,000 students have financed their studies at BYU-Hawaii by working at PCC".[33] In fact, the inhabitants of the villages are played by LDS students.[34] Showcasing Polynesian cultures thus helps to support students at an LDS educational institution; their education goes along with displaying a way of life they no longer belong to and most of them had not even been aware of prior to their career as performers.[35]

The Mormon anthropologist Terry D. Webb holds that the preservation and display of pre-contact Polynesian cultures is grounded in LDS theology both with regard to the theological idea of restoration of the lost greatness of Polynesian civilization (Webb 2001, 130) and the genealogical-mythical conception "that Polynesians are descended from the ancient civilisations whose histories are contained in the *Book of Mormon*" (Webb 2001, 137). Webb also points to a performative reversal in that the students, by performing the lifestyle of their ancestors in costumes, comedy and servility within a cage-like setting, negate the principles of modesty and dignity that are otherwise of fundamental importance for Mormon conduct and in particular to behavior within the temple, so that the PCC appears "[l]ike an anti-temple" that "reverses the sacred" (Webb 2001, 140).

Beyond commercialization of culture and moneymaking, however, the Center is devised as a religious space meant to positively affect all visitors, as stated by the PCC's third strategic aim: "Demonstrate and radiate a spirit of love and service which will contribute to the betterment, uplifting and blessing of all who visit this special place."[36] According to Webb, the PCC also functions as "an extraordinary space with religious significance" (Webb 2001, 140) for the students performers. In his analysis, the park "is an expressive restatement of the temple ceremony; it plays on temple themes, and reinforces Mormon beliefs" (Webb 2001, 141). Moreover, successful and satisfactory performances can be perceived in religious terms; consider this quote from the personal journal of one villager/student:

> I could really feel the spirit of God with us today as we performed. I think that if we had not asked Him of His presence and thanked Him for all He'd done for us, we would not have performed as well as we did. Everyone put their faith in Him.[37]

Let us move on to Korea, where there are several folk villages. The best-known one, visited by domestic and international tourists alike, is the Korean Folk Village in Yongin, a rapidly developing satellite city some 40 kilometers south of Seoul. The Korean Folk Village is located near Everland, Korea's largest theme park (and one of the top ten theme parks of the world based upon attendance). The Korean Folk Village was opened in 1974 as an open-air museum and has the character of a living museum that displays architecture, customs and lifestyles of the Joseon (Chosŏn) Dynasty (1392–1897). As part of the recreation of an earlier period, at certain times (weekends, holidays and from spring to fall generally), "traditional customs and ceremonies for coming-of-age, marriage, funeral, ancestor memorial, and other ceremonies are recreated".[38] The Korean Folk Village includes a "traditional marketplace" and numerous workshops where handicrafts are produced and sold, but also a proper amusement park section offering rides, games and several museums.

There are also several folk villages in the Korean countryside. While the Korean Folk Village is unashamedly museum-like, others offer more real-life scenarios. One example is the Hahoe Folk Village in Andong (the stronghold of Confucianism in Korea, with several Confucian schools serving as tourism destinations) which was submitted by the Republic of Korea as a tentative World Heritage Site for the following reason:

> Their time-honored residences, Confucian school, and many other ancient buildings are preserved intact, together with their unique folk arts, including the Hahoe Mask Dance Drama, called Pyolshin-gat, a shamanist rite venerating the tutelary communal spirits[,] Hahoe Folk Village contains rare and invaluable cultural vestiges that need to be preserved in good condition in this ever-changing era.[39]

With the village, its "shamanist rite" is thereby also to be preserved for posterity. Another Korean village which has recently caught international attention is Chonghakdong Village, referred to as "a Korean Shangri-La".[40] The villagers, it seems, voluntarily retain a pre-industrial lifestyle that allows only some carefully selected technical innovations. Apparently they adhere to Ilsimgyo, which in the media is often described as a 19th-century "syncretistic" movement combining Confucian, Buddhist and Christian elements with a strong emphasis on astrological and millennarian traits. It seems that the fossilized status of the village and its cultivation of "traditional" knowledge have made it a popular spot for summer camps for children who are supposed to be made familiar with "Korean ways and values".[41] Not surprisingly, Chonghakdong Village is also an attractive destination for international, but even more so for domestic tourists – and it is reported that "busloads of tourists" arrive in the village via a new road.[42]

Folk villages can be found in various other countries. David Chidester has recently drawn attention to the South African Bantustan of Bophuthatswana, a client-state of apartheid South Africa, where, beginning in 1983, adobe villages, each purportedly representing one tribal people, were constructed as part of the Lotlamoreng Dam Cultural Park. Among the displays at this park, "clay statues of African deities, most prominently a twenty-foot-tall African goddess" (Chidester 2005, 180), were erected. The building of this folk village thereby also created new religious artworks as a form of religion-on-display. Besides status of African deities, the Lotlamoreng Cultural Park also housed a reproduced Victorian mission complex and, in a remarkable contrast, a number of statues depicting Biblical scenes were erected in the churchyard.[43] Folk villages do not necessarily display indigenous religions only. The Lotlamoreng Cultural Park was politically outdated soon after being opened to the public shortly before the end of the apartheid regime. "Bereft of its founding impetus, it was an instant anachronism" (Comaroff and Comaroff 1997, 2). Then it came to be inhabited by new residents, but this time "more real than authentic" ones (Comaroff and Comaroff 1997, 3).

Some folk villages are referred to as cultural parks. Tjapukai Aboriginal Cultural Park near Cairns, on Australia's north-eastern coast, is an example. Located next to a rainforest cableway, this park was started in 1996 as a successor project to a successful dance theater (Moscardo and Pearce 1999, 421). This cultural park, which highlights the culture of the indigenous rainforest people of Tropical North Queensland, includes a cultural village besides three theaters where one can watch dances, history and the "creation theatre", "which combines live performances and laser technology to present an Aboriginal perspective on the creation of humans" (Moscardo and Pearce 1999, 421).

In 2007, Tjapukai Aboriginal Cultural Park made a sacred site (Bare Hill) available to its visitors, in this way "offering detailed insight into the lifestyle and rituals of the indigenous culture", as a press release put it.[44] The park also holds evening shows, for which the brochure promises "entertainment and indulgence with a sumptuous buffet":

> Immerse yourself in the traditions of the Aboriginal people through traditional dances, music and the telling of dreamtime legends providing a powerful and personal insight into ancient Australian culture.[45]

Whereas cultural parks and folk villages are artificial, reconstructed or fossilized institutions, there are also some travel agencies and tour operators that offer exposure to selected real life ("authentic") villages. In this "village tourism", visitors stay with families overnight and share meals with them. This type of tourism is practiced in Nepal, where an operator (Nepal Village Resorts) offered to take their guests to "unspoiled villages where they spend a few days living with the local people and being treated as honoured family guests".[46] This is an extreme form of village and culture exposure. The guests were assured that "[t]hese warm and friendly people are always ready to perform their music and dance and to give an insight into their religion".[47] As religion features prominently in the life of the village – at least that is what we are told – it will likewise be a natural part of the exposure, and the tourists are promised that they will be able to take home a blessing:

> As the locals are all Buddhist, the village gompa, a simple but beautiful temple, will be a feature of your stay. There will be the chance to get a blessing from the resident lama before you leave.[48]

Tourists are also invited to live in Ainu homes in the Ainu tourist villages on the island of Hokkaido (Japan). For many Japanese living on Honshu, the main island of the Japanese archipelago, going to the northern island of Hokkaido is "like going abroad" (Hiwasaki 2000, 397). For a majority of Japanese tourists relaxing at hot-spring baths and viewing the beauty of nature are main attractors; accordingly, there is an emphasis on nature (mountains, rivers, waterfalls, foxes, deer, bears) in tourism to Hokkaido, and the image of the Ainu is to some extent cast in this framework.[49] The history of the Ainu tourist villages goes back to the late 19th century, when one such tourist center was visited by members of the Imperial (Meiji) family, including the emperor himself (in 1881). However, the so-called tourist Ainu-boom occurred after World War II. At Akan, one of the Ainu tourist villages, "approximately 200 Ainu entertain 1,600,000 tourists a year" (Hiwasaki 2000, 399). Katarina Sjöberg (2004, 232) describes these villages as representing "centers or market places where not only material needs are fulfilled but also, in fact mainly, social, cultural, and religious ones". It seems that these tourist villages are spaces for the negotiation and expression of Ainu identity. The villages/centers are sites for:

• the production and consumption of Ainu-made products, mainly as souvenirs
• "demonstrations of Ainu beliefs customs" (Ohtsuka 1999, 94) and other educational activities, partly through museums and exhibitions
• the internal and external transmission of Ainu mythology
• the staging of all sorts of events (festivals) and the performance of Ainu rituals (Sjöberg 2004).[50]

In fact, "until recently, tourist villages were the only domain where the Ainu were permitted to practice their culture" (Hiwasaki 2000, 402). However, the "selling" of Ainu identity, while creating revenues, employment, visibility and public recognition, is not unanimously endorsed by all Ainu, and "[t]hose who are involved with tourism are often looked down upon by fellow Ainu, and many Ainu people do not like to have the term '*Kankô-Ainu*' (Ainu involved in tourism), attributed to them" (Hiwasaki 2000, 401).

Religious communities on display

In the cases already considered, religion is displayed as one element of culture – and it is the projected cultural totality that is showcased and consumed in folk villages. In the present section we will take a look at locations which function as tourism attractions in their capacities of representing religious groups. However, in many cases it is not so much the doctrinal content of their religious identity, but their particular, clearly distinguished and, judged from mainstream society, seemingly anachronistic lifestyles grounded in their religious doctrines and identity that warrant their status as tourism attractions. To some extent that is true for monasteries in Western societies.

Ultra-Orthodox Jews are gazed at in Jerusalem. The Meah Shearim neighborhood is an especially popular tourist site. Wikipedia describes its outer appearance as follows:

> Today, Meah Shearim remains an Old World enclave in the midst of a city that aspires to modernity. With its overwhelmingly ultra-Orthodox population, the streets retain the flavor of an East European shtetl. Life revolves around strict adherence to Jewish law, prayer and the study of Jewish texts. Traditions in dress may include black frock coats and black or fur-trimmed hats for men (although there are many other clothing styles, depending on the religious sub-group to which they belong) and long-sleeved, modest clothing for women.[51]

The exposure of the Meah Shearim neighborhood to tourism and intrusive/ inappropriate behavior of tourists has created tensions between tourists and inhabitants. Therefore, so-called neighborhood regulations have been passed which are put up as "modesty posters" at all entries to Meah Shearim. Here are the regulations.

(1) Modest dress for women and girls (knee-length skirts or longer, no plunging necklines or midriff tops, no sleeveless blouses or bare shoulders).
(2) Tourists should avoid visiting the neighbourhood in large, conspicuous groups.
(3) Residents should not be photographed or filmed without permission.

(4) During the Jewish Sabbath (from sunset Friday until it is completely dark on Saturday night), refrain from violating the Sabbath in any way. That means no mobile phones, no cigarettes, no photo or video cameras.

(5) Avoid wearing blatant Christian symbols or T-shirts with Christian slogans.[52]

Myra Shackley reports that tourists who had ignored these regulations were "frequently ... being stoned. A similar fate can befall cars which try to traverse the area on the Sabbath" (Shackley 2001, 145).

Let us turn to North America, where we find some minority Christianities that feature on tourism itineraries and are part and parcel of the tourism sector. Consider the Shakers (official name: The United Society of Believers in Christ's Second Appearing), who had moved to New York in 1774 (Bixby 2007). The Shakers became a tourist attraction already in the first half of the 19th century, as witnessed by descriptions of their appearance in guidebooks. It seems that the Shakers actively accommodated visitors even in their worship, but possible hopes that the visitors could be potential converts did not materialize. Around the middle of the 19th century new railroad connections made more remote Shaker villages accessible to tourism. The Shakers started to sell goods to tourists and eventually also began to run boarding houses that came to be used by travelers; they also charged tourists for meals. Towards the end of the 19th century, "Shakers began to emphasize production of fancy goods and foodstuffs, items that would appeal to the tourists visiting their villages" (Bixby 2007, 100). The presence of visitors in the villages, their showing off their fine clothes and unrestrained behaviors, evoked fears of "corrupting" the Shaker youth. Later on Shaker tourism seems to have declined, only to be revived after the 1960s, at a time when the Shaker communities had already largely declined or even disappeared and when Shaker villages were bought by investors and turned into Shaker museums. As such, several Shaker villages devoid of actual Shakers are now leading their own life as tourism remnants, helping "to foster the romantic Shaker image" (Bixby 2007, 107). Also the only remaining Shaker village with a minuscule community of some few believers at Sabbathday Lake, Maine, is a tourism attraction and the group seems to be quite reflexive of their ongoing exposure.[53] The Shakers have been called an "an increasingly fashionable element of the American cultural tourism industry" (Shackley 2001, 30).

Let us turn to another part of the United States. Soon after the American transcontinental railroad was completed, Salt Lake City turned into a popular tourist destination. While the landscape of Salt Lake Valley was praised and described as paradise-like, the Latter Day Saints, one of 19th-century America's most despised deviant religions, were regarded as something like an abomination. Initially, visits to Utah were meant to inspect a site of religious deviance and presumed perversion and their polygamy in particular fueled tourist attention. Since non-Mormon inhabitants of Salt Lake City initially controled the tourism business, middlemen such as drivers and guides reinforced anti-Mormon stereotypes. Eventually, however, Latter Day Saints' leaders

> came to believe that they could convince Salt Lake tourists of Mormon virtue even if the tourists had come to see Mormon vice ... LDS leaders responded to tourism by bringing virtues previously private into public display; Mormon cultural institutions such as religious services, musical performances and church members' education and civility assumed the additional role of serving as vehicles for portraying a public image consonant with outsiders' conception of gentility and morality.
>
> (Hafen 1997, 346)

After the official abolition of polygamy (in 1890) and the achievement of statehood for Utah, church leaders even adopted a more proactive policy to market their religion. From 1898 onwards "church authorities ... began targeting tourists as potential converts" (Hafen 1997, 375) and they set up a bureau of information.

More than a century later, the Salt Lake City 2002 Winter Olympics gave the Latter Day Saints' "faith international exposure, which indirectly and subtly allowed them to soft-sell their faith through self-promotion and education" (Olsen 2006b, 266). The church still targets tourists visiting Salt Lake City for "soft proselytizing" (Olsen 2006b, 260).[54]

The Anabaptist/Mennonite communities, in particular the Old Order groups that have maintained a lifestyle striking contemporary observers as fossilized, are a further important American example. Living within a few hours driving distance from larger metropolitan areas, the Old Order Amish in Lancaster County (Pennsylvania) and the Old Order Mennonites in the Waterloo region of Ontario are situated within the range of short term (weekend) visitors. Tourism to Lancaster County started around the time of World War II, while it is of a more recent date in Ontario (Wall and Oswald 1990, 4–9).

Besides the special character of these people's way of life including their dress, modes of transportation and architecture, the reputation of their agricultural produce and their domestic crafts contributed to their emergence as attractions in tourist terms. The tourists' interests are being catered to by different tour-operators, farmers' markets, roadside stalls, heritage shopping villages (for the purchase of "authentic" products in "historical" settings) (Mitchell 2003) and various sorts of attractions such as "living museums of Amish farms, and visitor centers, which purport to exhibit authentic evidence of Amish and Mennonite history and lifestyles" (Fagence 2001, 202).[55] Moreover, visitor centers offer the communities an opportunity to present their religious message. Employees at the Mennonite Information Center (opened in 1958) "explain Anabaptist theology and the Old Order way of life", they "answer questions the tourists may have concerning the Amish and Mennonites" and keep theological, inspirational and instructive literature available (Wall and Oswald 1990, 28).[56] The center also shows a 30-minutes three-screen feature on the Amish in its theater.[57]

As Michael Fagence has pointed out, not all Amish/Mennonite groups are actively involved in the tourist business and different segments are involved in different manners. While

the Old Orders try to retain a detachment ... [t]he less strict orders have become drawn into the commercialism of tourism with the development of souvenir and retail outlets, information and interpretation centers, tour and transport services, entertainment venues, multimedia staged events, commercial lodgings, restaurants, and especially the outlet stores for the famed quilts and furnishings and woodworks.

(Fagence 2001, 205)

To some extent, according to one interpretation, the less strict Orders seem to shield the Old Orders from tourist invasion[58] and possibly even "provide the barrier that safeguards the integrity of the Old Order communities" (Fagence 2001, 205),[59] which, together with their products, are the core attraction. Tourism may here contribute to community cohesion by generating a commitment of the less strict Orders to their stricter fellow believers, for the income they derive from visitors is built mainly on the special reputation of the Old Orders.

The exposure to tourists takes many forms. At the one extreme, there is intrusion in people's privacy such as gazing at people, photographing people who hold the belief that they should not be photographed, or entering their homes. At the other extreme, the Amish culture is systematically exploited in terms of commercialism. The horse with the buggy, for instance, is an omnipresent symbol used by hotels, restaurants, shopping malls and entertainment venues (Fagence 2001, 203–4; Wall and Oswald 1990, 23–29). It creates apparent links, even where there are none; the symbol themes the entire landscape.

The symbol can also be found on the homepage of the Pennsylvania Dutch County which reports that "[o]ver five million people visit Lancaster County each year".[60] And: "Many people return here year after year because they find Lancaster County so special."[61] The reasons for this special character clearly are the Amish and their lifestyle:

Here you'll discover Amish communities where life moves at a slower pace and centers around time-honored traditions and values. You'll find beautiful scenery dotted with one-room schoolhouses and wooden covered bridges, modern farm machinery being pulled behind four- and six-mule teams, homemade clothing and quilts gently blowing in the breeze, and where you'll hear the clip-clop of horses' hooves echoing down quiet country roads.[62]

The values and lifestyle of the Amish have thereby contributed to the idyllic landscape and atmosphere that the urbanites can enjoy for their relaxation and recreation. More than that, however, the trip is advertised as reminding the urbanites of existential alternatives, of different ways of life:

> These people as a whole are not as materialistic as modern society today. Instead, they adhere to more traditional ways and family values … take time to reflect on the values that make them so "different". There is a lot to be said for their slower-paced lifestyle.[63]

Faith tourism

The term "faith tourism" is sometimes used as a synonym for religious tourism.[64] Sometimes, the term is used as a catchword for a non-pilgrimage, multifaith style of tourism to religious sites mainly undertaken by Christians. Consider the widely quoted prediction that "faith tourism based on Christianity is one of the strongest growing sectors in international tourism today, generating at least US$1 billion per annum" (Woodward 2004, 173).[65] Note that this probably refers to any form of tourism "based on Christianity".

Here is one example of faith tourism. On 29 March 2006, Inter Action: American Council for Voluntary Action published the following piece of news:

> In a few months' time, St. Lucia will tap one of the hottest growth markets in the travel and tourism industry – the faith tourism market – when the award-winning journalist, author and speaker Andria Hall hosts a renewal retreat for women to refresh and renew their spirits.[66]

The write-up announced that the retreat group would be joined by a gospel choir from New York scheduled to give a public concert in the Caribbean. Hence, faith tourism may well operate in many directions: while "women of faith, excellence and integrity" from the New York area are refreshing and renewing their spirits at Coco Resorts in St. Lucia's Rodney Bay, the locals will have a chance to refresh their spirits by a US gospel choir. Hall's team, the write-up informs, is closely cooperating with Air Jamaica.

It seems that the Jamaican government seeks to benefit from "faith tourism". The following section from the official website of the Jamaican Tourist Board merits to be quoted in full:

> So you're coming to Jamaica and you wonder what Jamaicans do with their time. Well, given the complexities of Jamaican society, one can spend forever learning about our people and culture, but if you have one week and would like to "be" a Jamaican, here's what we suggest: / Attend a Religious Service. /Jamaica is listed in the Guinness Book of World Records as having more churches per square mile than any other country, a fact that many Jamaicans are proud of and quick to extol. In addition, we have created many fascinating forms of European and African forms of worship blended into Christianity, as well as creating unique belief systems such as Rastafari. Regardless of your own religious beliefs, attending service in Jamaica is certainly a most telling cultural experience. The options are wide and varied. There are the more formal traditional services of Christian churches such as the ones held at historic parish churches. There are also non-traditional services that take place anywhere from under huge circus-style tents, riverbanks and small one-room chapels to large modern worship halls, while Rastafarians sometimes hold large meetings to "chant". Religion is a central part of the lives of most Jamaicans, and most religious-minded people here would be more than happy to have you join them in worship. If you choose to go to any meeting, be sure to inquire about etiquette, and be prepared to meet some of the most welcoming Jamaicans and witness first hand the power of belief.[67]

Attending the rituals is here referred to as a *cultural* experience – and not as a religious one. Even the religious practices of ordinary people are thereby made accessible for tourist experience – with the only restriction of observing local "etiquette".

Visiting religion is occasionally also a feature in ethno-tourism. Booking a half-day trip to the Cachabri Indigenous Reserve in Costa Rica, where one will be visiting an Amubri, Bribri and Cachabri Indian village, the visitors are prepared to expect the following experiences:

> We will see cocoa plantations, bananas, thatch roofed huts and the simplicity of life of these people. In Cachabri we will be met by an AWA (indigenous medicine man) who will tell us about their traditions and religion.[68]

Another significant example for the tourist marketing of religious minority groups as a sort of "faith tourism" and the political and cultural reevaluation of these groups resulting from their new role as a precious good again comes from the Caribbean. Cuba's strategic commitment to international tourism following the end of the Soviet support of the Cuban economy in 1990 not only drew on the island's natural resources but also on its Afro-Cuban performance and religious culture. Already since the 1980s, Afro-Cuban floor shows could be seen in many hotels. Among the performative themes of these shows one would find "the anthropomorphic dramatization of a few of the major deities of Santería" and "a Tropicana-like cabaret extravaganza that refers to several African-based religious traditions simultaneously" (Hagedorn 2001, 8).

Semi-folkloric, semi-ritual performances continue to be held, in part for tourists, and Afro-Cuban religion has generated business opportunities for a number of Cubans including religious specialists (Argyriadis 2007). Since the early 1990s, "several high-ranking and well-respected priests of Ifá, Santería and Palo Monte became involved with government sponsored tours for foreigners who want to become initiated into Santería", generally known as Ochaturs[69] or Santurismo (a combination of Santería and *turismo*). Most of these tourists are Canadians and Europeans, but also Mexicans, Argentinians and (recently) Venezuelans. The previous official policy of scientific atheism, which had continued an earlier history of persecution of Afro-Cuban religions and the harassment of its practitioners, was changed towards a policy of selective support, partial legalization and "mainstreaming these religions and their adherents into the tourism trade" (Hagedorn 2001, 9). The Ochatur system provides for initiation packages that include airfare, food, lodging and a cut for tourism offices. In 2001, Katherine Hagedorn quotes a price of 7,000 USD for these initiation package tours, which was two to three times the price an independent traveler would have to pay in Cuba and around 12 times the amount Cubans would need to invest for getting initiated (Hagedorn 2001, 9, 222).

The participation in the Ochatur or Santurismo arrangements is lucrative in social, financial and material ways for the priests involved:

> If a priest or priestess of Santería agrees to participate in Ochatur, he or she may be offered a nice house in an attractive beach location (in which to perform comfortable, picturesque initiations), relatively "free" travel within and without Cuba, and a cut of the profit.
>
> (Hagedorn 2001, 222)

Hagedorn reports that her informants had continued to cater to their Cuban audiences and customers as well, but that they were occasionally dismissed by other practitioners as "tourist Santeros", a critique which was to a lesser degree expressed also towards those who initiated foreigners outside the framework of government-controlled agencies. Apart from the natural suspicion towards being bought by the government, the critique and suspicion of commercialism has been a matter of ongoing internal dispute in the recent history of Afro-Cuban religions (Argyriadis 2007).

Shaman tourism

Shamanism has long since served as a taxon for classifying a presumed form of early religion in Siberia and other parts of the world. For centuries, shamans and their practices have exerted a fascination on the Western imagination (Hutton 2001). However, from the late 1960s onwards, starting with Carlos Castaneda's *The Teachings of Don Juan* (1968) and the work of anthropologist-turned-advocate/practitioner Michael Harner (b. 1929), shamanism has been appropriated in such a way as to become an option available for anybody wishing to try it out.[70] As a globalized (glocalized) phenomenon, shamanism has turned into something like a post-modern "world religion".[71]

Besides attending courses and workshops offered by centers or foundations in Europe and North America, people started traveling to visit shamans "out there" – like others who travelled to be near gurus of various kinds. Apart from individual seeker-ship, small-scale operators started arranging trips to shamans, also for groups. Shamanism tours are among the types of trips offered by most New Age tour operators in the United States (Attix 2002, 54).

It seems that such tours of "participatory spiritual tourism, where the encounter between indigenous shamans and Western visitors is mediated by tour guides and travel agencies", and where "Westerners and shamans engage in a form of exchange, the goal of which is to deliver an *experience* of an *authentic* shamanic ritual to the visitors",[72] began concurrently. These trips followed the trails laid by American anthropologists and took their participants mainly to Central and Southern America.[73] Visual anthropologist Anya Bernstein states that "by the 1980s, fueled by the New Age explosion, shamanism was already properly packaged and promoted to the mainstream" (Bernstein 2005). While it may be an exaggeration to claim, as Bernstein does, that "today almost any packaged tour to Central and South America includes 'shamanic counseling'" (Bernstein 2005), the popularization of shamanism has obviously increased. Neo-shamanic discourses and practices are part of a symbiosis with eco-, ethno-, culture-, nature- and New Age tourisms as well as of general media representations including documentaries, travel reports and the like, where different elements in this symbiosis reinforce each other.

While there are some providers who offer "shaman trips" to destinations in South America,[74] shamanism is not necessarily the main attraction for all trips; nor are the shamans only visited by tourists and spiritual seekers from North America and Europe, but it seems that they serve as an attraction for domestic tourists as well. This is documented for the Pataxó Indians in Bahia (Brazil), who are in various ways engaged in ethnic tourism. According to the Brazilian anthropologist Rodrigo de Azeredo Grünewald, the Pataxós "themselves attempt to act as attractions and offer their culture for sale in the market" (Grünewald 2002, 1011). Their main "products" are handicrafts, but also other items produced as part of a cultural revival, including a type of dance, the Auê, "that has always been performed in their ceremonial gatherings to represent 'the spiritual reunion of Indians in happiness'" (Grünewald 2002, 1012). Apparently in order to meet the tourist demand, two Pataxó Indians proclaimed themselves to be shamans, "without finding any legitimacy among the Pataxó themselves, who disqualified their presentations as 'their personal marketing', meaning they were actually shamans-for-tourists" (Grünewald 2002, 1014).

While the self-proclaimed shamans did not gain a reputation as shamans within their group and were disregarded as tourist-fakes, their public legitimacy changed once they were explicitly framed in a tourist context. This was occasioned by the opening, in 1999, of a so-called "ecotourism" project in a part of a forest which, in 1997, has been "protected for environmental reasons, especially because it represented a source of raw materials for handicrafts, such as seeds for necklaces and bracelets" (Grünewald 2002, 1008). These "ethnic" handicrafts are mainly produced for tourist markets – once again illustrating the close ties between ethnicity, economy and ecology as a resource for ethnic-cum-tourist arts. The ecotourism-site

> involved the construction of a trail through it [= the forest] where bus-riding tourists get off and walk to a place in which several round, thatched roof huts were put up for them to experience a different Pataxó tradition. In the first hut, tourists listen to a talk on the traditional indigenous lifestyle; in another they meet the shaman, who explains about the forest's medicinal plants. Further on, there is a hut with Indians ... selling craftwork exclusively from forest raw materials.
> (Grünewald 2002, 1008–9).

Interestingly, this shaman on display in his hut is one of the two new shamans, whose status had been denied by the group previously. As a "shaman-for-tourists", it seems "that he has earned his (legitimate) place in the group" (Grünewald 2002, 1015). However, he is not recognized as a shaman because of his performative skills, but the kind of shamanism exhibited in the tourist context features explanations of the plants. In the tourism context, shamanism obtains a new meaning, status and legitimacy.

After the downfall of the Soviet Union, Siberian shamans once more entered the orbit of Western academic, spiritual and tourist interests. Hartner, the guiding spirit of much contemporary neo-shamanism, traveled to the Southern Siberian republic of Tuva in 1993, where he appointed a local shaman as "The Living Treasure of Shamanism" (Bernstein 2005). In the meantime, Siberian shamanism is almost as much on the tourist map as its Central and South American counterparts; on the internet it is quite easy to find trips with visits to famous sites of ancient and modern shamanism (i.e. shamanic power places) and also offering meetings with "real" shamans and participation in a "real shaman spiritual ritual".[75] Besides witnessing shamans, some trips take their participants also to Buddhist sites.

Some shamans have become celebrities and started to act as veritable tourism attractions in their own right. At Elansy settlement, Valentin Khagdaev, who features in Anya Bernstein's acclaimed documentary *In Pursuit of the Siberian Shaman* (2006; 75 minutes), not only performs rituals for local, multi-ethnic clienteles but also lectures, acts as guide and performs poetry, songs and rituals for groups of travelers from Russia and other parts of the world. It seems that by doing so, he strategically connects his shamanism to other aboriginal or indigenous "pre-religions" (pre-Orthodox, pre-Christian, pre-Islamic, pre-Buddhist), thereby building bridges to his audiences and contributes to establishing a global system of indigenous religiosity. In other contexts, however, local shamans seem to be threatened by the development of tourism. At Lake Baikal, for example, the expansion of tourism is of great concern to local shamans "because many of the most picturesque or stunning sites near the lake are also sacred sites where shamans carry out annual rituals" (Metzo 2008, 238).

In Mongolia the downfall of the Soviet Union likewise brought shamanism more into the limelight. The end of the age of repression (that affected shamans as much as Buddhists) is often described as having led to a revival of shamanism. Since 1998, the Mongolian government has made efforts to promote tourism to the country. Buddhist monasteries and traces of shamanic culture around Hövsgöl Lake are among the most popular tourist destinations (Yu and Goulden 2006). The government reports an annual 15–20 percent increase in the number of tourists visiting the country.[76] Apart from some shamanic sites, shamanism tourism has emerged as a niche within culture-, nature-, ethno- or special interest tourism to Mongolia (Schlehe and Weber 2001, 99).

Shamanism is practiced in several parts of Mongolia, including the capital, and among ethnic minorities of reindeer herding nomads living in remote areas. The economic and ecological decline of these nomads therefore also indirectly threatens the survival of shamanism. The German anthropologist Judith Schlehe has drawn attention to the example of a female shaman who, instead of following her group into the higher mountainous regions, stayed at a place where her tent could be more easily reached by Mongolian clients and foreign tourists. The shaman, who apparently was paid a small sum from the national park administration for remaining nearby, is reported to now receive regular visitors, most of them tourists, who are happy to pay money for taking a picture of the place, animals, tent and people and who give candy to the children. Moreover, sometimes she visited a tourist camp where she performed some rituals for money – which was a new thing to occur here as elsewhere. Tourism thereby has turned shaman practice into a monetary transaction. It generates new sources of revenue that allow the shaman to support her group while at the same time threatening her reindeer flock since she cannot take the animals to the higher regions, which would be out of reach for the tourists (Schlehe 2005).

Schlehe also points to an incident illustrating the globalization of shamanism: Julie Steward, alias Sarangerel Odigon (1963–2006), a woman with a Mongolian (Buryat) mother and a German father, born in the United States, started to practice shamanism (or what she would refer to as "Tengerism") as an adult; she then moved to Mongolia where she strived to restore and reconstruct the "ancient and original" religion of the Mongolians. Among her major moves was the founding of a Mongolian Shamans' Association (Golomt Tuv) which gave Mongolian shamans a common platform and brought them into touch with shamans in other parts of the world, with the prospect of starting a shamanic world organization. Through some books Sarangerel also spread her Mongolian message to Western audiences. She traveled widely, giving lectures and holding workshops on Mongolian shamanism. Moreover, she started a Mongolian shamanic association of America (The Circle of Tengerism).

Sarangerel, it seems, was also instrumental in setting up a solstice-ceremony in 1999 aiming at the revival of a 13th-century shamanic ceremony. The three-day event was remarkable because it was planned by a coalition of business people (including tour operators), practicing shamans and scholars of shamanism (Schlehe and Weber 2001, 100–105; Schlehe 2005). In order to defray the costs of the ceremony, the organizers hoped to attract foreign tourists to the event; they tried to market it accordingly, while at the same time pointing out that the ceremony was not merely "a show", but was meant to point to the fact that shamanism was a "real religion" (Schlehe and Weber 2001, 101). Wishing to meet the presumed demands of tourists, the shamanic ceremony proper was preceded by folklore-type performances (music, theater, dance and acrobatics). In the end, however, very few foreigners arrived, while many local participants brought munificent offerings. Schlehe and Weber note the simultaneity of two modes of participation: While parts of the audience were continuously taking pictures and filming the event, other perceived the shamanic performance as a religious ritual with immediate significance for their lives and problems (Schlehe and Weber 2001, 104).

I am not aware of the further history of that festival (especially after the death of Sarangerel), but Googling to current tourism events, it seems that shamanism is still propagated as an element in tours built around festivals. There is, for instance, the weeklong "Ice Festival Tour" (see http://www. bluemongolia.com/icefestivaltour.html) where Day 3 (corresponding to 20 February in the 2007 program) was supposed to provide the following schedule with a possible embedded "shaman ceremony":

Breakfast, Ice festival Opening, Ice creation competition, Ceremony of offering of Mountain of Ikh Khaan Saridag and Dalai Eej-Khuvsgul lake.

(Shaman Ceremony), National Concert, Lunch, Participate in snow festival, Free time, Dinner, Stay in the tourist camp.

For those preferring to come during summer, Blue Mongolia Tour offers the eight day long "Reindeer Festival" tour at the end of June. While tourists are taken to the Gandantegchilen Monastery ("Present biggest monastery, which houses for giant standing Buddha statue" [sic]) on day 7, day 5 has the following program:

> Breakfast, Explore marching of reindeer herds, fire worshipping festival, Lunch, shaman rituals, display about tepee people and their reindeer herd, Dinner, Stay overnight in tourist camp.[77]

While it would be easy to criticize such programs as a commercialization of indigenous religions and their ritual practices, one should recall that the tourists do not meet an unbroken chain of tradition, but a religious culture that is concurrently being renegotiated and redefined (Schlehe and Weber 2001, 114), and that tourism may well be a factor in that process. Based on their fieldwork, Judith Schlehe and Helmut Weber point out that they have not met a single shaman who had perceived the presence of tourists as in any way causing problems. One shaman even explicitly stated that even those who were attending just out of curiosity were welcome (Schlehe and Weber 2001, 109, 111). Intuitive concerns of authenticity and related problems appear to be more an issue for Western intellectuals than for Mongolian shamans.

Interestingly, contrary to many private operators, the Official Website of the Ministry of Roads, Transport and Tourism, Mongolia, does not once mention the words "shaman" or "shamanism". Instead, the strategy of the Ministry focuses on Genghis Khan, nature and scenery and, to some extent, on the Buddhist monasteries.[78] Even where it highlights nomadic cultures and where it features events as attractions, shamanism is not part of this presentation.[79]

Moving further south, one encounters shamanism and shamans as tourist attractions in Nepal,[80] Thailand and Korea. In Korea, where shamanism is on the one hand widely practiced, but on the other hand generally despised, it has in recent years gained public legitimacy under Cultural Conservation Law terms as part of a cultural preservation policy (Kim 2003). Shamanism is not officially acknowledged as a religion in Korean society and does not appear in official religion statistics, but the cultural preservation policy and demands from the performing arts industry as well as from tourism have created new performative spaces (Kim 2003, 218–19). Shamans are now performing publicly in their role as carriers of traditional arts and several shamans earn their livelihood as performing artists. Contrary to ordinary shamanism, arts shamanism is not a performance of healing, and it is concluded by applause from the audience (Kim 2003, 216). Traditional arts performances also cater to the tourism market. In tourism contexts, shamans are also hired by luxury hotels and are performing in folk villages (Kim 2003, 204, 210).

For Northern Thailand, where ethnic (highland) tourism has boomed, it has been observed that "in urban Chiang Mai, where several highland ethnic groups have been brought to perform their cultural activities for tourists, a Mien man pretends to perform a shaman ritual every night, since this group does not have many activities that can be seen as entertainment like the other groups" (Leepreecha 2005, 12). From Prasit Leepreecha's account it seems that this is an example of outright commercialization of shamanistic performances. Here shamanism is neither preserved nor revived as a cultural practice, but invented as a mere spectacle in order to compensate for the absence of other attractions.

SOUVENIRS FROM CHAPTER 6

- Tourism is a major arena for the encounter of and exposure to other religious traditions.
- Such encounters can be accidental or intended.
- Tourism can stimulate learning about religions, formal and informal interreligious learning and the expansion of people's religious repertoire.
- The spectrum of encounters reaches from voyeurism to immersion.
- The display of indigenous cultures is embedded in global power structures, but also provides agency and stimulates cultural and religious revival.
- Elements of indigenous religions that were despised in colonial and nationalist contexts can become re-evaluated as precious cultural capital.
- The global appropriation of indigenous spiritualities can lead to their de-ethnicization and de-territorialization.
- Past and traditional religious practices are performed and preserved in folk villages/cultural centers that have sometimes served as refuges for such traditions.
- Folk villages are sites for the erection of religious buildings, the production of religious art and religious education.
- At least one such cultural center, which is operated by a religious organization, can be a space with religious significance for visitors and workers alike.
- Sometimes supported by means of modern technology, religious traditions of indigenous cultures are transmitted as part of acts of consumption and shows.

- The tourist exposure of religious groups in their native habitat can lead to tensions and requires negotiations of boundary maintenance.
- Touring religious groups can amount to inspecting religious deviance and confirming prejudices, whereas toured groups may wish to proselytize the tourists; visitor centers provide stages for religious (self-)representations.
- Given its expected economic benefits, tourism to religious groups and experts is sometimes actively supported by governments, resulting in their selective official recognition and support; within these groups suspicions of illegitimate and undesirable commercializing can arise.
- In recent decades, shamanism has developed from a (presumed) type of religion to a religious option open to everybody; shaman tourism has emerged as one mode of religious appropriation.
- The world over, shamans make themselves available to (domestic and international) tourists, sometimes resulting in new opportunities for shamans; there are "tourism shamans", international shaman celebrities, traditional arts shamans and invented shamanisms; shamanism becomes part of monetary transactions.
- At the same time, at other places, tourism can threaten the continuation of shamanist practice.

Chapter 7

Performances

Entertainment is part of the expected leisure tourist experience. Holidays may be relaxing (not all in fact are, and some are not meant to be), but in any case they should not be boring. In Chapter 5, we have discussed tourist spaces such as theme parks that were created to entertain (and in the examples we visited even to some extent to enlighten) their visitors; performing arts shamans do not heal, but educate and entertain (see Chapter 6; p. 163 f.). In economic terms, entertainment and tourism are both distinct and overlapping spheres of economic activity. Some entertainment businesses would not survive without tourists, and tourist resorts are provided with entertainment facilities.

Religion is traditionally held to be a "serious business". While it was, and often still is, hard for many scholars to accept that religion is, in fact, business, the entertainment dimension, if not function, of religion is even more rarely explicitly acknowledged. Presumably this is because it is held to be a byproduct, if even that, of whatever is perceived as religion's core concerns, functions or origins. This almost universal neglect is surprising given the obvious fact that myths, rituals, singing, festivals, pilgrimages, and other features of religion actually did and do entertain people. Boring rituals may appeal to intellectuals or else be sustained by force. However, preaching and even religious controversy can to some extent be entertaining.[1] Religions therefore have enormous potential for entertainment, and religious events often use several media.

The few instances of scholarship addressing the entertainment dimension or function of religion at all (at least those I am aware of) mainly refer to contemporary mass media or US American religious history (see, for example, Robertson ed., 2002).[2] In both cases, the subtext is that of an anomaly – of religion entering the media landscape or blurring the boundaries between religion and media[3] (as if entertainment was not religious before the age of electronic media) or of the US as a special case. In her book *The Domestic Manner of the Americans* (1832) the English novelist Frances Trollope polemically remarked that "religion and entertainment in the United States were virtually synonymous, especially for women" (Moore 1994, 120–21).

On the other hand, many "American Protestant ministers never uttered the word 'entertainment' with an approving tone without placing it next to the words 'useful' and 'instructive'" (Moore 1994, 19). The neglect of religions' entertainment potential may thus well be another instance of often decried Protestant legacies in the study of religion(s), reinforced by culture critical attitudes towards a commercialization of religion and its perceived degradation to "nothing but entertainment".

Religions also provide entertainment for tourists – not only by supplying attractions including sites, places, and spaces or the display of religious groups and specialists, but also by staging performances. In the context of indigenous cultures one may think of so-called "aboriginal arts performances".[4] Data from the 1990s "indicate that about half of all German and a third of British tourists [to New Zealand (MSt.)] attended a Maori performance" (Ryan 2002, 955). In many places such "aboriginal performances" are regular features of folk villages and cultural or ethnic tourism (see Chapter 6).

The entertainment tourists may derive from such performances does not always go along with appreciation or respect, but can also be perceived as offensive. Visits to the Western Wall to see and to photograph Jews praying were part of the guided tour ever since tourism discovered Palestine in the late 19th century; when visiting, "the tourists had little respect for the Jews' piety, knew nothing of their rituals, and often voiced anti-Semitic or sceptical commentaries. The Jews, for their part, certainly did not enjoy being stared at by lounging, giggling foreigners" (Shepherd 1987, 190). Compare the following quote from a *Tourist Guide to Ainu Life* published by the Hokkaido government in 1927: "Many thoughtful Ainu people are ashamed to perform the old manners of their ancestors for money amidst the laughter of spectators. They consider it disrespectful to their forefathers." The guidebook therefore exhorts the tourists to more appropriate behavior: "You are therefore requested, while looking at them, to refrain from laughing without any reason, or assuming an attitude of mockery" (quoted by Sjöberg 1993, 134).

In the present chapter, the reader will be invited on a tour de force around the world. We will take a closer look at various instances of ceremonies and rituals, worship, religious variety shows, and dances before moving on to more complex events such as holidays and festivals.[5]

Rituals

Occasionally, tourism has led to the reintroduction of ceremonies that were about to die out. This is what has happened with the famous *iyomante* (bear sacrificial ceremony) among the Ainu. The *iyomante* had been prohibited by the Japanese authorities after the annexation of the Ainu territories in the late 19th century, but was practiced secretly in the 20th century until the restrictions against it were lifted in the late 1970s. The official reintroduction of the ceremony has to be seen in the context of the flourishing Ainu tourism (Sjöberg 1993, 53). In line with the changed context, when it was reintroduced in some tourist villages, the timing of the period was changed from February to August in order to match the tourist season in Japan (Sjöberg 2004, 242). Moreover, dances typically performed in the framework of the *iyomante* were lifted out of this context and came to be performed in tourist villages under the title "bear festival" (Hiwasaki 2000, 399 and n. 27).

In an exhibition hall of one tourist village, documentary films on different Ainu practices, rituals and ceremonies such as the *iyomante* are on display (Sjöberg 1993, 164). Apart from live or staged rituals, this form of mediatization of ritual practice is common in various tourism contexts; the mediated double can be shown at or close to a given ritual site, for example in visitor centers, in near-by locations that represent local or regional culture such as museums. Travel magazines or travel films and the internet provide national or global channels of mediated spread of the respective ceremonies.

Some performances can be explicitly directed at tourists. This was the case with the weekly *powwow* performed by Blackfeet Indians in a camp set up close to the Glacier Park Hotel near Montana (Shaffer 2001, 69). Other performances are shared by tourist audiences. Among the shared audiences, tourists and tourism may eventually turn into a dominant factor. This, however, is not a unidirectional development (Sjöberg 2004, 241), as it often gives rise to negotiations, redefinitions, and changes of the performance and the local group. At many places one encounters a worry – often expressed more vociferously by scholars and critics than by performers and participants – concerning the possible profanization and commercialization of religious ceremonies and discomfort with them being subjected to the tourists' gazes and cameras. In some instances, performances are straightforwardly touristified. The transition does not necessarily occur abruptly. Moreover, given that there are several interested parties apart from tourists and the tourism branch, there are various attempts at striking a balance between different interests and preferences.

While local participants invariably may find the presence of tourists a challenge, sometimes the tourists are exhorted to redefine their roles. This is what happened at Ubud (Bali), where a magazine aimed at tourists invited them to take part in the "cultural events" of the region "not as tourists but as villagers" while at the same time informing them "that the religious ceremonies are not tourist attractions and that their participants are not there simply to provide a colorful décor for exotic photographs" (Picard 1996, 87–88 [quoted from the *Ubud Post*]).

Consider the following example for the dynamic effects of tourism on ritual practice from Thailand. Once a year, in August, the Akha who migrated to Thailand from China and Burma in the early 20th century hold a festival that involves offerings, sacrifices, music, dancing, and – most famously – the construction of large swings, which are subsequently used for ritual swinging. Apart from more mundane reasons such as serving as pastime, play, and entertainment, a study of the ceremony suggests that it works as a thanksgiving to the ancestors and deities for protection of the crops or "the celebration of the maturation of planted rice" (Kacha-ananda 1971, 120).[6] Because of the performance of songs and dances this ceremony has become quite popular with tourists. (The Akha have been a tourist attraction for more than 20 years.) In a tourism village in Chiang Rai, the swinging is now performed day in and day out, whenever groups show up and ask for it to be performed. It has been de-contextualized and turned into a tourism amenity. Moreover, the children, for whom the swinging seems to have become a sort of serious play, have assumed performative new roles (Leepreecha 2005, 11).

Where this chapter focuses on ritual activities and events at places visited by tourists, tourism may also result in the transfer of ritual practices, gestures or elements witnessed when back at home.[7] In my own research in Norway one informant, a Dean in the national church, referred to a "revolution" that had occurred in the church over recent decades. As one example he pointed to the fact that almost all Norwegian churches now have orb-shaped candle stands on which people light candles. This practice, he believed, was introduced as a result of Norwegians traveling to Catholic countries, where they had first begun to like it.[8] Unfortunately, very little more data is available to me at the time of writing.

Apart from the transfer of ritual practices, rituals can be transferred in a discursive manner. Here is an example. Since 1945, Japan has been a destination for American tourists where most travelers visit at least some temples or roadside shrines, in many of which they can see hundreds or thousands of brightly bibbed statues of the bodhisattva Jizō associated with fetal spirits (*mizuko*) often represented by children's pinwheels. The Jizō statues are dedicated to *mizuko kuyō*, a ritual practice that seeks to placate fetal spirits in the aftermath of an abortion or pregnancy loss. The *mizuko kuyō* is mentioned in all major English travel guidebooks. Jeff Wilson describes the typical reaction of travelers as follows:

> Time and again, the American tourist surveys a field of hundreds or thousands of *mizuko* Jizō statues, intrigued but unsure of their meaning. Informed by a companion or passerby, she or he is suddenly stuck fast in their tracks, arrested by the disorienting knowledge that the Japanese memorialize their abortions and miscarriages in such a public and religious way. ... This freezing effect is often followed by a rush of emotion – wonder, grief, thankfulness or some combination of the three. Although these visitors are not Buddhist, the image haunts them, and they feel compelled to paint the scene for readers and friends later on. Sometimes this simple encounter with the unexpected is sufficient to transform their feelings around abortion and other pregnancy losses;

sometimes the moment goes further and the American visitor actually conducts a brief *mizuko kuyō* by leaving a talisman, ritually washing a statue, and/or saying a prayer over one of the *mizuko* Jizōs.

(Wilson 2009, 13)

An exposure to these rituals sites can trigger powerful emotions and lead to transformative experiences and actual ritual engagement. However, from what I understand, the ritual practice as such is not transferred to the United States (American Buddhists aside), but the ritual is rhetorically appropriated by non-Buddhist Americans from both camps in the US abortion debate (pro-life and pro-choice advocates) as an argument for their respective cause.

Worship

According to available statistic material, around nine percent of Germans traveling abroad claim to take part in a religious service during their travels; for domestic tourists that rate doubles to 18 percent (Lukatis and Hieber 1996, 1, n. 4). In a survey conducted on the islands and in bathing resorts of Ostfriesland (Germany) in 1994, 14 percent of the tourists said that they had attended a service during their holidays. Among the reasons given for this behavior, 32 percent agreed with the statement that they find it interesting to experience something like this at a different place. Twenty-four percent referred to their attachment to the church, while 12 percent held that attending a service provides welcome variety to the holiday, and another 12 percent said that they previously had positive experiences with attending services (Lukatis and Hieber 1996, 48–52). A more recent study from the German federal state of Sachsen-Anhalt found that 22 percent of day-trippers were interested in attending a service, as against 25 percent of those spending at least one night in Sachsen-Anhalt (Seidel 2006, 32).

Since rituals and worship often take place during holidays such as Easter and on weekends, which also happen to be preferred periods for traveling, groups engaged in the performance of rituals during these times or on such occasions often find themselves exposed to the gaze, the camera flashes, the smell, and the noise of tourists. Already in 19th-century Rome, an observer estimated that "three fourths of the crowd at the Easter service he attended [in St. Peter's] was British" (Withey 1997, 90).

Apart from such special timings, tourists may just happen to be around when the performances are held or make it a point to be at the spot when something "goes on". At some places, many tourists seem to expect some sort of ritual activity to take place. For the English World Heritage Site Avebury, known for its large prehistoric stone circle and a popular site for pagan ritual activities, Jenny Blain and Robert Wallis (2007, 55) report of some tourists complaining "if *no* rituals are evident". Moreover, they "have seen the observers gather not only for larger 'public' celebrations but even when a single practitioner engages in chanting or other less intrusive practices in an out-of-the-way part of the circle" (Blain and Wallis 2007, 55).

The performing community, however, has different requirements. Some communities and some individual members are more used to being exposed to tourists than others. Some try to protect privacy, while others are clearly aware of performing, as it were, on a stage and are more or less happy to be documented by cameras (Blain and Wallis 2007, 55). The Sunday services of the Shakers, which were a well-known destination after being publicized by newspaper reports and travelogues, are an early example. At one point during their services,

> a Shaker speaker would offer a sermon that often was directed to the visitors, expounding on their sinful state and explaining the virtues of Shakerism. (The Shakers were aware of the effect a good speaker could have, and have designated speakers at least as far back as 1807.) Other Shakers might rise up and testified to their face, as the spirit moved them.
>
> (Bixby 2007, 88)

In this case, the services were designed as stages for proselytism – greatly needed for a group renouncing natural means of reproduction. Yet, it seems that this strategy did not produce the desired effects.

As we have seen earlier, management practices as to how to deal with this intrusion vary. The behavior of visitors varies likewise; at many places one hears complaints about inappropriate behaviors. An early example is reported from 19th-century Rome, where visitors were observed "munching sandwiches and even popping champagne corks during services. At one point during the 1820s, the pope felt compelled to issue an appeal against using St. Peter's as a fashionable promenade" (Withey 1997, 94).

The ongoing performance of time-honored rituals often contributes to the aesthetical appeal of the place and enhances the visitor experience. Attending the performance of a festive liturgy makes a church come to life and may lead to other sorts of emotional reactions.

Reactions of the visitors may vary from repulsion, outrage, suspicion, and laughter to sympathy and enchantment.[9] Again the boundaries between experiences deemed aesthetical and religious are blurred. The perpetuation of old traditions may well be in the interest of tourists and tourism agencies. In many cases the presence of groups of performers "as ongoing, contentious communities of worship pales in contrast to their value as archaic relics of the past" (Bremer 2004, 114). Bremer (2004, 114) describes that as a process of "archaization". One could also refer to it as musealization of ritual practice, as long as this is not taken to imply that the performers thereby necessarily perceive their own performances as less authentic, meaningful or efficacious. Being on display may have various impacts on their self-awareness and reflexivity.[10] It can also be perceived as the price to be paid for gaining revenues in the form of donations, etc.

Participation is a term with a broad range of meanings covering the roles/ experiences of bystander and spectator with free-floating attention as much as that of becoming deeply immersed with focused attending. Visitor-participants may stay for just a few minutes or remain throughout the entire ceremony. While the former option – the bystander/spectator dropping in by accident and staying just for a short while with attention primarily directed towards the aesthetics of the space – may be the rule when religious performances are subjected to the tourist gaze, exceptions to the rule are also reported by anecdotal evidence: the attention and body of tourists getting immersed in or captivated by unfamiliar situations.[11]

Religious variety shows

Just as themed spaces are devised for tourists (besides religious places that are exposed to tourism), performances were and are created especially for tourists. Based on a recent study by Aaron Ketchell we will take a brief look at variety shows that have emerged in Branson/Missouri, the second largest "drive-to" destination of the United States (second to Orlando/Florida, home of the Walt Disney World Resort and other themeparks) (Ketchell 2007, 92–93). As a destination, Branson, a city of only 6,500 permanent residents, especially appeals to Christians and families.

In 2004 Branson "hosted forty-seven variety show theaters with more seats than New York City's Broadway district and more than a hundred different live productions" (Ketchell 2007, 86). While music entertainment was provided by local artists until the 1970s, during the 1980s numerous bigger names made their appearance on stages in Branson – be it as guest artists or by establishing their own venues. The shows make use of country, southern gospel and pop music, and while very few are framed as explicit gospel acts, religion is a standard theme in most shows in that they include at least a number of gospel numbers and Christian testimony. The musical entertainment shows resonate with the Christian religiosity of the spectators but also address the "nonbelievers by offering the possibility of conversion mediated by experiences of leisure" (Ketchell 2007, 98). Apart from Christianity, many of these shows invoke notions of home, family, rurality and country (Ketchell 2007, 98). All these topics are also assembled in Branson's many Christmas productions (Ketchell 2007, 107–11).

Branson offers several other forms of religious entertainment, including a musical *(The Promise)* based on the life of Jesus staged since 1995; this "show is patterned after Broadway style musicals and places a pious spin on big stage song and dance that the entire family will be sure to enjoy".[12] The actor, who has portrayed Jesus throughout all the years, regards his acting as a ministry, and the cast members "often express their work in terms of

Christian vocation" (Ketchell 2007, 219). There are reports of conversions and healings surrounding the show (which latterly seems to have become less popular) (Ketchell 2007, 219–21).

A less overt, but more implicit or embedded approach to evangelism is provided by the shows of the magician Kirby Van Burch[13] who concludes his shows (as described by Ketchell) by revealing some of the secrets behind some of his tricks and pronouncing his act as a great illusion, while at the same time pointing to God as the ultimate source of the magician's capacities and talking about reading Bible stories with his grandmother (Ketchell 2007, 221–22).

While Christians have always been the core constituency for Branson tourism, Ketchell points to the emergence of tour operators who are more explicitly catering to a Christian clientele. The more overt targeting of this group is also reflected in the recent emergence of so-called "show-services" held at theaters transformed into churches on Sundays. A typical feature is their adoption of elements of comedy or show. Some of these services highlight gospel music without the use of sermons, while others are something like more explicitly Christian variants of the ordinary shows (with more gospel singing and comments on such issues as prayer and the teaching of evolution in public schools) (Ketchell 2007, 208–16). While theaters are temporarily assuming church-like functions on Sundays, churches and other worship sites are increasingly relying on the patronage of tourists (see also Chapter 2).

Dances

Dances are common tourist entertainment performances, be it in the North or in the South of the globe. Dances are attractive performances because of their (synæsthetic) qualities of combining different senses and media such as drumming, singing and other forms of music and rhythm, recitation, display of objects, masks and other special clothes, etc. Tourist dance performances can occur in "traditional" settings, in staged environments especially erected for the purpose (which often contain quotes from or simulacra of backstage performance sites) or even in tourist spaces such as hotels.

Pictures of dancing people are a familiar motif in tourism advertising since the early history of the modern tourism. Dances, it seems, are a tourism resource worldwide, with especially spectacular and famous ones (such as the Dogon masked dances and the Hawaiian *hula*) serving as tourism attractions in their own right. The anthropologist Jane Desmond argues that songs and dances

> are believed to be representative of, and since expressive, to be especially revealing of, a culture or a people (both of which are conceived as unitary things). They are portable and can be brought to the audience,

unlike other cultural practices which are less easily detached from their broader social and physical contexts.

(Desmond 1999, 17)

In tourism contexts, dances have thus become a precious cultural capital. The "portable" character of dances implied that dances and dancers could also travel from the tourist peripheries to the centers of power. The first Maori performers from Aotearoa (New Zealand) toured Australia and Europe in 1862,[14] and Hawaiian *hula* dancers started to tour California from the 1850s onwards. A poster advertising the dance as the "Greatest Attraction of the Season" also includes a list of the dances on the program. According to that program, the first set opened "with a Pula ia Laka (Prayer to Laka, goddess of hula)" (Desmond 1999, 61). The entertainment program did not yet renounce the religious dimensions of the *hula*. However, it seems that this sort of religious framing was discontinued when the *hula* later began its success on Broadway, in tent shows, during the 1893 world exposition, and in supper clubs, night clubs and showrooms.[15] By presenting an embodied vision of Hawaii, such performances did their share to prepare the ground for the successful development of Hawaiian tourism (Desmond 1999, 79) (as did the Maori companies for New Zealand), long since the main source of income for the state (especially since the shutdown of the sugar industry). Live performances of the *hula* are a central feature of tourism in Hawaii, to the extent that the *hula*-girl is the main destination image of Hawaii.[16] The image of the female dancer is invariably linked to the Edenic imagery cast on the islands: "unspoiled by modernity yet willing to be its entertaining hostess" (Desmond 1999, 88).

Apart from tapping extant dances, tourism appears as a major impetus for the "revival" or "renaissance" of dancing and related musical performances. This has been observed at many places around the globe, partly by outside observers, but also by governments and other interested parties.[17] The fact that many dances, especially among indigenous people, have been re-contextualized into tourist settings has obviously raised the issues of "authenticity" and "commoditization" (e.g. Daniel 1996; Xie 2003; Wall and Xie 2005). In several places, dances first came to enjoy a specific prestige – both in local, national, and tourism contexts – after becoming part of the tourism system.[18]

Most dances performed for the entertainment of tourists, especially in Western destinations such as Paris and New York, are non-religious. Dancing in general is classified as a secular activity on Western mainstream mental maps. However, in many cultures dancing belongs to the repertoire of religious forms of expressions. Such dances have likewise become exposed to tourism.

Christian missionaries in Hawaii began arriving in 1819, and branded the *hula* as "lascivious, and circumscribed it heavily" (Desmond 1999, 61–62), an attitude which was shared by parts of the indigenous elite. Although the public performance of the *hula* had become restricted in 1859, King David Kalākaua revived court patronage of the *hula* from the 1860s, and for his coronation in 1883 dances and chants were presented that included non-Christian religious elements. In the early 20th century, the *hula* had become "part of the entertainment for the developing tourist trade in the islands" (Imada 2004, 118). Apparently, at this time the *hula* religious varieties of the dances were performed only in a folk village (see Chapter 6; p. 147) or in non-public performances for Native Hawaiians, whereas the mainstream *hula* had become assimilated to "the taste of tourists: shorter skirts, fewer verses, and English-language lyrics" (Imada 2004, 122). The dances became disconnected from the religious dimensions they reportedly had in pre-contact times, when it was "a religious practice performed at temples" by dancers "trained under strict rules and the protection of the female goddess Laka" (Imada 2004, 117). Besides tourism, the Latter Day Saints offered some kind of shelter for the performance of the *hula*. Nevertheless, even for Mormons "indigenous dance was benign and even beneficial so long as it was divorced from religious rituals such as the *kuahu* (hula altar) to the goddess Laka" (Imada 2004, 123). At the same time, some Mormons were *hula* masters who also had knowledge of the religious dances; while these practitioners and teachers modified the dances in the framework of their church, it is possible that they have exposed their non-Mormon "hula students to some Hawaiian religious practices, such as chants to hula gods" (Imada 2004, 123). During the 1930s religious varieties of the *hula* reappeared in public (Imada 2004, 122–23). More recently, dances that were earlier disclaimed as unreligious came to be appreciated: "the *kahiko* hula style was cast as anti-Christian and dangerous; today *kahiko* is celebrated as an authentic tradition "revived", even though most of the dances performed have been newly created" (Linnekin 1997, 228).

Apart from various so-called indigenous religions and performances often classified as "shamanic", among the so-called world religions dance as a religious activity appears in Hinduism, Buddhism, and Confucianism.[19] In Western Christendom, the Shakers are a group that performed dances as part of their worship, and they also displayed their dances for tourist audiences who eagerly grasped the occasion:

> Offering the chance to see the odd sectaries and watch their elaborate dances, they could attract hundreds of visitors on a Sunday, so many that some could not be accommodated to the Shaker meeting houses.
>
> (Bixby 2007, 92)

Yet, it seems that most visitors remained unconvinced by this practice. Some, if not many, appear to have reacted in negative terms and some negative judgements ("disgusting") are reported (Bixby 2007, 92).

In tourism contexts, religious dances are often conceptually framed as "folklore".[20] In Brazil, the Bahia Folklore Company (Balé Folclórico da Bahia) performing in a theater in Salvador has a number of Candomblé dances such as the *puxada de rede* in honor of Yemanjé, the deity of the sea, in its repertoire. Tourists are among the audience at the theater. A travel agent advertising on the internet offers a trip called "Afro Salvador" which invites its customers to "[l]earn traditional rhythms, dance, religion and cuisine of the black heart of Brazil". Apart from attending the performance of the Balé Folclórico da Bahia (also offered by other travel agents), this trip allows participants to take part in percussion and drum workshops. Moreover, it promises trips to the Museo Afro, a visit to "a traditional Candomblé house of worship", focusing "on the religious and social traditions of the temple", but also schedules visits to two churches, one of them (the Bonfim church) reportedly being "one of the most important churches of pilgrimage in Brazil and deeply synchronized with Candomblé".[21]

Exposure to tourism has led to various degrees of change both with respect to the context and the texture of the dances. Such changes pertain to:

- the composition, role, spatial setting, and participation of audiences
- timing, duration, location, staging
- complexities of structure and performance
- performative roles and behavior (e.g. with regard to display of individual skill and interaction with the audience)
- gender roles
- social functions, and expected (religious) rewards.[22]

Dances may be abbreviated and adapted to suit the tourist demand and context, for example by giving more floor time to the more spectacular elements such as masks, music,[23] costumes and stage decorations. Improvised sections are often shortened or replaced by fixed sets and the format is "condensed structurally" (Daniel 1996, 794). Several sets of performance are shortened and compressed into time frames suitable for tourist consumption (Xie 2003; Wall and Xie 2005). In some cases, there occurs a duplication, where the changed dances are performed for tourists, while the other format (with no or minor changes) is continued in the traditional settings as "insider events".[24]

While the dances on the one hand emphasize conventional structures, not the least in order to appear "authentic", tourism in many cases first provides performers the means, time, and space to develop the format and work creatively with given formats (Daniel 1996, 793–94). Tourism does not necessarily lead to standardization – although it often does – but certainly triggers processes of professionalization.

When dances are lasting for many hours and there are no visitor facilities that provide visitors a chance to appreciate the working, background or meanings of what is going on, attention and initial fascination readily fade away and the "authentic experience" turns into prolonged boredom.[25]

A stronger emphasis on rhythm to please and entertain tourist audiences occasionally goes along with an obliteration of the religious significance and meaning of the structure[26] or key elements of the dances. This has been pointed out for the bamboo-beating dance among the Li on the island of Hainan, off the coast from China, where the apotropaic and religious significance of the color red has lost in importance while the bamboo-beating rhythms with "intimate team play and smiling faces" are being emphasized (Xie 2003, 11). At the same time, tourism is a medium for these dances to be revived after several decades of suppression by the Communist government. This public reemergence of the dances, it seems, is achieved under different auspices: the dances are viewed as "cultural" rather than "religious" (Xie 2003, 11).

In another part of China the transfer from religious contexts into a colorful display of ethnic culture has taken even more extreme forms. Among the Tai, practitioners of Theravada Buddhism who live in Sipsongbanna in the south of the province of Yunnan (in the borderland with Laos and Burma), dances are performed for Han-Chinese audiences on a daily basis. However, some of the so-called ethnic dances were created by government dance troupes, and "[t]he dancers are often majority Hans clad in halter tops and tight 'ethnic' skirts" (Davis 2001, 28). Although the peacock does not seem to have a special status among the Tai, peacocks have become the main tourism symbol of Sipsongbanna. Peacock heads theme restaurants, buses, and hotels. One explanation of the choice of the peacock as the main symbol may be the famous peacock dance, which is nowadays "performed by a woman twirling in a white tutu decorated to look like peacock feathers". Outside tourism display culture, however, "the only peacock dance performed by Tais is a slow and stately *kinnaree* dance, performed at temple festivals by elderly men in masks" (Davis 2001, 28).

Dances can be lifted out of their context and transferred to other settings. This, in turn, may lead to further transfers. Bruce Kapferer[27] reports how the dances that are part of the exorcisms he has studied over the years in Sri Lanka have, apparently under the impact of tourism, gained an increasing importance to the extent of eventually being lifted out of the ceremonial ensemble altogether. As independent units they have since been performed in other venues such as hotels, for different audiences and with different functions. As a consequence of their tourist performance, these events were then separated from the control of the low caste community that had hitherto performed them. Their dramatic and exotic features were often expanded. In what is a sort of spiral feedback loop, they were then often copied by non-specialists as part of the creative development of exorcist practice.

In Korean Buddhism several types of dances are performed today, mostly by monks in a large temple in the capital (Van Zile 2001, 11–12). There have been some attempts to transfer Buddhist dances to other audiences. This has occurred as part of a Buddhist ceremony, Yongsanjae (Yŏngsanjae), which in turn was much abbreviated; in the abbreviated format dancing gained a more prominent place, obviously because it was held to be particularly appealing to the new target audience:

> Pongwon-sa Temple, located near Ewha Womans University in western Seoul, reenacts Yongsanjae, a Buddhist ritual offering with music and dance by monks for groups of visitors that make prior reservations. While the whole ceremony runs for three days and nights, tourists can sample it for 40 minutes or so with an exposure to ascetic dances such as the cymbal dance, drum dance and butterfly dance. Also they are served traditional temple food that the nuns at Pongwonsa Temple have been making for hundreds of years.[28]

The changes implied by a transfer to a tourism pattern are here consciously engaged as part of what can be described as a Buddhist outreach program.

Vodun dances are an established phenomenon in tourism to Haiti. *Vodun* dances are staged regularly in major hotels in Port-au-Prince. Such shows, it seems, have a history going back to the occupation by United States marines (1915–34). In the literature, it has been observed that the performers fall into a trance even in performances targeted at tourists. It seems that the presence of the tourists is not necessarily detrimental to the performative logic of the event to unfold itself for the performers. This, in turn, makes such performances particularly attractive for tourist audiences. See the following "Destination guide" for Haiti, unmistakably spiced by tropes of exotics, alcohol, adventure and religious value-judgments marking "the other":

> Haiti, with its eerie voodoo (vodun in Haitian Kreyol) drums breaking the evening silence, is a land of superstition. Seeing a vodun ceremony, even if staged strictly for touristic reasons, is an adventure you may never forget. Worshippers, dressed in white, go into a trance as they use handfuls of flour to trace symbols of Afro-Haitian gods on dirt floors. There is a strong scent of rum (world-class Barbancourt rum has been distilled in Haiti since 1765) as worshippers chant names of important deities, especially Baron Samedi. The Baron wears black, formal attire and a top hat. This popular deity is believed to have powers regarding death, funerals, and zombies. The latter comprise Haiti's walking dead and are de rigueur ingredients for Hollywood horror films.[29]

While we in other cases have found a re-contextualizing of religious practices in terms of "folklore" or "culture", the religious character of the performance is here from the point of view of an outside description denied by casting it as evidence for "superstition". The description fuses notions of

Western popular culture with a description of *vodun*. The passage reflexively acknowledges the tourist staging character of the event while at the same time twisting the expected conclusion: albeit purely touristic, it is nevertheless a possibly unforgettable "adventure".

In the case of Cuban Santería (as analyzed by Katherine Hagedorn), prior to becoming exposed to tourism, ritual/religious performances had first been transformed into "folklore". The songs and dances of the Afro-Cuban religious traditions came to be performed by "grupos folklóricos" such as the famous Conjunto Folklórico established in 1962. The performances of this ensemble seem to be a hybrid of different genres, "somewhere between religious ritual and nightclub floor show", where "sequence and texture of the performance" remain similar to religious sessions (Hagedorn 2001, 57). Hagedorn describes the reactions of the audience to a typical performance as ranging "from delight to light entrancement and mesmerization" (Hagedorn 2001, 57). These hybrid performances are now an important tourist attraction. The audience is typically composed of four distinct groups: young foreign tourists, older Cuban religious practitioners, young Cuban black marketeers and the young dancers and singer hoping to perform with the troupe (Hagedorn 2001, 58). Accordingly, the performances entail a situation of heterogeneous simultaneous communication.

Not only outsiders have an interest in denying the religious character of dances, but even insiders and performers have devised strategies to distinguish between dances performed for different audiences (tourists/non-tourists; uninitiated/initiated) and in different spatial and temporal settings. These strategies may involve the texture of the performance or its taxonomy. In her pioneering study of the anthropology of dance, Anya Peterson Royce mentions to three such strategies: the identical dance is referred to by a different name when performed for an audience mainly consisting of tourists (Haiti); the dances performed for the uninitiated are "borrowed" from other groups (Taos Pueblos [according to Donald Brown]); the third strategy (observed for the Tongan Islands) is to take an old dance, modify its form, give it a new name, thereby transforming its identity (Royce 2002, 84–85).

In the case of Santería, the use of sacred or consecrated drums is one way of distinguishing a "real" and "powerful" performance from a folklore/tourist one. Where the drums look the same and cannot be distinguished by onlookers their "abilities" and efficacy are clearly different in the view of the performers (Hagedorn 2001, 99). Another way of distinguishing religious from folkloric/tourist performances is the intent of the performers, whether it is to "bring down" the divine agent (*orisha* or *santo*) as in the religious/ritual version or whether it is a reflexive, mimetic re-presentation of this prototype in the folklore/tourism variety (Hagedorn 2001, 100–101). These distinctions on the side of the performers notwithstanding, the very dynamics of the performance and the rhythm regularly lead to the occurrence of trances and possessions among the audience even in "profane" places like theaters – which made the lead percussionist of the Conjunto Folklórico refer to such experiences as "inappropriate possessions" (Hagedorn 2001, 108).

It is impossible to discuss dance and tourism without a reference to Bali, where tourism has emerged as a major arena and patronage system for dances, some of which have been partly based on the performative register of exorcisms created in tourism contexts.[30] It may be worthwhile recalling that performances held in the villages, or in hotels, also attract Balinese spectators, who often stand behind the tourist audiences sitting in rows of chairs or in an amphitheatre. Note that the staging often refers to a religious framework by having the scenery formed as a temple gate (Picard 1996, 139).

Here, we will limit ourselves briefly to one case, in order to point to the interplay of different agents and genres such as travel literature, photography and the production and display of exotic art. The Russian-born German artist and musician Walter Spies is a good example of a middleman: living on the island from 1927 to 1938 he produced his own works of art and at the same time he encouraged indigenous people to explore their music and dance. In this way, he influenced the formation of the hybrid *kecak*, which integrates the ritual chanting of *sanghyang* with a narration from the Ramayana (originally just one episode, but later extended to cover the entire epic). In allusion to "the male chorus playing the role of the army of monkeys sent by the prince Rama to rescue the beautiful Sita" (Picard 1996, 150), the *kecak* is also known as the Monkey Dance. Not quite unlike the equally famous *barong*, the Monkey Dance is a creation of the 1930s catering to the entertainment needs of American and European tourists (Johnson 2002, 14–15).

The Monkey Dance is nowadays advertised as tourism commodity, generally classified under "Night Life". One tour operation (indo.com) provides the following "description":

> [T]he Kecak Dance is a spectacular choreographic accomplishment that showcases another aspect of Balinese artistic excellence. One hundred or so bare-chested men sit down on the ground surrounding a bonfire or a fire made from coconut husks, led by a priest or a female dancer in the middle. The only music to accompany them are the beats of their palms clapping or hitting their chests, their thighs, or other parts of their bodies, rhythmically accompanied by shouting and chanting. The dancers move in unison, creating a spectacular sequence of hands stretched out, pulled in, rested on the shoulder of the next person, and waists gyrated left and right. All in a dizzying tempo.[31]

Apart from the priest (who is obviously regarded as optional), no mention is made here of any religious dimension of the spectacle. The performance is regarded as dance-music entertainment. The religious dimension will, however, in all probability remain very much present for the performers who by their performance please the gods even when entertaining the audience. Such performances can therefore be described as communication with a multitude of messages and receivers (audiences).[32] The performances create a tourist-religious hybrid. Michel Picard also comments on the reluctance of Balinese dancers to do without consecrated implements such as masks when performing other dances; contrary to the Cuban drummers, it seems that they do not consider making a distinction between "real" and "tourist" performances but that they insist on performing all dances in the same manner. Moreover, in Bali even the events created and performed especially for tourists "tend to use similar ritual procedures as the ceremonies that inspired them, be they the presentation of offerings or the use of consecrated accessories" (Picard 1996, 160).

Yet, there are limits to the touristification of dance-performances. Social anthropologist Leo Howe reports the following incident:

> [W]hen the Bali Beach Hotel used the *péndét* – a dance in homage to the gods when they descend into their temple shrines – as a welcome for their tourist audience it brought condemnation from religious authorities, who were concerned that this use of the dance appeared to treat tourists as if they were gods, and was thus tantamount to a desecration of an important ritual dance.
>
> (Howe 2005, 136)

Subsequently, a choreographer at the Conservatory of Music was commissioned to create an alternative dance to replace the ancient religious one at the opening of tourism performances. In Balinese, this new composition is called *Panyembrama* (literally, "that which is offered to guests"); the Indonesian name is *Tari Selamat Datang* (literally, "welcome dance"). Eventually, however,

> ... this tourist version of a ritual dance returned to the temples, where it originated [in its previous reincarnation (MSt.)], after a number of dancers who had learned the *Panyembrama* at the Conservatory came to perform it instead of the *Pendet* in the course of temple ceremonies.
>
> (Picard 1996, 143)

The transfer from temple to tourism contexts here is a two-way process. The issue whether it is appropriate to perform religious dances in non-religious contexts (for tourists) presupposes a conceptual classificatory scheme that is not available in all cultures. But one can attempt to devise one. In Bali, in 1971 the authorities gathered academics with the task of determining the "sacred" or "profane" status of dances. This, however, was no easy task since this and similar distinctions developed subsequently did not make sense in the different Balinese contexts and the suggested classificatory scheme was eventually dropped (Howe 2005, 137–38; Picard 1996, 121–33). Between 1971 and 1974 the Governor launched three decrees, among them one prohibiting "sacred" dances to be performed outside of their traditional religious context, and another one that forbids access to temples to all non Hindu-Balinese during the temple-ceremonies (Picard 1996, 130–31). However, a study by Udayana University found that the government's concern to shield the religious/ritual sphere from tourist interference was not shared by the performers themselves, for "while dancers in general deplored the commercialization of dance, they wanted to promote cultural tourism by staging the most authentic Balinese dances specially for the tourists" (Howe 2005, 138) – and these happened to be the religious/ritual dances.

In the meanwhile, it seems that indigenous Balinese culture has fused with tourist culture to such an extent that festivals are now held to promote such presumably "traditional" performances devised as tourist performances in the first place. The aspects identified as "traditionally Balinese" by agents of tourism have apparently been adopted as positive markers of identity by some/the Balinese themselves (Howe 2005, 143). This points to the process whereby "cultural tourism" has turned into a "tourist culture" where "the brand image of their tourist product" has become "the marker of their cultural identity" (Picard 2008, 162), a process described as a "dialogical" identity construction by Michel Picard.

The case of the so-called Hopi Snake Dance points to rather different processes and solutions. Here, tourism exposure eventually led to an anti-tourist counter-reaction that restored the privacy of the performance. At the same time when the event was fenced off from tourism, it became re-publicized in an act of performative mimicry and appropriation, which eventually was challenged. Here is what has happened.

The Hopi Snake Dance, in which participants handle live snakes, occurs as one of several ritual performances on the final day of a nine-day ceremony (Dilworth 1996, 22). Shortly after the subduing of the Indians in New Mexico and Arizona, accounts of the Snake Dance began to reach larger audiences, in part via ethnographical accounts and photographs.[33] "By the early 1890s it had become a national ritual for newspapers and magazines to report on the 'Weird Arizona Snake Dance' or 'Hideous Rites' in their August issues" (Dilworth 1996, 21). During the 20th century, however, adjectives such as these were dropped; instead public perception shifted to the " 'noble' bearing of the dancers and the profundity or 'archaic mystery' – in place of 'savagery' – of the rites" (Howes 1996, 141).

In the age of the expansion of modern transportation networks, the Snake Dance was promoted as a tourist attraction by the Atchinson, Topeka and Santa Fe Railways, whose routes went through these regions (Dilworth 1996, 54). The railway companies also sponsored guidebooks and press reports that provided information about the Indian cultures and stimulated the desire to see them. While the fame of the Snake Dance spread across the world, thousands of outside visitors came to witness it and to take snapshots of it every year; in turn, their images were disseminated on postcards and via other media.[34] By the turn of the century, "[t]he proliferation of cameras began to cause conflicts between photographers vying for the best spots from which to shoot the public parts of the ceremony" (Dilworth 1996, 71). Apparently, this led to some adjustments by the performing Hopis, such as avoiding the cameras when drinking an emetic at the end of the ceremony (Dilworth 1996, 71). Eventually, the Hopi started to charge a fee for bringing a camera; in the 1920s, sketching and taking pictures at the ceremonies were forbidden.[35] Some decades later, the Snake Dances were closed to visitors altogether (Dilworth 1996, 22, 72). After being opened and mediated in the form of a monetary transaction, the event was subsequently sealed off first from the reproductive gaze and then from the tourist presence altogether. It thereby regained the status of an insider event and resumed cultural privacy.

Concurrently, however, the Smokis, "a virtual tribe" (Howes 1996, 141) made up by Arizona businessmen and professionals in the early 1920s, created a mimicry version of the Snake Dance. Painting their bodies in red and putting on Hopi ceremonial dress, they performed their simulacrum since 1921 every year in Prescott (Arizona). What probably started "as a racist parody" (Howes 1996, 141) eventually took on more ambivalent modes to the point where this dance "came to be taken seriously by its perpetrators" (Howes 1996, 142).[36] In 1991, however, "the Hopi Chairman Vernon Masayesva called for an end to this sacrilege. The Smokis' White leader, known only as 'Chief Ponytail,' ceased the imitation snake dance following the Hopi protest" (French 2003, 36). Not only public photographic representation, viewing and participation, but also acts of performative mimicry we de-appropriated.

Holidays and festivals

We have seen some examples (and many more could be added) that dances and dancing often occurs as part of larger ceremonial structures such as holidays, seasonal celebrations, feasts and festivals. In tourism contexts, dances may gain in prominence in their overall structure, and holidays and festivals may turn into events featuring the display of dances. The lines of demarcation between pilgrimages and festivals are often blurred. Festivals can be part of pilgrimages, the celebrations are often the "pull factor" putting pilgrims on the track; alternatively, traveling to festivals may be framed as "pilgrimages".

Holidays and festivals are here defined as cyclically recurrent public (religious) events typically involving several interconnected celebrations, displays and performances such as rites, rituals, meals, processions and fairs. In tourism contexts, some elements are often lifted out of these complex structures. Holidays, for example, tend to be listed in tourism materials because of the special foodstuffs prepared for them, or like Ramadan may be considered noteworthy because of the nightly activities and bustling night markets (Henderson 2008, 141–42).

Festivals are routinely put on tourist itineraries (Kirshenblatt-Gimblett 1998, 59). Their dates, occasions and presumed "content" are usually listed in tourism-related information resources such as the sites set up by tourism agencies and bureaus on the internet.[37] Of course, not all of the festivals listed in such places actually attract tourists. However, feasts and festivals traditionally celebrated at what now are peak times of the tourist schedule are particularly affected by the interface with tourism. Off-season festivals may be less exposed, unless they themselves become an attraction. Sometimes companies time their tours to match a festival event (Shackley 2001, 53). When festivals are recurring at very large intervals, these intervals can be shortened for tourist purposes. This is, at any rate, what has happened among the Dogon, where shortened versions of some festivals "have been developed for tourism, for which the visitor pays both in cash and in kind, by providing beer for the troupe" (Shackley 2001, 53).

Given the attractiveness of festivals for tourism, "festivals of all kinds have proliferated with the explicit intention of encouraging tourism" all around the world (Kirshenblatt-Gimblett 1998, 61). Apart from promoting extant festivals, new festivals are designed,[38] often in order to attract tourists.[39] Most of these new creations are not explicitly religious events, but they can appeal to religious traditions. For Thailand, Erik Cohen has observed that:

> [M]any touristically marginal communities have in recent years invented new festivals in order to gain a place on the "tourist map". In many of these new festivals secular themes prevail, though they may be tenuously related to Buddhism.
>
> (Cohen 2004b, 155)

Attention to tourist demand has led to tapping the Buddhist heritage as cultural capital for further performative investments. Sometimes, religion is more directly tapped into the creation of special festival events. In Macau, for example, in 2001 the "government organized a Mazu festival to promote tourism" (Liu 2003, 391). This was held at the site on Macau's Coloane Island, where a large (20 meter) marble statue of the goddess Mazu had been erected in 1998, as a duplicate of one on the mainland. For the event, performers were brought from Fujian and pilgrims from Taiwan also participated.

As we shall see, the exposure of traditional holidays and festivals invariably leads to changes. Let us begin our discussion by looking at an example from one relatively small-scale case from Central America, which picks up the thread from our previous discussion of dances. Around the change of the year the Boruca, an indigenous people living in (south-west) Costa Rica with reportedly some 2,000 members,[40] celebrate a festival known as Fiesta de los Diablitos. This festival annually recalls and performs the fight between the Spanish, represented by a bull and the Boruca, or the little devils (Diablitos). The festival lasts for three days, from 30 December to 2 January, but at some places it is held a month later. The timing of the event and some of its elements such as the robbing of food especially prepared for the occasion give it the appearance of an ancestral festival. In recent times, apparently in tune with the exposure of the festival to tourism, the dances, previously the end-point of a sequence of actions involving music (partly with drums made of skins) and spatial dislocations, have become its main focus. Accordingly, the event is now often referred to as Danca de los Diablitos. The dancers wear a kind of sack clothing made from the leaves of a specific tree as well as masks. The festival-cum-dance is listed in all major tourism events calendars for Costa Rica (but also on a global scale). The tourism exposure of the event has resulted in several changes: the dances are now performed during all three days of the festival rather than on the last day only, some performers stopped wearing the sack-like clothing, and more and more masks are being painted with acryl. The masks are now also produced and marketed as handicraft and souvenirs and can even be ordered online.[41] The dances are nowadays also performed on request throughout the year by school children.[42]

In Bhutan, two festivals that involve mask dances "account for 50% of all arrivals".[43] This has called the government into action, and the Department of Tourism is now "actively involved in the management" of these festivals.[44]

Bank holidays present good opportunities and occasions for travel. Consider the large number of non-resident-Indians traveling to India during the Christmas and New Year season. For some holidays and festivals such as Thanksgiving in the United States or Christmas in Europe, North America and Australia (where it also coincides with the summer holidays) many people, especially from the younger generations, travel to join their families or friends. This is an important factor for domestic, but to some extent also within international tourism.[45]

Bank holidays at home may coincide with celebrations at the destination,[46] and in some cases the celebration of the festival at a particular destination is in itself an important attraction. A well-known example is Easter in Rome, which has almost become a "brand" in its own right. According to reports from German media, in 2006 about half a million pilgrims and tourists, most of them from the United States, spent Easter in that city.[47] Probably only a portion of this number intends to witness any of the public performances traditionally held by the Pope in various locations during the celebration of that festival, such as the Way of the Cross procession in the Colosseum, one of the main tourism attractions of the city, on Good Friday. The mass celebrated in St. Peter's Square on Easter Sunday has in the age of television turned into a global media event – and does its share to broadcast the Easter-in-Rome tradition around the world.

While the Catholic Easter celebrations are an additional attraction to the prime destination of Rome and Christmas shopping is a major stimulus for short-term trips, the city of Turku (Åbo in Swedish) on the south-west coast of Finland with a population of some 175,000 declared itself the City of Christmas Peace in 1996. As Tuomas Martikainen explains, "[t]he background for that project was an interest to improve the image of the city, to increase tourism in the winter period and, thus, to bring money into the local economy" (Martikainen 2008, 139). Apart from the incoming dimension, of course, the project also, if not mainly, targeted the local inhabitants (Martikainen 2008, 139) and their image of their city and the holiday.

Another kind of coincidence of tourism season and religious celebration can be observed in various parts of the Spanish speaking Catholic world, especially in Andalusia. The spectacular processions held during Holy Week are part of the holiday program of many tourists, even if they did not come to Andalusia in order to attend them; many take advantage of the occasion to gaze at – and in the gazing manner participate in – the unfolding spectacle. The processions are described in guidebooks and other travel literature while tourism agencies point to them in order to promote their landscapes as having more to offer than sun, beaches and food.

The Oberammergau Passion plays, which since 1633 have taken place every ten years, are an international tourism highlight. More than half of the participants in that event, which is of major economic importance for the village and its surroundings, are from the United States and Britain (47 and 23 percent respectively) (Steinecke 2006, 140).

A massive tourist participation at festivals leads to social, ecological and economic pressures similar to those observed at religious sites (see Chapter 4; pp. 89 ff.). Such effects include noise, litter, congestion, etc. as well as overcrowding and massification, with the local residents in some cases becoming the minority of congregants. In some cases, over 80 percent of the festival audience is made up by tourists.[48] Demands of changing the timing of the performance and giving privileged seating to tourists are not uncommon. These changes are often made in order to generate more revenues, and the effects not only change the ceremonial sequence but may also disrupt social hierarchies and give rise to questions of power and control.

In extant scholarship, festivals are therefore often presented as a prime example (alongside dances) of the presumed disruptive and authenticity-annihilating effects of tourism. It is argued that from being a "display" or a "practice" they are transformed (i.e. commodified) into a "product" which is being packaged and marketed in order to be sold and meet the demands and needs of the tourists (Hall 1994, 176; Robinson 2001, 43). Mike Robinson, head of the Centre for Tourism and Cultural Change (now at Leeds Metropolitan University), has observed that "[r]eligious rites, festivals, and ethnic traditions are often reduced and shaped to meet tourist expectations to the point where the host culture loses the deeper meaning and social function of such practices" (Robinson 2001, 43). Sometimes, one may add, the organizers of festivals, especially governments that have no interest in publicizing religion, may consciously downplay religious elements.[49] Nevertheless, statements such as the one by Robinson, imbued with rhetoric of nostalgia, need to be qualified. To begin with, one wonders whether there ever was a well-defined, fixed meaning of such festivals at all; one can surmise that such "deeper" (= religious or otherwise?) meanings were disputed or negotiated and were far from unchanging even in the pre-tourist era. Moreover, apart from suffering a "loss" of meaning, festivals may at the same time acquire new meanings.[50] Similarly, while they may lose their pre-tourist social functions they may gain new ones in the interface with tourism. These new meanings and functions may involve issues of nationhood, politics, ethnic relations and cultural identity, as social anthropologist Leo Howe has shown with regard to Bali.[51]

One has to be careful not to present the developments described by Robinson as if they were universal and unavoidable. On the one hand, there are cases that "would seem to suggest that internal value systems are sufficiently resilient to cope with and confront tourism in the subtle or blatant emblems embodied in cultural displays" (Bendix 1989, 144). On the other hand, the line of conflict is often not between tourists and locals, but between various fractions of "insiders" or locals. Tourism and tourists may be an argument used in other discursive contestations. In a case study of the feast of Holy Week in León (Spain), Mark Tate has vividly illustrated how locals often, among themselves, disagree on vital matters including the question whether the festival in question is to be classified as "folklore" or "religion" (Tate 2004).

By their very nature, feasts and festivals are complex events that attract and cater to different types of audiences. Festivals require and allow for various modes of participation. Therefore, as Michael Roemer (2006) has shown for the Gion festival in Kyoto (one of Japan's largest festival events), in festivals religious elements may be simultaneously explicit and implicit, visible and invisible. The elaborate artifacts, dances, parades and other forms of entertainment attract the tourists but are at the same time, even by many tourists, held to please the *kami*. Even the crowd-pleasing acts have a sometimes more and sometimes less acknowledged religious significance. It seems impossible to say that the festival is either a secular or a religious event. The "mix of divine rituals and fun entertainment" (Roemer 2006, 214) is probably not only typical for Japan, but can be found at many festivals the world over. Contrary to Roemer, I would not speak of a "dualistic structure" (Roemer 2006, 215) but rather of a selective simultaneity of religious and other elements in such events.

The Gion festival in Kyoto was one of the attractions that the modernizing project of the Meji era had opened "to lure Western visitors and boast of its rich cultural history" (Roemer 2006, 198). Many European festivals had tourists among their audiences and participants already since the beginnings of modern tourism. In other settings, however, especially in the Global South, the exposure to tourism has happened more rapidly, which has potentially more disruptive consequences. Many politicians, public administrators or religious leaders – persons in power – actively seek to make money or to create new economic opportunities by opening festivals to tourism. In some cases, the participation of tourists is encouraged in the hope of promoting the principles of the respective religion to the tourist audience[52] or to obtain other benefits. It is not quite clear whether the economic and religious rewards always outnumber the cultural and social costs, but the outcome is not necessarily negative.

Money earned by tourist participation at festivals may be reinvested in these very events. Available extra funds can be used "to add adornment and splendor" or to "encourage spectacularity, extravagance, and exoticism".[53] While such changes may well put authenticity-seekers off, for many locals committed to the festivals this appears like a natural and desired option and actually enhances the quality of their experiences (or at least in part makes up for the intrusion of the tourists).

Some festival traditions cope better with tourists than others. Factors such as the speed of the transition to tourist participation and the size and number of the local community will influence that balance sheet. In any case, the assumption that tourism automatically has a disastrous impact on festivals is not confirmed by available studies. Anthropologist Jeremy Boissevain's long-running research on religious festivals in Malta, for instance, has concluded that while tourism indeed "does affect popular celebrations" its "role is neither as crude nor as spectacular as the critics of cultural commoditization have suggested" (Boissevain 1996a, 114). While the occurrence of commoditization as part of selling the island to tourists cannot be doubted, this process has not destroyed the festivals but rather it has "imbued them with new meaning" (Boissevain 1996a, 116). To some extent, and by some actors, commoditization is even encouraged because tourists increase the audience and can be used as markers in the competition between different groups of actors in order to increase their respective prestige (Boissevain 1996a, 117). The genuine interest shown by some tourists in these festivals even contributed to making them "more acceptable to the urbanized middle-class who previously denigrated many parochial pageants" (Boissevain 1996a, 115).

One way to cope with the touristification of festivals is to create what Boissevain terms "insider events" (Boissevain 1996b, 16). These are public events celebrated either during the off-season, before tourists arrive, or after they have left.[54] Engaging a terminology by Ervin Goffman (already applied by MacCannell for the study of tourism), such additional discrete insider events can be called "back-stage" festivals. Presumably these alternative events have adopted some of the social functions previously fulfilled by the touristified festivals. Or they display forms of behavior that are deemed inappropriate for the tourist showcases. In some cases (documented for the Italian Val di Fassa village of Penia), all outsiders (and not only tourists) are now physically barred from the festivals (Boissevain 1996b, 18).

Sometimes traditional festivals are embedded in staged festivals, resulting in different intertwined frames. Here are two examples. In Cusco (Peru), the Day of the Indian (later renamed as Cusco Day), a celebration of the Indian identity claimed by many as part of local and regional culture, is annually held since 1944. More recently, apparently to support Cusco's tourism appeal, a theatrical rendition of the former Incan Festival of the Sun (*Inti Raymi*) became part of the Cusco Day program, and the state agency in charge of tourism promotion has even staged other Andean religious rituals as part of special events (Hill 2007, 449–50). Another staged meta-framework is The Smithsonian Folklife Festival (previously known as Festival of American Folklife), reportedly the largest annual cultural gathering in the United States, which was launched in 1967 and is held annually for two weeks around the Fourth of July (the US Independence Day) on the National Mall in Washington, D.C. With over one million visitors, this festival is a major tourist event. The festival, which usually features several nations, states, regions or themes, displays living cultural heritage in an educational and participatory manner. With the exception of a program on "Sacred Sounds: belief and society" (1997), religion has so far not explicitly featured on the list of programs, but religious practices and objects are parts of several programs and exhibits. For example, in addition to prayer flags and other religious objects, the Bhutan program from 2008 even displayed a temple erected for the occasion. The 1989 program on Hawaii included religious performances, where "visitors were invited to participate by praying or drinking, and thus were recruited to be supporting actors reifying and sacralizing re-contextualized performance" (Diamond 2008, 152). In 1985, the festival mimetically embedded an Indian *mela*, where (among many other things) religious objects were prepared and religious practices were performed and at the same time educational materials on Indian religions displayed (Kirshenblatt-Gimblett 1998, 66–69).

CASE-STUDY: THE ROUSING DRUM

Some of the issues addressed in the present discussion on festivals and religion can be exemplified by a Shinto shrine festival (*matsuri*) in the small provincial town of Furukawa studied by the American anthropologist Scott Schnell (1999). A *matsuri* comprises a series of celebratory events centring on the procession of a guardian deity, otherwise worshiped in a shrine, across the territory of the community protected by the deity; at the end of the celebration the deity is transferred back to the shrine.

The Furukawa *matsuri* is traditionally performed in April (19–21). It is a large-scale public event mobilizing the entire town. Formerly, the deity descended from its mountain shrine on special vehicles (*yatai*). By day, the tutelary deity is entertained by various solemn rituals. It moves across the territory on a portable shrine (*mikoshi*) pulled (formerly borne) by groups of attendants. Nowadays, the special vehicles (*yatai*) have been replaced by banners in the procession. At the same time when the procession marches through town, the vehicles with their intricate carvings and joinery are displayed and they are made to perform some of their mechanical tricks. At home, the women prepare and host lavish meals (involving the consumption of alcoholic beverages) attended by friends, relatives, business partners and other acquaintances. By night, from around 10pm to 2am, the *okoshi daiko*, a much wilder form of display takes place, involving a huge drum on a massive structure carried by 170 bearers and protected by guards against aggressive onslaughts of neighborhood teams that in their turn jointly carry large sticks with drums attached to them; the atmosphere of frenetic and somewhat dangerous revelry is animated by conspicuous consumption of alcohol (*sake*) and loud drumming, but is preceded by a formal religious service performed by a Shinto priest. The festival is concluded by the return of the deity (or its spirits) to its shrine to the accompaniment of music and dance.

Festivals are by no means static events celebrated in the same manner since time immemorial. The Furukawa *matsuri* likewise has an extended history. When the village became connected to transportation networks such as railroads and highways this made the festival accessible to non-local audiences. Tourism, however, is not the only, but certainly a major factor in the more recent developments of the festival and its context. As complex public events festivals serve many functions. The strategy of encouraging tourism as a means of economic development of peripheral regions led to marketing the *matsuri* as an economic resource. Accordingly, some structural elements of the festivals were adapted to suit the non-local spectators. Already in 1952, the starting time for the nightly *okoshi daiko* was moved from 1am to 10pm at the request of the Furukawa Chamber of Commerce in order to facilitate attendance by tourists. A series of other changes were also implemented that affected the flow and the structure of the event. The attacks performed by rival neighborhood teams during the nightly *okoshi daiko* came to be restricted to certain places. The structure on which the heavy drum is placed was furnished with wheels, thereby greatly easing the physical effort of the bearers. Acrobatics began to be performed atop the large sticks with the attached drums – and these acrobatic performances have turned into an attraction in their own right.

The number of tourists attending the festival has greatly increased since 1965. At roughly the same time parts of the event, namely the nightly *okoshi daiko*, and its related material culture, the *yatai* vehicles, were listed as cultural properties, culminating in the designation of both these elements as "important intangible cultural properties" by the Japanese government in 1980. The vehicles were replaced by banners in the actual processions in 1961, apparently because their safety and preservation as tourist attractions had become an important concern; the prime function of the *yatai* now seems to be that of cultural artifacts rather than as ceremonial implements. The popularity of the festival creates a sustained need for material implements such as the special lanterns and candles carried during the processions; apparently it is only the tourist sponsorship of the events that safeguards the continued local production of these items. Moreover, the popularity of the event has encouraged the transmission of the specific dances and music performed during the festival.

In 1969, the Japanese Broadcasting Corporation (NHK) filmed a documentary program on the festival involving the daytime staging of the nightly *okoshi daiko*. The limited duration of the festival restricts the advent of tourists to a very short period. In the meanwhile, however, several additional attractions have been built around the festival, including culture and handicraft centers and a museum (completed in 1992) with a special theater where a 3D film on the *matsuri* shot in 1991 by the Sony Corporation is shown at regular intervals; the museum also displays three ceremonial vehicles *(yatai)*. These new buildings and the rise of new hotels have changed the structure of the town into "an integrated tourist complex" (Schnell 1999, 273).

The popularity of the *matsuri* has brought obvious economic benefits to Furukawa. The exposure of the festival to tourism has sustained its vitality, and to the locals the high number of visitors seems to confirm the perception of the festival's uniqueness and nationwide importance. At the same time, there is some amount of unease about the packaging of the event and changes in the ecology of the town, which make it appear like a museum. Moreover, the increasing presence of tourists and the decreasing number of active local participants, a by-product of continued migration to larger cities, has led to some tensions and frictions between different interested parties. On the one hand, for local participants the huge number of spectators can interfere with the progress of the drum-procession and the unfolding of the fights during the nightly *okoshi daiko*. The aggression that is built up in the event therefore sometimes targets the automobiles of tourists. On the other hand, there has been some friction between the administrative personnel who regard it as their duty and in Furukawa's best interest to make the festival attractive to visitors and the shrine officers who insist on the religious qualities of the event which should not be compromised.

SOUVENIRS FROM CHAPTER 7

- Religious performances and events can serve as entertainment for tourists, sometimes resulting in the genesis of hybrid genres.
- Many tourists find it interesting to attend rituals in tourism contexts.
- Religious entertainment shows are developed at some destinations.
- The participation of tourists raises issues of respect, appropriate behavior and role-definition.
- Participation covers a wide range of possible roles and involvement; performances held for tourists often entail a heterogeneous blend of forms of religious communication.
- Tourist participation can give rise to the transfer of practices; performances originally devised for the entertainment of tourists can occasionally be appropriated into religious contexts.
- Some religious groups have tried to proselytize tourist audiences.
- In many cases, practitioners and other stakeholders draw upon classificatory schemes and techniques that distinguish tourist from religious performances; in some cases, tourism audiences have been effectively fenced off.
- Previously prevailing negative attitudes towards performances such as dances are reevaluated in tourism contexts leading to a renewed appreciation and changes in power structures.
- Exposure to tourism leads to various sorts and degrees of changes in performances, holidays and festivals; not all of these changes are considered negative by the stakeholders.
- Sometimes dances or other elements of ceremonies are lifted out of their previous contexts; in other cases, different kinds of performances are sampled together; sometimes they are transferred into meta-events.
- Apart from live performances, religious performances are mediated in various ways.
- Festivals are often sponsored in order to attract tourists and the presence of tourists is often appreciated by "locals".
- Tourist participation at festivals typically requires negotiations; this can lead to fractions and tensions, but also to the formation of new alliances between different interested parties.

Chapter 8

Mediations

While tourism, as pointed out in Chapter 6, is the main global arena for the encounter of people with different/other religious traditions, the interfaces of tourists with other religions are always mediated. As little as in other areas of human contact, in tourism there are no "pure" (= unmediated) encounters. "Others" are invariably situated on pre-existing mental maps. Images of the other, often amounting to stereotypes, are of primary importance for tourism, an industry to a considerable extent based on image making, since images often generate the desire to visit other places which are embedded in imaginary geographies (Hennig 1997, 95). In addition to being concerned with actual travel, tourism is therefore embedded in media industries.

Expectations of visits are created and mediated by various media including promotional materials such as brochures, posters, calendars, etc. The tourist gaze is prepared by an abundance of prior views and is reproduced ad infinitum in various media such as photography. In many, if not most, cases the tourist gaze amounts to reproductive recognition.

There are very few places that do not offer any information intelligible to tourists. Some sort of information is provided at most places regularly visited by tourists. Leaflets, pamphlets, brochures and other types of information aimed at visitors can nowadays be found even in relatively unimportant sites and at remote places. Audio tours are offered at many attractions. The information provided in these materials does not necessarily emphasize their religious dimension, but often highlights the artistic and historical features of the respective sites.

Alongside guards and attendants many places also have guides who operate as culture mediators. To some extent, they frame interactions by selecting what will be seen, by directing attention, providing explanations and by acting as role models. Guides are local mediators, while guidebooks are part of the global system of tourism communication; guidebooks rely on prior validation and anticipate posterior confirmation (or correction) (Grimshaw 2008, 23). Reading and gazing often go hand in hand, turning some forms of travels into veritable hermeneutical projects (Gregory 1999, 116).[1] In the past decade, the internet has opened new avenues for global tourism communication.

Towards the end of the chapter we will touch upon a more material trace of mediated encounters. A souvenir is at the same time local – it has to be purchased on the spot in order to function as souvenirs – and translocal, both because it is carried away from its place of purchase, and since souvenirs are often not produced at the place where they are sold and whose aura they are meant to capture.

Apart from the media of tourism communication briefly explored in this chapter, other could, and eventually should, be discussed. Let us here at least acknowledge their existence and point to the need of extending this line of inquiry. To begin with, self-produced ways of remembering travels such as diaries, or – more widespread and visual – watercolours, photographs, photo books and videos mediate the travel experiences of tourists. Apart from making memories, such mementos create (fragments of) narratives of identities for individuals and families, friends or even nations.[2]

Long before the actual travel, one becomes a virtual tourist, equipped with imaginations and expectations. For some icons of global tourism the secondary images, promulgated by pictures and in a seemingly endless cycle of representations (Jenkins 2003) continuously reproduced in photographs, videos, etc. long since overshadow the "original" sights; paradoxically, their infinite replication seems to cheapen them and to make them priceless at the same time. Yet virtually everybody seems to feel compelled to gaze at these sights in physical proximity (hence the metaphor "attraction").

There is an abundance of travel literature including popular magazines. Thomas Cook started the first travel magazine, later called *Cook's Excursionist*, which was used as "the firm's main publicity vehicle" (Hazbun 2007, 9). Travel columns are features of most newspapers. In addition, there are travelogues and publications including books that describe experiences of individual travelers.[3] These sometimes cover religious groups, sites, rituals and personalities. Travel literature plays a part in creating views, attitudes, expectations and emotions about traveling, attractions and destinations. Some genres of travel literature create "spaces of nostalgia" and utopian anticipations of renewal, often in contrast to everyday realities and sometimes linked to religious or spiritual tropes (Wemhöner 2004). However, the extant academic bibliography, as far as I can tell, only rarely takes the wide range of travel writings in non-Western languages into account.

Apart from directly tourism-related literary genres, fiction is an important medium for tourism because fiction often "themes" places and landscapes. Images of Prague, for example, are for many people coloured by the work of Franz Kafka. We have already encountered one example of such a process, namely the impact James Hilton's 1933 novel *Lost Horizon* on the mythologization of various landscapes (see Chapter 5; p. 125). For Branson/Missouri and the Ozarks (in the central United States), Aaron Ketchell has pointed to the effects of the bestselling novel *The Shepherd of the Hills* (1907; film starring John Wayne in 1941) by Harold Bell Wright (1872–1944). According to Ketchell, "Wright clothed Branson, its surroundings, and its residents in a spiritualized aura and connected this portion of the Ozarks with religious sentiments that still drive the tourism market" (Ketchell 2007, 25). There are also other, more contemporary, examples. James Redfield's bestselling novel *The Celestine Prophecy* (1993) may well have stimulated New Age-inspired tourism in the Peruvian Andes.[4] Another global bestseller, Dan Brown's *The Da Vinci Code* (2003) has brought many tourists to the pilgrimage center of Les Saintes-Maries-de-la Mer in the Camargue (southern France) (Badone 2008, 35–36), but it has also attracted regular tourists to specific places mentioned in the novel such as St. Sulpice Church in Paris. Currently several *Da Vinci*-walking tours are on offer, not only in Paris but also in London and other cities.[5]

While books such as these colour the perception of destinations, literature also reflects on travelers, traveling and tourism. The novel *Paradise News* (1991; translated in various languages) by the British author David Lodge is a well-known example. *Paradise News* portrays the experiences of different sorts of travelers (with a laicized Catholic priest as the main character) to Hawaii. The novel reflects on the metaphor and mythology of paradise that theme Hawaii as a destination and contrasts it with the experiences of people who came to live in Hawaii. One of its characters is an anthropologist of tourism whose theory clearly reflects academic work in that field, also with regard to religion[6] – fiction here popularizes academic scholarship on tourism.

Tourism managers may consciously develop the effects of fiction on the imagery of places, thereby turning them into sights and destinations. Another management strategy is to create media attention in the first place. From its earliest stages, the developing tourism industries hired visual artists, photographers and journalists to publicize their products (Shaffer 2001, 81–86). Television is another influential medium for travel and tourism. Apart from travel programs in ordinary channels, there are now many specialized holiday and travel television channels in all major languages. Many travel programs are also available as DVDs. I am not aware of any studies on such programs and their presentation of religion(s), and it would be audacious to come up even with the most preliminary generalizations at this point. So, let's turn to the guides.

Guides[7]

There have always been guides accompanying travelers. The tour managers-cum-tutors, known as governors or bear leaders, who accompanied the young aristocrats on the Grand Tour during the 17th and 18th centuries have been regarded as harbingers of the modern tourist guides. Erik Cohen points to the roles of the pathfinder, who helps people to find their way in unknown geographical territories, and the mentor, a spiritual advisor or leader, as the precursors of the roles played by the tourist guides (Cohen 1985).

There are professional and non-professional guides – the latter category often comprises volunteers or part-time guides such as local students or other marginal natives and academics who act as tour leaders. In the course of the development of tourism in given areas, "original guides" are often replaced by professional ones (Cohen 1985, 16–22). In the context of the widescale development of tourism during the past decades, being a tourist guide has become a more widespread occupation and in many countries working as a guide is among the more attractive economic employment opportunities provided by tourism (besides managers, watchmen, waiters, trackers, drivers, maintenance and construction works, kitchen personnel, etc.). Sometimes one and the same person adopts different but overlapping roles: one may act as porter, guide, souvenir salesperson and souvenir contractor at the same time. Even where they do not sell souvenirs, guides often direct their customers to souvenir shops.

The increasing number and professionalization of tour guides and leaders resulted in the formation of national and subsequently also professional organizations. In 1986, for example, a European Federation of Tourist Guides Association (FEG) was founded (see www.feg-touristguides.com) and one year later, in 1987, a World Federation of Tourist Guide Associations (www.wftga.org).

However, there are different types of tourist guides. According to one mainstream definition, quoted on Wikipedia, a tourist guide is a "person who guides visitors in the language of their choice and interprets the cultural and natural heritage of an area, which person normally possesses an area-specific qualification usually issued and/or recognized by the appropriate authority",[8] whatever such an authority might be. Apart from being qualified and approved, which seems to require some sort of education or training, this definition highlights the linguistic mediation and the interpretation of heritage monuments, a category that often includes religious structures.

The tourist guide may be a local guide, i.e. a native or resident of the respective are or an outsider. In some countries one needs to have a license to act as a guide and only licensed guides are allowed to show visitors around at certain places. Other countries do not impose such rules.

Yet another category of guides is the tour manager, a "person who manages and supervises the itinerary on behalf of the tour operator, ensuring the program is carried out as described in the tour operator's literature and sold to the traveler/consumer and who gives local practical information".[9] The tour manager may or may not actually take the group to any sites. This task is similar and to some extent overlaps with that of a tour leader who stays with a group during a given period. While the task of the (local) tourist guide pertains to specific local attractions, the task of the tour manager or group leader refers to the respective group on the one hand and to the respective destinations on the other, where the destination, which are often regions or countries, encompasses several attractions. While the tourist guide provides access to, information about, and interpretation of specific attractions (such as religious buildings), the tour leader/manager gives leadership to the group, a process which involves issues such as animation, control, integration, moral and organization (Cohen 1985, 11–16). The role of the tour leader/manager is a challenging and complex one which involves several tasks and levels of mediation, and there are quite different kind of groups and tours which each require different solutions. Apart from attractions and destinations, events provide another category that often necessities specific guidance requirements. In theme parks and other tourism settings, there are also animators.

Given all these tasks, tourist guides and tour leaders play important roles in mediating and negotiating cross-religious encounters. Extant research seems to vaguely indicate that many groups opt for guides who share their own religious preferences (Olsen and Timothy 2006, 10) and structure the trips according to their own needs and expectations.[10]

Cook's Eastern Tours used handpicked native guides as part of its service package on its trips to the Holy Land. The tour leaders were eager to provide biblical illustrations for all sorts of places visited (Shepherd 1987, 180–81).[11] Apparently the tour leaders partly acted as lecturers and partly as preachers. This was perceived as appealing for tourists "seeking a spiritual experience with the Holy Land" (Messenger 1999, 104).

Guides may transmit or contribute to constructing mythologies surrounding landscapes, cities and places. The information shared by them originates from various sources including folklore, hearsay, other guides, training provided by schools, universities, specialist agencies or their employers, brochures, guidebooks, magazines, the internet and occasionally even from anthropology or religious studies literature.[12] A study of English cathedrals from 1977 revealed, much to the dismay of the church, that not all guides were found to give correct information; many were also criticized for disturbing religious services or for their "bad manners" (Hanna, Marris and Lefley 1979, 64). A relatively early study of the Khajuraho temples in India mentioned the "fanciful or belligerently chauvinistic interpretations" made by some guides (Ichaporia 1983, 84). While some guides are seen and present themselves as "scholars", other try to capture the attention of visitors by playing the roles of animators or entertainers (Ichaporia 1983, 84).

At large tourist attractions, many guides are professionals. At smaller churches, local parishioners volunteer as guides, who may or may not get formal training. In Germany, churches offer weekend training seminars for church guides. A recent German evaluation report points to contrasting attitudes between tourism agencies and the churches: whereas the church representatives regard it as a main aim of guided tours that participants become familiar with the symbolism of the building in order to be brought closer to the Christian faith, the majority of representatives from the tourism branch felt that matters of faith should be avoided during guided tours. When evaluating the performance of the guides, it seems that their charisma and their ability to give a vivid presentation were considered to be of prime importance (Hoburg 2007).

At religious sites, especially in monasteries, guides are often from the religious personnel of the respective institutions.[13] Even where that is not the case, guides based at religious sites are often perceived as ambassadors, representatives or embodied representations of the religious place and group in question. Some local guides engage a religious way of speaking, which is not appreciated by all travelers.[14]

At sites belonging to less well-known religions such as ethnic and new religions, "native" guides may perform the task of presenting basic understanding and creating sympathy for these unfamiliar religions. On the other hand, we have already encountered one case – the Baha'i gardens at Haifa – where the guides belong to other religions. These non-Baha'i guides do provide a basic sketch of the Baha'i religion, but in general they tend to downplay the religious character of the site (Gatrell and Collins-Kreiner 2006, 774; Collins-Kreiner and Gatrell 2006, 43).

In contrast to tourist guides working at given attractions, tour leaders spend more time with the groups in their charge, which may give them more ample opportunities to introduce "their" groups to the religious traditions they encounter at the destination. They often also prepare "their" groups for visits to religious sites or events, for example by giving background information and by practical advice on issues such as appropriate behavior and dress or how and when to take part in religious rituals. Apart from formal instruction, tour leaders often educate in informal settings such as over dinner.

Attempts at eliciting respect or encouraging understanding may sometimes be (mis)understood as inappropriate role-switching on behalf of the guide, who can be criticized for being overly sympathetic with respective to the other, especially when that other is Islam(ic). The boundary role of the tour leader can also feature prominently in cases where the tour leader has to mediate between the local guides and the tourist group. However, individual guides and tour leaders have very different approaches, education, personalities and personal relationships to the places and religions visited.

In some cases, the information provided by indigenous guides is advertised as part of trips. Participants at a half-day tour ("Kèköldi and the Cacao goddess!") to the Kèköldi Indigenous Reserve in Costa Rica are promised: "Your guide will tell you interesting mythological stories from the Bribri culture and the special connection of the people with the nature that surrounds them."[15]

The activity of the guides is often linked to other educational displays such as museums. Apart from educating about religions, guides can sometimes adopt religious or spiritual tasks. The role of the tourist guide is then conflated with that of the mentor (which in fact is one of its antecedents), the spiritual guide to the inner self or to other worlds. At Machu Picchu, for example, local shamans operate as "spiritual guides" to the New Age "pilgrims" (Arellano 2007, 91), resulting in a complex set of glocalized hybrid identities including "aboriginal", "indigenous", "shamanic" and "New Age" elements. Especially among tour operators belonging to "alternative religious" scenes, the tour guides, who likely also act as the tour operators in small-scale agencies, tend to assume the roles of religious guides; in these cases, the charisma or achievements (as healer or otherwise) of the guide/operator are as much of an asset as the places visited.[16]

In tours arranged by religious organizations or by operators with close ties to such institutions, it can be seen as an asset if religious specialists such as priests or pastors accompany or guide the group. Established religions have realized the educational, inspirational or even apologetic potentials of the role of the tourist guide. According to news in the press, Korea's largest Buddhist order found that foreign visitors to Korean Buddhist temples often fail to provide insights into Korean Buddhism. According to a write-up, Buddhist monks "are becoming involved in enhancing Korean tourism by acting as tour guides, assisting in meditation, serving tea and simply talking about Buddhism in English".[17] Visitors from Japan seem to be the main target group.

Guidebooks

Knowledge about destinations and sites is also transmitted by guidebooks; travel guides and guidebooks can be complementary, but the guidebook can also be considered as a replacement for the actual guides.[18]

Travel guidebooks have developed concurrently with the growth of the modern tourism industry. The first specimen of the famous series by Murray and Baedeker, generally regarded as the prototypes of the modern guidebooks, were published in 1836 and 1839 respectively. Thomas Cook also produced his own travel guides.

To some extent, medieval Pilgrim's Guides are precursors of the modern tourist guidebooks. Even the mediaeval Pilgrim's Guides such as the 12th-century *Liber Sancti Jacobi* (Book of St. James) contained practical advice such as descriptions of stages of the route, hostels, river crossings, places to visit on route, tolls and alerts on avaricious innkeepers. Also during the age of the Grand Tour a vast amount of travel literature was published that combined practical information and personal recollections.[19]

By providing practical information about the travel and the destinations, guidebooks were, and still are, an important medium for creating an awareness of the developing practice of tourism and for creating a conscious attitude among travelers. Guidebooks "provide a security of evidence ... not only of what is encountered, but more so that it 'will' be encountered" (Grimshaw 2008, 24). In their claim to authority, guidebooks are often compared to the bible – and this charisma is sometimes reinforced by their very format; in an interesting material homology, from 1872 Baedeker started to print its guidebooks on the same extra-thin paper used to print bibles (Grimshaw 2008, 21).

Guidebooks are normally handy and often illustrated volumes which are meant to be consulted before, during and after the trip, but they are rarely read cover to cover. Selecting and taking along a guidebook therefore is one way of framing travel as a tourist trip in the first place, whether the book is actually used or not. There are different types of guidebooks, and guidebooks have various functions such as signposting routes, helping to organize the trip, interpret the destination and animate the travelers. Moreover, guidebooks combine maps, illustrations, sketches and text; they conflate different genres such as the directory, the atlas, specialized books and travel narrative (Steinecke 1994), where the individual voices of the authors are usually not featured individually.

Guidebooks put places on the mental map of travelers and re-present them as tourist destinations. They mediate between the tourists and the places they visit. They create patterns of perception and expectations among tourists (Fendl and Löffler 1993). Just as souvenirs, guidebooks are instrumental in creating destinations. In the emerging tourism industries, the development of guidebooks was often part of conscious marketing strategies seeking to establish places on the tourist itinerary. To take one example, when Northern Pacific tried to promote Yellowstone, the Wonderland guidebook series created a very special imagery of the place: "Metaphors linking Yellowstone's geothermal wonders and natural spectacles to Greek, Christian, and pagan mythology reinforced this landscape of otherness" (Shaffer 2001, 50).

Many guidebooks include sections on the culture of the regions and countries.[20] For countries such as Egypt, India and Thailand this often also includes short descriptions of the past and present religions in these respective countries.[21] Information on religion is often situated next to information on arts, architecture, food, transportation, tariffs, accommodation and much more. In guidebooks to countries such as Egypt and Thailand, but also Italy, elements of religions are almost omnipresent both with regard to text and images. Many guidebooks feature religious motifs on their covers.

Many guidebooks tend to sweep away boundaries between "high" and "low" culture and, like brochures, they literally open up the destination to tourist consumption; they provide a sense of expectation of access. Religious places may also be included in guidebooks in order to create a "local coloring" of the destination, while tourists may actually not visit these places.[22] On the other hand, guidebooks often actively exhort their readers to visit religious sites. By providing information on opening hours, entrance fees (if any) and suggestions about best views and times to visit, the guidebooks facilitate such visits. Guidebooks also routinely list feasts and festivals or other religious events.

I think it is difficult to dismiss the hypothesis that guidebooks are – possibly with the exception of school books – one of the genres of literature in which most people obtain information about religions other than their own and maybe also about aspects of their own religion (for instance with regard to its artistic heritage, history and spatial variety). Many guidebooks feature religion prominently and/or contain vast amounts of information on religions.

Apart from being produced by commercial publishers, guidebooks are often prepared by the owners of religious tourism attractions. Many parishes, for example, produce small and relatively inexpensive guidebooks about their churches. A study of English parish churches from 1983 estimates that over 70 percent of the parish churches had a guidebook; "there must be well over a million copies of church guidebooks being distributed by churches every year" (Hanna 1984, 36) – and this figure does not cover the large cathedrals. Over the decades these guidebooks have increasingly become professionally produced and illustrated. There now are guidebooks for special groups such as children, families or for people interested in brass (Hanna 1984, 36). Guidebooks are not only purchased to get actual information on the places during a visit, but also as souvenirs – especially the glossy ones with many pictures (Hanna, Marris and Lefley 1979, 14). The sale of guidebooks is also a source of revenue. Most churches have a small bookstall, and many larger ones even have a bookshop attached to them.

The Norwegian scholar of religion(s) Siv-Ellen Kraft has recently published an analysis of the representations of religions, philosophies and spiritualities in the *Lonely Planet India* (11 editions since the first one published in 1981), where, as she points out, religious motifs are much more present than in the *Lonely Planet* guidebook on California (although Californians are statistically very religious people). Kraft discusses the voices of authors and the construction of authority in the *Lonely Planet India* as well as the introductory sections on the different religions presented and the visual materials on the different religions. She notes, for example, that Hindus and Muslims are usually portrayed as crowds, whereas Buddhism (consistently classified as a philosophy and not as a religion) is illustrated with pictures of individuals or small groups of people. Many pictures show Indians engaged in performing rituals. Kraft finds that "Indian religions are described as exotic, colourful and extremely different, and for these reasons interesting and entertaining. But they are not offered as truths to be taken seriously by travelers" (Kraft 2007, 234). The religions are presented as timeless entities and are detached from their contexts.

At the same time, Kraft argues, there is a second storyline to the *Lonely Planet India* (which, from a cursory look at guidebooks to other countries, may well be a peculiar trait for travels to India). This is the unbounded spirituality of the (ideal) mature and independent traveler contrasted to the static religions of the somewhat childish locals. According to Kraft, *Lonely Planet India* repeatedly invites the (ideal) reader to "dip into" or "check out" the "spirituality" (rather than the religion) at places such as Rishikesh or McLeod Ganj (Kraft 2007, 238). The guidebook thereby reflects developments in and meets expectations among their Western readership. *Lonely Planet India* operates with a parallel dichotomy (Kraft 2007, 239):

Spirituality (+) // religion (-)
Traveling (+) // tourism (-)

Whereas religion is part of a given (compulsory) identity (of the locals), spirituality is characterized by choice and quest of the mature traveler (Kraft 2007, 237). While not in itself offering spiritual guidance, the guidebook shows paths where one may find it. According to Kraft, *Lonely Planet India* "promotes the individuality of the traveler as a spiritual goal" (Kraft 2007, 241).

In the chapter on Varanasi, *Lonely Planet India* exhorts its readers to walk the steps (ghats) to the Ganges at dawn for a "unique, world-class 'people-watching'" (and religion-watching!) experience.[23] This seems to be a recurrent topic in the guidebooks, for all the seven German and English guidebooks to India published between 1907 and 1998 that I have looked at invariably suggest an itinerary of religious sites of the city. European travelers are thereby actively encouraged to visit Hindu and Muslim religious places. Apart from occasional comments on unpleasant smells the descriptions refrain from religious value judgments.

The Danish tourist researchers Anette Therkelsen and Anders Sørensen have warned that guidebooks should not be naively read as scripts. Content analysis of guidebooks should not obscure the facts that different tourists may have very different experiences even when using the same guidebook, that "tourists do not blindly reproduce what they read" and that most tourists actively "seek out additional information about destinations, attractions, accommodation, etc." (Therkelsen and Sørensen 2005, 58). This may also hold for tourists' perception of religious places, events and people, but again all this is not yet studied.

While the travel guides to India and other non-Western countries have characteristically been written by Westerners, other guidebooks are produced locally and written by locals. Different guidebooks to the same places may well point to struggles over public representation. Therefore, they can be analyzed "as a vibrant form of public discourse", for instance with regard to "what is to be seen and what is to be ignored" (Gencarella 2007, 272) with regard to religion in a place. Obviously, this involves various (often conflicting) interests and values. Far from only serving the needs of tourists, guidebooks may likewise be of importance for the residents' perceptions of their own place, including its religious scenery (Jacobs 2001, 315).

In addition to general guidebooks from the well-known national and international series (Lonely Planet, Baedeker, Guides Bleus, etc.) there are special guidebooks catering to special areas of interest. Guidebooks to cemeteries, which also served as powerful tourism attractions, have a very long tradition going back to the 19th century (Seaton 2002). Since the 1950s, several guidebooks have been published "for Jewish travelers wishing to visit various parts of the United States. These books cater mostly to secular or moderate Jewish travelers, many of whom make a point of visiting Jewish sites during their vacation" (Ioannides and Cohen Ioannides 2002, 21). Most of them list synagogues, Jewish shops, hotels and places where to find kosher food (Ioannides and Cohen Ioannides 2002, 21).

The recent segmentation of the tourism branch in general and accordingly of the guidebook market in particular have in turn led to the emergence of specialized guidebooks. For Berlin, to take just one example, a study from 1989 could already point to guidebooks on churches of Berlin, Jewish parts of Berlin and a guide to "occult Berlin" (Lauterbach 1989, 215). The New Age scene is also very productive in producing guidebooks (Attix 2002, 54), and there are specific guidebooks (and directories) for resorts, retreats, workshops and spas. In the context of the burgeoning Christian travel market, travel guides addressing Christian tourists have recently been published. The international media and publishing house Zondervan, a founding member of the Evangelical Christian Publishers Association, has in 2001 launched a series of Christian travel guides. Irving Hexham, a Religious Studies professor at the University of Calgary, has written several of these volumes and supervised the production of several others. The volumes are to be read as supplements to standard guidebooks.

There are also guidebooks to pilgrimage sites. Suzanne Kaufman has argued that early guidebooks to the emerging pilgrimage town of Lourdes were imitations of guidebooks to secular travel destinations (Kaufman 2005, 27). They likewise functioned as promotional materials and helped people of limited means and with limited time to arrange their trips by suggesting accommodations, restaurants and other services as well as by suggesting a schedule for people who only had two days so that they would not miss out on anything important that the town had to offer (Kaufman 2005, 33–36). Many guidebooks presented and advertised Lourdes as an opulent tourist town, promising "an enticing tourist adventure for pilgrims" (Kaufman 2005, 34), who were encouraged "to behave like savvy tourists, providing expert advice on how to make the most of short days" (Kaufman 2005, 35).

The internet

Many publishers of guidebooks have developed a strong web presence and their websites combine downloads and shops with travel magazines, community and travel services. At present, the internet has, if not completely replaced, assumed many of the same functions of the guidebooks.[24] Apart from, or instead of, consulting guidebooks, one now surfs the net in order to retrieve information about destinations (Hashim, Murphy and Hashim 2007). "Word of mouse" has developed into a key domain of information. Services such as Google Maps and Google Earth are used by travelers; both have some options for religious sites in their places of interest layer.

Many tourists surf the net while holidaying, be it to stay in touch with the wider world or to share pictures or experiences and also to get more information on the place where they are – and one is increasingly getting used to the sight of tourists carrying print-outs from the net.[25] Others browse relevant sites with their increasingly sophisticated mobile gadgets. Again the tourists and the scholars follow the same path: The reader will have noted the pervasive use of the internet as my cicerone into the world of contemporary tourism.

A short Google-search (made in February 2008) reveals a host of virtual tours that are now available on the net. On the first pages with results, virtual tours to China, Florence, Rome, Oslo and The 1,000 islands popped up.[26] The website www.travelingonline.com was created "as a way to visit the cities and countries of your dreams and to glimpse places of wonder and mystique" and promises "wonderful travel tales that only come from the true adventure of traveling" as well as "stories that are honest personal experiences and not the hype of travel agencies and promotional writers".[27] Among the virtual trips one also encounters religious sites, including a "Historical enchantment" with "The Temple of the Magician, the tallest structure in Uxmal",[28] or, "Simple and unadorned, a pink stucco colonial-styled church" in virtual Celestun, Yucatan.[29] The virtual world can also help to overcome real handicaps, for instance by giving access to sites which are difficult to access for the disabled, virtually available. The Armchair Travel Company has started a site (which in 2008 claimed to have had over 3,000,000 visitors since 2000) that specializes "in producing superb Virtual Tour Systems and kiosks for venues which have difficulty providing access to the disabled. This often includes listed buildings, where installing lifts would be too costly or disruptive, or for more unusual sites such as naval museums with ships and submarines."[30] In the World Heritage category, the site also offers virtual tours to a number of religious sites such as the Taj Mahal, St. Paul's Cathedral and Westminster Abbey.

The emergence of travel blogs has diversified the accessible information on places (and could in future be used much more systematically in studies such as the present one). Travel blogs have also drastically reframed the relation between the travelers and their social networks, between home and travel (and so have social networking websites). Last but not least, they provide a new forum and stimulate new forms of travel writing. Many tourists now make their travel photographs available on the internet, and YouTube is a rich source of short travel videos.

Souvenirs

Purchasing souvenirs is as much part of tourist behavior as visiting attractions, taking pictures and buying (if not sending) postcards. It is part of the shopping pursuit which "is a major component of tourist experiences in many destinations" (Goss 2005, 60). It has been observed that pilgrims in Asia tend to spend money liberally on their trips (Reader 2005, 240), which also to some extent accounts for the economic benefits accruing from pilgrimages; similar observations can of course be made for tourism, which for many is a time where one spends money more freely and some(times) even conspicuously.

Postcards, generally only available at destinations, validate and communicate the visit; by sending them they serve as shared trophies of spatial conquest. Postcards – often depicting religious sites, objects or performances – can also function as souvenirs when taken home rather than sent to others. At the same time, postcards also help creating the tourist gaze and the recognizable feature of the respective sites. Postcards are also sent from pilgrimages. Suzanne Kaufman's study of Lourdes highlights the kind of mediatization achieved by postcards from that town:

> Often juxtaposing these modern marvels of transportation [i.e. trains, tramways and the funicular (MSt.)] alongside pilgrims marching in traditional peasant costume, the cards asserted the routinized compatibility of traditional religious practice and modern technology. Even the partaking of Lourdes water became an activity that resembled secular thermalism.
>
> (Kaufman 2005, 40)

The pilgrims and the shrine are presented as part of a tourist scenario:

> Postcards also depicted bustling street scenes, attesting to the vibrant commercial life of Lourdes. In these imagined urban landscapes, pilgrims stroll along the boulevards like tourists, gazing into shop windows

> as in any other popular resort towns. Indeed, at times the shrine recedes, pushed into the background by the cluster of shops, hotels, tramways and promenading pilgrims.
>
> (Kaufman 2005, 40)

Souvenirs can be bought as gifts for those who did not share the travel experience or for the travelers themselves. In that case, souvenirs serve as objects of memory; they may create continuity of memory and experience;[31] they "evoke polysensual memories" (Morgan and Pritchard 2005, 42). They can function "as mnemonic devices around which to tell stories" (Graburn 2000, xiv). Souvenirs extend the actual time-frame of travel. They are fragments of biographical narratives and help to transform "a public act (seeing a sight) ... into a private history (what I saw) with social meaning (look at what I saw)" (Desmond 1999, 43). Obviously, souvenirs can also be valued for their social and aesthetical functions.

Souvenirs entertain various semiotic relationships to attractions, destinations, sights. Some souvenirs have a contiguous and intrinsic relationship to the site; the very fact of being purchased *in situ* gives them a metonymical quality, even if the object itself was produced somewhere else. Physical fragments, indexical souvenirs as it were, are considered the "most powerful and significant souvenirs" (Shackley 2006, 101). Sometimes this power takes revenge: the Kīlauea, a volcano on the Big Island of Hawaii, is considered to be inhabited by the fire goddess Pele whose *mana* is considered to be present there, in particular at the Halema'uma'u-crater, where people regularly place offerings to the deity. Many tourists who visit the Hawaii Volcanoes National Park take away some pieces of lava or stone as souvenirs, a practice which is discouraged by the locals, since Pele's *mana* inhabits these materials, and some travel guides warn against doing this as the materials contain a curse. In fact, there are reports that more than two thousand souvenirs are sent back to the National Park every year by people who report to have experienced Pele's curse, with due apologies (Crowe and Crowe 2001, 43–44).[32]

Souvenirs help to create sights and promote travel. As pointed out by MacCannell in his classical study, sights require souvenirs or other markers such as guidebooks, postcards, signposts, information tablets to establish their status as attractions or destinations in the first place (MacCannell 1999 [1976], 41). Souvenirs have also been described as belonging to the category of "identity merchandise", i.e. "consumer products that represent cultural groups by means of graphic paragons, archetypes and key symbols" (Linnekin 1997, 216). Souvenirs are indeed tools for identity construction.

Different types of souvenirs involve various media and materials. Souvenirs are often designed in the form of modified functional objects such as ashtrays, cups, spoons, key and napkin rings or paper knives, often illustrated with some kind of motif that links them to the respective places.

Foodstuffs can also be used and marketed as souvenirs. In Lourdes, lozenges made with sugar and water from the grotto were marketed as souvenirs, and they were packed in special tins decorated with the imprint of the basilica and of the spring (Kaufman 2005, 48). The pilgrimage-cum-tourist town developed a vibrant souvenir industry with hundreds of small shops and several large emporiums (Kaufman 2005, 45).

Many objects tend to be cheap kitsch or purely markers (such as T-shirts giving the name of a place), but can also include expensive handicraft.[33] A variety of religious motifs, signs and symbols are being used to decorate such items. From Egypt, one may recall desk ornaments or wall decoration with the Sphinx, obelisks and pyramids; miniature obelisks in brass or soapstone, small busts of deities in various materials; pendants, bracelets and small boxes ornamented with pictures of divine agents such as Horus; miniatures of masks, thrones[34] and goddesses (Isis at Luxor); a wide range of papyrus reproducing or mixing ancient religious arts. Among the Dogon, calabashes are engraved predominantly with motifs "drawn from the repertoire of traditional mythical figures and mask types" (Lane 1988, 67).[35] For Hawaii, Linnekin reports that the volcano goddess Pele was featured on T-shirts apparently appealing to female customers (Linnekin 1997, 238). Nowadays, one finds T-shirts stating "I'm blessed by fire goddess Pele"; the T-shirts indicate the spatial origin of this blessing: "Volcano Kilouea, Big Island, Hawaii".[36] In a shop in a hotel in Havana (Cuba) tourists can buy T-shirts with an artist's rendition of several Santería gods. Other Santería-related souvenirs include colored glass bead necklaces (so-called *collares*, received after the first degree of initiation), small, dark-skinned dolls in old-fashioned long puffed dresses representing female deities and *batá* drums (Hagedorn 2001, 224–25). In Sri Lankan tourist shops, the motif of "bulging-eyed demons swathed in serpents and flames" taken from masks used in Sinhalese rituals, especially exorcisms, is omnipresent not only on masks but also on vases, key fobs and batiks (Simpson 1993, 169).

Souvenirs may include religious or "magical" objects such as amulets, talismans, votive papers, figurines, miniature statues, prayer books, rosaries, prayer beads and other devotional materials or other objects such as textiles, ritual masks, foodstuffs, books and prints, paintings and pictographs.[37] Objects (religious or otherwise) produced as souvenirs can sometimes be recognized by visible markers such as "made in ... " or "souvenir from ... ".

Religious objects are being used as souvenirs even in places where they legally may not be taken out of the country (which is the case in Burma).[38] Attempts have also been made to foreclose the "souvenirization" of religious objects. Consider the example of Bali, where the Dutch colonial government "duly collected and inventoried artifacts of Balinese culture, not only to put them at the disposal of scholars, but also to prevent them from being sold as souvenirs to tourists" (Picard 1996, 21).

The following example points in a different direction. Bear carvings are an early specimen of Ainu tourist art sold as souvenirs. One theory has it that this practice originated as a result of the travel of a rich Japanese landowner to Switzerland in 1922 where he saw Swiss farmers carving bears as a means of supplementing their income; on his return he advised Ainu farmers to follow suit (Ohtsuka 1999, 93). Whether that theory is true or not, the fact remains that the choice of the bear motif for souvenir art is somewhat surprising, since "the carving of images of bears and other animals considered to be spirits was previously restricted to religious implements" and "[t]he creation of animal images in paintings and carvings, especially the image of bears, was never taken lightly" (Ohtsuka 1999, 93). Also implements used in rituals were reproduced as souvenirs. Kazuyoshi Ohtsuka argues that this art together with the folk village performances "strengthened the view held by many visitors to Hokkaido that even modern Ainu people continued to live in a traditional – i.e., 'primitive', fashion" (Ohtsuka 1999, 94).[39]

Souvenirs are often provided with brief explanations on the mythological, ritual or spiritual background of the object in question. For artists on Rapa Nui (aka Easter Island) it has been observed that when tourists ask questions about their carvings "the right story can facilitate a figure being sold, and different artists may fabricate different explanations" (Eggertson 2008) – increasing sales prospects to tourists apparently stimulating ad hoc mythologization.

Salespeople in souvenir shops often act as representatives of the respective groups and the first point of contact. Observing them may give visitors clues to modes of behavior, ways of speaking, gestures, clothing, etc.[40] They also often operate as interreligious brokers, for example by explaining the symbolism, meaning and possible use of objects. That these explanations are not always correct from a normative or theological (if any) or even from a scholarly point of view and that they may be modified in order to enhance the sales prospects of the respective items is a different matter.[41] Consider, however, that even producers and indigenous users may have different interpretations of the object and that they may use it in manners not endorsed by the respective authorities (if any).

Souvenir shops – usually found in good numbers in close proximity to attractions[42] – are nowadays major retailers of religious objects.[43] Souvenir shops often serve as something like free museums, and museums are generating some of their revenue by operating as souvenir shops. Sometimes, shops, galleries, museums, handicraft workshops and other forms of services are integrated into encompassing structures.[44]

Handicrafts sold to tourists as souvenirs sometimes can not be adequately replaced by contemporary craftspeople resulting in a depletion of cultural heritage including ritual or religious artifacts (such as Dogon masks) (Shackley 2001, 42–43). Relic hunting and tomb-plundering were, from early on, business opportunities provided by "archaeologists", historians and tourists traveling to Egypt and other countries.[45] In order to serve the market of mass tourism handicraft items are now mass-produced.[46] The world over, tourism has sustained the demand for and production of "traditional" arts and crafts, and in some cases re-invigorated those on the verge of extinction (Hennig 1997, 145). Apart from religious objects being directly used as souvenirs, contemporary and past religious traditions are sources of inspiration for the design of souvenirs.

Some studies of the souvenir are grounded in a structural-functionalist approach to the study of religion and tourism (see Chapter 1; pp. 22ff). Beverly Gordon, for example (Goss 2005, 57), sketches three structural explanations of the omnipresence of the souvenir. One builds on gift theory as well as on ritual theory and regards souvenirs as an entry or re-entry fee on coming home (Gordon 1986, 138); another hypothesis expands on the idea of inversion ("explaining" why souvenirs often are playful or childish); the third explanation builds on ideas of Graburn and Cohen and reads as follows:

> People feel the need to bring things home with them from the sacred, extraordinary time or space, for home is equated with ordinary, mundane time and space. They can't hold on to the non-ordinary experience, for it is by nature ephemeral, but they can hold on to a tangible piece of it, an object that came from it.
>
> (Gordon 1986, 136)

If this explanation were to hold one would need to assume that souvenirs, as messengers from the sacred, would possess a special agency. This would put them on the same footing with relics. As a matter of fact, building on a casual remark by Walter Benjamin, this comparison has become a recurrent topic in the literature.[47] Since relics are often the focus for pilgrimages, this brings us back to the ideal–typical distinction between pilgrimage (relic) and tourism (souvenir). In reality, however, we once again encounter a continuum. To begin with, as we have seen souvenirs have long since been sold at sanctuaries and pilgrimage sites.[48] Purchasing souvenirs seems to be no less a natural part of pilgrimages than of other tourist travels. Many, if not most, pilgrimage centers, therefore have a souvenir industry attached to them. Pilgrimage centers like Fátima are characterized by the omnipresence of religious articles sold in shops around the sanctuary but also in souvenir shops in hotels.[49] Besides shops there are often, especially in economically less developed countries, street vendors, hawkers, usually operating from stalls on the street. There is a wide range of retailing services and the prizes for items may vary considerably depending on where they are purchased.[50] For some sites, haggling is reported, and the massive commercialization of sacred sites by the souvenir trade is sometimes seen as going against the spirit of the site.[51] On the other hand, there are pilgrims who actively seek to avoid tourism related merchandise. At the same time, many despisers of tourist souvenir kitsch hunt for memorabilia that seem more authentic and valuable to them.[52]

Typically, souvenirs tend to be kitsch of the worst kind. Countless examples immediately spring to mind. It seems that the modification, some would say perversion, of properties of objects adequately fulfils the function of acting as a mnemonic or memetic devise and to distinguish them from other objects and experiences.

Souvenirs are not only sold in souvenir shops, but at various religious sites, from the local parish church to international pilgrimage centers. Even relatively small churches sell souvenirs, with a leaflet, brochure or guidebook and a postcard as the minimal assortment. However, as early as 1983 it has been noted that English churches were widening their range of stock. As an example, the report referred to one parish church that had "over a hundred different items for sale", while another one sold "thousands of pens, pencils, plastic badges, satin badges and metal badges, and hundreds of leather bookmarks, car stickers, memo pads and local guidebooks" (Hanna 1984, 50–51). The merchandise sold at shops located within or next to churches and monasteries in Germany typically includes printed materials and information materials, musical supplies such as CDs recorded at the respective place, devotional items such as candles, crucifixes, icons, cymbals, singing bowls, incense sticks, regional products including food items (often fair trade products) and handicraft articles, and games such as jigsaw puzzles (Neumann and Rösener 2006, 140).

As already mentioned, the same objects may be purchased by pilgrims and tourists alike.[53] While one would expect that pilgrims and tourists ascribe different sorts of meanings and agencies to these object, in actual fact this assumption may be difficult to ascertain, particularly when one takes into account that many of the objects so purchased are used as gifts to other people who did not participate in the trip. When the pilgrimage entitles the pilgrim to an upgraded social or religious status, it is very important that the pilgrim bring home some visible proof. Thus, pilgrimage signs, certificates, plaques or other testimonials are not uncommon.[54] The tourist souvenir (like the postcard) may fulfil a similar function. It indicates that the owner has been "there"; it serves to authenticate and to internalize the experience – just like having photographs taken with the attraction/site clearly visible in the background. This documentation may provide social capital.

It has been pointed out that purchasing a souvenir "imparts tangibility" to an otherwise intangible experience (Shackley 2001, 43). The knowledge and experience of "having been there", of having conquered and appropriated the place, may likewise imply the desire to take home part of the cultural heritage of the group visited. Souvenirs may also encapsulate the presumed mystique of the place. Consider the following description of Lourdes, a wonderland of religious kitsch in all its forms:

> Judging from conversations over the years with those who buy the souvenirs, the items are seen as brightly attractive and evocative of the shrine and town. The Madonna festooned with coloured lights will stand in a place of prominence to remind family members and guests of the visit, perhaps cheek by jowl with secular mementoes of other trips abroad – the flamenco dancer doll from the Spanish seaside holiday or the statuette of the Eiffel tower.
>
> (Eade 1992, 27)

Tourist art may introduce new forms, designs and techniques, unrelated to local traditions – called "heterogenetic style" by Erik Cohen; other styles are modifications of traditional products ("ortho-heterogenetic"), to be distinguished from the traditional ("orthogenetic") style (Cohen 1993a, 153). An example for the continuity from production for "traditional" clients to that for tourists is the making of religious figures by Nepalese craftsmen who have a long tradition of supplying their products to different religious groups and demands, both within Nepal and abroad. Tourist markets merely continue that practice (Teague 2000). Other cases, however, point in a different direction; let us consider one example. In the 1970s, artists of Kambot (Papua New Guinea, East Sepik Province) developed so-called storyboards, i.e. carved and painted wooden boards depicting both mythological stories and scenes of everyday life, for sale to tourists and art dealers. The people of Kambot have been exposed to missionary efforts since the 1920s. As a consequence, ritual objects were removed from their ceremonial houses and initiations were discontinued. The newly developed storyboards, however, often depict non-Christian indigenous mythological stories and apart from being for sale to foreigners, these carved and painted wooden boards are now also being used "as visual support for the transmission of myths to the younger generation" (Colombo Dougoud 2000, 224). The demand for souvenirs has thereby created a new medium allowing the transmission of the mythological tradition. Canoes often are a key motif on the storyboards, and Roberta Colombo Dougoud has suggested that this may allow tourists to connect the pictures to their own experiences as travelers, where "carvers tell about their life and myth" (Colombo Dougoud 2000, 233).

In other cases, souvenirs are produced by people who do not belong to the same religious or ethnic group as those who may claim traditional religious, ethnic or cultural ownership of the objects being reproduced.[55] Although buyers of Tibetan Buddhist scrolls (*thangkas*) in Nepal will routinely believe that they were made by Tibetans, the majority are actually crafted by Newars and Tamang (Bentor 1993, 118–20). Tibetan origins are also assigned to "[q]uite a few other tourist arts in Nepal, from images of

Confucius to necklaces of imitation gems, both imported from Hong Kong" (Bentor 1993, 118). The souvenir industry has become a global enterprise with regard to production, repertoire and distribution.

Studies of souvenirs have emphasized the ritual, aesthetic, semantic and material transformations of the religious motifs and ritual objects that are being produced as souvenirs, shifting their context from "internal" to "external" audiences. Navajo ritual sandpaintings, for example, first had to be put into permanent form in order to be sold to tourists, and the change of the material shape corresponded to their transfer from ritual and religious to artistic and tourist contexts (Parezo 1991). In several cases it has been observed that religious objects are generally left unconsecrated when produced for tourist markets. Moreover, the religious and mythological meaning dimensions of artistic designs, art and craft forms have a general tendency to disappear in the tourism context (Smith 2006, 131).

Here is a list of further typical transformations that have been observed especially with regard to mass produced items:[56]

- stereotyping (with less attention to details often held to be crucial in prior contexts)
- deviation from the iconographic canon
- simplification, alteration and fusion of symbols
- invention of new genres or borrowing of motifs
- liberation from given sizes and proportions (resulting in miniaturization or sometimes magnification to gargantuan dimensions)
- changes in the colors used and techniques of making new things appear ancient
- changes in the materials used (with a preference for cheap and light materials such as plastic)
- technical sloppiness.

Apart from the artifacts themselves, the social and religious organizational frameworks of their production and the property and power structures and family networks in which they are embedded can be subject to change. For some Sri Lankan specialists in mask making, for example, the production of masks for outsiders has become the central economic activity; accordingly, "the provision of services within the caste itself became a dispensable aspect of their work" (Simpson 1993, 172). In this case, gender restrictions were also relaxed so that girls joined in painting masks, which had previously been a male domain (Simpson 1993, 172).

The dominant theoretical approach to describing these transformations has been that of commercialization of religious art. However, in a comparative analysis Erik Cohen has challenged the common assumption that the commercialization of ethnic crafts invariably has pernicious consequences. In many cases "commercialization may have a rehabilitating and, to a limited extent, even revitalizing, rather than destructive impact" (Cohen 1989b, 165). This conclusion probably also applies to the production of religious popular arts. From religious points of view popularization is not necessarily a bad thing. At least some religions have long traditions of adopting various means to put their message across in order to reach different people and other worlds. Moreover, protagonists may come up with various rationalizations. One is that unconsecrated tourist souvenirs do not qualify as religious objects at all, but are mere "decorations" (and hence there is no perceived harm in popularizing them). Moreover, as Myra Shackley has pointed out for pilgrimage retailing, the "fashionable intellectual pose to disapprove of commoditization at sacred sites" is "usually articulated by people who are unaware of the emotions stirred up in the pilgrim by the act of visiting such a site" (Shackley 2006, 99). Similar conclusions should not be a priori excluded for tourists.

The "cultural biographies" (Morgan and Pritchard 2005, 44) of souvenirs as they move through different hands and contexts, their transformation into household goods, have to my knowledge not been studied. Their perceptions can be expected to range from frivolous to almost reverential attitudes. Here is a testimonial by the tourism scholar Annette Pritchard:

> In the kitchen, we've got two wall sculptures of the Indian god Kokopelli. They really remind me of Arizona, of the desert and the colours of the rocks, of the spirituality of the people and their special places like Sedona.
>
> (Morgan and Pritchard 2005, 38)

The image of the (Pueblo) flute player deity Kokopelli is nowadays encountered on a broad range of gadgets, knick-knacks and souvenirs in the south-west of the United States. It is omnipresent on Native American crafts. This "total commoditization" (Malotki 2000, 2) notwithstanding, sculptures of this deity placed in a kitchen in England can invoke important memories for the travelers, especially since the objects were not the usual small kitsch items, but relatively large sculptures which were expensive and difficult to transport, entailing a challenge and a commitment. The sculptures trigger sensual memories of landscapes and places, but they also invoke a spirituality, which has become re-territorialized and has found a new home, albeit as an iconic reality rather than as a matter of religious belief or practice, in a kitchen in a different part of the world; this kitchen is at the same time spatially linked to a planetary geography of power places (Sedona).

In the disguise of souvenirs, then, religious motifs and objects from a wide array of religious traditions from all around the globe are finding new homes in other parts of the world. This amounts to a veritable globalization of religious material culture. Implicitly, it is generally taken for granted that these products do not function as objects of piety or devotion and that they are domesticated (= profane) with respect to any possible religious agency. This may well be true, but there may also be various shadings of the presence of superhuman agency, from "hot" to "cold", "thick" to "thin", "serious" to "playful", "conjunctive" to "subjunctive". Objects carried as necklaces on the body may occasionally assume the function of amulets. At any rate, future analyses of the "multireligious" landscape of contemporary tourist societies should, in my opinion, pay close attention to these "things" and the religious pluralization of home decorations.

What happens with the souvenirs in their new "home" contexts, how are they interpreted and used by the people who have purchased them?[57] In order to take some modest first steps in addressing these issues, my former research assistant Janemil Kolstø conducted, in December 2008 and January 2009, telephone interviews with a random sample of 412 persons in Bergen (Norway) about their understanding and use of souvenirs.[58] The sample consisted mainly of experienced travelers. Only 18 percent of the respondents had traveled fewer than three times during 2008, the average being slightly more than four trips during that year.

Twenty-three percent of our respondents said that they did not bring home anything from their previous three trips. When referring to the things they took home, 28 percent used the term "souvenir", while 26 percent spoke of a memento and 14 percent of a gift and another 7 percent of a commodity. Others simply said that they liked taking something home. (Multiple answers were permitted.)

Around 10 percent stated that they deemed it very important to bring home something, and that they would not come back from a trip empty-handed. Fifteen percent, on the contrary, stated that they never took home anything. Forty-five percent found that taking home things was not that important, but it could happen, while 30 percent found it important, but held that it ultimately depended on the prevailing conditions. There is no statistically significant correlation between travel frequency and the ascribed importance of bringing home souvenirs.

The most decisive factors on buying something were the nature of the purchased item (25 percent of 447 answers, where multiple answers were permitted) and the destination (23 percent). Somewhat less frequently mentioned were the distance from home (13 percent) and the mood (10 percent). The most important quality of an item, which our respondents would consider to buy, was its authenticity (26 percent of 739 answers, with multiple answers permitted). Other, but significantly less important criteria were its relation to the visited attraction or destination (10 percent), and the item's utility and its size (9 percent each). Forty-four percent of the answers to the question which items they would definitely not consider purchasing referred to mass produced, bulk goods, followed by junk/paraphernalia as the second most listed answer (17 percent of 572 answers).

Turning to religion, 81 percent of our respondents were members of the Church of Norway, the Lutheran state church. Only 3 percent referred to themselves as atheists and 9 percent as agnostics. Thirty-one percent stated that they were not interested in religious matters. Nine percent said that they were spiritual, while 47 percent classified themselves as religious. Around half of our respondents stated that they attend church at least once a year, while 9 percent said that they went to church once a month and as many once a week.

Eighty-six percent of our respondents stated that they had visited a religious or spiritual site on their travels; 41 percent out of these had bought a souvenir, a gift or token, at that site (or such sites). In addition, even apart from such visits, 29 percent of our respondents stated that they purchased objects which they themselves somehow considered to be religious or spiritual during their travels. We did not find a statistically significant correlation between their consumption of such objects and their self-assessed religiosity; also atheists bought souvenirs which they considered to be religious/spiritual objects.

A total of 438 "religious" or "spiritual" objects were mentioned, but some 48 percent of these were not qualified in any specific manner. A total of 361 items were identified, with 14 percent being postcards and 19 percent images of religious/spiritual places or motifs. The largest category of responses referred to figures of various kinds (33 percent), followed by items of decoration such as jewelry (15 percent), and books and other publications (7 percent) including publications about the visited sites. The category other (9 percent) comprised such different kinds things as a Tibetan prayer wheel, a Chinese spirit catcher, a prayer card from the United States, materials such as tarot cards, energy stones, papyri, an "occult box", recordings of religious/spiritual music, various kinds of textiles (a prayer rug, a carpet with an image of a deity from South America), liquids such as wine from a monastery, herbs from a monastery, drugs and medicines such as a Buddhist ointment from Thailand, and objects of utility such as glasses, plates, lighters or bottle openers which in one way or the other were either decorated or modified by religious motifs.

When it comes to the "figures" they had purchased, people mentioned 120 examples. (Many of these items were classified as "other" by others; consider such examples as a prayer rattle purchased in a Buddhist temple in Thailand, a string of Islamic prayer beads, a Jewish candle holder, a candle brought from a church in Iceland, various candles of unspecified provenience as well as different kinds of pots and jugs.) The example of figures mentioned most often were figures of the Buddha (brought home from various countries in Asia, but also purchased in Turkey and Cyprus), crucifixes, figures (and statues) of Maria and Jesus, figures of gods and deities (mainly from Greece and India), and representations of angels and saints. At religious or spiritual sites people bought miniatures of these respective places (such as St. Peter's Basilica and Cologne Cathedral). Some respondents could not recall where they bought the miniature and which place it represents.

When asked about figures, some respondents also mentioned icons – which are the main example in the category images. (Icons are becoming increasingly popular even in Lutheran church buildings in Norway.) The Norwegian tourists brought icons from a variety of countries such as Croatia, Estonia, Germany, Greece, Italy, Poland, Russia, Serbia and Spain. Other examples of pictorial souvenirs included a poster with religious motifs from Australian aborigines, a picture with Islamic saints, a representation of the Dome of the Rock, a picture with Biblical sites in Jerusalem, a poster with several cathedrals, a picture of St. George slaying the dragon, and a triptych with Jesus and Mary.

Crucifixes are also the main items among the 55 pieces of jewelry listed by our respondents. Some respondents, however, clearly stated that they would not consider buying a crucifix, which as an object apparently was too closely identified with Christianity or categorized as a religious object and hence not suitable as a souvenir. Several respondents had bought a rosary – mostly in Italy – or similar objects of Islamic and Chinese provenience. (One respondent explicitly pointed out that the rosary bought in the Middle East was not to be considered a religious object in this context.) Lockets were mentioned sometimes. Other items mentioned were a shell, an Indian orna- ment bought in a church in the United States, a Thor's Hammer purchased in a Norwegian museum, a guardian angel (also from Norway), a Hindu bracelet from India and a Buddha ornament from Thailand.

Some respondents reported that they lost the souvenirs they had purchased. Others stated that they had given them as gifts. Yet the over- whelming majority reported that they kept the souvenirs at home, often by fixing them on walls or by prominently displaying them in bookcases and showcases, mostly in the living room area, often as a kind of eye-catcher, but sometimes, as in the case of icons, in the bedrooms (with the icon right over the bed). Some respondents stated that some of the items created quite an impression with visitors. When a lady, who works in IT and referred to herself as a spiritual person, put up a, to her eyes, female looking Buddha statue from China she was taken by surprise when she found that the statue was luminescent; she stated that this came as a shock and resulted in some kind of a religious experience. Several respondents reported that they put the souvenirs away after a while, probably to make place for a new purchase.

Some souvenirs that were classified as religious/spiritual were put to practical use. The jewelry, bracelets and crucifixes can be worn, the incense is burned, and stories are told about some images. Nativity sets bought while traveling are taken out and displayed during the Christmas season.

When asked about the significance of the souvenirs to their own reli- giosity/spirituality, many respondents spurned any such interpretation and stated that these objects did not mean anything to them in terms of religion.

For others, however, this was very much the case – in particular to Christians, who by having the souvenirs around them would be reminded of Jesus and places such as Jerusalem. Other responses pointed to a religious significance of the objects, even though not in terms of a specific creed but rather as recalling the significance of the quest or the existence of something between heaven and earth, of powers inspiring humans, of a larger view of the world and of myths, of inner peace, of miraculous things happening all over the world, of the belief that traces of truth can be found in all religions, and of a certain sense of security. While most of these statements remained rather vague, the concept of memory was of central importance since the objects "reminded" these people of the varied realities of religion. For others, the souvenirs created a certain atmosphere, and the vagueness of many statements was made explicit by some others who said that the objects meant something to them without them being able to verbalize this meaning.

Our study of outbound tourists from Bergen revealed the extraordinary extent of glocalization of religious objects, with religious/spiritual objects from a wide range of religious traditions finding their way into Norwegian homes, sometimes in visually prominent positions. Whereas the religious/spiritual souvenirs did not carry any religious meaning for many, for others their meaning was rather straightforward and positive; for a third category of respondents the souvenirs materialized the memory of the reality of religion in an unspecific but potentially important way.

SOUVENIRS FROM CHAPTER 8

- Tourist guides and tour leaders are key-mediators in cross-religious communication.
- They transmit a variety of information on religions obtained from various sources.
- Representatives of religions can act as tourist guides, and some tourist guides adopt religious roles.
- Guidebooks contain representations of religions (which should be subject to critical scrutiny); guidebooks to long-distant destinations can contain separate sections on different religious traditions.
- Religious motifs are prominent in illustrations including book covers.
- For many people, travel guidebooks are an important source of information on "distant" religions.
- By advising readers to visit places, guidebooks typically stimulate their readers to religious exposure.
- Guidebooks are produced for many religious attractions and sites.

- Some guidebooks cater to the needs of religious groups or specialize in religious attractions including pilgrimage sites.
- On the internet, religious sites become virtually accessible to virtual tourists.
- Many people purchase souvenirs when visiting religious sites.
- The design of souvenirs sometimes makes use of a repertoire of religious motifs, objects and symbols.
- Religious objects can be used as souvenirs; souvenir shops serve as major retail institutions for religious objects, especially in pilgrimage centers.
- Even modest religious attractions nowadays have an assortment of souvenirs on offer.
- Souvenirs can be produced by outsiders or by manufacturers of religious objects for non-tourist use; selling religious objects to tourists can have repercussions on the traditional economy of producing such objects.
- When produced as souvenirs, (religious) things are subject to a series of transformations.
- In the form of souvenirs a broad variety of religious material culture has effectively spread across the globe; a micro-study from Bergen (Norway) shows the broad range of objects, where figures such as icons (bought at many different places) feature prominently.
- Travelers from Bergen put souvenirs they classify as religious to various uses, often on display in their homes.
- For some respondents such objects did not imply any religious meanings; for others it did; for a third category religious souvenirs serve as a vague reminder of (religious) alterity, the possible reality of "something real out there".

Chapter 9

Terminal reflections

Looking back at the itinerary drawn up by this book, it needs to be pointed out that there are various stations at which we have not halted. Although the present itinerary may appear quite extensive, it is far from complete. While some may find it excessive to devote an entire book to what some may consider (contrary to my own view) a marginal subject, the topic in fact is far from exhausted. Many issues could well have benefited from (further) explorations; consider business, backpacker or third age tourism, postcards, photographs and photographing, advertisements and brochures, and the vast fields of travel literature, to mention only a few topics. Moreover, all chapters could have been supplemented by various other examples and by engaging additional theoretical perspectives. Last but not least, while this book portrays tourism as some kind of a homogeneous system, social analysis may well differentiate the subject through various categories such as class, ethnicity, gender, race, and historical and geographical contexts.

Despite its admitted limitations, the present book has aimed at providing a multiplex first account of the busy intersections and reciprocities between religion – on institutional, private, and individualized levels – and (leisure) tourism, which by now is a highly diversified sphere. Note that both key terms are used here, out of convenience, as shorthand signifiers for complex formations of networks of agents, structures of communication, and systems of objects. On theoretical and empirical grounds, we have rejected the general thesis that tourism has taken the place of religion in the modern world, or that the tourist is ultimately a religious/spiritual figure. Nevertheless, it is impossible to ignore the fact that many tourists (although not all), including those traveling without any prior religious or spiritual motivations, are in one way or the other, either physically or through a wide range of travel-related media, exposed to religion in several of its varieties and diverse material qualities. Clearly, a renewed interest in religion or religious topics emerges among some people when traveling, and religious attitudes and values can contribute to tourist behavior, starting with the selection of destinations. Conversely, our analysis has pointed to a new touristic layer of religion. Evidently, several aspects of religions (most prominently places but also performances and holidays and festivals) are more or less profoundly affected and hosted by tourists and tourism – sometimes to the extent that they are mainly advertised to and consumed by tourists and that they are maintained or produced for tourism. The same is true for religious objects produced and sold as souvenirs. Indigenous people and religious groups as well as traditions or religious experts such as shamans are visited by tourists. Moreover, religious tropes and metaphors are, often playfully, engaged by tourists and both inventively and stereotypically used, often hyperbolically, by promoters of tourism when referring to (potential) attractions and destinations.

Hopefully, then, the present book has made it abundantly clear that tourism is a major arena and context for the unfolding of religion in the contemporary global world, so that tourism no longer appears as a marginal subject for those who study religion(s) – nor religion for those who study tourism. The reciprocity between the two spheres entails that both relate to each other – the agency being on both sides, each being both subjects and objects in this mutual relationship. Tourism bears upon religions, while religious groups, organizations, and individuals in different ways use tourism facilities for their purposes, and religion is in various shadings (explored in greater detail in the different chapters of the present work) engaged by tourism, tourists, and governments. These developments can result in a "touristification" of religious structures, while tourism can appear as a playground for religious activities.

When religion, in its ideological, material and performative instances makes its appearance in the arena of tourism, religion is being displayed and staged; by being part of tourism as a system of communication, religious events, groups, metaphors, performances, and places are being subjected to its code, for which the notion of "attraction" is a defining feature. In other words, by being absorbed within or entering the tourism system, aspects of religion(s) such as events, groups, and sites are being converted or translated into attractions to be appropriated by the tourist gaze and typical tourist activities such as visiting, photographing and buying souvenirs. These aspects of religion(s) serve as opportunities for amusement, distraction, diversion, education, entertainment, fun, pastime, and spectacle or may otherwise appear as heritage. Inversely, if such material instances of religion are not convertible or translatable into attractions, they will most likely not appear on (official) tourism circuits and routes. Ordinary religion is mostly of interest to scholars and fieldworkers; to tourists it becomes of interest as elements of an attraction or a destination, often as some kind of scenery. At the same time, even relatively minor structures are increasingly being dressed up as attractions. While aspects of religions, as we have seen throughout this book, can in some cases be a major element of the *mise en scène* of travels and places, in other cases they merely serve as a background prop contributing to the creation of a favorable ("authentic", "scenic") atmosphere. Religion is represented *in situ* or in museums, theme parks or various electronic or print media, including advertisement materials.

More specific key findings with regard to the busy intersections between religion(s) and tourism have been flagged in our travel diary throughout the itinerary; since they were collected as "souvenirs" (reflecting the reduction in complexity typical for this kind of objects), which are displayed as text boxes within each chapter, they will not be reiterated here. From the various arguments, examples and issues covered by our voyage through global tourism, it is clear that the complexities of the confluences should restrain one from drawing overtly ambitious general conclusions. Not every tourist is immune to religion, nor is every tourist a spiritual seeker; by being opened to and submerged in tourism, religious events, performances, places and things do not as such become degraded and inauthentic – to mention some stereotypical misconceptions. Whereas religion for some tourists in some countries may be consumed as a practice of nostalgia and vicarious memory, enacted at sites and events where an active minority of performers looks after the perpetuation of religion on behalf of a listless majority (Davie 2000), such an interpretation would not necessarily lend itself to tourism in other part of the world. While many religious events and objects change once they function as tourist attractions and are "touristified" in the sense of becoming adjusted to the *modus operandi* of mass tourism, this cannot be said to be the case everywhere. In many cases, however, negotiations or even conflicts occur at the busy intersections between religion(s) and tourism. Since both religion and tourism are often subject to value judgements – in the sense of being considered as inherently good or evil – a scholarly perspective would be well advised to carefully avoid the trap of merely confirming prejudices. Moreover, although (or because) it is easy to provide a, technically speaking, relatively unambiguous definition of tourism that allows for an unequivocal identification of some kinds of activities (travels) as touristic, and people engaging in this mode of traveling as tourists, this very act of classification, which also can include pilgrims/pilgrimages, does not as such trigger valid inferences concerning the attitudes and behaviors of these people (at least when understood as "real" people rather than as metaphors for theorizing social processes). With regard to religion, for example, the very fact of being a tourist does not predict any specific religious (or anti-religious) attitudes and behaviors. This is why the present book has focused on the systemic qualities of tourism.

In the following, rather than once again proudly displaying our findings (souvenirs), let us tentatively place the topic of tourism on the map of some recent theoretical work in the social sciences and the study of religion(s) where tourism, to my eyes, so far has for the most part been unduly neglected. Of course, all these issues could be discussed much more extensively than is possible here.

Consumption

In the West (as in much of the world), we find ourselves living in a capitalist consumer society/culture/civilization. To a large extent, therefore, our lives revolve around the purchase and enjoyment of various sorts of goods, and for many persons, processes of consumption are ways of constructing meaning and identity (Campbell 2004). Besides creating pleasure, consumption also conveys agency (Appadurai 1996, 7). Tourism is an inherent part of (global) consumer culture. The tourism sector sells travel and in order to generate the necessary interest and desire, its advertisements promise "unique" travel experiences, sometimes with images grounded in mythological and religious tropes (e.g. "paradise") used as strategies of branding and packaging. Moreover, tourism offers many sites of consumption. By merging into the experience industry (Richards 2001) and the tourism sector, aspects of religions become a matter of consumption by more than their local users. The present study has pointed to a variety of religious sites, objects and performances that are advertised, sold and consumed in tourism contexts, in many cases subsumed under the category of (tangible and intangible) cultural heritage and administered by the heritage industry. Treated in this way, religious sites, objects and performances become a kind of commodity and are subsumed under an interactional framework of commoditization and packaging that may involve processes such as aestheticization, exoticization, folklorization, fossilization, musealization, Orientalizing and/or romanticization. This may require a reformatting that often results in their simplification in order to be suitable for consumption by tourists (who may or may not be religious and who may or may not have religious interests and motivations). Religions and the various forms of symbolic capital associated with them are by no means immune to this form of commercialization. In fact, consumption as such is not foreign to religion and commerce may be a legitimate way of practicing religion; accordingly, it has been noted "that the commodification of religion happens to a large extent as an internal process within the church and not only because of outside pressure or exploitation" (Martikainen 2008, 142) – an observation that is applicable to tourism as well and also is true of other religious organizations. Thus, as long as one does not hold a romantic notion of religion, there should be nothing revolting in the tourism consumption of religious objects, performances, and sites as such.[1] By being transformed into a different code, they will certainly change their meaning, but unless one believes that meanings are metaphysically enshrined in the world (including the meaning of religion and spirituality), or unless one rejects consumer capitalism in itself based on certain persuasions (Marxist or otherwise), such changes may not appear deplorable, as long as the people who can legitimately claim ownership over cultural and religious property are not denied their rights and as long as tangible or intangible cultural and religious property is not damaged. This, of course, has in several cases turned out to be a matter of intense negotiations and dispute.

Mobility

Danièle Hervieu-Léger (1999) distinguishes between two figures of religion in the destabilized, moving world of modernity: the pilgrim and the convert. We will now have to add a third figure: the tourist. Contrary to the other two, the tourist is a truly (post-)modern character. Where the convert chooses to switch from one religion to another and the pilgrim returns home, typically with a changed (solidified, transformed) religious identity, the tourist visits different religious destinations in a never-ending round trip, which may or may not be described as a quest. Apart from the tourist being a theoretical metaphor for the dynamism, flow, flux, hybridity and versatility of religious identities in the context of late modern societies, many tourists, even those with stable and deeply committed religious identities, in fact expose themselves in bodily form to the material reality of religious variety or even diversity, allowing for a wider spectrum of interactions, from the repugnant or curious gaze to explorations of various kinds, including the taking home of impressions, memories and objects. Tourism is a modern system of mobility enabling "the movement of people, ideas and information from place to place, person-to-person, event to event" (Urry 2007, 12). Tourism puts religious people, objects and ideas on the move; it contributes to the cultural and religious traffic, provides points of entry into other rounds of meaning, uproots elements of religions, and immerses them in a horizontal flow that in turn takes them beyond the organizational control of religious groups. While the ordinary believer, situated in static contexts, be it homeland or in diasporic settings, is still very much the ideal type of the religious person, this no longer necessarily reflects social realities of religion and religious identities.[2]

Globalization

Tourism is a major (albeit often marginalized) dynamic factor in the process generally referred to as globalization, major characteristics of which include long-distance connectivity, increasing awareness of this interconnectedness, and time–space compression or "flattening" of the world.[3] When it comes to religion, the impacts of globalization are typically discussed with reference to diaspora and migration, pluralism, politics, transnational networks and organizations. Probably reflecting a widely shared theoretical contempt for tourism (but not for travel in practice!), tourism is hardly ever mentioned in the standard theoretical literature on globalization and religion. Yet, as a social sphere, tourism is a prime example and mover of global flows, and the unspecific characteristics of tourists as a group (see above) reflect the fluidity of these global flows. Long-distance tourists encounter various religions along the routes they are traveling. Given the worldwide occurrence of elements of religion(s) in tourism (as analyzed in the present book), tourism appears to be a dynamic of considerable significance for the global visibility of religions (as attractions). Moreover, it is also through tourism that religion is being globalized as a category and a model (Beyer 2006 [without reference to tourism]). In tourist guidebooks, for example, (potential) tourists can read about the religions and religious attractions of various countries. Tourism contributes to the objectification of religion, its representation as something out there, which in turn needs to be conserved and displayed. Not only being an abstract notion, religions, mediated by tourism, have become materially and physically accessible on a worldwide scale. This does not necessarily imply their homogenization, but at the same time opens spaces for emergence and invention (see also Clifford 1988, 17). Whereas religions are communicated globally in tourism contexts, in the form of attractions and souvenirs, religion always appears in a local form; while tourists (as "guests") take home memories and memorabilia from given local contexts, the presence of tourism and tourists are significant factors for the "hosts", namely the many "local" religious events, groups, or places; likewise, as we have seen, tourism in many ways stimulates the production of localities.[4] While tourism can be perceived to threaten the integrity of local identities, it can also be said to enhance their endurance and creativity.

The popularization of religion

Like mass media, sports, music, etc., tourism is part of popular culture. Just like other varieties of popular culture, tourism, sometimes in confluence with religion, renders spaces of identities for individuals, communities and nations. Being public, tourism creates, forms, sustains and changes public space(s); it "publishes" and popularizes religion. As we have seen, the touristic advertisement, consumption and selling of religion, like that of other forms of popular culture, provides entertainment, information and points of reference for various ideologies and practices. While, on the one hand, it may disenchant religion, on the other, tourism relies on and celebrates the enchantment ascribed to religion as a quality and source of attractiveness; tourism can in turn become an arena of religious enchantment. The appearance of religion in the arena of tourism can hold "the potential of perplexity and the delight of the unexpected", to borrow a phrase from a recent study of religious games and toys (Bado-Fralick and Norris, 2010, 185–86).

Besides being part of popular culture and sharing many of its issues, when floating in the flow of tourism, religion can become popularized beyond the organizational walls of the respective religious organizations and traditions. Tourism popularizes religion, and due to tourism, religious events, groups, performances and places become accessible as subjects of consumption far beyond the boundaries of religious communication and its organizational sphere as well as participants qualified as adherents, believers, members or worshipers. From the point of view of some (but far from all) religious organizations and participants this may appear inappropriate, amounting to "trivialization" of religion, and maybe it was the religionist bias deeply ingrained in the study of religion(s) which has so far debarred it from addressing tourism as a context of communication about and an arena for constructing religion. Considering sport, music, dance, games, health, holidays and media, in fact tourism is not alone in challenging or even removing the barriers around religion as a clearly demarcated sphere governed by "the sacred" or related semantic codes under the control of religious specialists and other producers of religious communication (Knoblauch 2009). Yet, as we have seen in this book, tourism in various ways engages religion, and even though tourism does not operate according to the code of religious communication, it does not as a matter of principle exclude it either – religious souvenirs or religious places can trigger religious communication, even if that is not their *raison d'être*. The confluence of pilgrimage and tourism or hybrid forms such as religious theme parks may point to the impossibility of clearly distinguishing religious communication from communication about religion in the arena of tourism. Tourism is taken for granted by many religious groups as a medium for religious communication when arranging a variety of trips for their members. While tourism may or may not be a principal arena of religious communication, it certainly is a main context of communication about religion – and as such it clearly merits attention from scholars of religion.

Notes

Introduction

1 For some European countries such as Bulgaria, Austria, Estonia, Portugal, and Switzerland the travel and tourism/GDP rate is between 15–20 percent, but it is somewhat lower for main European industrial nations such as the UK, France and Germany (between 12 and 10 percent), but it is slightly below 10 percent for countries such as the USA, Israel and Japan (Aramberri 2009).

2 For fuller accounts see e.g. Ryan (2003, 1–22); Chambers (2000, 12–17). For general histories of tourism see e.g. Löfgren 1999; Inglis 2000; Boyer 2005; Hachtmann 2007.

3 Hibbert 1969 remains the classical study. See also Brilli 1995. For an online exhibition on The Grand Tour, see http://www.getty.edu/art/exhibitions/grand_tour/what.html.

4 Urry (2002, 124–30, 148–49) argues for the crucial role played by photography for the development of tourism.

5 The *UNWTO World Tourism Barometer* is a regular publication of the Market Intelligence and Promotion Department of UNWTO aimed at monitoring the short-term evolution of tourism and providing the sector with relevant and timely information. The *UNWTO World Tourism Barometer* is published three times a year (January, June and October). The first issue was published in June 2003. The issue I refer to here is available at http://www.unwto.org/facts/eng/pdf/barometer/UNWTO_Barom09_1_en.pdf.

6 Here is an estimate from The World Tourism Organization: "By 2020 international arrivals are expected to surpass 1.5 billion people"; http://www.world-tourism.org/aboutwto/why/en/why.php?op=1 (accessed 16 February 2009).

7 Picard (1996, 53) notes the rapidly increasing domestic (Indonesian middle class) tourism to Bali.

8 http://www.world-tourism.org/aboutwto/statutes/en/pdf/statutes.pdf (accessed 16 February 2009).

9 http://www.world-tourism.org/aboutwto/eng/menu.html (accessed in 2005).

10 Picard (1996, 158, 162) challenges the metaphor of "impact" as an exogenous force that strikes passive host societies like a projectile; he rightly points to the inherent disputes about and negotiations of tourism.

11 For a summary see Steinecke (2006, 96–107).

12 For a case study see Hill 2008.

13 http://www.linkbc.ca/torc/downs1/WTOdefinitiontourism.pdf (accessed 19 August 2010). This definition is widely quoted in the literature and on the internet.

14 Day trippers or other short-term travelers are also called excursionists.

15 There has been some discussion about that issue in anthropology, see, e.g., Badone (2004, 180–89).

16 See (among others) McCabe (2005, 85–106), who points to the methodological implications of these rhetorical and discursive practices for social research. Enzensberger (1996, 117–33; originally published in 1958), maybe the first theory of tourism, notes that "critique is part of tourism itself since its inception" (121). Enzensberger understands tourism as "nothing but a gigantic escape from the kind of reality with which our society surrounds us" (135), a clearly dated theory, be it only because tourism nowadays is the kind of reality with which our society surrounds us.

17 In the opening editorial to the journal *tourist studies* (2001/1), the editors ironically state: "Indeed at times it has been unclear which was growing more rapidly – tourism or tourism research" (Franklin and Crang, 2001, 5).

18 Hospitality management, planning and marketing may be the tourism studies' equivalent to practical theology in the field of religious studies.

19 The book covers a wide bibliography and the author claims: "All the literature available at this moment has been used in this book" (Vukonić 1996, xii). However, in his review, Leiper (1998, 261–63) points to some omissions in the bibliography.

20 Vukonić's book is divided into two main parts. Part One addresses general issues such as "Spiritual Life and Leisure Time" (3–19), the argument of which is difficult to summarize; "Religion as a Cause and Result of Migration" (21–30), which sketches a rather unspecific long-term scenario; "Tourism – A Form of Seasonal Migration" (31–39); "The Motivation of Tourist Journeys" (41–50), where he reviews the earlier literature and concludes "that tourist journeys determined by just one motive are very rare" (50). Part Two more specifically deals with the relationship between tourism and religion. The first chapter of that part discusses "Religious Feelings and Needs as Motives for Tourist Migrations" (53–60); then follows a chapter on "Religious Contents in Tourism" (61–68), which briefly alludes to many aspects more fully discussed in the present work (buildings, events, souvenirs); the following chapter is devoted to the concept of the religious tourist ("*Homo Turisticus Religiosus*"; 69–78); a further chapter presents a synthetic overview of the main ways in which "religion as concept and as a phenomenon is present in almost all the theoretical studies of tourism, and that it is present in none of them" (78) ("Tourism Theorists"; 79–93); "The Theological View of Tourism" (95–115) mainly concentrates on Catholic theology; there follow several chapters addressing pilgrimage ("Pilgrimage – Common to All Religions", 117–34; "The Touristic Determinants of Pilgrimages", 135–43; "Međugorje – A Tourism Case", 145–56); the next chapter analyzes the official attitudes of the Catholic church to tourism ("Tourism in the Institutionalized Forms of the Church", 157–68); the next chapter briefly explores "The Economic Repercussions of Religious Tourism" (169–76); the book ends with some "Future Scenarios" (177–90) where he comes up with the following convictions/predictions: "Today there are no signs indicating that the religious motive for travelling might become weaker in the future ... It seems that religion and belonging to a church have finally become separated and in the future will no longer be considered two sides of the same religious life. That is why in the future religious tourism will develop primarily on an individual basis, on the interest and the prompting of the individual believer's feelings and less in the organization of the church." (189) To some extent this is what seems to have happened. "On the other hand, it is realistic to expect that, in the near future, the alternative tourist with a certain religious conviction will, in the new tourist-receiving milieu ... ,

establish a useful dialogue with the local population of the same religion or a different one. The basis of such a dialogue should be the recognition of pluralism" (190). Ultimately, Vukonić has a very positive view of tourism and is convinced of its positive effects in terms of economy, civilization and religious culture.

21 For pilgrimages, similar to Spanish, Portuguese distinguishes between *peregrinação* (Spanish *peregrinación* and *peregrinaje*) and *romario* (Spanish *romería*). According to Steven Engler (email), *peregrinação* is only used in academic circles. On the history of this semantic distinction see also Sanchis (2006, 85–97).

22 See my review of this volume in *Religion* 38 (2008, 96–98).

23 For a review see M. Collins in *Implicit Religion* 10 (2007, 307–10).

24 Another recent American case study (without any larger conceptual or theoretical agenda) from a religious studies scholar is Ketchell 2007.

25 A similar distinction is proposed by Cohen (1998, 1–10; reprinted in Cohen 2004a, 147–58). He adds the following comment to the second approach: "This interface is largely unexplored." A first step towards this exploration is attempted in the present work. I had originally referred to the two approaches as "deep structures" and "dynamic interferences", but have then (partially) adopted Cohen's terminology. Vukonić (1996, 80) also notes that "[t]here has been almost no serious interest in studying the interrelationship between tourism and religion in the literature on tourism." The present work expands the analytical framework compared to the book by Vukonić. I also disagree with his statement that "[r]eligion and tourism are intertwined: the activity of one creates the conditions of the other."

26 The entry on Wikipedia (http://en.wikipedia.org/wiki/Religious_tourism; accessed 10 February 2010) was first created in 2007; also in 2007, an entry "Turismo religioso" was created on the Portuguese Wikipedia (http://pt.wikipedia.org/wiki/Turismo_religioso; accessed 12 February 2010); the Spanish entry was created in 2009 (http://es.wikipedia.org/wiki/Turismo_religioso; accessed 12 February 2010). On the French and German Wikipedias, when entering the synonymous terms one is automatically directed to the respective pages on pilgrimage (as of 10 February 2010). In Germany, the term "spiritual tourism" is more common than "religious tourism"; this preference, which may indicate an attempt to include non-institutional forms of religiosity/spirituality and reflect an often negative perception of the term religion, is also manifest on the German Wikipedia, which since 2008 has an entry on this term (http://de.wikipedia.org/wiki/Spiritueller_Tourismus; accessed 10 February 2010). The popularity of both terms (religious/spiritual tourism) reflects the increasing importance of this segment of tourism for the tourism sector.

27 Note that since its 19th edition (2007) the Brazilian tourism fair Festival do Turismo de Gramada has a separate Hall of Mystic, Religious and Esoteric Tourism ("Salão do Turismo Místico, Religioso e Esotérico").

28 The author acknowledges the impure quality of that category, its "intrinsic heterogeneity" (77), which he regards as a good metaphor for the crushed nature of modernity. Nevertheless, the book concludes by giving some practical suggestions to improve this branch of tourism. As an appendix, it offers an inventory of associations and organizations in the field of religious tourism in Italy (165–83), mainly in the area of pilgrimages.

29 Cohen (2004b, 157) seems to define religious tourism as the ministry (outreach) to tourists undertaken by various churches. The term "spiritual tourism" has also gained currency in recent years. The term is often not well-defined, but reproduces in one way or another the distinction between religion and spirituality.

30 Typologies of tourists have been criticized as somewhat arbitrary from methodological points of view; see Steinecke (2006, 66–67).

31 Religious tourism is here understood as a sub-form of cultural tourism. For an analysis of the potentials of religious sites for cultural tourism see McGettigan (2003, 13–26).

Chapter 1

1 For a much more far-reaching interpretation see Berger (2004, xii), who suggests "that tourism can be understood as a modern manifestation of ancient mythic beliefs". He builds this interpretation on a reading of Eliade and Barthes.

2 Based on his extensive fieldwork on pilgrimages in Japan, Reader (2005, 37) regards "any attempt to differentiate between 'pilgrims' and 'tourists' to be unsound". Davie (2000, 157) acknowledges that "the line between pilgrimage and tourism (even religious tourism) is extremely difficult to draw. Pilgrims and tourists must be recognized as overlapping categories".

3 For an early discussion see Cohen (1992b [1981], 47–61).

4 The classical statement is Turner (1969, 94–130; "Liminality and Communitas"). For an interesting critique with regard to a pilgrimage/tourism center see Eade (1992, 18–32).

5 The Turnerian theory of pilgrimage has been widely used but also severely criticized on theoretical and empirical grounds be several scholars; some important studies are referred to and summarized by Eade and Sallnow (1991, 4–5). According to Margry (2008, 21) the theory "has been falsified over and over again on the basis of ethnographic case studies".

6 Selänniemi, an expert in the study of sustainable tourism, now works for a large tour operator.

7 I remain, however, unconvinced of some of these interpretations (for instance regarding communitas).

8 Space does not permit a more penetrating methodological critique.

9 "[T]ourists generally remain unchanged and demand a lifestyle not too different from that at home" (Graburn 2001, 50).

10 For a later discussion see Graburn 2001.

11 This assumption seems to be confirmed by some empirical studies, which point to the primacy of regenerative motives (relaxation, absence of stress, distance from everyday life, leisure) and the fundamental need of regeneration and relaxation (Steinecke 2006, 50–51). For methodological reflection on the study of travelers' motives see Hirtenlehner, Mörth and Steckenbauer 2002. On the basis of an Austrian sample these authors conclude that there were three fundamental motives for tourist traveling: discovery, regeneration and entertainment.

12 "Vacations involving travel (i.e. tourism) are the modern equivalent for secular societies to the annual and lifelong sequences of festivals and pilgrimages found in more traditional, God-fearing societies" (Graburn 2001, 43).

13 The idea that sightseeing is a substitute ritual has by now become commonplace (see David Lodge; p. 251, note 6 to Chapter 8).

14 Note that MacCannell engages elements of Ervin Goffman's theory of ritual and style of social analysis.

15 Authenticity has been a major issue in the study of tourism ever since. Relevant literature is legion.

16 See Grimshaw (2008, 15): "Tourism was presented as the *de facto* new opiate of the masses in a reading combining the Marxist critique and disdain of both religion and capitalism."

17 Other theories of tourism refer to categories such as festivals, play, flow, ritual, consumption, etc.; see Hennig (1997, 72–101) and Steinecke (2006, 48–49).

18 Tresidder is also inspired by Eliade (and by Graburn and MacCannell). In his view, "[t]ourism provides the opportunity to live outside both time and space for a limited period" and "whenever society agrees to release us, the sacred becomes an attainable entity available to us all. If we accept the notion of the sacred … we have to accept that there has to be a place in which we can consume this sacred time, it has to be 'different' or 'special'" (Tresidder 1999, 140–41); he then proceeds to apply this idea to national parks.

19 Katie Alegro (2004) distinguishes five phases of place making with regard to the Mammoth Cave (which is still visited by between one and two million tourists annually). The reactions analyzed by Sears fit into the Romantic interpretations (phase 2) in Alegro's reconstruction.

20 Sears seems to regard tourism attractions as a kind of early civil religion.

21 In her study of the period 1880 to 1940, Shaffer (2001, 6) interprets tourism as a ritual of American citizenship, as a patriotic duty within emerging nationalism, which "was central to the development of a nascent national culture in the United States", especially in the context of the establishment of a national transportation and communication network as well as the emergent consumer culture.

22 On the underlying framework of such shifts see Urry 1995.

23 Interestingly, this terminology is developed by once again contrasting the tourist with the pilgrim. A pilgrim, Brown states, would not even consider such deals where "you look the vendor into the eye and complete the deal, he knows that you know it is a fake (despite its protestations), and you know that he knows that you know, and so on" (Brown 1996, 46, note 6). His assumptions about pilgrims and pilgrimages may be somewhat naïve, though.

24 I therefore disagree with Urry (2002, 12) when he stipulates that tourism "results from a basic binary division between the ordinary/everyday and the extraordinary", as long as this implies something more than a purely spatial translocation. In fact, many tourists happily return to the same destination every year and they look forward to having their dinner in exactly the same restaurant they had dinner before. Eugenia Wickens, (2002, 841) calls these "home-comers" the "Lord Byron Type" ("the annual ritual return to the same place").

25 There is specialized scholarly literature on each of the following branches of tourism. References seem unnecessary in the present context.

26 To some extent, culture tourism encompasses several of the other forms of tourism singled out in the present list; for a summary of cultural tourism studies see Melanie K. Smith 2006; Timothy and Nyaupane 2009.

27 I.e. tourism to "sites, attractions or events that are associated with death, violence or disaster" (Sharpley 2005, 216). Holocaust tourism is the classical example. Recent examples include travels to Ground Zero and New Orleans. See also the war grave travels studied by Walter. Visits to disaster sites often trigger religious responses. Dark tourism is by no means a modern development; Thomas Cook already had visits to battlefields (Waterloo) in his program; see Hachtmann (2007, 59).

28 See also Chapter 5.

29 See Mustonen 2005. With regard to motives and aspirations, the concept of the liminoid, and reflections on the nature of postmodern, Mustonen claims "that contemporary volunteer tourism is a continuation, a kind of rebirth of traditional pilgrimage" (174). I find his arguments not really compelling. For the two communities in North India of his sample, Mustonen notes that "India in general played an important part in tourists' experiences. Many tourists seek inner peace through Indian spirituality" (167).

30 The recent diversification of tourism is thereby reflected in postmodern theorizing about tourism; see also Uriely 1997.

31 Allcock 1988 suggests studying tourism as a form of "implicit religion", but his program remains somewhat shallow.

32 Grimshaw engages the tropes of tourist, traveller and exile in an attempt to construct a post-modern, post-religious, profane, secular, inter-cultural theology. The main method "is to read texts on tourism, travel and exile as if they were theological writings because so often they seem to offer a possible location and experience of grace that is deeply attractive for a secular western modernity that locates the real, the authentic – or even grace – as that which has been lost, relocated or found only over there: anywhere but here" (2008, 11).

Chapter 2

1 *The Oxford English Dictionary* (http://dictionary.oed.com), s.v. interference, definition 2.

2 Part II of Timothy and Olsen eds (2005) presents tourism in relation to various religious traditions (East Asian "philosophies", the New Age, Judaism, Buddhism, Islam, Sikhism, Hinduism, Catholicism, Latter Day Saints) and the attitudes of these religions towards travel. None of the authors of these chapters is a trained historian of religions.

3 See a report on the Allgäu region in Bavaria published at http://www.sonntags-blatt-bayern.de/dekanate/dekanat9.htm (accessed 27 August 2007). According to this report 25–30 additional priests are active in pastoral care during the tourist season in the tourist centers. One dean is quoted as saying that there are tourists attending services held in the open countryside who had not been in touch with the church for 25 to 30 years. Similarly, a reportage on a German pastor (from the former GDR) ministering the Protestant tourist community on the island of Gran Canaria refers to the fact that many people attending Sunday worship do not go to church at home; one female participant is quoted as saying that the experience makes her appreciate the religious message in a new way; the reportage was published in 2000; see http://www.berlinonline.de/berliner-zeitung/archiv/.bin/dump.fcgi/2000/1002/blickpunkt/0007/index.html (accessed August 27, 2007).

4 This is based on interviews with tourists in Bergen (summer 2007).

5 I am grateful to Bjørn-Ola Tafjord for this reminder.

6 Interestingly, some hotels excluded Jewish guests during the summer holidays, but admitted them during other seasons when they stayed to attend conferences or congresses; see Bajohr (2003, 158).

7 Albeit especially widespread in the US, seaside anti-Semitism was an international phenomenon; in Germany, Jews were increasingly discriminated against in many seaside resorts, while other resorts such as Norderney, Helgoland and Bad Kissingen acquired fame as quasi-Jewish resorts; after 1933 holidaying became increasingly impossible for Jews in Germany; see Bajohr 2003.

8 Black Americans faced the same kind of discrimination at holiday resorts.

9 See http://www.goingonfaith.com/ (accessed 10 July 2009); http://www.travelwithspirit.com/index.html (accessed 10 July 2009).

10 See http://www.wrtareligioustravel.com/NR/rdonlyres/97134A3D-F95A-4832-9B02–04C3EB5B75D6/0/WRTA2009Brochure.pdf (accessed 19 July 2009). Access to this PDF document now requires username/password.

11 Reference kindly provided by Hans Schmalscheidt.

12 This is also known as seasonal retirement migration.

13 See http://www.ev-kirche-teneriffa.es (accessed 14 January 2009).

14 While we by now have a fair number of studies of the creation of religious institutions and "sacred space" in the diasporas, I am not aware of any

study discussing the religious infrastructures catering to the needs of leisure displacements.

15 See http://hotelkadampa.com/es/spain (accessed 25 February 2010).

16 Francisco Diez de Velasco, email to the author, 6 January 2010.

17 In 1999 it started its own internet-church: www.nettkirken.no.

18 Interview with the Dean, 1 September 2008.

19 Information and hypothesis kindly provided by Mark Chaves (email to the author, 5 January 2009).

20 There are also ministries and religious facilities at transitional spaces such as train stations.

21 Information kindly provided by the IACAC secretary, Mary Holloway (email to the author, 15 January 2010).

22 See http://en.wikipedia.org/wiki/World%27s_busiest_airports_by_passenger_traffic (accessed 14 January 2010) for continuously updated stastistics.

23 Translation and observation generously shared by Ian Reader (Manchester).

24 The prayer room signifier sometimes carries a different logo. At some other airports, one speaks of "religious reflection room" or of "meditation room"; in these cases, often also the logo shows a figure in meditation posture. In Islamic countries, religious facilities are naturally referred to as "mosques".

25 See Marion Bowman, "Religion in context: airport chapels and chaplaincy", course material kindly provided by the author.

26 Accessed 16 January 2010. The chapel also has its own website: http://www.airportchapel.org (same date).

27 http://www.airportchapels.org/ (accessed 15 January 2010).

28 See also Bowman, "Religion in context".

29 See http://www.flickr.com/photos/stormdaemon/806603065/ (accessed 3 April 2010).

30 See http://www.vatican.va/holy_father/john_paul_ii/apost_constitutions/documents/hf_jp-ii_apc_19880628_pastor-bonus-index_en.html (accessed 9 February 2010).

31 http://www.cef.fr/catho/culture/tourisme/index.php (accessed 3 April 2008).

32 http://www.byegm.gov.tr/yayinlarimiz/kitaplar/turkiye2008/english/350-351.htm (accessed 19 August 2010).

33 Also for tourists without a definite religious agenda, Turkey has much to provide in terms of religious attractions, most famously the Hagia Sophia in Istanbul. In Ephesus, the temple of Artemis and other temples as well as the (reconstructed) house of the Virgin Mary have to a great extent contributed to the revival of the town through tourism, according to Scarce (2000, 29).

34 The scheme also targeted Jewish tourists. Izmir is recognized and developed as a potentially major Jewish destination; see Cohen Ioannides and Ioannides (2006, 167).

35 http://www.chnpress.com/news/?section=1&id=1839 (accessed 19 May 2008).

36 http://www.chnpress.com/news/?section=1&id=1839 (accessed 19 May 2008).

37 *Promotion of Buddhist Tourism Circuits in Selected Asian Countries* (2003, 1).

38 *Promotion of Buddhist Tourism Circuits in Selected Asian Countries* (2003, 2).

39 Note that the choice of the study site (the Western Wall in Jerusalem) to some extent predicts and predicates the results.

40 There are some studies confirming the idea that national cultures have an effect on tourist behavior, albeit only as a moderating variable; see Abraham Pizam 1999.

41 Cohen himself sketches some evidence in his study of pilgrimage centers in Thailand, where he states (a) that "[w]ith the development of modern tourism,

both domestic and foreign, some of the traditional festivals at popular pilgrimage centers tend to become highly commercialized". Commercialization, however, does not automatically amount to secularization. Furthermore, Cohen observes (b) that: "New touristic fairs and festivals with an utterly secular character cropped up in a variety of … locations; these are completely unrelated to any religious center." This observation, then, refers to the emergence of a new type of public events. Finally, Cohen claims that: "Thai festivals as a whole undergo secularization and their touristic character is strengthened at the expense of the religious one."Apart from examples, where due to changes in the political structure, former politico-religious centers have become popular pilgrimage-cum-entertainment centers, this statement comes as a bit of a surprise and is not really substantiated in Cohen's foregoing analysis. All quotations are from Cohen (1992a, 48).

42 Theories predicting that increasing (awareness of) religious diversity is one factor leading to secularization could point to tourism as exposing travellers to the fact that there are other religious options available out there. In that sense, tourism could trigger indirect secularizing effects on tourists. However, I would not think that this is a promising theoretical approach, if only for the simple reason that the exposure to diversity first of all puts defense mechanisms in motion, leading to a strengthening of religious identity.

43 For some examples of an alleged negative impact of tourism on Malaysian culture that refer to Islamic groups, see V. King (1993, 113).

44 Religion is only addressed in some few chapters.

45 See Hanna (1984, 22) for visitors from former colonial countries to parish churches in Britain.

46 Delaney 1990 suggests that the *hajj* serves as a symbolic model for the annual return journeys of (first generation) Turkish migrants living in Belgium; as such a model the *hajj* might be able to explain "why, against any rational calculus, thousands of Turks living in Europe undertake the arduous journey back to Turkey year after year, at vast expense, in physical discomfort, and at risk of life" (513). While this comparison offers some interesting analytical perceptions, its explanatory value is diminished by the fact that many migrants from other religious traditions undertake similar return journeys.

47 For a Canadian example see the Bronfman Israel Experience Center Monreal: http://www.biec.ca/biec-about.html (accessed 19 August 2010).

48 Unfortunately, the authors fail to comment on another interesting finding of their study: fewer (!) people agreed with the following statements/views after their trips than before: "Israel serves as a national, cultural center of the Jewish people"; "Israel as a source of pride for North American Jewry" (Ari, Mansfeld and Mittelberg 2003 21).

49 For the Jewish community in the United States it has also been observed that "even those Jews who travel primarily for recreational purposes will often seek out Jewish sites" such as old Jewish neighborhoods, homes of famous Jewish personalities, synagogues, graveyards, etc. (Ioannides and Cohen Ioannides 2002, 24). Even ordinary travel thereby gains some ethnic features.

50 http://www.ghanaweb.com/GhanaHomePage/features/artikel.php?ID=59447 (accessed 21 October 2007).

51 http://www.ghanaweb.com/GhanaHomePage/features/artikel.php?ID=59447 (accessed 21 October 2007).

52 For analyses and descriptions see Schramm 2004. The interesting case of queer "pilgrimages" to the "queer homeland" of San Francisco is discussed by Alyssa Cymene Howe 2001. Note her comment (53): "Although all pilgrimages involve

leaving 'home' to find spiritual redemption, the unique quality of queer tourism is that a reversal of religious pilgrimage is at play. Many queer tourists leave home because it is there that they have undergone spiritual exile; a 'homeland' offers the sanctuary that many 'back homes' do not."

53 http://www.ghanaweb.com/GhanaHomePage/features/artikel.php?ID=59447 (accessed 21 October 2007).

Chapter 3

1 Based on the example of Koyama-san, a retired insurance broker from Osaka in his late 60s, as reported by Reader (2005, 100–101).

2 This is the case with the British war grave travels, see Tony Walter (1993, 67). For Graceland in the context of American pilgrimage sites see, e.g., Juan Eduardo Campo 1998.

3 Among other publications, see Margry ed. 2008. For dark tourism, see Ryan, Aicken and Page 2005.

4 Such a scheme seems to be implied in book titles such as Gladstone (2005) *From Pilgrimage to Package Tour* and Swatos and Tomasi (eds), *From Medieval Pilgrimage to Religious Tourism: the social and cultural economies of piety* (2002).

5 See also Olsen and Timothy (2006, 3) and Davie (2000, 157).

6 Here is a telling example: in 1999, the year after a cable car had started to operate to the pilgrimage temple of Manakamana in Nepal, the number of visitors almost doubled; a similar structural development had taken place in the aftermath of opening a new highway in the late 1960s; see Bleie 2003. According to a report from AP (28 November 2007), the 2006 opening of a rail line connecting Lhasa with the rest of China has resulted in a dramatic increase of travel to Tibet.

7 Vukonić, 2002, regards, as the title says, the relationship between religion, tourism and economics as a "convenient symbiosis"; at the same time he argues that the economic side of pilgrimage should be studied more intensely.

8 For a comprehensive study see Nolan and Nolan 1989.

9 Note that Wiley's article is anti-tourist: he regards the tourists as "a threat to the village" (Wiley 2005, 154) and speaks of "the modern triumph of tourism over Christianity" (152).

10 For a case study see Shinde 2007.

11 One of the most visited pilgrimage locations of the world (allegedly 7.5 million visitors annually, surpassing even Lourdes) is San Giovanni Rotondo, the residence of the Capuchin priest Padre Pio (1887–1968), famous for his stigmata, who was declared a saint in 2002; see Reader (2007, 221).

12 For information published by the Baha'i World Center for pilgrims and about pilgrimage to Baha'i holy places see http://pilgrimage.bahai.org/ (accessed 3 January 2008). A comprehensive study of Baha'i pilgrimage is lacking; for a scholarly perspective on one site see Collins-Kreiner and Gatrell 2006.

13 For a case study of a small new French religious group in which pilgrimage plays a crucial role, see Mayer 2001. The author also pays attention to the interface with the local tourism branch.

14 See http://en.wikipedia.org/wiki/World_Youth_Day (accessed 7 January 2009).

15 See http://www.topnews.in/catholic-world-meeting-families-starts-mexico-city-2109919 (accessed 16 January 2009).

16 The websites set up for such events usually provide lists of hotels; discounts with some airlines are often negotiated for such events.

17 The Old Town of Santiago de Compostela was inscribed in the list in 1985.

18 Santos also discusses several theories that would explain the reasons behind the revival.

19 Sá Carneiro 2003, 259 mentions 60 books written by or for Brazilians about the Camino.

20 For the island of Selja (off the West Norwegian coast) with the ruins of the former St. Sunniva Abbey see Mikaelsson 2005.

21 See www.pilegrim.no

22 Interestingly, the head of the association has taken some courses in the history of religions.

23 For these discourses see Mikaelson 2008.

24 For Christian pilgrimages to Israel see Collins-Kreiner *et al.* 2006.

25 "The typical visit of the Catholic pilgrims is short and focused on sacred sites … The Protestants, on the other hand, come for a longer period and are also interested in sacred sites" (324–25). Previous studies reviewed by Fleischer (2000, 315–16) point to similar differences with regard to tour structures and activities.

26 See http://www.unitours.com/index_pilgrimages.html

27 See http://www.coesima.eu/portal/index.php?id=1146 (accessed 18 January 2009).

28 The book lists main religious/spiritual attractions country wise (covering 42 countries) and supplies statistical and historical information. For the United Kingdom Fournier covers London (Saint Paul's, Westminster Abbey, Methodist Central Hall, Westminster Cathedral), Canterbury, Walshgbam (sic!=Walsingham), Whitby, Glastonbury, Epworth, York, Caldey, Stonehenge, Iona, with pictures from Bolton Abbey, Canterbury Cathedral, Stonehenge, a brief text on the Oxford Movement and provides a list of main sanctuaries as well as all UNESCO World Heritage Sites.

29 See http://www.sacred-destinations.com (accessed 19 August 2010).

30 http://www.insight-travel.com/question.html (accessed 6 February 2008).

31 http://www.insight-travel.com/question.html (accessed 6 February 2008).

32 In the case of Lourdes, older thermal stations in that region benefitted from the increasing popularity of the pilgrimage center, see Kaufman 2005, 31: "Older thermal stations, such as Gavarnie and Cauterets, were now indebted to the sanctuary for bringing new customers to their spas; in fact, between 1860 and 1906 nearly half the clientele of Pyrenean thermal resorts were also on a pilgrimage to Lourdes."

33 Walter (1993, 72) speaks of "unintentional pilgrims" for those war grave travelers "finding that for a few moments they have ceased to be tourists and have connected with something very deep". Of course, one can discuss Walter's criteria for distinction between tourism and pilgrimage, but this is not the issue here.

34 This was observed for Santiago de Compostela by Santos (2002, 49).

35 For an example, see Badone (2008, 35).

36 For a case in point see the contributions to Swatos ed. 2006. For an early instructive example see also Eade 1992. Vukonić 2002, 62 frames it maybe somewhat too undifferentiated: "Without doubt, religious and touristic features interweave with few, if any, signs of them harming each other." Students of pilgrimages in the ancient world have likewise emphasized the conflation of pilgrimage and tourism; see Williamson 2005. Margry (2008, 28–29) tries to reverse this trend.

37 pdf on CD. For similar observations see Singh (2004, 57–60).

38 See also Gladstone (2005, 178–94).

39 The *pandas* also perform other functions for the pilgrims, and there is increasing competition among the *pandas*, who "generally have a bad reputation with pilgrims, who often perceive them as corrupt, lazy and greedy" (Gladstone 2005, 189).

40 For a tourist-presentation of the fair see http://www.pushkar-fair.net (accessed 27 May 2006).
41 http://en.wikipedia.org/wiki/Pushkar_Camel_Fair (accessed 27 May 2006).
42 See Gladstone (2005, 186–88) for an analysis of the resulting "dual tourism industry" (different hotels and restaurants catering to both groups and changes in the real estate sector).
43 For the different terms that can be used in modern Japanese in order to distinguish pilgrimage and religion see Graburn (2004, 132; 1983, 71–82, glossary).

Chapter 4

1 For a coherent attempt in that direction see Knott 2005.
2 The landmark publication is Smith 1987.
3 Tourism can both be both "locative" and "utopian" in the sense of Smith 1993. However, even when tourism is locative it is simultaneously trans-locative, and even when utopian, the utopias are located and part of itineraries.
4 It seems that tourist itineraries and flows are relatively understudied in Tourism Studies; for a summary of available hypotheses see McKercher and Lew 2004.
5 This is not meant to imply that religious places have an inherent "magnetic pulling power". Given that attractions are often considered as key ingredients of tourism, the term "attraction" has been discussed in Tourism Studies. More recent studies have rejected earlier notions of "gravitational influences", "magnetic" forces or "intrinsic attracting power" exerted by attractions. Several definitions have been suggested, sometimes within larger theoretical frameworks. For a brief summary and a reflection on current changes see Benckendorff 2006.
6 In Tourism Studies vocabularies this can be referred to as a "core resource".
7 Chapter 6 (pp. 146ff.) will look at one category of tourist or touristified villages.
8 Reader (1991, 134–61) emphasizes the beautiful location and landscape setting of many Japanese pilgrimage places, making them interesting travel destinations in their own right. Many travelers (pilgrims and/or tourists) also undertake their journeys in order to learn more about Japanese history. Sacred forests are a border-zone between sites and landscapes. Sacred forests can also become tourism attractions. An African example is the sacred forest in Ouidah (Benin), which simultaneously serves as a *vodun* ritual site.
9 Vukonić (1996, 66): "There are more visitors to larger and more grandiose buildings, in the architectural sense, although their religious significance is not greater than that of some much smaller sacred buildings."
10 A study of English parish churches has identified no fewer than "155 different types of features which were thought to be of most interest to visitors … No one type of feature was mentioned by more than 14 percent of incumbents. Top of the league were the monuments, followed by the architecture, stained glass, towers, fonts, associations with people and the brasses" (Hanna 1984, 24).
11 See Hazbun (2007, 33) for the de-development of villages near Pharaonic sites.
12 See Shackley (2001, 1–7) for an attempt to classify sacred sites.
13 http://fr.wikipedia.org/wiki/Cath%C3%A9drale_Notre-Dame_de_Paris#Le_tourisme (accessed 3 April 2008).
14 Shackley (2001, 1) puts the figure at 12 million visitors. Vukonić (1996, 67) refers to a study from 1985 according to which there were between 9 and 10 million visitors annually. On a peak day that meant some 4,750 people passed through the cathedral in just one hour.
15 However, there are also different statistics available on the internet which may paint a different picture.

16 See http://en.wikipedia.org/wiki/Sagrada_Fam%C3%ADlia (accessed 9 April 2008).
17 See http://ca.wikipedia.org/wiki/Temple_Expiatori_de_la_Sagrada_Fam%C3% ADlia (accessed 9 April 2008).
18 See Rotherham (2007, 70–74) for case studies of churches in rural tourism in Britain.
19 For these terms see Leiper (1990, 374).
20 This is the case with the majority of parish churches; see Hanna (1984, 26).
21 See Sharpley and Sundaram 2005.
22 From Asia, the Temple and Cemetery of Confucius in Qufu in Shandong Province (China), since 1994 listed on the UNESCO World Heritage Site, is one of the most important examples; one of the most well-known cemeteries in the Western world serving as a tourist attraction is Père Lachaise in Paris, mainly because of the celebrities buried there. For a virtual tour see http://www.pere-lachaise.com/ (accessed 20 January 2009). The site has a very interesting intro-duction claiming that the website as well as the cemetery itself can be defined by the relations they establish between the living and the dead. The text seems to avoid religion at all cost and claims that it is the arts and dreams that offer a consolation in the face of death! For rural cemeteries as tourist attractions (and their religious significance) in 19th century, America see Sears (1998, 99–115). Another interesting case is war grave travel; see Walter 1993. For tour-ism to cemeteries and churchyards in general see also Seaton 2002. The cata-combs in Rome and Palermo are another interesting example.
23 A region in south-western France markets itself as Pays Cathare (see, e.g. http://www.payscathare.org [accessed 9 March 2009]), in memory of the medieval religious group of the Cathars that were persecuted and extinguished. *Le Sentier Cathare: De la Médterranée aux Pyrénées, à pied de château en château* (2005) is an example of a guide book inviting travelers to explore the Cathare past by providing an itinerary. (I owe this reference and further materials that cannot be discussed here in any detail to my colleague Einar Thomassen.).
24 Consider Salem, Massachusetts, the site of the 1692 witch trials. Salem has served as a tourist destination since the mid-19th century. In recent decades it is branded as the Halloween Capital of the World; it attracts "hundreds of thousands from all over the world" (Gencarella 2007, 281). There is also an increasing tourism to cities known for their history of violent clashes between religious groups. Both Beirut and Belfast have in recent years been emerging as "hot" destinations. For Belfast, see Dépret (2007, 137–62, 269–72).
25 I am not aware of any study on this topic. The prominent place of religious sites in many brochures is mentioned in passing by Selwyn 1993.
26 *Faraway Holidays 1983* quoted by Dann (1996, 75).
27 Referring to a document from 1994.
28 http://www.unesco.org/courier/1999_08/uk/dossier/txt21.htm (accessed 5 June 2010).
29 See *Promotion of Buddhist Tourism Circuits in Selected Asian Countries*, (2003,71) for the case of Vietnam. The decision to invest in the rehabilitation or preservation of religious buildings sometimes requires a new classification of sites according to their value as heritage.
30 See http://www.frauenkirche-dresden.de/ (accessed 17 February 2008).
31 This is an allusion to the Cathedral of Our Lady of the Angels in Los Angeles (completed and dedicated in 2002), designed and constructed by Spanish architect José Rafael Moneo Vallés.
32 *Promotion of Buddhist Tourism Circuits in Selected Asian Countries* (2003, 33) (based on a report prepared by the National Tourism Authority of Lao PDR).

33 http://en.wikipedia.org/wiki/Sh%C5%8Ddoshima (accessed 1 February 2010).

34 Gothóni (1994, 179) describes this in the context of visits to Mount Athos within the conceptual framework of pilgrimages – when a visit inadvertently acquired a religious dimension, it gets classified as pilgrimage: "The field tales show that visitors, foreigners and Greeks alike, when asked before their journey to Athos, generally say that they are just going to see the place because they have heard and read so much about it. [MS: They initially had framed their visits and expectations as tourism.] After returning to Ouranopolis, most of them clearly realize that they have just made a pilgrimage. They are indeed deeply impressed by what they have seen and what they have experienced, and they are moved." See also Andriotis (2009, 79).

35 See also Hanna (1984, 9) for the following statement of one incumbent at a parish church: "I feel strongly that parish churches have tremendous potential for proclaiming the Christian faith to visitors, who often are impressionable and have to look and think."

36 Whether that is a clever strategy is a different question.

37 It is unclear whether the emergence of religious interest and experience only comes to effect when visiting places that one to some extent is familiar with, or whether similar experiences also occur at "alien" places.

38 Vukonić (1996, 63) presents a more one-dimensional analysis when he says that religious buildings have "lost their religious function" once they have been turned into tourist attractions.

39 See the discussion in Bremer 2006 and 2004.

40 See also Bremer (2004, 143–44) for similar observations.

41 Woodward (2004, 182) refers to a 1999 community survey from the Buddhist Temple of the Tooth Relic in Kandy (Sri Lanka) that "found only 50 percent of local residents in favour of foreign tourists (i.e. non-Buddhists) visiting the Temple, 40 percent were concerned at the inappropriate clothing worn by international tourists and indeed 13 percent wanted no tourists at all (Kandy Municipal Council, 2000)."

42 Note that even beaches – the prototypical tourist space – can serve as ritual spaces, e.g. in Bali, where they function as sites for rituals of purification. However, "the presence of curious and scantily clad bathers has proven to be a source of exasperation for the Balinese" (Picard 1996, 76).

43 At the Buddhist Shaolin Monastery in Dengfeng (China) two luxury public bathrooms measuring more than 150 square meters were recently installed for three million yuan (= US$430,000). The bathrooms are free of charge for tourists and monks alike. They are equipped with LCD televisions in the foyer, an area for diapers/ nappy changing and provide access for the disabled. Predictably there was some criticism of this development. For a report from the *Window of China* see http://news. xinhuanet.com/english/2008–04/08/content_7940163.htm (accessed 9 January 2009).

44 In many cases, especially in less economically developed countries, damages caused by environmental or other factors are far greater challenges than tourist impact. Also the ritual engagement of sites (e.g. by depositing or burning offerings) often creates "ritual litter" and damages sites.

45 The pyramids of Giza have been covered with graffiti since antiquity. An Arabic writer noted in the early 13th century that the inscriptions travelers made on the then still extant surface would fill over 10,000 pages; see Künzl and Koeppel (2002, 39). On the vandalism of Egyptian sites by tourists, collectors and archaeologists, see Fagan 1975.

46 A case study from Nepal reports findings that pilgrims rather than tourists are "responsible for most of the physical pollution and degradation of the site" (Sofield 2001, 259).

47 See the case from the Greek Island of Skyros as reported by Zarkia (1996, 143–73, 167): "Tourists' behaviour in the churches was the second big problem. 'They went there with their sleeping bags, they used this holy place for camping. Now we keep all the churches locked during summer … ' The custom is that the church should be open at all times … Now this strategy of defense keeps the churches locked during the presence of strangers." This strategy is viable because the island has a very short tourist season.

48 For the four main churches of Paris, see Pearce (1999a, 85).

49 For a survey of management issues also see Olsen 2006a.

50 Woodward (2004, 178–79) points to coach access as a major management challenge at UK cathedrals.

51 See also Bremer (2004, 79) for an example.

52 See the interesting observations by Bremer (2004, 141–43).

53 Interview with the Dean, Bergen, September 1, 2008.

54 Quoted by Woodward (2004, 180).

55 This is part of the transformative (not to say destructive) impact tourism often has on landscapes.

56 http://www.tanahlot.net/home/index.php/index.php?option=com_content&view=article&id=473&Itemid=3 (accessed 19 August 2010).

57 Apart from the routes of independent international travelers (very few of whom currently travel in that region), Zoroastrian sites are on the programme of international travel agencies. Touran Zamin, an Iranian travel agency catering to the international market, offers a 14 days/13 nights tour "Tracing Zoroastrian Roots". The attractions covered on this tour include natural sites (mountains, caves), archaeological sites, imperial palaces, city visits (with visits to tombs, squares, bazaars, mosques), and visits to four Zoroastrian shrines, two fire-temples and some Zoroastrian villages; www.touranzamin.com (accessed 22 May 2008). The agency also offers "Iran Church Tours" (to Iranian Armenia) and "Iran Nomads Tours".

58 I don't know how this figure, which is reported on the visual history website of the temple (www.bahai.us/bahai-temple), was established, but it does not seem implausible given the number of visitors present when I visited the temple.

59 See Jonathan Adams, "A Falun Gong welcome for mainland visitors to Taiwan", *International Herald Tribune* (July 3, 2008); http://www.iht.com/articles/2008/07/03/asia/taiwan.php (accessed 13 January 2009).

60 See http://whc.unesco.org/en/list (accessed 11 April 2008).

61 For a tour description combining culture, nature, shopping and religion see http://www.mysticvibration.com/Egypt/Egypt.html (accessed 15 May 2006). The director of Purple Mountain Healing Center and Purple Mountain Tours who arranges Sacred Journeys and Goddess Tours to Egypt (and several other places) where she (as advertised on www.purplemountaintours.com/egypt.htm [accessed 1 February 2008]) has special permission to enter several sacred sites (e.g. The Great Pyramid and the Temple of Ramses II and Nefertiti at Abu Simbel) and perform rituals in there with her groups. In fact, it seems that the Egyptian Antiquarian Organizations rents out interior chambers of the Great Pyramid at Giza to New Age tour groups, see Attix (2002, 55). During his activities as a tour guide to the Egyptian pyramids Jørgen Podeman Sørensen (University of Copenhagen) has experienced different encounters with several groups of people who would perform their own rituals inside and outside the temples (email to the author).

62 http://whc.unesco.org/en/about/ (accessed 11 April 2008).

63 For the history and an analysis of tourism/pilgrimages to these places see Ivakhiv 2003.

64 For the mystical tourism (*turismo místico* as the locals call it) linked to Cusco (where restaurants, gift shops and child street vendors alike capitalize on the "mystical" theming of the place), see Hill 2007.

65 For Cusco, see Hill (2007, 437).

66 See Reader (2007, 223) who notes that "[t]he spread of 'New Age' ideas among pilgrims has clearly affected pilgrimages such as Santiago and Shikoku".

67 For some people it is that mixture which makes Glastonbury appealing. But the diverse claims for the sacredness of the space have occasionally also resulted in tensions. At other places there have been outright conflicts.

68 See (without reference to religion or religious practices) Ryan, Aicken and Page eds. 2005.

69 http://www.kscourts.org/ca10/cases/1999/04/98–8021.htm (accessed 10 July 2007).

70 http://www.kscourts.org/ca10/cases/1999/04/98–8021.htm (accessed 10 July 2007).

71 http://www.kscourts.org/ca10/cases/1999/04/98–8021.htm (accessed 10 July 2007).

72 A similar conflict between "traditional practices" (greatly revived since the late 1960s) and tourists is documented for the Chief Mountain in Montana by Reeves 1994.

73 See Shackley 2004 for a case study of the Uluru.

74 Quotations taken from Ingram (2005, 26–27).

75 At least for those who have positive experience during their trips. Eight of Ingram's respondents reported predominantly positive experiences of Aboriginal culture, while nine reported predominantly negative reactions, see Ingram (2005, 26).

76 See in detail Digance 2003. Attix (2002, 55) has pointed out that "[a]lmost none of the New Age guidebooks, as yet, are providing their readers with ideas of appropriate protocols of behavior or etiquette to be observed in the practice of pseudo-traditional ceremonies, let alone indicating that such attempts at replication are unwelcome, and indeed have been banned by tribal organizations in recent years".

77 See http://www.hawaiiweb.com/maui/html/sites/honokahua_preservation_site.html (accessed 30 January 2010) for pictures of the stone and the site; see http://www.allbusiness.com/north-america/united-states-hawaii/113569–1.html (accessed 30 January 2010) for the dispute. (Florian Jeserich drew my attention to this case.).

Chapter 5

1 Pretes discusses this project as an example of the consumption of intangible concepts such as Christmas and the paradoxes of authenticity in post-modernity.

2 Pictures can easily be found via Google images.

3 http://icom.museum/ethics.html#intro (accessed 29 January 2009).

4 See the example of the Hupa dance regalia that were repatriated from the Peabody Museum of Archaeology and Ethnology at Harvard University in 1998; the regalia eventually found their way into another museum, the Hoopa Tribal Museum, and are occasionally brought to attend the dances (Gaskell 2003, 157–59).

5 See the preceding note and the case of the Virgin of Vladimir icon discussed by Gaskell (2003, 154–57).

6 See the consecration of the new Tibetan altar consecrated by the Dalai Lama at the Newark Museum discussed by Gaskell (2003, 151–54).

7 The Museum Schnütgen (a collection of sacred/liturgical art) housed in the Romanesque church of St. Cecilia in Cologne is an example of a liturgical arts museum. For other uses, consider the following examples of museums housed in former churches from across the world: the Museum of Czech Music (Prague), the

Tycho Brahe Museum of Ven (Sweden), the Museum of Garden History (London), the National Tile Museum (Lisbon), the Angel Museum in Beloit (Wisconsin), the Lavahe Islands Marine Museum (Canada), etc.

8 Apart from the Kazan Cathedral and the Museum of Atheism, "[i]n the early days of the Soviet Union many anti-religious museums were created from the collections of pre-revolutionary church archaeological museums, and from the contents of closed churches" (Koutchinsky 2005, 154).

9 For the early international expositions see Burris 2001.

10 For a panorama focusing on the exhibits see Grossman 2003; for Germany and Austria with a focus on their cultural and religious significance see Offe 2000.

11 http://www.creationmuseum.org/about (accessed 1 February 2009).

12 See http://en.wikipedia.org/wiki/Creation_Museum (accessed 1 February 2009).

13 There are some older creationist museums in the United States such as the Museum of Creation and Earth History in Santee (California) run by the Institute of Creation Research and the Creation Evidence Museum in Glens Rose (Texas) founded in 1984.

14 See http://www.glencairnmuseum.org/ (accessed 31 January 2009).

15 For a critical discussion of this museum see Pantke 2004. For the impact of tourism on urban regeneration in general see Smith (2006, 153–70).

16 See http://www.yamasa.org/japan/english/destinations/aichi/meijimura.html; http://www.time.com/time/magazine/article/0,9171,689508,00.html; http://en.wikipedia.org/wiki/Meiji_Mura (all accessed 1 February 2010).

17 http://www.ancientcity.com/?q=/en/objective (accessed 1 February 2010).

18 http://www.ancientcity.com/en?q=/en/facilities-and-activities (accessed 1 February 2010).

19 http://www.ancientcity.com/en?q=/en/index (accessed 1 February 2010).

20 Sometimes, extant churches are integrated in open air museums; one example is the Fränkisches Freilichtmuseum in Bad Windsheim (Germany).

21 http://www.tepapa.govt.nz/TePapa/English/WhatsOn/LongTermExhibitions/The Marae.htm (accessed 1 February 2009).

22 See Otto's letters quoted by Bräunlein (2004, 55–56).

23 See http://museedesreligions.qc.ca/fr/about/index.asp (accessed 31 January 2009).

24 http://www.glasgowmuseums.com/venue/index.cfm?venueid=13 (accessed 1 February 2009).

25 For a critical analysis see Lanwerd 2004.

26 See Hendry 2000 for a global perspective on theme parks.

27 Religious motives occur in some amusement parks such as Dreamland, opened in 1904, on Coney Island (in southernmost Brooklyn, New York City). This amusement park had "an Orient section with gardens, temples and a re-creation of the destruction of Babylon", Lukas (2008, 61). Moreover, the park had some attractions based on religious themes: "Creation featured a biblical tale that included the Garden of Eden and Adam and Eve, while End of the World offered an unapologetic missive for potential sinners among the crowds, and Hell Gate featured a woman being dragged down to the depths of hell" as described by Lukas (2008, 62).

28 Opened in 1946, Holiday Worlds, previously (until 1984) known as Santa Claus Land (because of its location in Santa Claus, Indiana), lays claim on being the first theme park. The park mainly offers various rides and is themed around major festivals such as Christmas, Halloween, Fourth of July and Thanksgiving. "The park's Christmas section takes the idea of Christmas and makes it an everyday, if not less symbolic, event. Children can talk to Santa Claus year round and gaze up at a large Christmas tree" (Lukas 2008, 87).

29 For a much quoted attempt at pointing towards underlying ritual/religious structures see Moore 1980. Ryba (1999–2000) reads Disneyworld as a "degenerate
   utopia" (206) and as "an American heaven" (219), "achieving the reification of a
   broadly based, tacitly held eschatology at the heart of American mythical con-
   sciousness" (183). See Hendry (2000, 88) for other interpretations that engage
   religious tropes.

30 There have been tensions with religious organizations. In 1996, the Southern
   Baptist Convention decided to boycott the Disney company, among other reasons
   because of the company's "employee policy which accepts and embraces homosexual relationships for the purpose of insurance benefits" and its "[h]osting of
   homosexual and lesbian theme nights at its parks"; for the text of the declaration
   see http://www.religioustolerance.org/new1_966.htm (accessed 3 March 2008).

31 Heritage USA has changed hands and names several times after that; see http://
   en.wikipedia.org/wiki/Heritage_USA (accessed 11 July 2007). For a dossier of the
   Park (history/story; tour; pictures; links; etc.) see http://illicitohio.com/SBNO/
   heritage/heritage01.html (accessed 11 July 2007).

32 The combination of shopping mall and theme parks symbolically joins two prototypes of post-modern public spaces and focal loci of post-modern consumerism;
   see Smith (2006, 27).

33 When revisiting the website on 14 February 2010, a "World-Fest: America's
   Largest International Festival" had made its appearance.

34 http://www.bransonsilverdollarcity.com/rides-attractions/ride_detail.aspx?
   AttractionID=911 (accessed 3 March 2008).

35 The opening of the theme park happened under protests from the Jewish Defense
   League which was concerned that the park had the hidden agenda of seeking to
   convert Jews to Christianity (see http://www.jdl.org/action/action/park.shtml)
   (accessed 10 May 2006). As a matter of fact, the founder of the park, Marv
   Rosenthal, is a Jew who had converted to Christianity and become a Baptist
   pastor. In 1989, Rosenthal had relocated his ministry from New Jersey to Orlando
   (following an order of the Lord according to one version, or hoping to reach out
   to more people at a huge tourist destination according to another account). In
   Orlando, Rosenthal and his wife Marbeth founded "Zion's Hope", a Ministry that
   "seeks to graciously proclaim to the Jewish people their need for personal salvation through Jesus the Messiah and to proclaim the gospel of the Lord Jesus
   Christ to all men regardless of race, religion, gender, education, or national origin.
   Accordingly, Zion's Hope seeks to educate the Bible-believing Church concerning
   the place of Israel in both history and prophecy and assist it in fulfilling its
   God-given obligation to rightfully include the Jewish people in its program
   for world evangelism" (http://www.zionshope.org/about/index.htm; accessed
   14 February 2010). In 2005, Zion's Hope and The Holy Land Experience separated forming two distinct organizations. For a theologically antithetical account
   of the place and the ministry see Beal 2005. Janemil Kolstø drew my attention to
   this book.

36 Lukas (2007, 274–75) mentions that "much attention has been given to the park's
   policy against hiring charismatic or Pentecostal Christians and its policy against
   'disruptive behavior' such as speaking in tongues".

37 http://www.theholylandexperience.com/abouthle/mission.html (accessed 10 May
   2006).

38 http://www.theholylandexperience.com/discoverhle/liveshows.html (accessed 10
   May 2006).

39 The park is criticized for that by Beal (2005, 59). Note that analogous reproductions (place substitutions) of far off or past places are well established and have a

long tradition in the United States. The largest open air show of the 1904 St. Louis World's Fair was the Jerusalem Exhibit, a replica of Jerusalem for which even original inhabitants of Jerusalem and characteristic livestock were brought to St. Louis; residents held religious services and events on the spot; there were even items of special interests for Jews and Muslims; the Exhibit served in part as a surrogate event for all those who were unable to attend the simultaneous World Sunday School Convention in Jerusalem (Vogel 1996).

40 http://www.theholylandexperience.com/discoverhle/dining.html (accessed 10 May 2006).

41 Trinity Broadcasting Network (TBN), reportedly the United States' largest Christian television network (http://en.wikipedia.org/wiki/Trinity_Broadcasting_Network; accessed 2 April 2010), has studio facilities next to the park, and during my visit a show was broadcasted live from the park's indoor auditorium.

42 See http://www.tierrasanta-bsas.com.ar/ (accessed 10 March 2008).

43 Email to the author, 26 March 2009.

44 See http://eins.scm-digital.net/show.sxp/3670_religionspark–tierra_santa–das_bi blische–disneyl.html (accessed 20 January 2008); source: Christliches Medienmagazin jesus.de, December 16, 2007.

45 http://www.nazarethvillage.com/village.php (accessed 3 March 2008).

46 http://www.nazarethvillage.com/parable.php (accessed 3 March 2008).

47 http://www.nazarethvillage.com/booking.php (accessed 3 March 2008).

48 http://nazarethvillage.com/news.php (accessed 3 March 2008).

49 http://www.guardian.co.uk/israel/Story/0,2763,1677557,00.html (accessed 15 December 2006).

50 http://www.guardian.co.uk/israel/Story/0,2763,1677557,00.html (accessed 15 December 2006).

51 http://news.bbc.co.uk/2/hi/south_asia/4494747.stm (accessed 15 December 2006).

52 http://news.bbc.co.uk/2/hi/south_asia/4494747.stm (accessed 15 December 2006).

53 See also http://www.sagartv.com/gangadham.asp# (accessed 15 December 2006).

54 It seems that the company has in the meanwhile changed the project by relocating it to a place on the Mumbai–Pune highway. With its reported 18 million inhabitants and 10 million domestic as well as 1.35 million international tourists a year, Mumbai was apparently a more promising venue. The project is now advertised as "Sagar World", which among other things will include a mythological museum and a temple city. According to the company's website, this will only be the seed project, with nine further Sagar Worlds in the planning. See http://www.sagartv.com/sagarworld.asp (accessed 20 October 2007).

55 http://news.bbc.co.uk/2/hi/south_asia/4494747.stm (accessed 15 December 2006).

56 http://news.bbc.co.uk/2/hi/south_asia/4494747.stm (accessed 15 December 2006).

57 See also http://www.sagartv.com/gangadham.asp# (accessed 15 December 2006).

58 I am grateful to Christiane Brosius for drawing my attention to this complex.

59 http://en.wikipedia.org/wiki/Akshardham_%28Delhi%29 (accessed 4 February 2010).

60 Schlehe, email to the author (3 February 2010).

61 Sometimes, rides are given names that allude to deities: Parc Astérix in Paris (France) has a ride called "Tonnerre de Zeus" (Zeus' Thunder), chasing down from the Olympus, and a statue of Zeus; at Universal Orlando (Orlando, USA), there is an interactive ride called Poseidon's Fury; see Lukas (2008, 69, 90). There will probably be much more such examples.

62 Maybe the largest project of this kind is Dubai's Global Village that attracted some four million visitors annually during the past couple of years. There are several "world parks" in China; see Lukas (2008, 84–86).

63 An example of the former (The Ancient City/Thailand) has already been mentioned in the discussion of museums; to some extent folk villages/cultural parks as discussed in Chapter 6 overlap with the latter category.

64 A New Reoma World is in operation since 2004.

65 Peter Bräunlein first drew my attention to this park.

66 http://www.europapark.de/lang-en/c244/default.html (accessed 4 February 2010). While that may have appeared progressive at a time, the park seems to be somewhat lagging behind in reflecting more recent political developments: whereas there is a Russian section, Russia is not a member of the European Union; in contrast, the park has no sections themed around any of the countries that joined the EU during the recent waves of expansion – one may speculate whether this is a statement indicating that the park authorities are in any way uncomfortable with this development or whether that reflects expected visitor flows (from Russia, but not from other Easter European countries).

67 See http://www.europapark.de/lang-de/c276/default.html (accessed 4 February 2010).

68 Tourist motivation is sometimes studied as a dialectical interplay between "push" and "pull" factors; see Harrison (2003, 28).

69 http://en.wikipedia.org/wiki/Shangri-La (accessed 14 February 2010).

70 The Bhutan-Shangri-La nexus is continued in popular media such as YouTube.

71 These are discussed in the papers by Kolås and Hillman.

72 See http://www.honolulumagazine.com/Honolulu-Magazine/About-Us/ (accessed 27 January 2010).

73 See Hall and Tucker (2004b, 9–10), referring to a study by Douglas and Douglas from 1996 (non vidi). For the Edenic imagery of Hawaii see also Desmond 1999.

74 Nakedness in "tourist paradises" is a matter of contention: Paradise being conceived as "a place of innocence, without shame or inhibitions" by Western (youth) tourists, they take naked bathing for granted, while that is deeply resented by natives in some places (in this case in Southern Thailand); see Cohen (1982, 212).

75 http://www.lonelyplanet.com/worldguide/destinations/caribbean/saint-lucia (accessed 12 May 2006).

76 There now is also an Atlantis/Dubai.

77 http://www.nirwanabaliresort.com/location.php (accessed 30 May 2008).

78 For Bali; see Picard (1996, 27–38).

79 "Wedding firms facing local backlash produce ever more quasi-sacred spaces sealed from everyday life … Local residents must ultimately forfeit cultural space of their own for another form of tourist consumption. The destination wedding appears to be the rich, happy, transcultural displacement, but a place-conscious analysis will find alienation at the destination" (McDonald 2005, 192).

80 For a rich, complex and recent account see Smith and Puczkó 2009.

81 See http://www.redmountainspa.com/_health_education_fitness/personal_discovery.php (accessed 20 October 2009); see Johnston 2006, *Is the Sacred for Sale?*, 88 for appropriations of indigenous people in spa tourism.

82 See http://www.ananda.it/index.html (accessed 6 March 2009).

83 Interviews with 50 foreign tourists to Rishikesh and Haridwar conducted in 2007 have shown that these respondents "believe that religious places give a peace of mind and they feel spiritually satisfied"; "[a]pproximately half of the tourists believe in Indian religion and customs and enjoy the rituals followed in Indian tradition"; "[f]oreign tourists like Holy Ganges, prayers at night at the bank of Ganges, temples, Indian cuisines, sermons and interactions with monks"; they "are likely to celebrate and participate in Indian festivals"; some of them "are even eager to visit Satpuris"; "[t]hey believe that they are not looking for luxury

but their arduous journey to meet the divine goal to make life simple and more fulfilling and rewarding" (Aggarwal, Guglani and Goel 2008, 461).

84 For a Christianity-based apology of the spirituality of wellness and a reaction to negative statements by some spokespersons from the Churches see Jäger and Quarsch 2004.

85 See http://www.kloster-arenberg.de/index.htm (accessed 12 February 2009).

86 Check http://www.findthedivine.com/ (accessed 12 February 2009) for an extensive directory of over 1.700 retreat centres and over 300 retreat directors worldwide. Many abbeys and monasteries are offering retreat services, but there are also providers from a range of different religious (or non-religious) backgrounds.

87 The books by "travel expert" Eileen Barish (*The Guide to Lodging in France's Monasteries* [2006]; *The Guide to Lodging in Italy's Monasteries* [third edition, 2006]; and *The Guide to Lodging in Spain's Monasteries* [2006]), published by Anacapa Press, Scottsdale, AZ, are a case in point.

88 http://cse.comoshambhala.bz/default.asp (accessed 15 December 2006).

89 See Turner and Turner (1978, 6): "All sites of pilgrimage have this in common: they are believed to be places where miracles once happened, still happen, and may happen again."

Chapter 6

1 In a technical sense the term "contact zone" has been introduced to point to colonial situations in which colonizers and the colonized are entertaining ongoing relations under "conditions of coercion, radical inequality and intractable conflict" (Pratt 1992, 6). The term is here used in a wider sense as "the spatial and temporal copresence of subjects previously separated by geographic and historical disjunctures, and whose trajectories now intersect" (7).

2 Smith (2006, 30) suggests distinguishing between indigenous tourism ("visiting native people in their own habitat which is different from that of the tourist") and ethnic tourism ("engaging in the cultural activities of a minority group within the tourists' own society").

3 There is also another category of persons involved to be mentioned here, known as "culture brokers" in Tourism Studies. These are basically (political and economical) decision-makers who in a way are devising the eventual tourist experiences; the WTO is a global culture broker; for the concept see Smith 2001.

4 This fact is widely ignored by scholarship in this area. There are massive handbooks of interreligious learning that do not mention tourism with a single word, for example Sieg, Schreiner and Elsenbast eds, 2005.

5 One former tour leader to China and India reported that not all tourists were willing to enter religious sites, especially after she insisted of a specific dress code or a certain mode of decorum. In her report, in the years after 9/11 (the attacks on New York's Twin Towers on 11 September 2001) this was especially true of Islamic sites.

6 Observation by Melissa Kelly (email to the author 11 November 2009).

7 See Hazbun (2007, 18) for the early period.

8 See Hanna (1984, 85), there referred to as "the main tour operator offering holidays based on visits to churches".

9 http://www.interchurch.co.uk/about-inter-church.asp (accessed 27 January 2009).

10 http://www.interchurch.co.uk/about-inter-church.asp (accessed 27 January 2009).

11 http://www.interchurch.co.uk/index.asp (accessed 27 January 2009).

12 For an interesting case study from Peru, see Hill 2007.

13 http://english.visitkorea.or.kr/enu/index.kto–navigationpath:Culture>Korean Buddhism>TempleStayforForeignersCulture>Religion&belief>Buddhism> TempleStay (accessed 21 August 2010).

14 Many Christian monasteries nowadays offer participation in monastic life for restricted periods of time. This is a comparatively recent development.

15 This is how the workshop is being announced: "Daoist Immersion, Sept. 11–18, 2010 / Come to a spectacular mountain in New Mexico and explore how living a Daoist life can make a difference in the world today, how Daoism can provide a more appropriate worldview, conceptual structures, and behavioral guidelines that allow us to treat self, society, nature, and the cosmos as one interconnected webwork and thereby bring healing to the people and harmony to the world. / To immerse ourselves in Dao, our day begins with qigong stretches. ... In the afternoon, we experiment with a form of Daoist cultivation"; http://daoiststudies. org/dao/node/11674 (accessed 16 February 2010).

16 Azarya (2004, 951) finds an increasing "curiosity for the other" in international tourism, which is facilitated by the shrinking distances and travel times, growing prosperity, lower air fares, etc.

17 For a North American example, which illustrates the process of increasing tour-istification of ethnic heritage, see Hoelscher 1998.

18 Note the phrasing "custom and architecture", which avoids religious idioms; terms such as "ritual and sacred space" could have likewise been chosen.

19 The native being "on show" is the hallmark of what is generally regarded as "ethnic tourism"; see van den Berghe and Keyes 1984; on the concept of "cultural tourism" see Ryan (2002a, 953).

20 "[T]here is immense profit by association for countries branding their tourism industry with Indigenous images" (Johnston 2006, 12).

21 Examples include Mirante 1990, a scaring account involving the taking of hostage of two tribal ladies who were supposed to act as tourist attractions; van den Berghe 1995 on Mayas; Cohen 1989a and 1993b (= 2004a, 275–94) on hill tribe trekking in Thailand; Linnekin 1997 on the small island of Manono in Western Samoa: "The public pathway around the island lies essentially in people's front yards, between the houses and the sea. Samoans engaged in their daily activities comprise a living cultural performance for visitors, and the human zoo analogy seems inescapable. As they walk around the island, the tourists gaze into the open-sided houses at Samoans eating, sleeping, dressing, or engaged in meetings and ceremonies" (Linnekin 1997, 234).

22 For some examples, see Selwyn (1993, 132).

23 http://www.drakensberg-tourism.com/zulu-culture-traditions.html   (accessed   7 February 2008).

24 http://www.drakensberg-tourism.com/zulu-culture-traditions.html   (accessed   7 February 2008).

25 Open-air museums often include church structures preserved from former times.

26 An extension is the themed design of hotels or resorts in the shape of "traditional" villages.

27 See Kirshenblatt-Gimblett (1998, 96): "Live ethnographic displays were a featured attraction at international expositions in Europe and America where entire envir-onments were recreated complete with inhabitants."

28 http://www.nzonline.org.nz/tamakiheritagevillagechristchurch.htm   (accessed   24 February 2008).

29 http://www.nzonline.org.nz/tamakiheritagevillagechristchurch.htm.

30 http://www.maoriculture.co.nz/Maori%20Village/Home (accessed 18 May 2008).

31 See http://www.polynesia.com/pcc_mission_statement.html (accessed 2 May 2008).

32 This is the access strategy: "Everyone is welcome to visit the beautiful grounds of the Laie Temple, including the Visitors Center and the Family History Center; however, only authorized members of The Church of Jesus Christ of Latter Day

Saints may enter the temple" (http://www.polynesia.com/hawaii-temple.html; accessed 2 May 2008).

33 http://www.polynesia.com/purpose-and-history.html (accessed 2 May 2008).

34 For the complex navigation between money-making, educational and doctrinal incentives of the PCC see Ross (1994, 56).

35 See also Kirshenblatt-Gimblett (1998, 146), who argues that the Mormon performers thereby "also exhibit their conversion".

36 http://www.polynesia.com/pcc_mission_statement.html (accessed 2 May 2008).

37 Quoted by Webb (2001, 138).

38 http://www.lifeinkorea.com/travel2/219 (accessed 25 February 2008).

39 http://whc.unesco.org/en/tentativelists/1106/ (accessed 25 February 2008).

40 http://www.skynews.co.kr/skynews_main/english/TOURISM/tourism_008.htm (accessed 25 February 2008; URL no longer active).

41 See http://cnntraveller.com/2007/03/01/ancient-of-ways/ [posted March 1, 2007] (accessed 25 February 2008).

42 See http://www.skynews.co.kr/skynews_main/english/TOURISM/tourism_008.htm (accessed 25 February 2008; URL no longer active).

43 For pictures see Comaroff and Comaroff (1997, 2–3,=plate 1.1. and 1.2.).

44 http://www.tjapukai.com.au/media_releases.html (accessed 17 January 2010).

45 http://www.tjapukai.com.au/brochures/TjapukaibyNight.pdf   (downloaded   17 January 2010).

46 http://www.nepalvillage.com/ (accessed 25 February 2008); the same text is now advertised under http://www.nepaletrek.com/citytour_4.php (accessed 21 August 2010).

47 http://www.nepalvillage.com/ (accessed 25 February 2008); the same line is now used by various agencies; see, e.g., http://www.adamtravels.com/tourism.htm and http://www.nepaltoursdestination.com/village_tours.php (both accessed 21 August 2010).

48 http://www.nepalvillage.com/ (accessed 25 February 2008); this line is now used at http://cosmictrekking.com/index.php?page=village-tourism (accessed 21 August 2010).

49 Hiwasaki (2000, 398) speaks of a "naturalisation of the Ainu", also "pervasive" in the Japanese media.

50 Hiwasaki (2000, 407) reports the number of 20,000 spectators for an *iyomante*.

51 http://en.wikipedia.org/wiki/Mea_She%27arim (accessed 13 July 2007).

52 http://en.wikipedia.org/wiki/Mea_She%27arim (accessed 13 July 2007).

53 Witness their website: http://maineshakers.com/ (accessed 14 March 2008).

54 The church, moreover, engages tourism for internal pastoral purposes.

55 See Wall and Oswald (1990, 17–19), who note a stronger emphasis on history with the Canadian (Old Order Mennonite) attractions.

56 see also http://www.mennoniteinfoctr.com/ (accessed 7 July 2009).

57 http://www.mennoniteinfoctr.com/amishfilm.html (accessed 7 July 2009); this URL is now outdated, but see http://www.mennoniteinfoctr.com/mennonite-movie.asp (accessed 21 August 2010) which advertises a "Mennonite Movie".

58 A similar line of argument is presented with regard to brochures diverting tourists from Amish backstage regions was presented by Buck 1977.

59 At the same time, it is wrong to assume that even Old Order Amish are in principle averse to interaction with tourists. Wilson (1993, 39) states that, "Many Old Order Amish are now inquisitive about their tourist guests and seem to enjoy meeting them." He also notes that some Old Order Amish are less concerned with shielding even their homes from tourists: "Many ... now allow tourists to visit their houses and farms (although not all – some lanes have 'tourists not welcome' signs posted)" (38).

60 http://www.800padutch.com/reasons.shtml (accessed 12 July 2007).

61 http://www.800padutch.com/reasons.shtml (accessed 12 July 2007).

62 http://www.800padutch.com/reasons.shtml (accessed 12 July 2007).
63 http://www.800padutch.com/reasons.shtml (accessed 12 July 2007).
64 See http://en.wikipedia.org/wiki/Faith_tourism (accessed 18 February 2010): "Religious tourism, also commonly referred to as faith tourism" (empty link).
65 These figures are taken from *Tourism Trendspotter* 2000.
66 http://www.interaction.org/newswire/detail.php?id=4914 (accessed 15 December 2006); see now http://www.sluonestop.com/news/Mar%2029%2006.html (accessed 21 August 2010).
67 http://www.visitjamaica.com/planning_your_trip/features_general.aspx?guid=de4b 2176–79d1–4cf4–8f88-d7abac8a008a (accessed 15 December 2006); see now http://www.congress.co.il/paragon/cla08/montego-bayjamaica.html (accessed 21 August 2010).
68 http://www.costaricantrails.com/tours/puerto-viejo/cachabri-indigenous-reserve30. html (accessed 28 January 2008).
69 *Ocha* is a truncated form of *oricha* (deity).
70 This shift in the discursive landscape is analyzed by von Stuckrad 2003. There are several, sometimes polemical, accounts of (neo-) shamanism, often discursively contrasting; see Wallis 2003 who also studies Celtic, Druid and other shamanism as well as debates about shamans engagement with sacred sites.
71 Shamanism shares in the global religious system as analyzed by Beyer 2006); see now http://www.sluonestop.com/news/Mar%2029%2006.html (accessed 21 August 2010).
72 Both quotes are from Bernstein (2005).
73 See www.sacredheritage.com (accessed 1 February 2008) as an example of a tour operator working with "[m]ore than twenty original healers of the Australian, Andean and Amazon rainforest cultures"; the agency operates since 1993, and many of their local partners since the 1970s and 1980s.
74 See, e.g., www.sacharuna.com (accessed 30 January 2010); www.boliviamistica. com (accessed 30 January 2010).
75 See, e.g., www.zetourz.com/tour.php?id_tour=276; http://www.nuove-esperienze.it/ sciamanismo%20siberiano.html (both sites accessed 3 February 2008).
76 http://www.mongoliatourism.gov.mn/index.php?action=menudata&id=7 (4 February 2008).
77 http://www.bluemongolia.com/reindeerfestival.html (accessed 4 February 2008).
78 http://www.mongoliatourism.gov.mn/index.php (accessed 21 August 2010).
79 See the description of the Nomad's Day Festival (held in September): http://www. mongoliatourism.gov.mn/index.php?option=com_content&view=article&id=261% 3Anomads-dayfestival&catid=53&Itemid=70 (accessed 21 August 2010).
80 See http://www.tibetanshaman.com/pil.html (accessed 30 January 2010).

Chapter 7

1 See Moore (1994, 120) writing about the 19th century: "Religious controversy became a species of paid amusements for Americans. ... Newspaper editors loved religious controversy."
2 This book has two sections: one pointing to the entertainment qualities of religion in the United States; and the other on the treatment of religion in various US American entertainment media. Another fruitful research landscape is Japan. Reader 1991, for example, uses the word "entertainment" throughout, but does not engage it as an analytical key term. Note its absence in the otherwise very useful index. The issue has recently been addressed in a special issue of the journal *Nova religio* on media and new religions in Japan. Tanabe 2006 provides some general reflections on religion and entertainment. Some of his reflections witness

the persistence of stereotypes rather than empirical studies. For instance, Tanabe claims (2006, 98) that religion is "marked by personal transformation, a real change in one's life, or at least a real impact making a difference in how one lives", whereas "[e]ntertainment is ephemeral, and while its impact can be powerful, personal transformation is unlikely". The underlying notion of religion seems deeply imbued by Protestantism, and computer games can point in a very different direction than the "ephemeral" reality Tanabe has in mind.

3 One of the best works from this field is now probably Meyer and Moors eds, 2006. The editors address the blurring boundaries between religion and media entertainment in their introductory essay.

4 On this category see Xie and Lane 2006. The lifecycle model suggested by these authors is not relevant in the present context.

5 Carnivals are another interesting case. Carnival celebrations are major tourism destinations. Some well-known examples include Rio, Mardi Gras in New Orleans and my home town Cologne. Caribbean carnivals are replicated around the world with some 50 "Caribbean carnivals" celebrated in Europe and America alone, see Mulligan (2007, 117). Notting Hill Carnival, which has its origins in the local African-Caribbean cultures, "is now the second largest carnival in the world after Rio" (Smith 2006, 149).

6 Kacha-ananda 1971 has some interesting pictures of the imposing swings.

7 On the general theoretical framework see Langer *et al.* 2006.

8 Interview, Bergen, 1 September 2008. Similar processes involve the use of candles at baptism and in cemeteries.

9 In 19th-century Rome, when Protestant tourists were offered the opportunity "to witness the ceremony of a young novice taking the veil, they went to that too, clucking their tongue about the tragedy of a young woman renouncing the world before she was old enough to make a rational decision" (Withey 1997, 90).

10 From the point of view of ritual theory, see also Stausberg 2006.

11 Consider also the case of the *mizuko kuyō* discussed on p. 169.

12 http://www.riegsecker.com/php/theater/his_life_musical.php (accessed 21 August 2010).

13 See http://www.kirbyvanburch.com (accessed 17 March 2008).

14 See Tahana and Oppermann (1998, 24).

15 For the tours since the 1930s see Imada 2004.

16 Elaborated by Desmond 1999.

17 For Ghana see Bruner (1996, 300); for Bali see Picard (1996, 165): "Accused not long ago of being a vehicle of 'cultural' pollution, tourism is now considered by the Balinese authorities to be a factor of 'cultural renaissance' (*renaissance cultural*)"; see Picard (1996, 198) for a critical discussion of the category of "renaissance of culture".

18 See Picard (1996, 135) for the case of Balinese dances (on which more later).

19 Dance is an understudied phenomenon in the study of religion(s); see Gundlach 2004.

20 At the same time the folklorization of religious practice antedates and parallels the emergence of tourism.

21 All quotes from http://www.viptourbrazil.com/TourDetails.asp?PackageID=42 (accessed 1 February 2008). This trip is now advertised here: http://www.brasi lianculturalcenter.net/wst_page12.php (accessed 21 February 2010). The wording on the Bonfim church can be found verbatim on various sites.

22 Most of these changes have been observed for the Dogon; see Lane (1988, 68).

23 So among the Dogon according to Shackley (2001, 53).

24 This is what seems to have occurred among the Dogon as analyzed by Lane 1988. Accordingly, he distinguishes between tourist dances and ritual dances. Both genres have different audiences, meanings and characteristics.

25 See Shackley (2001, 110–11) referring to the dances performed at the Tenchi festival of Lo Manthang in Nepal.

26 See Chow (2005, 301) for an example of the transformation of a religious rite into a dancing performance. Vukonić (1996, 64) makes this sort of change his main interpretation of dances in tourism contexts ("by 'opening up' to tourism and tourists, the originally religious character of these events has become completely profane, and much of the authentic quality of the original event has been lost. The reason for this is the commercialization of these events").

27 Personal communication, Bergen, 18 April 2008.

28 http://www.skynews.co.kr/skynews_main/english/TOURISM/trend_019.htm (accessed 24 February 2008; URL no longer available as of 21 August 2010). The information refers to the year 2000. See also Van Zile (2001, 12) for a (later abolished) version of the ceremony for paying visitors.

29 http://www.caribbean.com/haiti/ (accessed 20 February 2008).

30 For a detailed account see Picard 1996.

31 http://www.indo.com/active/night_life.html (accessed 25 July 2007).

32 McKean 1976 speaks of a triple audience of these dances: the gods, the locals and the tourists.

33 On the development of the visual representations of the Snake Dance see Udall 1992.

34 Some other dances also made their appearance on postcards; see Dilworth (1996, 96).

35 But in 1926, a group of Hopi dancers brought the dance to the capital, where "they performed before Vice President Dawes, Alice Roosevelt Longworth, and 5,000 other onlookers" with their cameras, Udall (1992, 37).

36 According to Howes, "a racist joke which backfired" (1996, 142).

37 Here are just two examples out of thousands: "Tibetan Winter Festivals" presented by the China Tibet Tourism Bureau (http://www.xzta.gov.cn/yww/Introduction/Festival/3768.shtml [accessed 26 February 2008]) and "Naga Festivals" presented by Nagaland Tourism (http://www.tourismnagaland.com/Festivals.html [accessed 26 February 2008]).

38 In Germany, this process is known as festivalization of urban space and society.

39 See Smith (2006, 140): "[A]round 56 percent of all festivals are created with a tourist audience in mind."

40 http://en.wikipedia.org/wiki/Boruca (accessed 16 March 2008).

41 See http://www.galerianamu.com/feature_artwork/dance_of_the_devils/2004–5/catalog.php (accessed 16 March 2008).

42 See *Ethnobiology Costa Rica 2004* (Organization for Tropical Studies Undergraduate Study Abroad Program, 2004), 208–9. The report can be downloaded here: www.ots.duke.edu/en/education/pdfs/usap/coursebooks/ et04.pdf; *Ethnobiology 2007* (Organization for Tropical Studies, 2007). This report can be downloaded here: ns.ots.ac.cr/en/education/pdfs/usap/coursebooks/et07.pdf (both accessed 16 March 2008).

43 *Promotion of Buddhist Tourism Circuits in Selected Asian Countries* (2003), 15 (based on a country report prepared by the Tourism Authority of Bhutan).

44 *Promotion of Buddhist Tourism Circuits in Selected Asian Countries* (2003), 17.

45 See Pearce and Moscardo (2006, 53) for Christmas travel in Australia.

46 See also Kirshenblatt-Gimblett (1998, 60): "The foreign vacationer at a local festival achieves perfect synchrony: everybody is on holiday, or so it seems."

47 http://www.tagesschau.de/ausland/meldung121962.html (accessed 17 April 2008).

48 Shackley (2001, 109), with an example from the Himalayas.

49 This is what Liu (2003, 392) reports for the boat races held as part of the Duanwu festival in Hong Kong: "Organizers successfully eliminated the religious element of the event". Jos Platenkamp (oral communication, Bergen, April 2008) made a similar observation with regard to the New Year's ritual of Luang Prabang (Laos), incidentally also centering on a boat race.

50 For tourists, on the other hand, the meaning of the festivals is often not apparent.

51 For interesting examples see Howe (2005, Chapter 7).

52 See Shackley (2001, 112), as an example: Buddhist monasteries in the Himalaya.

53 See Cohen (2004b, 154–55) with reference to studies on Bali, Singapore and Thailand.

54 Crain 1996 is an interesting case study for a pilgrimage festival.

Chapter 8

1 Gregory points to the scripting of tourism and travel, and the representation of other places and landscapes as text.

2 On tourist mementos as dialogues about personal and national identities in the US see Shaffer 2001. For various ways of bringing the Holy Land back home to the US for those who could not make the arduous journey to the Middle East in the late 19th century (including printed sermons preached on the basis of experiences of the visit to the Holy Land) see Messenger (1999, 104–10).

3 Unfortunately, it seems that "[t]he place of travel writing in tourism studies has been rather peripheral to date, partly due to the perceived tourist-traveler dichotomy" (Robinson 2004, 312).

4 Hill (2008, 267) cites a tourist who explicitly draws on ideas from the novel.

5 For Paris see http://www.classicwalksparis.com/tour/walking-tours/da-vinci-code-walking-tou.shtml (accessed 14 June 2010); for London: http://www.inetours.com/England/London/tours/Da_Vinci_Tour.html (accessed 14 June 2010; URL no longer available as of 21 August 2010); see also http://www.davincicodetours.eu (all sites accessed 21 August 2010).

6 See Lodge (1991, 61), quoting the anthropologist: "'The thesis of my book is that sightseeing is a substitute for religious ritual. The sightseeing tour as secular pilgrimage. Accumulation of grace by visiting the shrines of high culture. Souvenirs as relics. Guidebooks as devotional aids. You get the picture.'" Again quoting the anthropologist: "'It is no coincidence that tourism arose just as religion went in decline'" (64). He refers to sunbathing and immersion into the sea as "[a] kind of baptism" (90). Another motif is that of the priest as a kind of travel agent to paradise (153).

7 I wish to thank Melissa Kelly (Uppsala) for helpful discussions.

8 http://en.wikipedia.org/wiki/Tour_guide (accessed 8 February 2010).

9 http://en.wikipedia.org/wiki/Tour_guide (accessed 8 February 2010).

10 See Cohen (2006, 85): "One need only scan the multitude of tours available to the Holy Land to see that itineraries are constructed to impart very different perceptions (religious, political and historical) of the same region."

11 The guides hired by Cook almost immediately put the local interpreter guides, the so-called *dragomen*, out of business (Shepherd 1987, 177).

12 See Lane (1988, 66): "If the guide is good, tourists will be given an accompanying commentary on Dogon myth, history, and beliefs, which closely follows some of the more publicized anthropological summaries."

13 See Andriotis (2009, 78) for monks on Mount Athos who "can be considered as well-experienced tour guides. Not dissimilar to tour guides, they are able to provide interesting stories about the history of the monasteries, and direct visitors to some beautiful sites."

14 In religious tourism, however, tour leaders are often expected to be religiously inspirational.

15 http://www.kekoldi.org/index.php?option=com_content&task=view&id=53&Itemid =65.

16 One example is Rev. Hillary Raimo, a "non-denominational minister" (she studied with various shamans) who "now conducts her ministry work as a sacred guide to sacred sites", e.g. to Yucatan. The Yucatan-trip takes participants to various archaeological sites, but also includes "sacred teachings, rituals and cere-monies", but also, on demand, one-on-one sessions, healing circle ceremonies and other spiritual therapeutic activities; see http://www.powerplaces.com/Yucatan_ Hillary_Raimo.htm (accessed 6 March 2008).

17 http://www.skynews.co.kr/skynews_main/english/TOURISM/trend_019.htm (accessed 24 February 2008; URL no longer available as of 21 August 2010). The information refers to the year 2000.

18 Gorsemann (1995, 39) reports that between 6 to 15 percent of tourists use guidebooks.

19 For precursors of the modern genre see Gorsemann (1995, 44–79).

20 This holds true for printed guidebooks as well as for online resources; for an online-example see http://www.staedte-reisen.de (accessed 25 February 2008) whose content lists religious sites as a fixed menu under "sightseeing" for all of the cities it presents.

21 An analysis of guidebooks with regard to their content, rhetoric and other textual strategies including the use of illustrations with regard to religions would invari-ably bring to light issues such as authenticity, performance, staging, stereotyping, idealizing, exoticism, Orientalism/Occidentalism and tropes of representation. All these issues would require extensive discussion.

22 This has been shown with regard to the spiritual churches of New Orleans by Jacobs (2001, 323).

23 *Lonely Planet India* (387), quoted in Kraft (2007, 236).

24 I owe this observation to Bjørn-Ola Tafjord. The available scholarly literature on the internet and tourism seems mostly to be dominated by marketing issues from business and management perspectives.

25 Observation by Bjørn-Ola Tafjord.

26 For studies of virtual pilgrimages see MacWilliams 2002 and Hill-Smith 2009.

27 http://www.travelingonline.com/index.htm (accessed 13 February 2008).

28 http://www.travelingonline.com/uxmal/index.htm (accessed 13 February 2008).

29 http://www.travelingonline.com/celestun/index.htm (accessed 13 February 2008).

30 http://www.armchair-travel.com/home/index.htm.

31 Learning to perform a dance has been referred to as a "living souvenir" by Desmond (1999, 114).

32 Here is one example of a letter (Crowe and Crowe 2001, 43–44): "Dear Sir or Madam, Enclosed you will find what has become the biggest mistake we ever made. We ask the goddess, Pele, for forgiveness, to forgive our arrogance in thinking we could hold her raw, chaotic, elemental power. We ask that peace and harmony be restored to our lives in restoring these to her." Reference kindly provided by Florian Jeserich (Bayreuth).

33 Apart from serving as souvenirs, "[s]pecialist tours involving handicrafts form a small but increasing niche market" in the contemporary tourism industry (Hitchcock 2000, 1).

34 For examples see Hadidi-Feuerherdt (1987, 22–29).

35 Engraved calabashes seem to be a recent innovation (probably devised for the tourism market).

36 Information kindly provided by Florian Jeserich (Bayreuth).

37 Recordings of religious performances or multi-media presentations of religious places are also sold as souvenirs.
38 See Philp and Mercer (1999, 49) commenting on the emerging tourist trade in religious images and objects.
39 Hiwasaki (2000, 402) reports "that 5.2 percent of the Ainu population are involved in manufacturing folk arts, while 8.2 percent are involved in their sales".
40 This may also be explicitly advertised as in the following example: "While shopping for curios, you might purchase these from the Zulu women who crafted the goods. She will always pass the artefact to you using her right hand only. The palm of the left hand will be under the right forearm. This custom is significant, and serves to assure you that there are no hidden weapons and you have nothing to fear from her" (http://www.drakensberg-tourism.com/zulu-culture-traditions.html [accessed 9 February 2008]).
41 See Bentor (1993, 127) for a nice example of the inaccuracies of entrepreneurs and salespeople with regard to their explanations of the symbolism of the *thangkas*.
42 A map made in 1995/96 shows 19 souvenir shops in the roads close to Notre Dame; see Pearce (1999b, 55).
43 For a study of a souvenir shop (read in terms of a Geertzian approach) see Shenshav-Keller 1993.
44 For one example see the Glastonbury Experience as described by Bowman (1993, 53).
45 For Egypt see Fagan 1975.
46 The production and sale of souvenirs are often "major, and sometimes only, direct expenditures of tourists at the locality itself beyond the pre-paid package" Azarya (2004, 959).
47 See also Goss (2005, 59).
48 See Vukonić (1996, 170), referring to a study of medieval pilgrimages; Evans 1998 sketches the development of souvenirs from antiquity to the present.
49 For a case study see Yel 2006.
50 For the latter see Shackley (2006, 102). From her analysis of prizes, objects and different retail zones she observes a clear "relationship between the perceived sanctity of the object and the relationship between the location at which it is purchased and the shrine itself. Items purchased within the shrine are often regarded as the most holy and will be bought by visitors at an inflated price in preference to identical items being offered for sale outside the shrine, precisely for that reason. The further one gets from the shrine, the less holy the object."
51 This has been observed for the Wutai Mountain, see Shi (2009, 210).
52 For an example see Andriotis (2009, 76).
53 For an example see Knight (1996, 170–71).
54 In the boom period of pre-modern Christian pilgrimages in Europe the manufacture of "these fragile objects ran into many millions" (Spencer 1998, 13).
55 This may give rise to issues of intellectual property rights, see Hinch (2004, 252).
56 See the studies and materials contained in the exhibition catalogue *Exotische Welten/Europäische Phantasien: Airport Art. Das Exotische Souvenir*. Ausstellung des Instituts für Auslandsbeziehungen im Forum für Kulturaustausch, 2. September bis 22. November 1987 ([Stuttgart], Institut für Auslandsbeziehungen/ Edition Cantz, 1987); see also the various examples in Künzl and Koeppel 2002.
57 Bentor (1993, 116) mentions that *thangkas* are often read on Jungian terms in the West. Vukonić (1996, 68) remarks (without further references) that tourists use

some souvenirs, "on return from their journey, when performing their religious rituals".
58 Knut Melvær has kindly assisted in the analysis of the data.

Chapter 9

1 This is one of the points where the present book parts company with Carrette and King 2008 (2005), whose rhetoric seems to imply a view that implicitly objects to the process they describe as a "takeover" or a "hijacking" of spirituality – as if the latter were an originally unspoiled thing that was inappropriately dragged into the mud of consumer capitalism (which in an alternative interpretation may have set the stage for the remarkable category of "spirituality" to begin with). For a more ambivalent, differentiated, and self-positioned approach see the historian Leigh Eric Schmidt's study on the connections between commercialism and holidays, Christianity and consumer culture in the United States and its wrestling with the disapprobation, cynicism, and moralizing faced by the issue of commercialization and the highbrow form of aesthetic and academic elitism and its corresponding scholarly interpretive constructs (Schmidt 1995, 5–11, 14–15, 305–9).
2 See Tweed 2006 for a theory of religion that emphasizes the elements of crossing and of dwelling. Tweed also mentions "itinerant practices" such as "colonization, war, trade, tourism, and migration" (131).
3 I agree with Devji (2008, 9) that globalization, "despite its current celebrity, remains curiously undefined as an analytical or historical category".
4 See Appadurai (1996, 178–99) for this concept.

References

Abumanssur, Edin Sued (ed.). 2003. *Turismo religioso: ensaios antropológicos sobre religião e turismo.* Papirus: Campinas.

Adams, Jonathan. 2008. "A Falun Gong welcome for mainland visitors to Taiwan". *International Herald Tribune* (3 July 2008).

Aggarwal, Adarsh Kumar, Meenal Guglani and Raj Kumar Goel. 2008. "Spiritual & yoga tourism: a case study on experience of foreign tourists visiting Rishikesh, India". In: *Conference on Tourism in India – Challenges Ahead, 15–17 May 2008, IIMK.* 457–64.

Aktaş, Ahmet and Yakin Ekin. 2003. "The importance and place of Faith (religious) tourism in the alternative tourism resources of Turkey". In: Fernandes, Carlos, Jonathan Edwards and Francis McGettigan (ed.): *Religious Tourism and Pilgrimage: ATLAS – special interest group 1st expert meeting.* Tourism Board of Leiria/Fátima: Fátima, 151–73.

Alegro, Katie. 2004. "Mammoth Cave and the making of place". *Southeastern Geographer* 44: 27–47.

Al-Hamarneh, Ala and Christian Steiner. 2004. "Islamic tourism: rethinking the strategies of tourism development in the Arab World after September 11, 2001". *Comparative Studies of South Asia, Africa and the Middle East* 24: 175–86.

Allcock, J. B. 1988. "Tourism as a Sacred Journey". *Loisir et Société* 11: 33–48.

Andriotis, Konstantinos. 2009. "Sacred site experience: a phenomenological study". *Annals of Tourism Research* 36: 74–84.

Appadurai, Arjun. 1996. *Modernity at Large: cultural dimensions of globalization.* Minneapolis, London: University of Minnesota Press.

Aramberri, Julio. 2009. "The future of tourism and globalization: some critical remarks". *Futures* 41: 367–76.

Arellano, Alexandra. 2007. "Religion, pilgrimage, mobility and immobility". In: Raj, Razaq and Nigel D. Morpeth (eds): *Religious Tourism and Pilgrimage Festivals Management: an international perspective.* CABI: Wallingford, Cambridge/Mass, 89–97.

Argyriadis, Kali. 2007. "Le tourisme religieux à La Havane et l'accusation de mercantilisme". *Ateliers du LESC* 31: 24–46. [http://ateliers.revues.org/document672.html].

Ari, Lilach Lev, Yoel Mansfeld and David Mittelberg. 2003. "Globalization and the role of educational travel to Israel in the ethnification of American Jews". *Tourism Recreation Research* 28: 15–24.

Ashiwa, Yoshiko and David L. Wank. 2006. "The politics of a reviving Buddhist temple: state, association, and religion in Southeast China". *The Journal of Asian Studies* 65: 337–59.

Attix, Shelly. 2002. "New Age-oriented special interest travel: an exploratory study". *Tourism Recreation Research* 27: 51–58.

Azarya, Victor. 2004. "Globalization and international tourism in developing countries: marginality as a commercial commodity". *Current Sociology* 52: 949–67.

Bado-Fralick, Nikki and Rebecca Sachs Norris. 2010. *Toying with God: the world of religious games and dolls.* Waco: Baylor University Press.

Badone, Ellen. 2004. "Crossing boundaries: exploring the borderlands of ethnography, tourism, and pilgrimage". In: Badone, Ellen and Sharon R. Roseman (eds): *Intersecting Journeys: the anthropology of pilgrimage and tourism.* University of Illinois Press: Urbana, 180–89.

——2008. "Pilgrimage, tourism and *The da Vinci code* at Les-Saintes-Maries-De-La-Mer, France". *Culture and Religion* 9: 23–44.

Bajohr, Frank. 2003. *"Unser Hotel ist judenfrei". Bäder-Antisemitismus im 19. und 20. Jahrhundert.* Frankfurt: Fischer Taschenbuch.

Bandyopadhyaya, Ranjan, Duarte B. Moraisb and Garry Chick. 2008. "Religion and identity in India's heritage tourism". *Annals of Tourism Research* 35: 790–808.

Bar, Doron and Kobi Cohen-Hattab. 2003. "A new kind of pilgrimage: the modern tourist pilgrim of nineteenth century and early twentieth century Palestine". *Middle Eastern Studies* 39: 131–48.

Baumann, Zygmunt. 1996. "From pilgrim to tourist – or a short history of identity". In: Hall, Stuart and Paul Du Gay (eds): *Questions of Cultural Identity.* Sage: London, 18–36.

Beal, Timothy K. 2005. *Roadside Religion: in search of the sacred, the strange, and the substance of faith.* Boston: Beacon Press.

Beckerleg, Susan. 1995. "'Brown Sugar' or Friday Prayers: youth choices and community building in coastal Kenya". *African Affairs* 94: 23–38.

Bellows, Keith. 2008. *Sacred Places of a Lifetime: 500 of the world's most peaceful and powerful destinations.* Washington: National Geographic Society.

Benckendorff, Pierre. 2006. "Attractions megatrends". In: Buhalis, Dimitrios and Carlos Costa (ed.): *Tourism Business Frontiers: consumers, products and industry.* Elsevier Butterworth-Heinemann: Amsterdam, Boston, 200–210.

Bendix, Regina. 1989. "Tourism and cultural displays: inventing traditions for whom?". *Journal of American Folklore* 102: 131–46.

Bentor, Yael. 1993. "Tibetan tourist thangkas in the Kathmandu Valley". *Annals of Tourism Research* 20: 107–37.

Berger, Arthur Asa. 2004. *Deconstructing Travel: cultural perspectives on tourism.* Walnut Creek etc.: Altamira Press.

Bernstein, Anya. 2005. "Performing shamanism: from wild men to businessmen". http://hemi.nyu.edu/archive/studentwork/indigeneity/anya/final_paper-web.html.[hemi.nyu.edu/archive/studentwork/indigeneity/anya].

Beyer, Peter. 2006. *Religion in a Global Society.* London, New York: Routledge.

Birnbaum, Raoul. 2003. "Buddhist China at the century's turn". *China Quarterly* 174: 428–50.

Bixby, Brian. 2007. "Consuming simple gifts: Shakers, visitors, goods". In: Scranton, Philip and Janet F. Davidson (eds): *The Business of Tourism: place, faith, and history.* University of Pennsylvania Press: Philadelphia, 85–108, 259–64 (endnotes).

Blain, Jenny and Robert Wallis. 2007. *Sacred Sites, Contested Rites/Rights: pagan engagements with archaeological monuments.* Eastbourne, Portland: Sussex University Press.

Bleie, Tone. 2003. "Pilgrim tourism in the Central Himalayas: the case of Manakamana temple in Gorkha, Nepal". *Mountain Research and Development* 23: 177–84.

Bochinger, Christoph, Martin Engelbrecht and Winfried Gebhardt. 2009. *Die unsichtbare Religion in der sichtbaren Religion. Formen spiritueller Orientierung in der religiösen Gegenwartskultur.* Stuttgart: Kohlhammer.

Böhme, Gernot. 2006. *Architektur und Atmosphäre.* Paderborn: Wilhelm Fink.

Boissevain, Jeremy. 1996a. "Ritual, tourism and cultural commoditization in Malta: culture by the pound?". In: Selwyn, Tom (ed.): *The Tourist Image: myths and myth making in tourism.* Wiley: Chichester, 105–20.

——1996b. "Introduction". In: Boissevain, Jeremy (ed.): *Coping with Tourists: European reactions to mass tourism.* Berghahn Books: Providence, 1–26.

Bowman, Marion. 1993. "Drawn to Glastonbury". In: Reader, Ian and Tony Walter (eds): *Pilgrimage in Popular Culture.* Macmillan: Houndmills, London, 29–62.

——(manuscript) "Religion in context: airport chapels and chaplaincy".

Boyer, Marc. 2005. *Histoire générale du tourisme du XVIe au XXIe siècle.* Paris, Budapest, Torino: l'Harmattan.

Bräunlein, Peter J. 2004. "Shiva und der Teufel. Museale Vermittlung von Religionen als religionswissenschaftliche Herausforderung". In: Bräunlein, Peter J. (ed.): *Religion und Museum. Zur visuellen Repräsentation von Religion/en im öffentlichen Raum.* transcript: Bielefeld, 55–75.

Bremer, Thomas S. 2004. *Blessed with Tourists: the borderlands of religion and tourism in San Antonio.* Chapel Hill: University of North Carolina Press.

——2005. "Tourism and Religion". *Encyclopedia of Religion.* Second Edition 13: 9260–64.

——2006. "Sacred spaces and tourist places". In: Timothy, Dallen J. and Daniel H. Olsen (eds): *Tourism, Religion and Spiritual Journeys.* Routledge: London, New York, 25–35.

Brilli, Attilio. 1995. *Quando viaggiare era un'arte: il romanzo del Grand Tour.* Bologna: Il Mulino.

Brown, David. 1996. "Genuine fakes". In: Selwyn, Tom (ed.): *The Tourist Image: myths and myth making in tourism.* Wiley: Chichester, 33–47.

Bruner, Edward M. 1991. "Transformation of self in tourism". *Annals of Tourism Research* 18: 238–50.

——1996. "Tourism in Ghana: the representation of slavery and the return of the black diaspora". *American Anthropologist* 98: 290–304.

Brunet, Sandra, Johannes Bauer, Terry De Lacy and Karma Thsering. 2001. "Tourism development in Bhutan: tensions between tradition and modernity". *Journal of Sustainable Tourism* 9: 243–63.

Buck, Roy C. 1977. "The ubiquitous tourist brochure: explorations in its intended and unintended use". *Annals of Tourism Research* 4: 195–205.

Burris, John P. 2001. *Exhibiting Religion: colonialism and spectacle at international expositions, 1851–1893.* Charlottesville: University Press of Virginia.

Campbell, Colin. 2004. "I shop therefore I know that I am: the metaphysical basis of modern consumerism". In: Ekström, Karin M. and Helene Brembeck (eds): *Elusive Consumption*. Berg: Oxford, New York, 27–44.

Campo, Juan Eduardo. 1998. "American pilgrimage landscapes". *Annals of the American Academy of Political and Social Science* 558 (= Americans and Religions in the Twenty-First Century): 40–56.

Carrette, Jeremy and Richard King. 2008 [2005]. *Selling Spirituality: the silent takeover of religion*. Abingdon, New York: Routledge.

Chambers, Erve. 2000. *Native Tours: the anthropology of travel and tourism*. Prospect Heights: Waveland Press.

Chan, Selina Ching. 2005. "Temple-building and heritage in China". *Ethnology* 44: 65–79.

Chan, Selina Ching and Graeme S. Lang. 2007. "Temple construction and the revival of popular religion in Jinhua". *China Information* 21: 43–69.

Chang, Lan-Yun and Weining Liu. 2009. "Temple fairs in Taiwan: Environmental strategies and competitive advantage for cultural tourism". *Tourism Management*.

Chaves, Mark. 2004. *Congregations in America*. Cambridge/Mass., London: Harvard University Press.

Cheung, Sidney C. H. 1999. "The meanings of a heritage trail in Hong Kong". *Annals of Tourism Research* 26: 570–88.

Chidester, David. 2005. *Authentic Fakes: religion and American popular culture*. Berkeley, Los Angeles, London: University of California Press.

Chi-Tim, Lai. 2003. "Daoism in China today 1980–2002". *China Quarterly* 174: 413–27.

Chow, Chun-Shing. 2005. "Cultural diversity and tourism development in Yunnan Province, China". *Geography* 90: 294–303.

Clifford, James. 1988. *The Predicament of Culture: twentieth-century ethnography, literature, and art*. Cambridge/Mass., London: Harvard University Press.

——1997. *Routes: travel and translation in the late twentieth century*. Cambridge, Mass.: Harvard University Press.

Cohen, Erik. 1982. "Marginal paradises: bungalow tourism on the islands of Southern Thailand". *Annals of Tourism Research* 9: 189–228.

——1985. "The tourist guide: the origins, structure and dynamics of a role". *Annals of Tourism Research* 12: 5–29.

——1989a. "'Primitive and remote': hill tribe trekking in Thailand". *Annals of Tourism Research* 16: 30–61.

——1989b. "The commercialization of ethnic crafts". *Journal of Design History* 2: 161–68.

——1992a. "Pilgrimage centers: concentric and excentric". *Annals of Tourism Research* 19: 33–50.

——1992b (1981). "Pilgrimage and tourism: convergence and divergence". In: Morinis, Alan (ed.): *Sacred Journeys: The Anthropology of Pilgrimage*. Greenwood Press: Westport; London, 47–61.

——1993a. "The heterogeneization of a tourist art". *Annals of Tourism Research* 20: 138–63.

——1993b. "Hunter-gatherer tourism in Thailand". In: Hitchcock, Michael, Victor T. King and Michael J. G. Parnwell (eds): *Tourism in South-East Asia*. Routledge: London, New York, 275–94.

——1998. "Tourism and religion: a comparative perspective". *Pacific Tourism Review* 2: 1–10.

——2003a. "Tourism and religion: a case study – visiting students in Israeli universities". *Journal of Travel Research* 42: 36–47.

——2003b. "Contemporary tourism and the host community in less developed areas". *Tourism Recreation Research* 28: 1–10.

——2004a. *Contemporary Tourism: diversity and change*. Amsterdam: Elsevier.

——2004b. "Tourism and religion: a comparative perspective". In: Cohen, Erik: *Contemporary Tourism: diversity and change*. Elsevier: Amsterdam, 147–58.

——2006. "Religious tourism as an educational experience". In: Timothy, Dallen J. and Daniel H. Olsen (eds): *Tourism, Religion and Spiritual Journeys*. Routledge: London, New York, 78–93.

Cohen Ioannides, Mara W. and Dimitri Ioannides. 2006. "Global Jewish tourism: pilgrimages and remembrance". In: Timothy, Dallen J. and Daniel H. Olsen (eds): *Tourism, Religion and Spiritual Journeys*. Routledge: London, New York, 254–70.

Coles, Tim Edward and Dallen J. Timothy (eds). 2004. *Tourism, Diasporas and Space*. Routledge: London.

Collins-Kreiner, Noga and Jay D. Gatrell. 2006. "Tourism, heritage and pilgrimage: the case of Haifa's Baha'i Gardens". *Journal of Heritage Tourism* 1: 32–50.

Collins-Kreiner, Noga, Nurit Kliot, Yoel Mansfeld and Keren Sagi. 2006. *Christian Tourism to the Holy Land: pilgrimage during security crisis*. Aldershot, Burlington: Ashgate.

Collins-Kreiner, Noga and Dan Olsen. 2004. "Selling diaspora: producing and segmenting the Jewish diaspora tourism market". In: Coles, Tim Edward and Dallen J. Timothy (eds): *Tourism, Diasporas and Space*. Routledge: London, 279–90.

Colombo Dougoud, Roberta. 2000. "Souvenirs from Kambot (Papa New Guinea): the sacred search for authenticity". In: Hitchcock, Michael and Ken Teague (eds): *Souvenirs: the material culture of tourism*. Ashgate: Aldershot, 223–37.

Comaroff, John L. and Jean Comaroff. 1997. *Of Revelation and Revolution. Volume Two: The Dialectics of Modernity on a South African Frontier*. Chicago, London: Chicago University Press.

Crain, Mary M. 1996. "Contested territories: the politics of tourist development at the shrine of El Rocío in Southwestern Andalusia". In: Boissevain, Jeremy (ed.): *Coping with Tourists: European reactions to mass tourism*. Berghahn Books: Providence, Oxford, 27–55.

Crowe, Ellie and William Crowe. 2001. *Exploring Lost Hawai'i*. 'Aiea: Island Heritage Publishing.

Daniel, Yvonne Payne. 1996. "Tourism dance performances: authenticity and creativity". *Annals of Tourism Research* 23: 780–97.

Dann, Graham. 1996. "The people of tourist brochures". In: Selwyn, Tom (ed.): *The Tourist Image: myths and myth making in tourism*. Wiley: Chichester, 61–81.

——2005. "The theoretical state of the art in the sociology and anthropology of tourism". *Tourism Analysis* 10: 3–15.

Davie, Grace. 2000. *Religion in Modern Europe: a memory mutates*. Oxford: Oxford University Press.

——2003. "Seeing salvation: the use of text as data in the sociology of religion". In: Avis, Paul D. L. (ed.): *Public Faith? The state of religious belief and practice in Britain*. SPCK: London, 28–44.

Davis, Sara. 2001. "The Hawaiification of Sipsongbanna: orality, power, and cultural survival in Southwest China". *TDR – The Drama Review* 45: 25–41.

Delaney, Carol. 1990. "The 'hajj': sacred and secular". *American Ethnologist* 17: 513–30.

Dépret, Molly Hurley. 2007. " 'Troubles tourism': debating history and voyeurism in Belfast, Northern Ireland". In: Scranton, Philip and Janet F. Davidson (eds): *The Business of Tourism: place, faith, and history*. University of Pennsylvania Press: Philadelphia, 137–62, 269–72 (endnotes).

Desmond, Jane C. 1999. *Staging Tourism: bodies on display from Waikiki to Sea World*. Chicago: University of Chicago Press.

Devji, Faisal. 2008. *The Terrorist in Search of Humanity: militant Islam and global politics*. New York: Columbia University Press.

Diamond, Heather A. 2008. *American Aloha: cultural tourism and the negotiation of tradition*. Honolulu: University of Hawai'i Press.

Díaz Brenis, Elizabeth and Javier Hernández (eds). 2008. *Patrimonio cultural, turismo y religión*. Instituto Nacional de Antropología e Historia: México.

Diez de Valesco, Francisco. 2008a. "Introducción. La especifidad canaria: religiones entre continentes". In: Diez de Valesco, Francisco (ed.): *Religiones entre continentes. Minorías religiosas en Canaria*. Arc de Sant Cristòfol/Fundación Pluralismo y Convivencia: Barcelona/Madrid, 17–42.

——2008b. "Nuevas religiones y sus límites: nuevas espiritualidades y religiones alternativas en Canarias". In: Diez de Valesco, Francisco (ed.): *Religiones entre continentes. Minorías religiosas en Canaria*. Arc de Sant Cristòfol/Fundación Pluralismo y Convivencia: Barcelona/Madrid, 293–308.

Digance, Justine. 2003. "Pilgrimage at contested sites". *Annals of Tourism Research* 30: 143–59.

——2006. "Religious and secular pilgrimage". In: Timothy, Dallen J. and Daniel H. Olsen (eds): *Tourism, Religion and Spiritual Journeys*. Routledge: London, New York, 36–48.

Dilworth, Leah. 1996. *Imagining Indians in the Southwest: persistent visions of a primitive past*. Washington, London: Smithsonian Institution Press.

Dłużewska, Anna. 2008. "The influence of religion on global and local conflict in tourism: case studies in Muslim countries". In: Burns, Peter and Marina Novelli (eds): *Tourism Development: growth, myths and inequalities*. CABI: Wallingford, Cambridge/Mass., 52–67.

Domrös, Manfred. 2001. "Tourism in the Maldives: the advantages of the resort island concept". *Tourism* 49: 369–82.

Dubuisson, Daniel. *L'Occident et la religion. Mythe, science et idéologie*. Bruxelles: Éditions Complexe, 1998. [English as *The Western Construction of Religion* (2003)].

du Cros, Hilary and Chris Johnston. 2002. "Tourism tracks and sacred places: Pashupatinath and Uluru. Case studies from Nepal and Australia". *Historic Environment* 16: 38–42.

Eade, John. 1992. "Pilgrimage and tourism at Lourdes, France". *Annals of Tourism Research* 19: 18–32.

Eade, John and Michael J. Sallnow. 1991. "Introduction". In: Eade, John and Michael J. Sallnow (eds): *Contesting the Sacred: the anthropology of Christian pilgrimage*. Routledge: London, 1–29.

Ebron, Paulla A. 1999. "Tourists as pilgrims: commercial fashioning of transatlantic politics". *American Ethnologist* 26: 910–32.

Edensor, Tim. 1998. *Tourists at the Taj: performance and meaning at a symbolic site.* London: Routledge.

Eggertson, Svein. "Carving thoughts: some thoughts on Rapa Nui wood carving". (Unpublished paper presented at the 7th EsfO conference, Verona, 10–12 July 2008.)

Ellwood, Robert S. 1982. *Tenrikyo: a pilgrimage faith. The structure and meanings of a modern Japanese religion.* Tenri: Oyasato Research Institute, Tenri University.

Enzensberger, Hans Magnus. 1996. "A theory of tourism". *New German Critique* 68: 117–33.

Evans, Godfrey. 1998. "Mementos to take home: the ancient trade in souvenirs". In: Fladmark, J. M. (ed.): *In Search of Heritage as Pilgrim or Tourist? Papers presented at the Robert Gordon University Heritage Convention 1998.* Donhead: Aberdeen, 105–26.

Fagan, Brian M. 1975. *The Rape of the Nile: tomb robbers, tourists, and archaeologists in Egypt.* New York: Scribner.

Fagence, Michael. 2001. "Tourism as a protective barrier for Old Order Amish and Mennonite communities". In: Brent, Maryann and Valene L. Smith (eds): *Hosts and Guests Revisited: tourism issues in the 21st century.* Cognizant Communication Corporation: Elmsford, 201–9.

Fendl, Elisabeth and Klara Löffler. 1993. "'Man sieht nur, was man weiss'. Zur Wahrnehmungskultur in Reiseführern". In: Kramer, Dieter and Ronald Lutz (eds): *Tourismus-Kultur. Kultur-Tourismus.* Lit: Münster, Hamburg, 55–77.

Fitzgerald, Timothy. 2000. *The Ideology of Religious Studies.* New York, Oxford: Oxford University Press.

Fleischer, Aliza. 2000. "The tourist behind the pilgrim in the Holy Land". *International Journal of Hospitality Management* 19: 311–26.

Fournier, Jacques. 2004. *Guide touristique et spirituel de l'Europe.* Paris: Salvator.

Franklin, Adrian and Mike Crang. 2001. "The trouble with tourism and tourism theory?". *Tourist Studies* 1: 5–22.

French, Laurence Armand. 2003. "Wounded Knee II and the Indian prison reform movement". *The Prison Journal* 83: 26–37.

Frey, Nancy Louise. 1998. *Pilgrim Stories: on and off the road to Santiago.* Berkeley: University of California Press.

Gaskell, Ivan. 2003. "Sacred to profane and back again". In: McClellan, Andrew (ed.): *Art and its Public: museum studies at the millennium.* Blackwell: Malden, Oxford, Melbourne, Berlin, 149–62.

Gatrell, Jay D. and Noga Collins-Kreiner. 2006. "Negotiated space: tourists, pilgrims, and the Baha'í terraced gardens in Haifa". *Geoforum* 37: 765–78.

Gencarella, Stephen Olbrys. 2007. "Touring history: guidebooks and the commodification of the Salem witch trials". *The Journal of American Culture* 30: 271–84.

Gil, Angeles Rubio and Javier de Esteban Curiel. 2008. "Religious events as special interest tourism: a Spanish experience". *PASOS. Rivista de Turismo y Patrimonio Cultural* 6: 419–33.

Gladstone, David L. 2005. *From Pilgrimage to Package Tour: travel and tourism in the Third World* New York: Routledge.

Gonzáles, Roberto Carlos Rodríguez. 2008. "La diversidad cristiana en Canarias". In: Diez de Valesco, Francisco (ed.): *Religiones entre continentes. Minorías religiosas in Canaria*. Arc de Sant Cristòfol/Fundación Pluralismo y Convivencia: Barcelona/Madrid, 43–113.

Gordon, Beverly. 1986. "The souvenir: messenger of the extraordinary". *Journal of Popular Culture* 20: 135–46.

Gorsemann, Sabine. 1995. *Bildungsgut und touristische Gebrauchsanweisung. Produktion, Aufbau und Funktion von Reiseführern*. Münster, New York: Waxmann.

Goss, Jon. 2005. "The souvenir and sacrifice in the tourist mode of consumption". In: Cartier, Carolyn and Alan A. Lew (eds): *Seductions of Place: geographical perspectives on globalization and touristed landscapes*. Routledge: London, New York, 56–71.

Gothóni, René. 1994. *Tales and Truth: pilgrimage on Mount Athos past and present*. Helsinki: Helsinki University Press.

Graburn, Nelson H.H. 1983 (new edn 1993). *To Pray, Pay and Play: the cultural structure of Japanese domestic tourism*. Aix-en-Provence: Centre des Hautes Études Touristiques.

——1989. "Tourism: the sacred journey". In: Smith, Valene L. (ed.): *Hosts and Guests: the anthropology of tourism*. Second Edition. University of Pennsylvania Press: Philadelphia, 21–36.

——2000. "Foreword". In: Hitchcock, Michael and Ken Teague (eds): *Souvenirs: the material culture of tourism*. Ashgate: Aldershot, xii–xvii.

——2001. "Secular ritual: a general theory of tourism". In: Brent, Maryann and Valene L. Smith (eds): *Hosts and Guests Revisited: tourism issues in the 21st century*. Cognizant Communication Corporation: Elmsford, 42–50.

——2004. "The Kyoto tax strike: Buddhism, Shinto, and tourism in Japan". In: Badone, Ellen and Sharon R. Roseman (eds): *Intersecting Journeys: the anthropology of pilgrimage and tourism*. University of Illinois Press: Urbana, 125–39.

Graf, Jürgen. 2008. "Wellness und Wellnessbewegung". In: Klöcker, Michael and Udo Tworuschka (ed.): *Handbuch der Religionen*. Olzog: Landsberg am Lech.

Gregory, Derek. 1999. "Scripting Egypt: Orientalism and the cultures of travel". In: Gregory, Derek and James S. Duncan (eds): *Writes of Passage: reading travel writing*. Routledge: London, New York, 114–50.

Grimshaw, Mike. 2008. *Bibles and Baedekers: tourism, travel, exile and God*. London, Oakville: Equinox.

Grossman, Grace Cohen. 2003. *Jewish Museums of the World*. [Westport]: Hugh Lauter Levin Associates.

Grünewald, Rodrigo de Azeredo. 2002. "Tourism and cultural revival". *Annals of Tourism Research* 29: 1004–21.

Gundlach, Helga Barbara. 2004. "New approaches to the study of religious dance". In: Antes, Peter, Armin W. Geertz and Randi R. Warne (ed.): *New Approaches to the Study of Religion. Volume 2: Textual, Comparative, Sociological, and Cognitive Approaches*. Walter de Gruyter: Berlin, New York, 139–63.

Gunn, Clare A. 1997. *Vacationscape: developing tourist areas*. Third edition. Washington: Taylor & Francis.

Guo, Chao. 2006. "Tourism and the spiritual philosophies of the 'Orient'". In: Timothy, Dallen J. and Daniel H. Olsen (eds): *Tourism, Religion and Spiritual Journeys*. Routledge: London, New York, 36–48.

Gyllenhaal, Ed. 2006. "Glencairn Museum, Bryn Athyn, Pennsylvania". *Material Religion: The Journal of Objects, Art and Belief* 2: 132–36.

Hachtmann, Rüdiger. 2007. *Tourismus-Geschichte*. Göttingen: Vandenhoeck & Ruprecht.

Hadidi-Feuerherdt, Heidewig. 1987. "Aus dem Land der Pharaonen". In: *Exotische Welten/Europäische Phantasien: Airport Art. Das Exotische Souvenir. Ausstellung des Instituts für Auslandsbeziehungen im Forum für Kulturaustausch, 2. September bis 22. November 1987*. Institut für Auslandsbeziehungen/Edition Cantz: ([Stuttgart], 22–29).

Hafen, Thomas K. 1997. "City of saints, city of sinners: the development of Salt Lake City as a tourist attraction 1869–1900". *The Western Historical Quarterly* 28: 342–77.

Hagedorn, Katherine J. 2001. *Divine Utterances: the performance of Afro-Cuban Santería*. Washington, D.C.: Smithsonian Institution.

Hall, Colin Michael. 1994. *Tourism and Politics: policy, power, and place*. Chichester: Wiley.

Hall, Colin Michael, Allan M. Williams and Alan A. Lew. 2004. "Tourism: Conceptualizations, Institutions, and Issues". In: Lew, Alan A., Allan M. Williams and Colin Michael Hall (eds): *A Companion to Tourism*. Blackwell Publ.: Malden, Mass., 3–21.

Hall, Colin Michael and Hazel Tucker (eds). 2004a. *Tourism and Postcolonialism: contested discourses, identities and representations*. Routledge: London.

Hall, Colin Michael and Hazel Tucker. 2004b. "Tourism and postcolonialism: an introduction". In: Hall, Colin Michael and Hazel Tucker (eds): *Tourism and Postcolonialism: contested discourses, identities and representations*. Routledge: London, 1–24.

Hanna, Max. 1984. *English Churches and Visitors: a survey of Anglican incumbents*. London: English Tourist Board.

Hanna, Max, Tyrell Marris and Jenny Lefley. 1979. *English Cathedrals and Tourism: problems and opportunities*. London: English Tourist Board.

Hannam, Kevin. 2009. "Ayurvedic health tourism in Kerala, India". In: Smith, Melanie K. and László Puczkó (eds): *Health and Wellness Tourism*. Butterworth-Heinemann: Amsterdam etc., 341–44.

Harrison, Julia. 2003. *Being a Tourist: finding meaning in pleasure travel*. Vancouver: UBC Press.

Hashim, Noor Hazarina, Jamie Murphy and Nazlida Muhamad Hashim. 2007. "Islam and online imagery on Malaysian tourist destination websites". *Journal of Computer-Mediated Communication* 12: article 16. [http://jcmc.indiana.edu/vol12/issue3/hashim.html]

Hazbun, Waleed. 2007. "The East as exhibit: Thomas Cook & Son and the origins of the international tourism industry in Egypt". In: Scranton, Philip and Janet F. Davidson (eds): *The Business of Tourism: place, faith, and history*. University of Pennsylvania Press: Philadelphia, 3–33, 243–49.

Henderson, Joan C. 2008. "Representations of Islam in official tourism promotion". *Tourism Culture & Communication* 8: 135–45.

Hendry, Joy. 2000. *The Orient Strikes Back: a global view of cultural display*. Oxford: Berg.

Hennig, Christoph. 1997. *Reiselust. Touristen, Tourismus und Urlaubskultur*. Frankfurt am Main, Leipzig: Insel.

Hernández Ramírez, Javier. 2008. "Hiperespecialización turística y desactivazión del patrimonio. La gestión eclesiástica del Patio de los Naranjos de la Catedral de

Sevilla". In: Díaz Brenis, Elizabeth and Javier Hernández (eds): *Patrimonio cultural, turismo y religión*. Instituto Nacional de Antropología e Historia: México, 13–32.

Hervieu-Léger, Danièle. 1999. *Le pèlerin et le converti. La religion en mouvement*. Paris: Flammarion.

Hetherington, Kevin. 2000. *New Age Travellers: vanloads of uproarious humanity*. London: Cassell.

Hibbert, Christopher. 1969. *The Grand Tour*. London: Weidenfeld & Nicolson.

Hill, Michael D. 2007. "Contesting patrimony: Cusco's mystical tourist industry and the politics of *incanismo*". *Ethnos* 72: 433–60.

——2008. "Inca of the blood, Inca of the soul: embodiment, emotion, and racialization in the Peruvian mystical tourism industry". *Journal of the American Academy of Religion* 76: 251–79.

Hillman, Ben. 2003. "Paradise under construction: minorities, myths and modernity in Northwest Yunnan". *Asian Ethnicity* 4: 175–88.

Hill-Smith, Connie. 2009. "Cyberpilgrimage: a study of authenticity, presence and meaning in online pilgrimage experiences". *Journal of Religion and Popular Culture* 21:

Hinch, Tom D. 2004. "Indigenous people and tourism". In: Lew, Alan A., Allan M. Williams and Colin Michael Hall (eds): *A Companion to Tourism*. Blackwell: Malden, 246–57.

Hirtenlehner, Helmut, Ingo Mörth and G. Christian Steckenbauer. 2002. "Reisemotivmessung. Überlegungen zu und Erfahrungen mit der Operationalisierung von Urlaubsmotiven". *Tourismus Journal* 6: 93–115.

Hitchcock, Michael. 2000. "Introduction". In: Hitchcock, Michael and Ken Teague (eds): *Souvenirs: the material culture of tourism*. Ashgate: Aldershot, 1–24.

Hiwasaki, Lisa. 2000. "Ethnic tourism in Hokkaido and the shaping of Ainu identity". *Pacific Affairs* 73: 393–412.

Hoburg, Ralf. 2007. *Zwischen Ortsgemeinde und Tourismus. Der Markt der Kirchenführungen als Angebot und Ausbildung. Eine Markt- und Evaluationsstudie der Evangelischen Fachhochschule Hannover*. Hannover: Blumhardt-Verlag.

Hoefert, Hans-Wolfgang. 1993. "Kurwesen". In: Hahn, Heinz and H. Jürgen Kagelmann (eds): *Tourismuspsychologie und Tourismussoziologie. Ein Handbuch zur Tourismuswissenschaft*. Quintessenz: München, 391–96.

Hoelscher, Steven D. 1998. *Heritage on Stage: the invention of ethnic place in America's Little Switzerland*. Madison: University of Wisconsin Press.

Hoff, August. 1962. *Dominikus Böhm*. München, Zürich: Schnell & Steiner.

Howe, Alyssa Cymene. 2001. "Queer pilgrimage: the San Francisco homeland and identity tourism". *Cultural Anthropology* 16: 35–61.

Howe, Leo. 2005. *The Changing World of Bali: religion, society and tourism*. London: Routledge.

Howes, David. 1996. "Cultural appropriation and resistance in the American Southwest: decommodifying 'Indianness'". In: Howes, David (ed.): *Cross-cultural Consumption: global markets, local realities*. Routledge: London, New York, 138–60.

Huang, Jen-Hung, Shu-Ting Chuang and Yu-Ru Lin. 2008. "Folk religion and tourist intention avoiding tsunami-affected destinations". *Annals of Tourism Research* 35: 1074–78.

Hueneke, Hannah and Richard Baker. 2009. "Tourist behavior, local values, and interpretation at Uluru: 'the sacred deed at Australia's mighty heart'". *GeoJournal* 74: 477–90.

Huntsinger, Lynn and María Fernández-Giménez. 2000. "Spiritual pilgrims at Mount Shasta, California". *The Geographical Review* 90: 536–58.

Hutton, Ronald. 2001. *Shamans: Siberian spirituality and the Western imagination.* London: Hambledon and London.

Ichaporia, Niloufer. 1983. "Tourism at Khajuraho: an Indian enigma?". *Annals of Tourism Research* 10: 75–92.

Imada, Adria L. 2004. "Hawaiians on tour: Hula circuits through the American Empire". *American Quarterly* 56: 111–50.

Inglis, Fred. 2000. *The Delicious History of the Holiday.* London: Routledge.

Ingram, Gloria. 2005. "A phenomenological investigation of tourists' experience of Australian indigenous culture". In: Ryan, Chris and Michelle Aicken (eds): *Indigenous Tourism: the commodification and management of culture.* Elsevier: Amsterdam, 21–34.

Ioannides, Dimitri and Mara W. Cohen Ioannides. 2002. "Pilgrimages of nostalgia: patterns of Jewish travel in the United States". *Tourism Recreation Research* 27: 17–25.

——2004. "Jewish past as a 'foreign country': the travel experiences of American Jews". In: Coles, Tim Edward and Dallen J. Timothy (eds): *Tourism, Diasporas and Space.* Routledge: London, 95–110.

Ivakhiv, Adrian. 2003. "Nature and self in New Age pilgrimage". *Culture and Religion* 4: 93–118.

Jackowski, Antoni and Valene L. Smith. 1992. "Polish pilgrim-tourists". *Annals of Tourism Research* 19: 92–106.

Jackson, Richard H. and Lloyd Hudman. 1995. "Pilgrimage tourism and English cathedrals: the role of religion in travel". *Revue de Tourisme – The Tourist Review – Zeitschrift für Fremdenverkehr* 4: 40–48.

Jacobs, Claude F. 2001. "Folk for whom? Tourist guidebooks, local color, and the spiritual churches of New Orleans". *Journal of American Folklore* 114: 309–30.

Jäger, Willigis and Christoph Quarsch. 2004. *".denn auch hie sind Götter". Wellness, Fitness und Spiritualität.* Freiburg, Basel, Wien: Herder.

Jenkins, Olivia. 2003. "Photography and travel brochures: the circle of representation". *Tourism Geographies* 5: 305–28.

Jensen, Lionel M. 1997. *Manufacturing Confucianism: Chinese traditions & universal civilization.* Durham: Duke University Press.

Johnson, Henry. 2002. "Balinese music, tourism and globalisation: inventing traditions within and across cultures". *New Zealand Journal of Asian Studies* 4: 8–32.

Johnston, Alison M. 2006. *Is the Sacred for Sale?: tourism and indigenous peoples.* London, Sterling, VA: Earthscan.

Jonas, Raymond A. 2001. "Sacred tourism and secular pilgrimage: Montmartre and the Basilica of Sacré Coeur". In: Weisberg, Gabriel P. (ed.): *Montmartre and the Making of Mass Culture.* Rutgers University Press: New Brunswick, London, 94–119.

Joseph, Christina A. and Anandam P. Kavoori. 2001. "Mediated resistance: tourism and the host community". *Annals of Tourism Research* 28: 998–1009.

Kacha-ananda, Chob. 1971. "The Akha swinging ceremony". *Journal of the Siam Society* 59: 119–28.

Kaelber, Lutz. 2006. "Paradigms of travel: from medieval pilgrimage to the post-modern virtual tour". In: Timothy, Dallen J. and Daniel H. Olsen (eds): *Tourism, Religion and Spiritual Journeys.* Routledge: London, New York, 49–63.

Kane, Paula M. 2006. "Getting beyond gothic: challenges for contemporary Catholic church architecture". In: Nelson, Louis P. (ed.): *American Sanctuary: understanding sacred spaces.* Indiana University Press: Bloomington, 128–54.

Kaufman, Suzanne K. 2005. *Consuming Visions: mass culture and the Lourdes shrine.* Ithaca: Cornell University Press.

Ketchell, Aaron K. 2007. *Holy Hills of the Ozarks: religion and tourism in Branson, Missouri.* Baltimore: Johns Hopkins University Press.

Kim, Chongho. 2003. *Korean Shamanism: the cultural paradox.* Aldershot, Burlington: Ashgate.

King, Margaret J. 1981. "Disneyland and Walt Disney World: traditional values in futuristic form". *Journal of Popular Culture* 15: 116–40.

King, Victor T. 1993. "Tourism and culture in Malaysia". In: Hitchcock, Michael, Victor T. King and Michael J. G. Parnwell (eds): *Tourism in South-East Asia.* Routledge: London, New York, 99–116.

Kirshenblatt-Gimblett, Barbara. 1998. *Destination Culture: tourism, museums and heritage.* Berkeley: University of California Press.

Knight, John. 1996. "Competing hospitalities in Japanese rural tourism". *Annals of Tourism Research* 23: 165–80.

Knoblauch, Hubert. 2009. *Populäre Religion. Auf dem Weg in eine spirituelle Gesellschaft.* Frankfurt, New York: Campus.

Knoblauch, Hubert and Andreas Graff. 2009. "'Ich bin dann mal weg' – Säkularisierung oder Spiritualität". In: *Woran glaubt die Welt? Analysen und Kommentare zum Religionsmonitor 2008.* Verlag Bertelsmann Stiftung: Gütersloh, 725–46.

Knott, Kim. 2005. *The Location of Religion: a spatial analysis.* London, Oakville: Equinox.

Kolås, Åshild. 2004. "Tourism and the making of place in Shangri-La". *Tourism Geographies* 6: 262–78.

Kollandsrud, Mari. 1998. "Saint Olav of Norway: reviving pilgrim ways to Trondheim". In: Fladmark, J. M. (ed.): *In Search of Heritage as Pilgrim or Tourist? Papers presented at the Robert Gordon University Heritage Convention 1998.* Donhead: Aberdeen, 91–103.

Koutchinsky, Stanislav. 2005. "St. Petersburg's Museum of the History of Religion in the new millennium". *Material Religion: The Journal of Objects, Art and Belief* 1: 154–57.

Kraft, Siv Ellen. 2007. "Religion and spirituality in Lonely Planet's *India*". *Religion* 37: 230–42.

Künzl, Ernst and Gerhard Koeppel. 2002. *Souvenirs und Devotionalien. Zeugnisse des geschäftlichen, religiösen und kulturellen Tourismus im antiken Römerreich.* Mainz am Rhein: Verlag Philipp von Zabern.

Lane, Paul J. 1988. "Tourism and social change among the Dogon". *African Arts* 21: 66–92.

Langer, Robert, Dorothea Lüddeckens, Kerstin Radde and Jan A.M. Snoek. 2006. "Transfer of ritual". *Journal of Ritual Studies* 20: 1–10.

Lanwerd, Susanne. 2004. "Religion in Ausstellungen – Perspektiven einer kunstgeschichtlichen Kulturwissenschaft". In: Bräunlein, Peter J. (ed.): *Religion und Museum. Zur visuellen Repräsentation von Religion/en im öffentlichen Raum.* transcript: Bielefeld, 77–96.

Lauterbach, Burkhart. 1989. "Baedeker und andere Reiseführer. Eine Problemskizze". *Zeitschrift für Volkskunde* 85: 206–33.

Leepreecha, Prasit. 2005. "The politics of ethnic tourism in Northern Thailand". [http://www.akha.org/content/tourismecotourism/ethnictourism.pdf.]

Lehto, Xinran Y., Sally Brown, Yi Chen and Alastair M. Morrison. 2006. "Yoga tourism as a niche within the wellness tourism market". *Tourism Recreation Research* 31: 25–35.

Leiper, Neil. 1990. "Tourism attraction systems". *Annals of Tourism Research* 17: 367–84.

——1998. "Review of *Tourism and Religion* by Boris Vukonić (1996)". *Journal of Sustainable Tourism* 6: 261–263.

Linnekin, Jocelyn. 1997. "Consuming cultures: tourism and the commoditization of cultural identity in the Pacific Islands". In: Picard, Michel and Robert E. Wood (eds): *Tourism, Ethnicity, and the State in Asian and Pacific Societies.* University of Hawai'i Press: Honolulu, 215–50.

Liu, Tik-sang. 2003. "A nameless but active religion: an anthropologist's view of local religion in Hong Kong and Macau". *China Quarterly* 174: 373–94.

Lodge, David. 1991. *Paradise News: a novel.* New York etc.: Penguin.

Löfgren, Orvar. 1999. *On Holiday: a history of vacationing.* Berkeley: University of California Press.

Lukas, Scott. 2008. *Theme Park.* London: Reaktion Books.

Lukas, Scott A. (ed.) 2007. *The Themed Space: locating culture, nation, and self.* Lanham etc.: Lexington Books.

Lukas, Scott A. 2007. "A politics of reverence and irreverence: social discourse on theming controversies". In: Lukas, Scott A. (ed.): *The Themed Space: locating culture, nation, and self.* Lexington Books: Lanham etc., 271–93.

Lukatis, Ingrid and Astrid Hieber. 1996. *Tourismus und Kirche in Ostfriesland.* Kirchlicher Dienst in Freizeit, Erholung und Tourismus der evangelisch-luther-ischen Landeskirche Hannovers, Arbeitskreis Ostfriesland.

Lyon, David. 2000. *Jesus in Disneyland: religion in postmodern times.* Cambridge, Malden: Blackwell Publishers.

MacCannell, Dean. 1999 [1976]. *The Tourist: a new theory of the leisure class,* With a new foreword by Lucy R. Lippard and a new epilogue by the author. Berkeley, Los Angeles, London: University of California Press.

MacLaine, Shirley. 2001. *The Camino: a journey of the spirit.* New York etc.: Pocket Books.

MacWilliams, Mark W. 2002. "Virtual pilgrimages on the internet". *Religion* 32: 315–35.

Malotki, Ekkehart. 2000. *Kokopelli: the making of an icon.* Lincoln: University of Nebraska Press.

Marciniak, Katarzyna. 1994. "The perception and treatment of prehistoric and contemporary sacred places and sites in Poland". In: Carmichael, David L., Jane Hubert, Brian Reeves and Audhild Schanche (eds): *Sacred Sites, Sacred Places.* Routledge: London, New York, 140–51.

Margry, Peter Jan. 2008. "Secular pilgrimage: a contradiction in terms?". In: Margry, Peter Jan (ed.): *Shrines and Pilgrimage in the Modern World: new itineraries into the sacred.* Amsterdam University Press: [Amsterdam], 13–46.

Margry, Peter Jan (ed.). 2008. *Shrines and Pilgrimage in the Modern World: new itineraries into the sacred.* Amsterdam University Press: [Amsterdam].

Marschall, Sabine. 2004. "Commodifying heritage: post-apartheid monuments and cultural tourism in South Africa". In: Hallin, Colin Michael and Hazel Tucker (eds): *Tourism and Postcolonialism: contested discourses, identities and representations.* Routledge: London, New York, 95–112.

Martikainen, Tuomas. 2008. "Consuming a cathedral: commodification of religious places in late modernity". *Fieldwork in Religion* 2: 127–45.

Mattila, Anna S., Yorghos Apostoupoulos, Sevil Sonmez, Lucy Yu and Vinod Sasidharan. 2001. "The impact of gender and religion on college students' spring break behavior". *Journal of Travel Research* 40: 193–200.

Mayer, Jean-François. 2001. "La "Révélation d'Arès": naissance d'un pèlerinage dans la France contemporaine". *Social Compass* 48: 63–75.

Mazza, Carlo. 2007. *Turismo religioso. Un approccio storico-culturale.* EDB.

McCabe, Scott. 2005. "'Who is a tourist?' A critical review". *tourist studies* 5: 85–106.

McDonald, Mary G. 2005. "Tourist weddings in Hawa'i: consuming the destination". In: Cartier, Carolyn and Alan A. Lew (eds): *Seductions of Place: geographical perspectives on globalization and touristed landscapes.* Routledge: London, New York, 171–92.

McGettigan, Francis. 2003. "An analysis of cultural tourism and its relationship with religious sites". In: Fernandes, Carlos, Jonathan Edwards and Francis McGettigan (eds): *Religious Tourism and Pilgrimage: ATLAS – special interest group 1st expert meeting.* Tourism Board of Leiria/Fátima: Fátima, 13–26.

McKean, Philip F. 1976. "Tourism, culture change and culture conservation in Bali". In: Banks, David J. (ed.): *Changing Identities in Modern Southeast Asia.* Mouton: The Hague, 237–47.

McKercher, Bob and Alan A. Lew. 2004. "Tourist flows and the spatial distribution of tourists". In: Lew, Alan A., Allan M. Williams and Colin Michael Hall (eds): *A Companion to Tourism.* Blackwell: Malden, 36–48.

Messenger, Troy. 1999. *Holy Leisure: recreation and religion in God's square mile.* Minneapolis, London: University of Minnesota Press.

Metzo, Katherine. 2008. "Shamanic transformations: Buriat shamans as mediators of multiple worlds". In: Wanner, Catherine and Mark D. Steinberg (eds): *Religion, Morality, and Community in Post-Soviet Societies.* Woodrow Wilson Center Press / Indiana University Press: Washington, D.C. / Bloomington, 215–45.

Meyer, Birgit and Annelies Moors (eds). 2006. *Religion, Media, and the Public Sphere.* Indiana University Press: Bloomington.

Michel, Patrick. 1999. *La religion au Musée. Croire dans l'Europe contemporaine.* Paris: L'Harmattan.

Mikaelson, Lisbeth. 2005. "Locality and myth: the resacralization of Selja and the Cult of St. Sunniva". *Numen* 52: 191–225.

——2008. "Nidarosdomen og pilegrimsbølgen". *din* 41–59.

Mirante, Edith T. 1990. "Hostages to Tourism". *Cultural Survival Quarterly* 14: 35–38.

Mitchell, Clare J.A. 2003. "The heritage shopping village: profit, preservation and production". In: Wall, Geoffrey (ed.): *Tourism: people, places, and products.* Department of Geography, University of Waterloo: [Waterloo, Ont.], 151–76.

Mittelberg, David. 1999. *The Israel Connection and American Jews.* Westport: Praeger.

Moore, Alexander. 1980. "Walt Disney World: bounded ritual space and the playful pilgrimage center". *Anthropological Quarterly* 53: 207–18.

Moore, R. Laurence. 1994. *Selling God: American religion in the marketplace of culture.* Oxford, New York: Oxford University Press.

Morgan, Nigel and Annette Pritchard. 2005. "On souvenirs and metonymy: narratives of memory, metaphor and materiality". *Tourist Studies* 5: 29–53.

Morpeth, Nigel D. 2007. "Ancient and modern pilgrimage: El Camino Frances". In: Raj, Razaq and Nigel D. Morpeth (eds): *Religious Tourism and Pilgrimage Festivals Management: an international perspective.* CABI: Wallingford, Cambridge/Mass, 153–60.

Moscardo, Gianna and Philip L. Pearce. 1999. "Understanding ethnic tourists". *Annals of Tourism Research* 26: 416–34.

Mu, Zhang, Huang Li, Wang Jian-Hong, Liu Ji, Jie Yan-Geng and Lai Xiting. 2007. "Religious tourism and cultural pilgrimage: a Chinese perspective". In: Raj, Razaq and Nigel D. Morpeth (eds): *Religious Tourism and Pilgrimage Festivals Management: an international perspective.* CABI: Wallingford, Cambridge/Mass, 98–112.

Mulligan, Jackie. 2006. "Centring the visitor: promoting a sense of spirituality in the Caribbean". In: Raj, Razaq and Nigel D. Morpeth (eds): *Religious Tourism and Pilgrimage Festivals Management: an international perspective.* CABI: Wallingford, Cambridge/Mass, 113–26.

Murray, Michael and Brian Graham. 1997. "Exploring the dialectics of route-based tourism: the Camino de Santiago". *Tourism Management* 18: 513–24.

Mustonen, Pekka. 2005. "Volunteer tourism: postmodern pilgrimage?". *Journal of Tourism and Cultural Change* 3: 160–77.

Neumann, Birgit and Antje Rösener. 2006. *Was tun mit unseren Kirchen? Kirchen erleben, nutzen und erhalten. Ein Arbeitsbuch.* Gütersloh: Gütersloher Verlagshaus.

Nolan, Mary Lee and Sidney Nolan. 1989. *Christian Pilgrimage in Modern Western Europe.* Chapel Hill, London: University of North Carolina Press.

Offe, Sabine. 2000. *Ausstellungen, Einstellungen, Entstellungen. Jüdische Museen in Deutschland und Österreich.* Berlin, Wien: Philo.

O'Guinn, Thomas C. and Russell W. Belk. 1989. "Heaven on Earth: Consumption at Heritage Village, USA". *The Journal of Consumer Research* 16: 227–38.

Ohtsuka, Kazuyoshi. 1997. "Exhibiting Ainu culture at Minpaku: a reply to Sandra A. Niessen". *Museum Anthropology* 20: 108–19.

Ohtsuka, Kazuyoshi. 1999. "Tourism, assimilation, and Ainu survival today". In: Fitzhugh, William W. and Chisato O. Dubreuil (eds): *Ainu: spirit of a northern people.* Smithsonian Institution: [Washington, D.C.], 92–95.

Olsen, Daniel H. 2003. "Heritage, Tourism, and the Commodification of Religion". *Tourism Recreation Research* 28: 99–104.

——2006a. "Management issues for religious heritage attractions". In: Timothy, Dallen J. and Daniel H. Olsen (eds): *Tourism, Religion and Spiritual Journeys.* Routledge: London, New York, 104–18.

——2006b. "Tourism and informal pilgrimage among the Latter-day Saints". In: Timothy, Dallen J. and Daniel H. Olsen (eds): *Tourism, Religion and Spiritual Journeys.* Routledge: London, New York, 254–70.

Olsen, Daniel H. and Dallen J. Timothy. 2006. "Tourism and religious journeys". In: Timothy, Dallen J. and Daniel H. Olsen (ed.): *Tourism, Religion and Spiritual Journeys.* Routledge: London, New York, 1–21.

Organization for Tropical Studies 2004. *Ethnobiology Costa Rica 2004.* Organization for Tropical Studies Undergraduate Study Abroad Program. [www.ots.duke.edu/en/education/pdfs/usap/coursebooks/ et04.pdf]

Organization for Tropical Studies 2007. *Ethnobiology 2007.* Organization for Tropical Studies [ns.ots.ac.cr/en/education/pdfs/usap/coursebooks/et07.pdf].

Paine, Crispin. 2005. "Museums and religion". *Encyclopedia of Religion. Second Edition* 9: 6243–48.

Pantke, Christiane. 2004. "Kulturelle Identität und folkloristische Klischees. Die Bedeutung des 'Museums der afrobrasilianischen Kultur' im gesellschaftlichen und kulturellen Kontext Salvador da Bahias, Brasilien". In: Bräunlein, Peter J. (ed.): *Religion und Museum. Zur visuellen Repräsentation von Religion/en im öffentlichen Raum.* transcript: Bielefeld, 195–222.

Parezo, Nancy J. 1991. *Navajo Sandpainting: from religious act to commercial art.* Albuquerque: University of New Mexico Press.

Pearce, Douglas G. 1999a. "Tourism in Paris: studies at the microscale". *Annals of Tourism Research* 26: 77–97.

——1999b. "Tourist districts in Paris: structure and functions". *Tourism Management* 19: 49–65.

Pearce, Philip L. and Gianna Moscardo. 2006. "Domestic and visiting friends and relatives tourism". In: Buhalis, Dimitrios and Carlos Costa (eds): *Tourism Business Frontiers: consumers, products and industry.* Elsevier Butterworth-Heinemann: Amsterdam, Boston, 48–55.

Pernecky, Tomas and Charles Johnston. 2006. "Voyage through numinous space: applying the specialization concept to New Age tourism". *Tourism Recreation Research* 31: 37–46.

Persoon, Gerard A. 2004. "Religion and ethnic identity of the Mentawaians of Siberut (West Sumatra)". In: Ramstedt, Martin (ed.): *Hinduism in Modern Indonesia: a minority religion between local, national, and global interests.* RoutledgeCurzon: London, 144–59.

Petrillo, Clara S. 2003. "Management of churches and religious sites: some case studies from Italy". In: Fernandes, Carlos, Jonathan Edwards and Francis McGettigan (ed.): *Religious Tourism and Pilgrimage: ATLAS – special interest group 1st expert meeting.* Tourism Board of Leiria/Fátima: Fátima, 71–86.

Philp, Janette and David Mercer. 1999. "Commodification of Buddhism in contemporary Burma". *Annals of Tourism Research* 26: 31–54.

Picard, Michel. 1996. *Bali: cultural tourism and touristic culture.* Singapore: Archipelago Press.

——2008. "Balinese identity as tourist attraction: from 'cultural tourism' (*pariwisata budaya*) to 'Bali erect' (*ajeg Bali*)". *Tourist Studies* 8: 155–73.

Pizam, Abraham. 1999. "Cross-cultural tourist behavior". In: Pizam, Abraham and Yoel Mansfeld (eds): *Consumer Behavior in Travel and Tourism.* Haworth: New York, London, Oxford, 393–411.

Poria, Yaniv, Richard Butler and David Airey. 2003. "Tourism, Religion and Religiosity: A Holy Mess". *Current Issues in Tourism* 6: 340–63.

Pratt, Mary Louise. 1992. *Imperial Eyes: travel writing and transculturation.* London: Routledge.

Prentice, Richard. 2004. "Tourist motivation and typology". In: Lew, Alan A., Allan M. Williams and Colin Michael Hall (eds): *A Companion to Tourism.* Blackwell: Malden, Mass., 261–79.

Pretes, Michael. 1995. "Postmodern tourism: the Santa Claus industry". *Annals of Tourism Research* 22: 1–15.

Raj, Razaq and Nigel D. Morpeth (eds). 2007a. *Religious Tourism and Pilgrimage Festivals Management: an international perspective.* Wallingford, Cambridge/Mass: CABI.

Raj, Razaq and Nigel D. Morpeth. 2007b. "Introduction: establishing linkages between religious travel and tourism". In: Raj, Razaq and Nigel D. Morpeth (eds): *Religious Tourism and Pilgrimage Festivals Management: an international perspective.* CABI: Wallingford, Cambridge/Mass, 1–14.

Ramstedt, Martin. 2004. "The Hinduization of local traditions in South Sulawesi". In: Ramstedt, Martin (ed.): *Hinduism in Modern Indonesia: a minority religion between local, national, and global interests.* RoutledgeCurzon: London, 184–225.

Rauschenberger, Katharina. 2004. "Jüdische Museen in Kaiserreich und in der Weimarer Republik. Utopieersatz oder Selbstvergewisserung". In: Bräunlein, Peter J. (ed.): *Religion und Museum. Zur visuellen Repräsentation von Religion/en im öffentlichen Raum.* transcript: Bielefeld, 139–58.

Reader, Ian. 1991. *Religion in Contemporary Japan.* Basingstoke, London: Macmillan.

——2005. *Making Pilgrimages: meaning and practice in Shikoku.* Honolulu: University of Hawai'i Press.

——2007. "Pilgrimage growth in the modern world: Meanings and implications". *Religion* 37: 210–29.

Reader, Ian and George Joji Tanabe. 1998. *Practically Religious: worldly benefits and the common religion of Japan.* Honolulu: University of Hawai'i Press.

Reeves, Brian. 1994. "Ninaistákis – the Nitsitapii's sacred mountain: traditional native religious activities and land use/tourism conflicts". In: Carmichael, David L., Jane Hubert, Brian Reeves and Audhild Schanche (eds): *Sacred Sites, Sacred Places.* Routledge: London, New York, 265–96.

Reisinger, Yvette and Lindsay W. Turner. 2003. *Cross-Cultural Behaviour in Tourism: concepts and analysis.* Oxford: Butterworth-Heinemann.

Richards, Greg. 2001. "The Experience Industry and the Creation of Attractions". In: Richards, Greg (ed.): *Cultural Attractions and European Tourism.* CABI Publishing: Wallingford, 55–69.

——2002. "Tourism attraction systems: exploring cultural behavior". *Annals of Tourism Research* 29: 1048–64.

Richards, Greg and Carlos Fernandes. 2007. "Religious tourism in Northern Portugal". In: Richards, Greg (ed.): *Cultural Tourism: global and local perspectives.* Haworth Hospitality Press: New York, London, Oxford, 215–38.

Rinschede, Gisbert. 1986. "The pilgrim town of Lourdes". *Journal of Cultural Geography* 7: 21–34.

——1992. "Forms of religious tourism". *Annals of Tourism Research* 19: 51–67.

——1999. *Religionsgeographie.* Braunschweig: Westermann.

Rittichainuwat, Bongkosh Ngamsom, Hailin Qu and Jerrold K. Leong. 2003. "The collective impacts of a bundle of travel determinants on repeat visitation". *Journal of Hospitality & Tourism Research* 27: 217–36.

Robertson, C. K. (ed.). 2002. *Religion as Entertainment.* P. Lang: New York.

Robinson, Mike. 2001. "Tourism encounters: inter- and intra-cultural conflicts and the world's largest industry". In: AlSayyad, Nezar (ed.): *Consuming Tradition,*

Manufacturing Heritage: global norms and urban forms in the age of tourism.
Routledge: London, 34–67.

——2004. "Narratives of being elsewhere: tourism and travel writing". In: Lew, Alan
A., Allan M. Williams and Colin Michael Hall (eds): *A Companion to Tourism.*
Blackwell: Malden, 303–15.

Rocha, Cristina. 2006. "Spiritual tourism: Brazilian faith healing goes global". In:
Swatos, William H. (ed.): *On the Road to Being There: studies in pilgrimage and
tourism in late modernity.* Brill: Leiden, 105–23.

Roemer, Michael K. 2006. "Religious tourism in Japan: Kyōto's Gion festival". In:
Swatos, William H. (ed.): *On the Road to Being There: studies in pilgrimage and
tourism in late modernity.* Brill: Leiden, 187–218.

Rojek, Chris. 1997. "Indexing, dragging and the social construction of tourist sights".
In: Rojek, Chris and John Urry (eds): *Touring Cultures: transformations of travel
and theory.* Routledge: London, 52–74.

Rojek, Chris and John Urry (eds). 1997. *Touring cultures: transformations of travel
and theory.* Routledge: London.

—— 1997. "Transformations of travel and theory". In: Rojek, Chris and John
Urry (eds): *Touring Cultures: transformations of travel and theory.* Routledge:
London, 1–19.

Ross, Andrew. 1994. *The Chicago Gangster Theory of Life: nature's debt to society.*
London: Verso.

Rotherham, Ian D. 2007. "Sustaining tourism infrastructures for religious tourists
and pilgrims within the UK". In: Raj, Razaq and Nigel D. Morpeth (eds):
*Religious Tourism and Pilgrimage Festivals Management: an international perspec-
tive.* CABI: Wallingford, Cambridge/Mass, 64–77.

Rountree, Kathryn. 2002. "Re-inventing Malta's neolithic temples: contemporary
interpretations and agendas". *History and Anthropology* 13: 31–51.

——2006. "Journeys to the goddess: pilgrimage and tourism in the New Age". In:
Swatos, William H. (ed.): *On the Road to Being There: studies in pilgrimage and
tourism in late modernity.* Brill: Leiden, 33–60.

Royce, Anya Peterson. 2002. *The Anthropology of Dance.* New edition. Alton: Dance
Books.

Ryan, Chris. 2002a. "Tourism and cultural proximity: examples from New Zealand".
Annals of Tourism Research 29: 952–71.

——2002b. *The Tourist Experience.* Second edition. London: Continuum.

——2003. *Recreational tourism: demand and impacts.* Clevedon: Channel View
Publications.

Ryan, Chris, Michelle Aicken and Stephen J. Page (eds). 2005. *Taking Tourism to the
Limits: issues, concepts and managerial perspectives.* Elsevier: Amsterdam.

Ryba, Thomas. 1999–2000. "The utopics of Disney World's Magic Kingdom: a stroll
through a realized American eschatology". *Temenos* 35–36: 183–223.

Sá Carneiro, Sandra M.C. de. 2003. "Caminho de Santiago de Compostela: percurso,
identidade e passagens". In: Birman, Patrícia (ed.): *Religião e espaço público.* Attar
Editorial: São Paulo, 259–81.

——2004. "Novas peregrinações brasileiras e suas interfaces com o turismo".
Ciencias Sociales y Religión/Ciências Sociais e Religião 6: 71–100.

Sanchis, Pierre. 2006. "Peregrinação e romaria: um lugar para o turismo religioso".
Ciencias Sociales y Religión/Ciências Sociais e Religião 8: 85–97.

Santos, Maria da Graça Mouga Poças. 2003. "Religious tourism: contributions towards a clarification of concepts". In: Fernandes, Carlos, Jonathan Edwards and Francis McGettigan (eds): *Religious Tourism and Pilgrimage: ATLAS – special interest group 1st expert meeting*. Tourism Board of Leiria/Fátima: Fátima, 27–42.

Santos, Xose M. 2002. "Pilgrimage and tourism at Santiago de Compostela". *Tourism Recreation Research* 27: 41–50.

Scarce, Jennifer. 2000. "Tourism and material culture in Turkey". In: Hitchcock, Michael and Ken Teague (eds): *Souvenirs: the material culture of tourism*. Ashgate: Aldershot, 25–35.

Schlatter, Gerhard. 2006. "Tourism". *The Brill Dictionary of Religion* 4: 1904–7 [=*Metzler Lexikon Religion* 3 (2000): 515–19].

Schlehe, Judith. 2005. "Shamanism in Mongolia and in New Age Movements". In: Rasuly-Paleczek, Gabriele and Julia Katschnig (ed.): *Central Asia on Display. Proceedings of the VII. Conference of the European Society for Central Asian Studies*. Lit: Münster, 283–95.

——2009. "Zur Inszenierung nationaler, lokaler und religiöser Identitäten in indonesischen Kulturparks". In: Hermann, Elfriede, Karin Klenke and Michael Dickhardt (eds): *Form, Macht, Differenz. Motive und Felder ethnologischen Forschens*. Universitätsverlag: Göttingen, 165–77.

Schlehe, Judith and Helmut Weber. 2001. "Schamanismus und Tourismus in der Mongolei". *Zeitschrift für Ethnologie* 126: 93–116.

Schmidt, Leigh Eric. 1995. *Consumer Rites: the buying & selling of American holidays*. Princeton: Princeton University Press.

Schnell, Scott. 1999. *The Rousing Drum: ritual practice in a Japanese community*. Honolulu: University of Hawai'i Press.

Schramm, Katharina. 2004. "Coming home to the motherland: pilgrimage tourism in Ghana". In: Eade, John and Simon Coleman (eds): *Reframing Pilgrimage: cultures in motion*. Routledge: London, 133–49.

Schwilius, Harald, Ulrike Kasper and Anne Volgenandt. 2009. *Klosterlandschaft Sachsen-Anhalt. Machbarkeitsstudie zur Konzeptentwicklung im Rahmen des Spirituellen Tourismus*. Berlin: λογοζ.

Sears, John F. 1998 [1989]. *Sacred places: American tourist attractions in the nineteenth century*. New York: Oxford University Press.

Seaton, A.V. 2002. "Thanatourism's final frontiers? Visits to cemeteries, churchyards and funerary sites as sacred and secular pilgrimage". *Tourism Recreation Research* 27: 73–82.

Seidel, Anette. 2006. "Die Gästestruktur des Kulturtourismus in Sachsen-Anhalt". In: *Heilige Orte, sakrale Räume, Pilgerwege: Möglichkeiten und Grenzen des Spirituellen Tourismus*. Sachesen Anhalt/Ministerium für Wirtschaft und Arbeit: Magdeburg, Wittenberg, Bensberg, 22–35.

Selänniemi, Tom. 2001. "Plane Skin on Playa del Anywhere: Finnish Tourists in the Liminoid South". In: Brent, Maryann and Valene L. Smith (ed.): *Hosts and Guests Revisited: tourism issues in the 21st century*. Cognizant Communication Corporation: Elmsford, 80–92.

Selwyn, Tom. 1993. "Peter Pan in South-East Asia: views from the brochures". In: Hitchcock, Michael, Victor T. King and Michael J. G. Parnwell (eds): *Tourism in South-East Asia*. Routledge: London, New York, 117–37.

——1996. "Introduction". In: Selwyn, Tom (ed.): *The Tourist Image: myths and myth making in tourism*. Wiley: Chichester, 1–47.

Shackley, Myra. 1999. "The Himalayas: masked dances and mixed blessings". *UNESCO-The Courier* 28–29. [http://www.unesco.org/courier/1999_08/uk/dossier/txt21.htm]

——2001. *Managing Sacred Sites: service provision and visitor experience.* London: Continuum.

——2002. "Space, sanctity and service: the English cathedral as *Heterotopia*". *International Journal of Tourism Research* 4: 345–252.

——2004. "Tourist consumption of sacred landscapes: space, time and vision". *Tourism Recreation Research* 29: 67–73.

——2006. "Empty bottles at sacred sites: religious retailing at Ireland's National Shrine". In: Timothy, Dallen J. and Daniel H. Olsen (eds): *Tourism, Religion and Spiritual Journeys.* Routledge: London, New York, 94–103.

Shaffer, Marguerite S. 2001. *See America First: tourism and national identity, 1880–1940.* Washington, London: Smithsonian Institution Press.

Sharpley, Richard. 2005. "Travels to the edge of darkness: towards a typology of 'dark tourism'". In: Ryan, Chris, Michelle Aicken and Stephen J. Page (eds): *Taking Tourism to the Limits: issues, concepts and managerial perspectives.* Elsevier: Amsterdam, 215–26.

Sharpley, Richard and Priya Sundaram. 2005. "Tourism: a sacred journey? The case of ashram tourism, India". *International Journal of Tourism Research* 7: 161–71.

Shenshav-Keller, Shelly. 1993. "The Israeli souvenir: its text and context". *Annals of Tourism Research* 20: 182–96.

Shepherd, Naomi. 1987. *The Zealous Intruders: the western rediscovery of Palestine.* San Francisco: Harper & Row.

Shi, Fangfang. 2009. "Evaluation of visitor experience at Chinese Buddhist sites: the case of Wutai Mountain". In: Ryan, Chris and Gu Huimin (eds): *Tourism in China: destination, cultures and communities.* Routledge: New York, London, 197–212.

Shinde, Kiran. 2003. "Environmental crisis in God's abode: managing religious tourism". In: Fernandes, Carlos, Jonathan Edwards and Francis McGettigan (eds): *Religious Tourism and Pilgrimage: ATLAS – special interest group 1st expert meeting.* Tourism Board of Leiria/Fátima: Fátima, 87–101.

——2006. "Religious tourism: intersection of contemporary pilgrimage and tourism in India". In: Picard, David and Mike Robinson (eds): *Conference Proceedings "Journeys of Expressions V: Tourism and the Roots/Routes of Religious Festivity" (Belfast, Northern Ireland, March 13–15 2006).* Center for Tourism & Cultural Change: pdf on CD.

——2007. "Pilgrimage and the environment: challenges in a pilgrimage centre". *Current Issues in Tourism* 10: 343–65.

Sieg, Ursula, Peter Schreiner and Volker Elsenbast (eds). 2005. *Handbuch interreligiöses Lernen.* Gütersloher Verlagshaus: Gütersloh.

Silveira, Emerson José Sena da. 2004. "Turismo religioso popular? Entre a ambigüidada conceitual e as oportunidades de mercado". *Revista de Antropología Experimental* 4: 1–16.

Simpson, Bob. 1993. "Tourism and tradition: from healing to heritage". *Annals of Tourism Research* 20: 164–81.

Sindiga, Isaac. 1996. "International tourism in Kenya and the marginalization of the Waswahili". *Tourism Management* 17: 425–32.

Singh, Sagar. 2004. "Religion, heritage and travel: case studies from the Indian Himalayas". *Current Issues in Tourism* 7: 44–65.

Sjöberg, Katarina V. 1993. *The Return of the Ainu: cultural mobilization and the practice of ethnicity in Japan.* Chur: Harwood.

——2004. "Rethinking indigenous religious traditions: the case of the Ainu". In: Olupona, Jacob K. (ed.): *Beyond Primitivism: indigenous religious traditions and modernity.* Routledge: New York, London, 224–44.

Skrbiš, Zlatko. 2007. "From migrants to pilgrim tourists: diasporic imagining and visits to Medjugorje". *Journal of Ethnic and Migration Studies* 33: 313–29.

Smith, Jonathan Zittel. 1987. *To Take Place: toward theory in ritual.* Chicago, London: University of Chicago Press.

——1993 [1978]. *Map Is Not Territory: studies in the history of religions.* Chicago, London: University of Chicago Press.

Smith, Melanie K. 2006 [2003]. *Issues in Cultural Tourism Studies.* London, New York: Routledge.

Smith, Melanie K. and László Puczkó. 2009. *Health and Wellness Tourism.* Amsterdam etc.: Butterworth-Heinemann.

Smith, Valene L. 2001. "The culture brokers". In: Smith, Valene L. and Maryann Brent (eds): *Hosts and Guests Revisited: tourism issues of the 21st century.* Cognizant Communication: New York, 275–82.

Sofield, Trevor H.B. 2001. "Sustainability and pilgrimage tourism in the Kathmandu valley of Nepal". In: Smith, Valene L. and Maryann Brent (eds): *Hosts and Guests Revisited: tourism issues of the 21st century.* Cognizant Communication: New York, 257–71.

Spencer, Brian. 1998. *Pilgrim Souvenirs and Secular Badges.* London: The Stationery Office.

Stausberg, Michael. 2006. "Reflexivity". In: Kreinath, Jens, Jan Snoek and Michael Stausberg (eds): *Theorizing Rituals. Vol. 1: Issues, Topics, Approaches, Concepts.* Leiden: Brill, 627–46.

——2010. *Religion im modernen Tourismus.* Berlin: Verlag der Weltreligionen im Insel Verlag.

Steinecke, Albrecht. 1994. "Der bundesdeutsche Reiseführer-Markt. Ein Überblick unter beonderer Berücksichtigung der Mallorca-Reiseführer". In: Popp, Herbert (ed.): *Das Bild der Mittelmeerländer in der Reiseführer-Literatur.* Passavia Universitätsverlag: Passau, 11–34.

——2006. *Tourismus. Eine geographische Einführung.* Braunschweig: Westermann.

Swatos, William H. (ed.). 2006. *On the Road to Being There: studies in pilgrimage and tourism in late modernity.* Leiden: Brill.

Swatos, William H. and Luigi Tomasi (eds). 2002. *From Medieval Pilgrimage to Religious Tourism: the social and cultural economies of piety.* Praeger: Westport, London.

Tahana, Ngaroma and Martin Oppermann. 1998. "Maori cultural performances and tourism". *Tourism Recreation Research* 23: 23–30.

Tanabe, George 2006. "Playing with religion". *Nova religio* 10: 96–101.

Tate, Mark. 2004. "Tourism and Holy Week in León, Spain". In: Badone, Ellen and Sharon R. Roseman (eds): *Intersecting Journeys: the anthropology of pilgrimage and tourism.* University of Illinois Press: Urbana, Chicago, 110–24.

Teague, Ken. 2000. "Tourist markets and Himalayan craftsmen". In: Hitchcock, Michael and Ken Teague (eds): *Souvenirs: the material culture of tourism.* Ashgate: Aldershot, 194–208.

Teye, Victor B. 2009. "Tourism and Africa's tripartite cultural past". In: Timothy, Dallen J. and Gyan P. Nyaupane (eds): *Cultural Heritage and Tourism in the Developing World: a regional perspective*. Routledge: New York, London, 165–85.

Therkelsen, Anette and Anders Sørensen. 2005. "Reading the tourist guidebook: tourists' ways of reading and relating to guidebooks". *The Journal of Tourism Studies* 16: 48–60.

Timothy, Dallen J. and Paul J. Conover. 2006. "Nature religion, self-spirituality and New Age tourism". In: Timothy, Dallen J. and Daniel H. Olsen (eds): *Tourism, Religion and Spiritual Journeys*. Routledge: London, New York, 139–55.

Timothy, Dallen J. and Timothy Iverson. 2006. "Tourism and Islam: considerations of culture and duty". In: Timothy, Dallen J. and Daniel H. Olsen (eds): *Tourism, Religion and Spiritual Journeys*. Routledge: London, New York, 186–205.

Timothy, Dallen J. and Gyan P. Nyaupane. 2009. *Cultural Heritage and Tourism in the Developing World: a regional perspective*. New York, London: Routledge.

Timothy, Dallen J. and Daniel H. Olsen (eds). 2006. *Tourism, Religion and Spiritual Journeys*. Routledge: London, New York.

——2006. "Tourism and religious journeys". In: Timothy, Dallen J. and Daniel H. Olsen (eds): *Tourism, Religion and Spiritual Journeys*. Routledge: London, New York, 271–78.

Timothy, Dallen J. and Victor B. Teye. 2004. "American children of the African diaspora: journeys to the motherland". In: Coles, Tim Edward and Dallen J. Timothy (ed.): *Tourism, Diasporas and Space*. Routledge: London, 111–23.

Tresidder, Richard. 1999. "Tourism and sacred landscapes". In: Crouch, David (ed.): *Leisure/tourism Geographies: practices and geographical knowledge*. Routledge: London, New York, 137–48.

Turner, Victor Witter. 1969. *The Ritual Process: structure and anti-structure*. Chicago: Routledge & Kegan Paul.

Turner, Victor Witter and Edith L.B. Turner. 1978. *Image and Pilgrimage in Christian Culture: anthropological perspectives*. New York: Columbia University Press.

Tweed, Thomas A. 2000. "John Wesley Slept Here. American shrines and American Methodists". *Numen* 47: 41–68.

——2006. *Crossing and Dwelling: a theory of religion*. Cambridge/Mass.: Harvard University Press.

Udall, Sharyn R. 1992. "The irresistible other: Hopi ritual drama and Euro-American audiences". *TDR – The Drama Review* 36: 23–43.

United Nations 2003. *Promotion of Buddhist Tourism Circuits in Selected Asian Countries*. United Nations: New York.

UNWTO World Tourism Barometer. 7 (1), 2009. Available at http://www.unwto.org/facts/eng/pdf/barometer/UNWTO_Barom09_1_en.pdf.

Uriely, Nathan. 1997. "Theories of modern and postmodern tourism". *Annals of Tourism Research* 24: 982–85.

Urry, John. 1995. *Consuming Places*. London: Routledge.

——2002. *The Tourist Gaze*. Second edition. London: Sage.

——2007. *Mobilities*. Cambridge, Malden: Polity Press.

van den Berghe, Pierre L. 1995. "Marketing Mayas: ethnic tourism promotion in Mexico". *Annals of Tourism Research* 22: 568–88.

van den Berghe, Pierre L. and Charles F. Keyes. 1984. "Introduction tourism and re-created ethnicity". *Annals of Tourism Research* 11: 343–52.

Van Zile, Judy. 2001. *Perspectives on Korean Dance*. Middletown: Wesleyan University Press.

Vogel, Lester I. 1996. "Staying home for the sights: surrogate destinations in America for Holy Land travel". In: Le Beau, Bryan F. and Menachem Mor (eds): *Pilgrims & Travelers to the Holy Land*. Creighton University Press: Omaha, 251–67.

Von Stuckrad, Kocku. 2003. *Schamanismus und Esoterik. Kultur- und wissenschaftsgeschichtliche Betrachtungen*. Leuven: Peeters.

Vukonić, Boris. 1996. *Tourism and Religion*. Oxford, New York, Tokyo: Pergamon.

——2002. "Religion, tourism and economics: a convenient symbiosis". *Tourism Recreation Research* 27: 59–64.

——2006. "Sacred places and tourism in the Roman Catholic tradition". In: Timothy, Dallen J. and Daniel H. Olsen (eds): *Tourism, Religion and Spiritual Journeys*. Routledge: London, New York, 237–53.

Wall, Geoffrey and Barbara Oswald. 1990. *Cultural Groups as Tourist Attractions: a comparative study*. Aix-en-Provence: Centre des Hautes Etudes Touristiques.

Wall, Geoffrey and Philip Feifan Xie. 2005. "Authenticating ethnic tourism: Li dancers' perspectives". *Asia Pacific Journal of Tourism Research* 10: 1–21.

Wallis, Robert J. 2003. *Shamans/neo-Shamans: Ecstasy, alternative archaeologies and contemporary Pagans*. London: Routledge.

Walsh, Eileen Rose and Margaret Byrne Swain. 2004. "Creating modernity by touring paradise: domestic ethnic tourism in Yunnan, China". *Tourism Recreation Research* 29: 59–68.

Walter, Tony. 1993. "War grave pilgrimage". In: Reader, Ian and Tony Walter (eds): *Pilgrimage in Popular Culture*. Macmillan: Houndmills, London, 63–91.

Webb, Terry D. 2001. "The temple and the theme park: intention and indirection in religious tourist art". In: Hendry, Joy and C. W. Watson (eds): *An Anthropology of Indirect Communication*. Routledge: London, New York, 128–42.

Weidenfeld, Adi. 2006. "Religious needs in the hospitality industry". *Tourism and Hospitality Research* 6: 143–59.

Wemhöner, Karin. 2004. *Paradiese und Sehnsuchtsorte. Studien zur Reiseliteratur des 20. Jahrhunderts*. Marburg: Tectum Verlag.

Wickens, Eugenia. 2002. "The sacred and the profane: a tourist typology". *Annals of Tourism Research* 29: 834–51.

Wiley, Eric. 2005. "Romani performance and heritage tourism: the pilgrimage of the gypsies at Les Saintes-Maries-de-la-Mer". *TDR – The Drama Review* 49: 135–58.

Wilke, Annette and Esther-Maria Guggenmos (eds). 2008. *Im Netz des Indra. Das Museum of World Religions, sein buddhistisches Dialogkonzept und die neue Disziplin Religionsästhetik*. LIT: Zürich.

Williamson, George. 2005. "Mucianus and a touch of the miraculous: pilgrimage and tourism in Roman Asia Minor". In: Elsner, Jaś and Ian Rutherford (eds): *Pilgrimage in Graeco-Roman & Early Christian Antiquity: seeing the gods*. Oxford University Press: Oxford, New York, 219–52.

Wilson, David. 1993. "Time and tides in the anthropology of tourism". In: Hitchcock, Michael, Victor T. King and Michael J. G. Parnwell (eds): *Tourism in South-East Asia*. Routledge: London, New York, 32–47.

Wilson, Jeff. 2009. "*Mizuko kuyō* in the abortion cultural wars: The rhetorical appropriation of Japanese Buddhism by non-Buddhist Americans". *Religion* 39: 11–21.

Withey, Lynne. 1997. *Grand Tours and Cook's Tours: a history of leisure travel, 1750 to 1915*. New York: William Morrow.

Woodward, Simon C. 2004. "Faith and tourism: planning tourism in relation to places of worship". *Tourism and Hospitality Planning & Development* 1: 173–86.

Wuthnow, Robert. 2003. *All in sync: how music and art are revitalizing American religion*. Berkeley: University of California Press.

Xie, Philip Feifan. 2003. "The bamboo-beating dance in Hainan, China: authenticity and commodification". *Journal of Sustainable Tourism* 11: 5–17.

Xie, Philip Feifan and Bernard Lane. 2006. "A life cycle model for aboriginal arts performance in tourism: perspectives on authenticity". *Journal of Sustainable Tourism* 14: 545–61.

Yan, Hongliang and Bill Bramwell. 2008. "Cultural tourism, ceremony and the state in China". *Annals of Tourism Research* 35: 969–89.

Yel, Ali Murat. 2006. "Appropriation of sacredness at Fátima in Portugal". In: Arweck, Elisabeth and William Keenan (eds): *Materializing Religion: expression, performance and ritual*. Ashgate: Aldershot, Burlington, 221–36.

Yu, Larry and Munhtuya Goulden. 2006. "A comparative analysis of international tourists' satisfaction in Mongolia". *Tourism Management* 27: 1331–42.

Zarkia, Cornélia. 1996. "*Philoxenia* Receiving Tourists – but not Guests – on a Greek Island". In: Boissevain, Jeremy (ed.): *Coping with Tourists: European reactions to mass tourism*. Berghahn Books: Providence, 143–73.

Index

Compiled by Richard Bartholomew